Prototyping with Visual Basic

Rod Stephens

201 W. 103rd Street
Indianapolis, Indiana 46290

PROTOTYPING WITH VISUAL BASIC

Copyright © 2002 by Que

International Standard Book Number: 0-7897-2578-9

Library of Congress Catalog Card Number: 20-01090371

Printed in the United States of America

First Printing: September 2001

04 03 02 01   4   3   2   1

Trademarks

Warning and Disclaimer

Associate Publisher
Dean Miller

Acquisitions Editor
Jenny Watson

Development Editors
Sean Dixon
Maureen McDaniel

Managing Editor
Thomas F. Hayes

Project Editor
Karen S. Shields

Copy Editor
Molly Schaller

Indexer
Cheryl Landes

Proofreader
Plan-It Publishing

Technical Editor
Vince Mayfield

Team Coordinator
Cindy Teeters

Interior Designer
Ruth Lewis

Cover Designer
Anne Jones

CONTENTS

ABOUT THE AUTHOR

Rod Stephens started out as a mathematician but in the 1980s at MIT, he discovered the joys of computer algorithms and has been programming professionally ever since. During his tenure at GTE Laboratories, he used prototyping methods to build several large award-winning applications that are still in use today. More recently he has worked on projects ranging from tax software for the state of Minnesota to a training system for professional football teams.

Rod has written nine programming books that have been translated into several languages and more than 150 magazine articles covering Visual Basic, Visual Basic for Applications, Delphi, and Java. He is currently a columnist for Visual Basic Developer (www.pinpub.com/vbd).

Rod's popular VB Helper Web site (www.vb-helper.com) receives more than a million hits per month. VB Helper includes information on Rod's books, essays, tutorials, and hundreds of example programs for Visual Basic programmers, as well as example programs for this book.

DEDICATION

For Carol (1940-2000) and Amy (2000-) who barely had time get to know each other.

ACKNOWLEDGMENTS

Thanks to George Kocur and the other developers at GTE Laboratories who spent so much time in the trenches with me; Rob Merenyi who joined us just at exactly the worst possible moment (imagine the captain of the Titanic turning to you just after hitting the iceberg and saying, "Here, you take over"); Sandy Mundy and the others at GTE's billing centers who made ACE the easiest and most cost-effective prototyping project in history; and all of our other customers who made our jobs challenging, occasionally frustrating, but always interesting.

Thanks also to Jenny Watson, Sean Dixon, Karen Shields, Vince Mayfield, and all the other folks at Que who made writing this book a smooth and enjoyable experience.

INTRODUCTION

In this introduction

WHAT IS A PROTOTYPE?

Suppose you build simple wooden fences. After you've built a couple, they're pretty much all the same. If it took you 10 hours to build one fence, it will probably take you about 20 hours and twice as much wood to build a similar fence that's twice as long. It would be very surprising if it took you 200 hours and 100 times as much wood.

Unfortunately, planning a software project is not as simple. After you write a program, you can make perfectly accurate copies quickly, easily, and cheaply. If you build a wooden fence program and you need another one that's exactly the same, you make a copy of the first one and call it a job well done.

The only time you start a new development project is when you need something new. That means that whenever a development team starts a new project, they are entering uncharted territory. You can plan the completion of a fence, but how can you guess when you will be done inventing something completely new? Which parts of the project will be easy and which will be hard? What unexpected problems will you encounter? Will you be on time and within your budget?

Just remember the following rule, which seems obvious but is a simple statement with important consequences:

Every new software project has never been built before.

Experienced programmers and development teams can make educated guesses based on past experiences, but those are still guesses. If a team just built a report module for one application, it can make a reasonable guess as to how hard it will be to build another report module for a new application. But what if the team needs to build a Web-based charting tool and it has never done anything like that before? What if the team is using untested hardware? What if half the team members are new? A prototype can help answer these questions.

The most common form of prototype is a small version of a bigger project. It demonstrates most of the user interface so the customers can see what the program will look like. It contains some of the features that the final program will have. It demonstrates that any new software, hardware, and developers will work properly.

The following is what I mean by "prototype" in this book:

A *prototype* is a small test project designed to tell you something about another project that you have not yet built.

Some object-oriented languages such as C++ have a concept of prototyping that is very different from the application prototyping described in this book. A C++ prototype is a declaration of a routine or function that is defined elsewhere. The prototype lets one module or program know how to invoke a routine defined in another module without knowing how the routine is implemented. This is a useful concept but has nothing to do with this book.

WHY PROTOTYPE?

When an experienced developer estimates the time a project will take, the accuracy of the estimate depends on how similar the project is compared to others the developer has built. When done properly, a prototype is very similar to the final application it represents. The information gained by studying the prototype usually gives reliable information about the final project. By examining the team's experiences building the prototype, you can learn the following:

- How long the bigger project will take
- How many people (how much money) you need to build the bigger project
- Whether the design and development approach will work
- Whether the development team can even build the bigger project successfully

In addition to predicting the team's experiences working on the final project, the prototype can help make its development smoother. It can do the following:

- Win customer buy-in
- Ensure the final application meets the customers' needs
- Define the application so developers can stay focused on essential tasks
- Help developers become a more effective team

Although a prototype will not solve all of a development team's problems, it will help you understand how development of the related project will progress. A prototype can help developers build a better product with more features and fewer bugs more reliably and in less time.

WHY SHOULD YOU READ THIS BOOK?

If you are a developer, project leader, manager, or even a customer who works closely with medium and large software projects, you should understand prototypes and this book is a good place to start. It explains what you can learn from a prototype, how to decide which type of prototype to use, and how to get the most out of a prototype.

If you build only small programs that require little effort, you don't really need to build prototypes. If you run 100% over time on a four-hour project, you will end up spending eight hours on the project. Losing those four extra hours probably won't push you into bankruptcy.

On the other hand, if you build medium and large applications, prototypes can save you a lot of time, trouble, and money. Software development is extremely expensive. Even a modest development effort can cost millions. In the long run, maintenance costs can make the initial development costs look like small change. Investing a few thousand dollars in a prototype at the beginning can return huge dividends in improved usability and maintainability over time.

Other industries with high development costs, such as the aerospace and automobile industries, go to great lengths building prototypes before they attempt to build a finished product. They don't just toss their money into a project and hope for the best. Why should you?

WHY SHOULDN'T YOU BUY SOME OTHER BOOK?

Frankly, you should buy several other books in addition to this one. Right now there are no other books about building prototypes using VB.NET or earlier versions of Visual Basic. However, there are many books on general software design and project management, and these three topics go hand-in-hand.

Software design tells you what features to put into the prototype. The prototype helps refine the design and gives you information you can use for managing the larger project. At the same time, you need to use good project-management techniques while building the prototype so you can collect all the information you need to analyze the prototype later. The prototype is also a good place to practice the project-management techniques you will use during final development.

This book covers project management and software design briefly but it cannot cover them in the same depth as books dedicated to those topics. These topics also tend to be easily individualized so one author's software design style might be very different from another's. After you finish reading this book, read a few of these others. Pick out the ideas that you think will work best for you from each.

My bookshelf contains about a dozen books on project management, software design, and development techniques. When starting a new project, I skim through them checking the places I have bookmarked and making notes to refresh my memory of things to think about when starting the new project.

HOW THIS BOOK IS ORGANIZED

This book is organized into three parts: "Introduction to Prototyping," "The Prototype Lifecycle," and "Prototyping Techniques."

PART I: INTRODUCTION TO PROTOTYPING

This part of the book explains what prototypes are, what the most common types of prototypes are, how prototypes fit into a development lifecycle, and why you should care. These chapters discuss prototypes in general terms and do not include a lot of source code. If you are a manager or customer and don't generally get into the day-to-day details of application development, you will probably find these chapters the most important:

- **Chapter 1, "Reasons to Prototype"**—This chapter explains what you can learn from a prototype. It describes the things you should look for while prototyping to learn the most about the development effort still to come.

- **Chapter 2, "Kinds of Prototypes"**—There are several different kinds of prototypes, each with its own strengths and weaknesses. This chapter describes the most common types of prototypes and discusses the tradeoffs between them so you can decide which approach is best for your project.

- **Chapter 3, "Prototypes in the Lifecycle"**—This chapter explains how prototypes fit into the development lifecycle. If you use prototypes properly, you can get benefits from them long after an application's first release.

PART II: THE PROTOTYPE LIFECYCLE

The chapters in Part II of the book step through the four main phases of a prototype's life-cycle: analysis, design, development, and testing. They use an example application called VB NetLab to demonstrate some of the most important aspects of prototyping during each phase.

- **Chapter 4, "Analysis"**—This chapter explains how to analyze the customers' environment, assess their needs, and turn those needs into a requirements specification. The results of this analysis determine what features are included in the application's first release and therefore what features will be in the first series of prototypes. To provide a concrete example of the analysis process, this chapter examines the requirements for the VB NetLab application.

- **Chapter 5, "Design"**—There are four common application design approaches: user interface design, database design, object-oriented design, and procedural design. This chapter explains how each of these approaches works and tells how they complement each other. It applies each to the VB NetLab example so you can see how each method works.

- **Chapter 6, "Development"**—During the analysis and design phases, you can build very simple prototypes to show customers small pieces of what you have in mind for the final application. After you have finished analysis and design, you can start building much more sophisticated prototypes. This chapter describes some of the issues you face while building the application's main series of prototypes.

- **Chapter 7, "Testing"**—Even if you are building a throwaway prototype and don't intend to reuse its code, you need to perform a minimal level of testing. If a prototype is too buggy, the customers might not believe you can actually build the application. This chapter tells what kinds of testing you need to perform to ensure that customers can focus on the prototype's demonstration features and not on bugs.

PART III: PROTOTYPING TECHNIQUES

The chapters in this section explain some specific techniques for building prototypes. They describe code for performing some common tasks and they give some hints for managing aspects of prototype development:

- **Chapter 8, "Wizards"**—A wizard is a program that asks you questions to gather information. It then uses the information it gathered to build something. VB.NET provides a couple of wizards that can help you build prototypes. This chapter shows how to use some of these wizards to assemble a prototype quickly and easily.

- **Chapter 9, "Loading Data"**—Database programming is a huge topic. Fortunately, a prototype can often interact with databases in a more limited way than the final application. This chapter discusses ways a prototype can load and manipulate data without a lot of customized programming.

- **Chapter 10, "ADO Versus ADO.NET"**—ActiveX Data Objects (ADO) and ADO.NET are two powerful data access tools. Visual Basic 6 comes with ADO. VB.NET introduced ADO.NET. While both of these tools give you great flexibility and control over databases, they have slightly different strengths and weaknesses. This chapter discusses the advantages and disadvantages of ADO and ADO.NET and explains some of the issues you should consider when selecting a data access method for use in a prototype.

- **Chapter 11, "Database Tips and Tools"**—This chapter describes some specific data access techniques you might find useful while building prototypes. It explains tools that let you load data quickly and easily, save and restore application parameters, and manage user privileges.

- **Chapter 12, "Generating Reports"**—Every system I have worked on has required a large number of reports. This chapter explains how to add some simple reports to a prototype. It tells how you can display prebuilt reports, reports generated at runtime, and ad hoc queries.

- **Chapter 13, "Error Handling"**—This chapter explains how a prototype can handle errors. It discusses expected, abnormal, and unforeseen errors and tells how different kinds of prototypes should handle them. It explains how you can avoid terrifying customers running a prototype but still save plenty of information so developers can later analyze an error.

- **Chapter 14, "Wrapping Up"**—When a prototype is finished, it might seem like the work is over. Actually the work on the final application has just begun. This chapter describes some of the actions you should take after the prototype is finished but before you begin final development.

HOW TO USE THIS BOOK

The three parts of this book explain what prototypes are, the different stages of prototype development, and specific prototyping techniques.

If you are a manager or customer who doesn't plan on spending any time dealing directly with source code, focus on Part I, "Introduction to Prototyping," and Part II, "The Prototype Lifecycle." These chapters will give you the perspective you need to help plan the prototype and learn from it. They also explain how to help analyze requirements and design an application that does what you need. You might want to skim the other chapters at least so you can better understand what the developers will be doing when they build a prototype.

If you are a project manager or developer who will be working with the prototype design and development, you will need to spend most of your time on Part II, "The Prototype Lifecycle," and Part III, "Prototyping Techniques." However, don't ignore Part I, "Introduction to Prototyping." Although the chapters in that section don't contain a lot of code, they describe some fundamental concepts that all the developers should understand before anyone starts writing code.

SAMPLE CODE WEB SITE

You can find the source code for the examples in this book on the VB Helper Web site at www.vb-helper.com/proto.htm. Also look there for updates, corrections, reader discussions, and new code examples. E-mail your comments and suggestions to RodStephens@vb-helper.com.

BETA SOFTWARE

This book was written using a pre-release version of Visual Basic.NET. Many of the concepts and techniques discussed here are generic enough to work with the final Visual Basic.NET release or any other release for that matter. However, changes to the final version of Visual Basic.NET might break some of the examples.

Check the book's Web site for updates and corrections. If you spot something wrong, either because of changes made in the final Visual Basic.NET release or for any other reason, please let me know at RodStephens@vb-helper.com.

NECESSARY EQUIPMENT

This book is intended for those involved in building software with VB.NET. To get the greatest benefit, you should have VB.NET installed on your computer. Any computer that can reasonably run VB.NET should work.

If you are a manager or customer rather than a developer, you do not need VB.NET to read the material and understand the main concepts. You might not be able to run all the examples yourself, but you should come away with a good understanding of what prototypes are and how you can take best advantage of them.

If you use a previous version of Visual Basic, you will not be able to run all the examples described here and posted on the book's Web site. There were a lot of changes between Visual Basic 6 and VB.NET, so some of the code will work and some will not. The main concepts, however, should make sense whether you build prototypes using VB.NET, a previous version of Visual Basic, or some other programming language.

CONVENTIONS USED IN THIS BOOK

This book uses the following special elements to highlight text that expands on the main theme:

Tale from the Trenches
A "Tale from the Trenches" is an example drawn from real programming experiences. Learn from my mistakes before you make them your own, or just have a good chuckle at my expense. In my time as a developer, I've seen a lot of weird stuff.

Example
An Example is a possibly fictitious situation that illustrates some key point.

Note
A Note is some significant tidbit that expands on the current topic.

Tip
A Tip is a useful piece of advice for getting the most out of the current topic.

WHO IS THE CUSTOMER?

Most of the terms used in this book should be relatively easy to understand. The term "customer," however, can be a little confusing. The *customer* is the person or group who wants the final application you are going to develop. This can be a company or person who hires you to build a program. It can be a group of people who will buy your finished product from a mass-market software distributor. It can even be yourself when you build a program for your own use.

In many cases, the customer is in one part of a company and the developers building the application and prototype are in another.

During the years I worked at GTE Laboratories, our customers were usually other parts of the company. Those parts of the company had such diverse responsibilities as:

- Telephone service provisioning (designing circuits, assigning phone numbers, allocating physical wires, and so on)
- Customer billing
- Repair dispatching
- Telephone switch programming
- 911 service
- Company data and software maintenance

I also worked on a few projects for use within GTE Laboratories and some produced jointly with other telephone companies. I have also worked for customers building such diverse applications as component modeling software and professional football training systems. Customers are where you find them. The customers are not always the same as the final users of the application. In a large company, it is common to have management at a fairly high level buy software that will be used by lower-level users. In cases like that, you can sometimes run into adversarial relationships where the people paying for the software don't have the same goals as those who will eventually use it.

Most of my experiences have been relatively benign. When there has been a conflict, focusing on doing the best job for the company usually kept everyone on track. If that doesn't work for you, you'll need to perform a bit of a balancing act. You want to build the best software possible for the end user but you still have to satisfy the people who hired you.

In this book, I'm not trying to pin down exactly who the customer is. When the book says "customer," it usually means the users who will eventually use the system. Just hope they have the same goals as the people paying the bills.

INTRODUCTION TO PROTOTYPING

REASONS TO PROTOTYPE

In this chapter

In the most general terms, a *prototype* is a small test program designed to tell you something about another larger project that you have not yet built. You build the prototype and then use the information you learn from building and using it to predict things about the bigger project. A prototype can also let you try different approaches and perfect development techniques. The following are some of the most important uses of a prototype:

- Define application functionality
- Test application architecture
- Test untried technology
- Predict project duration
- Predict needed staffing
- Determine project feasibility
- Refine development techniques
- Build the development team

The following sections describe these prototyping benefits and how you can maximize their value. Some of the information you can gather during a prototype has subtle uses so it's not always obvious how to use what you learn. If you don't keep some of these in mind while you develop the prototype, you might miss out on important clues.

This information is as important for team leaders, project managers, and customers as it is for developers. For example, if the developers build a prototype containing too much user interface code, they will probably give you low estimates of the time and staffing needed to finish the application. You need to be aware of these issues so you can keep developers on track and so you know how much to trust their results.

Because some of these issues are subtle, you need to pay close attention to them during prototype development. Make a list of the things you hope to learn from the prototype and look it over frequently. Be sure to share the prototype's goals with the other developers and customers. If everyone stays focused on the goals, you can greatly increase your chances of success in relatively little time.

DEFINE APPLICATION FUNCTIONALITY

Probably the most important use of a prototype is to define the application's functionality. The goal is to ensure that the customers and the developers have the same view of what the final application will look like.

The project begins with a statement of what the application will do. The preliminary design suggests a possible method for performing the application's key tasks. A prototype solidifies that preliminary design so everyone can see what the developers have in mind.

The prototype shows what the application will look like and, to some extent, what it will do. At a minimum, the prototype should let the developers perform a carefully scripted walkthrough to explain the program's most important features to the customers. Ideally it also demonstrates those features so the customer can experiment with them and get a feel for how they will work in the final product.

Nonprogrammers often have trouble understanding what programmers mean when they describe a program. A programmer might say, "This form will display inventory in a grid control." The users might think they know what that means, but they often have trouble really understanding how that applies to their work until they see the form in action. A working prototype is the best way to give the customers a really good appreciation of what they are buying.

After they have seen and possibly experimented with the prototype, the customers can give feedback. The developers can adjust the development plan to make the product a better fit for the customers' needs. This greatly increases the chances that you will produce a product that the customer can actually use. This rule is completely obvious, but often ignored by developers. It's amazing how often developers build a product that no one wants.

Meeting with users gives developers more motivation. They see that they are building something that will actually be used by someone. They often get caught up in the customer's enthusiasm and want to do the best job possible. Working in isolation can be useful at times, but developers should stay focused on the end result.

If the feedback leads to major design changes, the developers can build a new prototype to let the customers see what the revised application will look like. You should repeat this cycle as often as necessary to ensure that the customers and developers all agree on the final system's functionality.

Incorporating feedback into new prototypes lets the customers know you are listening to them. It shows you take their concerns seriously and is a great way to win customer buy-in. A customer who makes a personal contribution to the project is more likely to do so in the future and is more likely to struggle for the project's success.

Tale from the Trenches
A few years ago I was working at GTE Laboratories, to assist dispatchers in routing several hundred repair trucks to their daily jobs. The workers at the work center where this new prototype was going to be installed were full of fear and resentment. Dispatchers were afraid they were being replaced and might lose their jobs. Operators and drivers didn't want to participate in something that might get their co-workers fired.

We picked out the dispatcher who was most traditional, anti-automation, and totally convinced that our system would never work. It couldn't possibly do a better job than he did! We sat him down in front of a prototype and showed him how to use it. We listened to his feedback and adjusted the prototype as quickly as possible, sometimes the same day. After a few sessions, he realized that this was not a replacement for him but a tool he could use to do his job better. He saw that we valued his input and became one of our strongest supporters. That convinced everyone else. If "Skeptical Steve" believed in the project, it must work!

In some applications, defining the functionality the customer needs can be difficult. Customers might not know exactly what they need or they might think they need one thing when they really need something else. Building a prototype can help clarify the customers' needs. Sometimes the project definition emerges incrementally as the customers see a series of prototypes and make evolutionary adjustments to each. Other times, after seeing an initial prototype, the customers realize what they really need and the design might take a completely new approach. In any case, prototypes let you get feedback early and often.

LIVING SPECIFICATION

After developers and customers have agreed that a prototype represents the system's functionality, the prototype can serve as a living specification. When customers have a question about what the final system will do, they can run the prototype and see.

Equally important, developers can look at the prototype to see what the final program should do. This lets them concentrate on writing code rather than trying to figure out what features to implement. It also helps prevent mismatches where one developer thinks a feature should work one way while another developer thinks it should work another way. If everyone understands what the prototype does, they will not need to argue about how things should work.

By defining the application's features, a good prototype lets several different tasks move forward in parallel. That lets you apply more people to the development effort at the same time so it can reduce total development time. The following sections describe some of the more important tasks that can run in parallel.

DETAILED SPECIFICATION

With an approved prototype in hand, you can begin preparing a detailed specification. Even the best prototype leaves some questions unanswered and the specification answers them. Writing the specification is a lot easier after the prototype is complete because it gives everyone a clear idea of how things will work. It's a lot easier to write about how an existing prototype works than it is to describe how a program that doesn't exist might work.

You can streamline the specification by referring to the prototype. Instead of describing every detail about how a scrolling list of inventory items works, the specification can say it works as demonstrated by the prototype. A programmer or customer who has a question about some detail during development can fire up the prototype and see.

The specification can also say one part of the system will be like another. Some large business applications contain dozens or hundreds of nearly identical reports. They are all very similar in format although they display different data. In that case, the prototype can demonstrate one of them and the specification can state that the others are similar.

If you use a series of prototypes, the specification should state which version it is referring to. For example, the specification might say: "The Work List Screen will look like the one in prototype version 0.09."

The specification should explicitly point out any features in the final application that differ from the prototype. Those are the main points where confusion might arise. Even with small features, if customers expect one thing and developers deliver another, the customers might feel betrayed. If the prototype cannot be trusted in this area, how do they know it can be trusted in other areas?

Tale from the Trenches

In one project, our team at GTE Laboratories built a prototype and then transferred it to GTE Data Services for implementation. That team went off on its own for several months and created what it considered the final application without any feedback from the customers or the prototyping team.

When the customers saw the final product, they noticed that the implementation group had made several "improvements." Our project leader sat through a series of meetings where the customers hammered the implementation team:

> CUSTOMER: With this version of the system, how would I do this?
>
> DEVELOPERS: Uh, we didn't think of that. I suppose you could use this roundabout method to do the same thing.
>
> CUSTOMER: What if you changed the application so it worked *this* way? It would be a lot easier.
>
> DEVELOPERS: I guess that would work.
>
> CUSTOMER: That's the way the prototype did it. Change it back.

In the end, the developers spent a lot more time making the program work the way it did in the prototype. The customers were very unhappy. They didn't see why they paid us to build a prototype, paid the development team to build the final application with improvements, and then paid the development team again to remove the improvements.

The development team had not learned from the prototype. If the developers had realized that the prototype defined the features that the customers wanted, they would not have added new features that had to be removed later.

DEVELOPMENT PLAN

After the customers accept the prototype, the developers have a fairly good idea of what the final application should do. You can then start designing the application's architecture and building a development plan. Some of the fine points might change as the detailed specification is fleshed out, but the overall design should be clear.

At this point, it's important to remember that the final program does not need to do things the same way the prototype did. The finished product should do what the prototype does, but it can use different methods. Often, prototypes are built using quick-and-dirty methods that are effective in the short term, but might not be easy to maintain over time. If you blindly follow the prototype's methods, you might be stuck with a poor design.

Step back and think about the problem again from scratch so you can build the best architecture possible.

DEVELOPMENT TOOLS

After seeing the prototype, you might be able to determine which tools you'll need to build the final application. For example, you might know that you will need an assortment of database-development tools. Even before the main programming effort begins, the database team can start buying or building those tools.

DOCUMENTATION AND TRAINING

User documentation and training depends only on what the program does and not how it works. That means you can begin preparing user documentation and training material as soon as the customer accepts the final prototype. These tasks always take a lot longer than developers expect and are often left to the last minute. The result is a product with documentation that is weak, incorrect, or missing entirely.

After you have a *final* prototype, you can begin preparing documentation and training materials. However, not all prototyping approaches produce a single final prototype. In one method, developers build an initial prototype and get customer feedback. They build a new prototype and get more feedback. The process repeats until the prototype does everything the final application should do. The developers then declare this last version of the prototype to be the final application. In that situation, documentation has to wait until features are finalized.

Chapter 2, "Kinds of Prototypes," talks more about the pros and cons of this sort of evolutionary prototyping as well as other approaches.

Tale from the Trenches
I've worked on several projects that used evolutionary prototyping and it can be very frustrating to the documentation and training people:

> TRAINING: Can you give me a rundown of how the user assigns an employee to a department so I can write it up?

> ME: Sorry, we don't know that yet.

> TRAINING: Can you at least tell me where the program gets the list of departments?

> ME: Nope. Perhaps in the next prototype.

This highlights one of the drawbacks to evolutionary prototyping: The functionality isn't completely set until the project is complete. At that point, documentation and training materials are already late.

You can help by keeping the documentation team aware of which functions are fixed in each version of the prototype. They may not be able to prepare all the materials, but they can at least get started.

Some companies require the developers to build a complete user interface prototype before they write any code. Documentation and development progress simultaneously. Although this makes it harder to accommodate last minute changes, it's a lot easier to release a program with a good set of documentation.

HOLLOW SHELL

A prototype does not necessarily implement features in the same way the final application will. The prototype might take huge shortcuts that make it less useable except in very specific instances. The goal here is to give the customer a feel for the application, not to build it yet.

Example
Many programs begin with a sign-on form on which the user enters a username and password. The prototype can compare the values entered to a username and password stored in the code. The final application will need to use a more flexible and robust system such as trying to log onto a database using the entered values.

Prototypes are often short on formatting and error-handling code. For example, phone number fields might not verify that entered values look like valid phone numbers so the user will need to use the right format.

Even so, the prototype should not be too stupid. It should save an invalid phone number into its test database or at least present a somewhat meaningful error message rather than crashing without warning. The prototype provides the first good chance for the customer to see what you are building. Making a good first impression is important, so don't mess it up with dozens of error messages and crashes.

If the prototype is too fragile to work safely, don't let the customer experiment with it. Instead, demonstrate it yourself following a thoroughly rehearsed script. Be sure you know what will work and what won't, and don't do anything you haven't tried before.

Tale from the Trenches
First impressions can mean life or death to a new project. One application I built for the state of Minnesota began with a logon form shaped like the state of Minnesota. Not just a rectangular form with a picture on it, but a form cut out to resemble the state.

When the users saw the first prototype, they loved it. When the demonstration was over, the first thing they asked was, "How did you make that logon screen?" They thought it was so cool. They also had a lot of useful feedback and we made a lot of changes to the design, but that one form had sold them. A little razzle-dazzle can make a powerful first impression.

One danger of a good prototype is that it might raise the customers' expectations. A good prototype looks like an almost finished program. After seeing a demonstration, the customer might say something like, "The prototype looks great! Just fix up those few bugs and formatting problems in the next week or so and we'll use that."

The customer doesn't understand that the prototype is like a movie studio set: It looks great in a carefully controlled demonstration but behind the facade, it's just a hollow shell.

Even if you convince the customers that you cannot just "fix up" the prototype, they might have trouble understanding why it will take you nine months to take the prototype from "almost done" to "done."

You should warn customers of the prototype's "hollow" nature before you show it to them so you don't raise their expectations prematurely.

TEST APPLICATION ARCHITECTURE

A prototype can test the application's preliminary architecture. While building the prototype, you can implement the overall framework you will need to build the final application. If it doesn't work for the prototype, it probably won't work for the final application, either.

Two of the most common application-design strategies are object-oriented design and stepwise refinement. The following two sections explain how a prototype can help you refine a project design using these two approaches.

OBJECT-ORIENTED DESIGN

In an object-oriented architecture, you begin by identifying the programming objects that make up the system. You determine how those objects interact and what sorts of features they need to have to do their work individually and as a group.

For example, a point-of-sale system might have objects representing customers, orders, order items, and inventory items. These objects have properties and methods for dealing with their own abstract data. The `Customer` object contains information about a customer: name, billing address, shipping address, account number, account balance, and so on.

The objects also know how to work together. The `Customer` object needs to know how to create a new `Order` object representing an order created by that customer. The `Order` object needs to know how to make `OrderItem` objects representing the items in the customer's order. One of these objects needs to know how to combine all the `OrderItems` to produce a bill for the customer.

Other objects might deal with controlling the application rather than the domain. These objects might include `User`, `Privilege`, `Form`, `Printer`, and `Report`.

In this kind of object-oriented architecture, the prototype should implement the most important objects. For this example, those would probably be the `Customer`, `Order`, and `OrderItem` classes. The prototype should define the main interactions among those objects and provide enough detail so it can display a reasonable imitation of the final application.

Some objects might provide only enough features to let the prototype work. When a user wants to create a new `Order` for a `Customer`, the new `Order` object might contain exactly four `OrderItems`. The final application would let the user add and remove `OrderItems` as needed but the prototype just needs to show what `OrderItems` look like.

The prototype might even omit some less important objects. In this example, the prototype might not provide real username and password checking. It also might not verify permissions before allowing the user to generate reports and view certain screens.

A prototype should definitely include any objects that you don't understand completely. If you plan to interact with a data acquisition system and you have not done so before, include the data acquisition classes in the prototype. The prototype gives you a chance to test things you don't understand in miniature before you try to implement them in the full-blown application. If you don't investigate these issues now in the prototype, you will have to handle them later when changing the system's design will be much harder.

As you build the prototype, you will learn more about the interactions among the objects. You might discover new features that an object should provide. You might find that some objects are unnecessary or that you need a new type of object that you didn't anticipate. Building the prototype will help you finalize your object architecture.

If you start making too many changes to the original design, you should probably step back and reevaluate. You will generally get a better result if you rewrite the design from scratch rather than incrementally patching it up to make the prototype work. When you have revised the design, you can start a new prototype.

After you have finished building the prototype, you should have the object model fairly well tested, at least at a high-level. If the prototype uses at least partial implementations of the system's most important classes, then your design is probably on track.

STEPWISE REFINEMENT

In the stepwise refinement development approach, you begin with a general statement of the program's design. For a point-of-sale system this might be something like the following:

> Store records describing customers, orders, and order items. Allow the user to create a new order and generate a bill automatically. Provide a lot of reports.

You then add more detail to this description to explain more about how the tasks will be accomplished. For example, you might mention that users need to log on with usernames and passwords, and that you will store data in a relational database.

When the system's description becomes too unwieldy, you group related tasks and break them into subsystems. You then add more detail to the descriptions of the subsystems. You continue this process—adding more detail and breaking the pieces of the system into smaller pieces—until you reach some level where you think you understand the complete solution.

At this point, you could start writing code to handle the smallest tasks. You could then combine them to solve higher-level problems, and so on until you had completed the entire application.

When you build a prototype, you need to decide which of the tasks you have defined should be included in the prototype. Usually those tasks include a large part of the application's user interface. That helps customers understand how they will interact with the program.

Building menus, buttons, and forms is relatively easy in Visual Basic, so including a lot of user interface in the prototype is not too difficult. It also lets you test any interface elements that are not part of the standard Visual Basic toolkit. For example, if you will be using a new ActiveX control that you just bought, you can try it out in the prototype to see whether it can do everything you need.

The user interface also provides a starting point for demonstrating deeper parts of the application. Pushing a button can launch code that tests pieces of the system that you need to study in greater detail.

You should include pieces of the design that you don't fully understand in the prototype. For example, if the final program must update a database on a Web server, the prototype should demonstrate that capability. The prototype need not implement every detail of this operation, but it should prove that you could accomplish the task. In this case, the prototype might connect to a database on a Web server and update a specific record. If you can do that much in the prototype, you will have some confidence that you can update records more generally in the final application.

As you build the prototype, you will probably discover new tools you need to build that you hadn't thought of before. You might also find you don't need other utilities that you thought would be necessary. Building the prototype will help you finalize your project architecture.

If you start making too many changes to the original design, you should probably step back and reevaluate. You will usually get a better result if you rebuild the design from scratch rather than incrementally patching it up to make the prototype work. When you have revised the design, you can start a new prototype.

After you have finished building the prototype, you should have the overall architecture fairly well tested. If the prototype demonstrates basic features from each of the program's major subsystems, then your design is probably on track.

TEST UNTRIED TECHNOLOGY

A prototype gives information about the system that you are about to build. When you plan to use untried technology, you need all the information you can get. The prototype should exercise any hardware, software, algorithms, or other technology that you have not used before. If a software tool you wanted to use won't do the job, it's better to find out in the prototype before you have spent a lot of effort preparing to use that tool.

The prototype does not need to exercise every feature of the new tool. It just needs to give you enough experience so you know how to use the tool to build the final application.

After you know how the tool performs, you can decide whether you should use that tool or replace it with something else. If no replacement is available, you might need to change the application's design to eliminate the related features entirely. Eliminating paths doomed to failure now can save a lot of time during final development.

The prototype can also help you test new activities that are not directly related to writing source code. For example, you can use a new source code control system, series of code reviews, or progress-tracking tools while building the prototype. This will help you learn whether these tools will work for you in the bigger project.

The prototype will also give you some experience with these tools while it is still easy for you to change their use. For example, after using a progress-tracking tool in the prototype, you might decide that you only need to track progress on a weekly instead of daily basis.

If you test every unknown feature of the system thoroughly in the prototype, you will know how to implement everything during final development. It can be a lot of work, but there will be no surprises. You might decide to switch graphing tools, change the frequency of code reviews, and drop a whole subsystem during prototype development. Building the final application, however, will be a matter of sitting down and writing code to do things you understand.

PREDICT PROJECT DURATION

After you have defined the tasks needed to build the final application, you need to assign durations to each of the tasks. This is usually done in a somewhat ad hoc manner with the lead developers guessing how long each task should take based on their prior experience. The quality of these estimates depends on the experience of the person making the predictions and the people writing the code.

You can compare the time needed to implement the tasks in the prototype with the predicted times and make adjustments if necessary. If you find that most of the prototyped tasks took longer than anticipated, then you should expect the nonprototyped tasks to take longer than expected, too. If most of the prototyped tasks are easier than anticipated, you might want to shorten the development schedule.

Although comparing prototype times to predicted times like this can be a useful scheduling technique, there are several ways it can backfire.

EASY PROTOTYPE TASKS

Many prototypes include the easiest tasks in the project's development. This is particularly true when developers run out of prototyping time or face tight deadlines. In that case, developers often work on the easiest tasks first because that way they finish as much of the prototype as possible.

If an easy task turns out to be a little harder than expected, it will take a little longer to complete. On the other hand, a problem in a complex task can affect the solution in several different ways, possibly spawning other problems. When a complicated task is harder than expected, it might take disproportionately longer to finish.

You should think about the tasks actually completed in the prototype and determine whether they are similar in difficulty to the project's other tasks. If they are generally easier, you might want to implement some of the harder tasks before you revise the project schedule.

Example

Suppose you want to build a routing application for a fleet of trucks. The prototype demonstrates the user interface and uses some prebuilt tables to simulate routing assignments. The prototype tasks are all done in roughly the expected time, so you assume your current schedule estimates are correct.

Building a user interface is relatively simple using Visual Basic. Building a complex routing algorithm can be extremely complicated. If you don't thoroughly understand the algorithm, it could take a lot longer than you expect to get it right. While you finished the prototype in the expected amount of time, you might have trouble meeting the application's final deadline.

To prevent this kind of problem, give extra thought to the application's hardest tasks. Prototype some of them if possible to get a better idea of how hard they really are.

The 80/20 Rule

Typically about 80% of a project's features are implemented in just 20% of the code. To put this a different way, about 80% of the code implements the most complex 20% of the tasks. Look for those difficult tasks and be sure they are represented in the prototype.

INSUFFICIENT PROTOTYPING TIME

Sometimes pressure from customers, marketing, or company executives limits the amount of time allowed for prototyping. The previous section explained how that might lead developers to implement the easiest tasks first and skew your time estimates.

Often not having enough time to finish the prototype is a sign of unexpected time pressure. If the prototyping period is cut short, you should ask yourself about the chances of the main application's schedule also being shortened. Make sure you have time to finish the application based on your current best total time estimate.

For similar reasons, you need to be careful about making predictions before the prototype is finished. If you have built half of the prototype's features, you cannot assume you have spent half of the time you will need. Consider the prototype tasks that are finished, and decide whether they are the easiest half of the tasks. The user interface is often built first and is often one of the easier parts of the prototype to build. In that case, you need to think hard about the relative difficulty of the remaining tasks before you can draw any reliable conclusions.

INCOMPLETE WORK

Chapter 2 describes several different approaches to building prototypes. Depending on which approach you select, much of the functionality in the prototype might be incomplete. Text boxes might not perform validations, lists might contain hard-coded values instead of getting their values from a database, and password checks might not really look up passwords.

In that case, you cannot count these incomplete tasks as finished. Suppose you predicted that the logon screen would take six hours to build and it took only three hours. If the prototype version of this screen does not actually validate passwords, you cannot assume that your schedule allocated twice as much time as necessary.

In cases like this, you need to guess how much of the final task was actually implemented by the prototype. If the prototype logon screen is about half finished, then your estimate of six hours is right on target.

This seems obvious when you spell it out like this but it underscores the danger of raised customer expectations described earlier in this chapter. If customers think the prototype's logon screen was finished early, they might try to convince you to shorten the project's time-line accordingly.

NONPROTOTYPED TASKS

A lot of important development tasks are not included in a prototype. Things like online help, documentation, and training material are rarely included in a prototype, but they can take up a lot of time. All too often, an application ships with terrible documentation, documentation based on an earlier version of the product, or no documentation at all because the development schedule didn't allow time for it.

You cannot multiply the time needed to build the prototype by some number and expect that to be the time needed to complete the whole project. You need to allow extra time for these items.

You also need to allow for extra development tasks that appear only when you start building the final project. Staff meetings, presentations for company officials and customers, and miscellaneous paperwork tend to take more time during application development than during prototype development. Even if a prototype task finished in the time you predicted, you need to allow extra time for these things. Plan for them.

INSUFFICIENT TESTING

It's extremely rare to test a prototype as thoroughly as a final application. After the prototype has come far enough to demonstrate certain design features, it is declared finished and work on the main project begins. Any bugs in the prototype are left for repair during the final implementation.

I can't argue that this is the wrong approach. Thorough testing of any application is a grueling process that can take a long time. Tracking down the last few bugs can take far longer than finding the first couple. Few organizations would be willing to spend four weeks on a prototype and four more weeks testing and debugging it before starting final application development.

Be aware that the final application will need a lot more time for testing and debugging than you are likely to give the prototype. Even if a task finishes on time in the prototype, it might still need extra testing.

FEATURE CREEP

During project development, new features commonly creep into the system. For example, the customer might think of things that were not included in the initial design. If these things are necessary, you have little choice but to add them.

Unfortunately, items added to the prototype can complicate schedule predictions. Suppose a prototype task requires twice as long as you thought it would but the extra time is due to a new feature. The extra time might affect only this one task. In that case, the rest of your schedule might still be fine.

Developers also tend to add new features to applications. They find some interesting or clever new feature that doesn't take a lot of work, and they tack it on. Usually these add-ons are fairly easy to build so they tend to weight the prototype with simpler code.

The easiest way to prevent these features from confusing the issue is to prohibit them. Tell developers not to add new features without prior approval. If someone suggests a really important addition, add it. Otherwise you can filter out unnecessary noise from the product. That will probably give you a better product in the end anyway.

Adding new features during development can also raise customer expectations. Nontechnical customers often don't know what's easy and what's hard for programmers. If you give them something easy, they might assume that something similar is also easy and they might ask for it. Stick with your initial design as much as possible to prevent this sort of thing.

UNEXPECTED PROBLEMS

Every software project encounters unexpected problems. You need to leave some time in the project schedule to let developers handle them. Similarly, you need to leave some time in the prototype schedule for emergencies.

The extra time you need usually does not scale well from the prototype to the final application. Prototypes tend to use a lot of untested technology so unexpected setbacks are common. After you finish the prototype, you should understand most of the formerly untried technology and not need quite as much slack time.

CHANGING DEVELOPMENT TEAM

For one reason or another, the developers working on final application development might not be the same as those who built the prototype. One developer might quit, another might be needed on a more urgent project, or you might be able to add new people to final development or even have completely separate prototyping and development teams.

In any case, if the developers who built the prototype are different from those who build the final application, whatever you learn from the prototype might not transfer directly. Some programmers are faster than others. Some write code that is easier to maintain and causes fewer bugs.

Individual developers might even work differently on different phases of a project. Some are particularly good at building a quick-and-dirty prototype interface, but are bad at building bulletproof code for the final application. If you apply too much pressure during prototype development, some programmers will burn out and their productivity will suffer during final implementation.

These kinds of differences in developer productivity are hard to measure, but you must take them into account when you plan the development schedule.

NOT TRUSTING THE RESULTS

A silly but remarkably easy mistake to make is to not trust the results of the prototype. If you went to all the trouble of building the prototype, you better learn from its results.

Example
Suppose you spend four weeks developing about 10% of the application's features and nothing else has occurred to make you question your predicted schedule. Then it will probably take you around 40 weeks to build the application. Forty weeks? That can't possibly be right! Besides, you only have six months. Surely you can reuse pieces of the prototype. And you learned things during the prototype, so they won't take as long in the final application.

It's easy to fall into this sort of trap, particularly if the project already has established deadlines. The pressure to ignore the prototype's results to meet those deadlines can be tremendous.

If you build the final application the way you built the prototype, you are likely to be wrong if you don't trust the prototype's results. Just declaring "we *will* have the project done by the due date" will do little except demoralize the developers, possibly reducing productivity and making matters worse.

Instead of ignoring the prototype's results because they don't tell you what you want to hear, modify your development plan to take them into account. Defer some of the program's features until the next release. Redesign the system architecture so you can add more developers. Most importantly, track progress carefully during development so you can tell if your changes are making any difference or if you are still headed for disaster.

SUMMARY OF TIME ISSUES

The previous sections describe a lot of ways a prototype can fail to predict the time needed to build the final application. It might sound like a grim picture, but usually these things happen in minor ways and don't seriously damage the prototype's usefulness. Some untested technology will be harder to use than you thought it would be, but something else will turn out to be easier. The customer will insist on one or two new features, but they won't radically change the application's purpose.

In the end, you'll examine the work you did in the prototype and make a guess about what fraction of the whole project that covered. Then you'll scale the results, add some extra time for testing, documentation, staff meetings, and unexpected problems and you'll arrive at a predicted length for the finished application. It will not be perfectly accurate because software development is an inexact science. However, it will be a lot better than the half-baked guesses that many software projects use for their timetables.

PREDICT NEEDED STAFFING

Staffing and duration are related closely but not in a simple way. Doubling the number of developers on a project does not necessarily cut development time in half. In some cases, it can greatly increase development time. However, sometimes you can shorten a project's duration by carefully adding extra developers.

The ideal time to add staff is right after you have finished the prototype and before you begin the main development effort. It is important to do this right away rather than taking a "let's wait and see" approach. If you wait until deadlines are looming, it will be hard or impossible to change the project's architecture to accommodate extra developers. At that point, throwing more people at the project might actually slow development while you get the new team members up to speed and try to repartition tasks in ways that do not fit the original architecture.

When you add developers to a project, you need to find things for them to do that do not interfere with what the other developers are doing. You need to somehow redefine or rearrange the project's tasks so they can be divided up differently.

Rearranging a project's tasks has dangers of its own. Tasks tend to group together naturally. If you break the natural groupings, you might cause more work. The developers working on the tasks must spend extra time coordinating their efforts. The related tasks must work consistently and should not contain duplicated code. Sometimes changes to one routine force changes to others.

Repartitioning the application might also make it so complex that the developers can no longer understand it. That can bring development to a standstill.

One of the simplest ways to rearrange a project's tasks is to split one into two or more pieces. This might create interactions among the pieces, but at least the rest of the project's tasks should interact with this group of tasks in the same way as before.

Another strategy is to pull out key parts of the most time-consuming tasks and put them in a tool library. Then you can assign other developers to build the tool library. If you define the interface between the tools and the routines that use them carefully to eliminate confusion, the tool team can work in parallel with the rest of the developers.

No matter how you change the development plan, the final programming effort will not follow the pattern set by the prototype. Predictions you make using the prototype data are less likely to hold if you don't do things exactly the same way—so you should track them closely as development progresses. If you see that you are not making up enough time to meet deadlines, you might have to try other measures.

DETERMINE PROJECT FEASIBILITY

A prototype can test untried technology and help predict a project's duration. If you learn that the new technology won't do what you need, or if you conclude that the application will take too long to build, you can decide to cancel the project.

Many companies consider canceling a project after the prototype stage to be a failure. Actually this is probably the way a prototype can save your company the most money. For a few thousand dollars worth of prototyping, you can save hundreds of thousands or even millions of dollars of development. The payback can be enormous.

A huge number of software projects are canceled late in the development process after spending a fortune in development money. More are finished and then declared failures because they don't do what the customers need properly and reliably. Canceling a project after the prototype is cheap.

Of course, if you cancel the project, you still haven't built the software the customers need. Many projects start with the assumption that the software is necessary. In that case, you might not be able to cancel the project. If the prototype makes the project seem unfeasible, however, you should step back and take another look at the problem. You might need to reduce the scope of the project or redesign the application architecture. You might even need to build another prototype to see if the new solution will work. Such major changes might be painful now, but they will be far less painful than having 20 developers spend a couple years building a system that is then totally scrapped.

REFINE DEVELOPMENT TECHNIQUES

While you build the prototype, you can refine your development techniques. You can hold code reviews and design meetings, practice using the source code control system and bug tracker, and set up the project's code directories. You can define the project's standard coding style, naming conventions, indentation rules, commenting formats, and so on.

After finishing the prototype, the developers should get together and decide on any changes they want to make before starting the main development effort. These things are a lot easier to change at this point than in the middle of development.

BUILD THE DEVELOPMENT TEAM

An often-overlooked advantage to building a prototype is that it lets you test and build the development team in a mini-project. As you build the prototype, you can identify the fastest developers, those who need the most supervision, and those who are natural leaders. Before you begin the final development effort, you can redefine peoples' responsibilities to best fit their abilities.

Tale from the Trenches

In a rather complex CAD system I worked on, one developer built a truly elegant design for one of the application's communications subsystems. It might have been worthy of an article in some development magazine, but it was too complicated for the programmer assigned to implement it. To make matters worse, that programmer thought he would get in trouble if he asked for help. In progress meetings he always said he was doing fine even though he was falling hopelessly behind schedule. Meanwhile, the developer who designed the subsystem was reassigned to another project so he couldn't help.

We did not build a prototype for that project. If we had, we would probably have noticed the problem in that subsystem right away. We could have simplified the design or reassigned a more experienced developer to cover that part of the project. As it was, that part of the application dragged on and became the time-limiting task for the whole project.

One common approach to staffing during a prototype is to begin with a small number of senior developers who work closely with the customers to define the application. They design the application architecture and define the project's major tasks. These will become the project's main subsystems.

At that point, each of these senior developers is assigned to one major task. Other senior developers might be added if the initial design team is too small to assign a developer to each major task. These developers later become the team leaders for their subsystems.

The developers each work on the design for their own subsystems with the project leader coordinating to minimize the relationships between the subsystems and to ensure that all the pieces fit together.

After the design is complete, the developers build prototypes of their subsystems and assemble them into the application prototype. Now is the time to reassign any developers who cannot handle their subsystems. Some subsystems might turn out to be more complex than expected. You might need to reassign them to more experienced developers or break them into smaller pieces.

The prototype lets you match developers with tasks that take full advantage of their abilities. It also lets the developers grow professionally. Over time, basic programmers can become team leaders. Team leaders learn to handle more complex subsystems and can become application architects and project leaders. The prototype lets the developers prove their skills in a situation where mistakes are correctable.

After the prototype is finished, the team studies the prototype and makes any needed adjustments. Using the information in this chapter, they might refine the design, pick replacements for tools that didn't work, adjust the development schedule, reduce the application's functionality, and so on.

By now, the team leaders should be intimately familiar with the system as a whole and their subsystems in particular. They have built prototypes of their pieces of the system and they have a good idea of how development should proceed.

At this point, the project staffs up for final development. Less-experienced developers are assigned to the subsystem teams. With the guidance of the team leaders, they work efficiently and harmoniously to build perfect subsystems that assemble into a perfect application.

At least in theory. There is still plenty of room for mistakes, tools that don't work, change requests from the customers, staffing and budget cuts, changes to deadlines, and other surprises. At least you've set yourself up for the best development experience you can have given the information you had at the time.

Summary

A prototype is a software microcosm. It is a miniature version of the final application you want to study. By building a smaller version of the program, you can learn a lot about the larger application in a much smaller amount of time. A prototype lets you make mistakes in miniature where they are easy to fix rather than waiting and making the same mistakes in the final application. You can use a prototype to define an application's features, verify that the program will satisfy the customers' needs, test untried technology, and hone the development team's skills.

You can even use a prototype to predict the final application's overall success. If you use a prototype correctly to guide development past potential mistakes, your success is almost assured.

KINDS OF PROTOTYPES

In this chapter

Most prototypes fall into one of two categories: throwaway prototypes or evolutionary prototypes. Which you should use depends on your general development strategy and what you hope to accomplish with the prototype.

This chapter describes these and other types of prototypes and discusses their strengths and weaknesses. It also explains how to pick the right kind of prototype for your application.

THROWAWAY PROTOTYPES

When you build a throwaway prototype, you plan to discard all of its code and start writing the final application from scratch. You get all the benefits of prototyping described in Chapter 1, "Reasons to Prototype," but you don't keep any of the code you wrote for the prototype.

Sometimes it makes sense to build more than one prototype. You start with an initial design and show it to the customers. Using their feedback, you modify the prototype and show it to them again. You repeat this process, possibly several times, until you have a prototype that everyone agrees defines the right features. Then you use it as the specification for building the final application.

Figure 2.1 illustrates this process graphically. Dashed lines indicate the quick-and-dirty development process used while building different versions of the prototypes. The prototype versions spiral in on the set of features that will be included in the final application. The solid arrow from the prototypes to the final application indicates the production-quality code developers use to implement the application.

Figure 2.1
In throwaway proto-
typing, a series of
prototypes define the
application's function-
ality but their code is
thrown away before
final development.

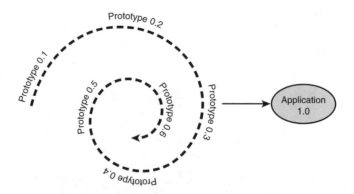

Tip

It's worth giving each version of the prototype a new version number and saving them in an archive for later use. Then if you need to refer to an earlier version, or if the customers change their minds and decide they liked an older version of the prototype better, you can easily go back.

Writing "quick-and-dirty" code is faster than writing solid production-quality code that can be used in a real application. The idea is to build a prototype quickly to define the application's features. Then developers build the actual application much more carefully.

To build a prototype as quickly as possible, developers can skimp on quality. The prototype code is just good enough to make the prototype work. It doesn't contain unnecessary error handling and doesn't demonstrate any more features than necessary to define the application. The prototype code is no more general than it needs to be. It is not necessarily extensible and it might be next to impossible to maintain over any length of time. It just needs to look good.

This doesn't mean developers should be intentionally stupid. They should still use comments to document the code, declare variables properly, and follow whatever coding conventions you have established. They do need to maintain and modify the prototype code during the prototyping period. They just don't need to worry about the code lasting forever.

Because quick-and-dirty programming is fast, it is often possible to build a series of throwaway prototypes that refine the initial design. Each version uses customer feedback and developer experiences to improve on the one before. Eventually, the prototype approaches what the customers need in their application. When everyone agrees the latest version of the prototype defines the application correctly, you can throw it away and start the final development phase.

It sounds weird that a prototype must be good enough to throw away but it is important that the last prototype be as nearly perfect as possible. Writing production-quality code takes a lot longer than writing quick-and-dirty code. If you must make changes to a prototype, you haven't lost a lot of work. Changes to the final application's code can have a much bigger impact.

This is particularly true because you can fine-tune the application architecture after you have finished the prototype. After you start the final development, changes to the architecture can cause major setbacks.

If the final prototype is solid, you can start preparing documentation and training materials when you begin development. Some changes to the application might pop up during the final stages, but the big questions should be answered.

ADVANTAGES

When you build a throwaway prototype, it might seem as if you waste a lot of time. After all, the code you wrote for the prototype is discarded and you have to start over from scratch.

This really isn't as bad as it seems. After all, you didn't spend as much time on the prototype code as you will spend on the final application's code. The following sections describe some of the advantages that make throwing away all this code worthwhile.

CODE QUALITY

The main advantage to a throwaway prototype is in the quality of the final code. When you build any complicated program, code tends to be written and rewritten. As the customers experiment with the prototype, they ask for new features and enhancements. No matter how carefully developers write their code, some of it will change and change again. After enough changes, the code becomes harder to manage. Bugs are more likely to appear and the code becomes even harder to modify in the future. If the changes are large enough, you might need to rethink the whole application architecture. In that case, a lot of existing code might be wasted.

When you build a throwaway prototype, you spend as little effort as possible initially. Only after you have a reasonable belief that the prototype defines the right application features do you start writing production-quality code. Although you might need to rewrite prototype code several times, you have spent as little time as possible on that code, so you haven't lost much.

When you start building the final application, the design has been concretely demonstrated by the prototype to eliminate ambiguity. The developers know exactly what the program needs to do so they will not need to rewrite the new code as much. Changes will still undoubtedly pop up as developers discover some things are harder than they thought, but the major design and feature changes should be over.

Building a throwaway prototype gives developers a chance to learn about the system. Then, when they implement the final application, they can get it right.

DEMONSTRATES MORE FEATURES

Building high-quality code takes a lot of time. Routines must be designed, written, tested, fixed, and rewritten.

Building a quick-and-dirty throwaway prototype is much easier. Developers should still begin with a good application design. After all, the prototype is supposed to resemble the finished application as closely as possible.

After the design stage, however, throwaway prototyping is very different from building a final application. After writing a routine, the developer only needs to test it enough to ensure it will work in the limited prototype setting. The routine might perform little error handling and it might not handle special cases. It might not even work in the same way that the final application will.

Example

A small shipping company is building an order-entry system. Each order has a shipping address that includes a name, apartment or unit number, street number, city, state, and Zip code.

The final application will use a database with a table listing Zip codes and the states they are in for the areas served by the company. When it starts, the program queries the table to get a list of states served and then uses that list to initialize the address form's state ComboBox. When it creates a new order, the program verifies that the order's Zip code has the proper format and that it lies within the state entered by the user.

The prototype uses code that explicitly sets the values listed in the state ComboBox to some of the states the company serves now. When it creates a new order, the prototype verifies that the Zip code has the proper format but doesn't verify that it lies within the state entered by the user. It demonstrates the final application's behavior but using methods very different from those the final application will use.

All these shortcuts mean that building a throwaway prototype is a lot easier and faster than building production-quality code. Developers can write more code in less time so the prototype can demonstrate more of the final application's features. The more features the prototype can demonstrate, the easier it is for customers to understand the application's design. That lets you get better feedback sooner so you can quickly zero in on what the customers need and produce a solid final specification.

PART
I
CH
2

QUICKLY INCORPORATE CHANGES

Normally a change to an existing program requires a lot of planning. Hasty changes are more likely to break a program than to fix it. To avoid adding subtle bugs to the code, a developer must study the code carefully, understand how the code relates to other pieces of the system, make the change, and then thoroughly test the code and any related routines.

The code in a throwaway prototype will not be maintained for a long period of time so some of this caution is unnecessary. Testing only needs to verify that the changes do not break the prototype, not that the new code can handle every possible situation.

In many cases, the prototype's code can insulate routines from changes in others. The previous example used prototype code instead of a database to build a list of states. That makes the prototype less flexible and harder to maintain but it separates the list of states from the database routines that the final program will use to load this information. If you make changes to the database routines, you do not need to worry about breaking the prototype code that builds the state list. Similarly, if you change how the state list works, you won't break the database code.

MORE PROTOTYPE VERSIONS

The ability to incorporate changes into the prototype quickly lets you be more responsive to customer feedback. Making fast changes lets you build more versions of the prototype so you can try new things. It encourages developers and customers to explore more options instead of sticking to their first ideas. That helps you produce a final application that does the best job possible.

Quickly incorporating customer feedback into the prototype also helps win buy-in. The customers learn that their opinions matter and that you listen to what they say. People whose suggestions make it into the prototype usually become enthusiastic about the project and often defend it when times are tough. A little customer goodwill can go a long way when the schedule slips.

Tale from the Trenches

When I worked at GTE Laboratories, I got to see a lot of the company's existing computer systems. Several of them were more than a decade old and included more than 5 million lines of source code!

Making changes to these huge and ancient systems is very dangerous. One false move could take customers out of service and introduce a bug that could take weeks to find.

To keep changes manageable, the company required several layers of approval before one of these systems could be touched. Users had to fill out a change request and get it approved from management before anyone would even look at the code.

Maintenance engineers would implement the change and test it on a special software build running on a separate test computer with a massive test database. If everything worked absolutely perfectly, they would load the change onto the production system days or even weeks after the original change request was filed.

In our prototypes, we were able to implement customers' change requests much more quickly. We could often install a change and show it to customers within hours. Sometimes the change was so simple, the customers stood behind us and watched us enter the new code.

Because we were not working with live customer databases and we were planning to rewrite the prototype code anyway, we were able to act much more quickly than the engineers maintaining the massive production systems. Our customers felt that we took their needs seriously and moved quickly to satisfy them, particularly when they compared our nearly instant changes to the process they needed to change their existing systems.

EASES PROJECT TRANSFER

Sometimes the group that builds the prototype is not the same as the group that builds the final application. A research group might build the prototype, get customer feedback, and write the specification. Then a development group takes over and builds the final application. In that case, the development group does not have any preconceptions they might have developed while building the prototype. They can start with clearly defined goals and without prejudice.

A similar case might arise if a small group of team leaders builds the prototype and then more developers join the project for the final development. The new developers can start fresh with the prototype as a specification and without any preconceptions about how the code should be built.

In some cases, a development team knows the final application will not be written in Visual Basic. Depending on the language and the developers' skills, it might be faster to build the prototype in Visual Basic rather than that other language. In that case, the prototype will be thrown away almost by definition because the Visual Basic code written for the prototype cannot be reused in an application written in C++ or Fortran.

Using Visual Basic for the prototype and another language for the final application has the advantage that it forces the developers to commit to throwing the prototype away. They cannot be tempted to reuse low-quality prototype code in the final application.

HELPS TEAM BUILDING

Throwaway prototypes give a development team time to improve their skills. It lets less-experienced programmers learn in a relatively safe environment. Any mistakes they make will be discarded before final application development anyway.

A throwaway prototype also gives the team a chance to match developers to the tasks they can handle best. It gives you a chance to identify the best programmers so you can assign them to the most difficult tasks during final application development. Similarly it lets you identify developers who might need extra supervision or training.

DISADVANTAGES

Unfortunately throwaway prototyping has a few disadvantages. The following sections describe some of the most important.

OVERENTHUSIASTIC CUSTOMERS

Throwaway prototypes are relatively easy to modify so you can quickly incorporate changes requested by customers. Sometimes the customers get so enthusiastic about their ability to modify the prototype that they get carried away. They make request after request and tie you up making endless revisions to the prototype. This has several bad consequences.

First, the customers might continue changing things that the prototype already covers. They might come up with more and more new ways to do the same things. The prototype keeps changing as customers insist that you try something new so it never settles down into something developers can use as a living specification.

If you see this problem looming, sit down with the customers and explain the problem. Brainstorm with them and come up with as many possible solutions to the problem as you can. Then pick the best one and use it in the prototype. Discard the others and move on.

A closely related problem occurs when the customers make too many change requests in general. They might not be redesigning features already present in the prototype, but there still seems to be no end to changes in sight.

In this situation, you cannot necessarily draw the line and accept some requests while rejecting others. It is possible that the customers' requests are all valid. In that case, you must decide whether the development schedule allows enough time to implement all the requests in the final application. If there isn't enough time, ask the customers to make a prioritized list of the enhancements they want. Customers tend to be better at this than most developers think. After you have the list, you can implement the most important features and save the others for the program's next release. If customers insist on all the changes, tell them the schedule will slip.

Eventually, you might need to set a date by which all change requests must be made. If you don't stop prototyping sometime, you'll never finish the final application.

PART

I

CH

2

Tale from the Trenches

In one project, our customers did exactly this. They kept coming up with new features they wanted and changes to existing features. The project leader told them we didn't have enough time to do everything and that further changes would need to wait until the next release.

The customers understood, at least in theory, but they couldn't keep their hands off the system. They knew our team leader would defer any new changes until the next release so they started calling the developers directly.

Developers generally want to be helpful and one or two changes don't usually cause much trouble so the developers gave in and promised new features. Eventually this got so far out of hand that it was starting to affect the project completion date.

Our project leader explained the problem to the customers and laid down the law. The customers were no longer allowed to talk directly to the developers. Any change requests or status reports had to go through him. And he would only answer phone calls and emails between 4:00pm and 6:00pm.

This worked. Deep down, the customers really did understand our problem. They just couldn't bring themselves to sit back and let the project take its natural course. After the new ground rules were established, they left us alone and we finished on time.

The customers were even happier with the new system. They really didn't want to spend all their time pestering the development team; they just wanted to be sure they were doing everything they could to make the project a success. After they understood that they would help us the most by letting us finish the job, everyone was happier.

TEMPTATION TO REUSE CODE

When you build a throwaway prototype, you must be sure that it is really thrown away. It is extremely tempting for developers to reuse the prototype's code. It already does what they need to do so why should they have to reinvent everything?

Reusing prototype code is particularly tempting when the developers who built the prototype also build the final application. It's not too hard to convince a new team of developers that they can rewrite the code better than it was written in the prototype. It's difficult for the prototype developers to admit that the code they worked so hard on isn't the best possible way to do things.

The prototype code was not written with reuse in mind. It was patched together as quickly as possible without proper coding style, documentation, or error handling. Some of it probably uses temporary methods that violate the overall project design. For example, the earlier example included Zip codes in the source code. Adding this quick-and-dirty code to the final application would be a huge mistake. At best, the developers would need to rewrite all this code. At worst it would cause subtle bugs that only appear much later when they are hard to diagnose.

Sometimes developers can take ideas from the prototype's code. Because the prototype's code is not up to production standards, however, they should rewrite anything they use. Cutting and pasting code from the prototype will introduce enough problems to offset any time savings.

Tale from the Trenches

Even if you know you should not reuse the prototype's code, it can be hard to resist the temptation. In several projects I worked on at GTE Laboratories, the plan was for us to build a prototype and then transfer it to a development group at GTE Data Services for final implementation. We would build the prototype using four or five programmers. The development would start with half a dozen team leaders and then staff up to 40 or 50 developers for final implementation.

In some cases, the development team reused prototype code with only minor modifications. They rewrote much of the interface code but they left a lot of the core algorithms unchanged. This can allow bugs from the prototype code to sneak into the final system without the developers knowing they are there.

The application developers also did not understand the code as well as they would have if they had rewritten the code from scratch. You learn a lot more building a system yourself than you do reading someone else's code.

Fortunately we suspected that a lot of code would be reused, particularly in the core algorithms. Some of that code was very tricky and we were better able to understand it than the development team. We were at a research lab studying these algorithms on an ongoing basis while they were a more traditional development and maintenance organization.

To make the system as robust as possible, we spent extra time on the final prototype versions. We made the entire system as solid as possible, paying particular attention to the core algorithms. We ended up with a semi-evolutionary prototype where the final development team rewrote some but not all of the application. Later sections in this chapter have more to say about reusing prototype code in evolutionary prototypes.

NO HELP SCHEDULING

A throwaway prototype does not give you much help in validating the development schedule. If the prototype doesn't use the same methods that the final application will, it cannot help you predict the project's duration.

Example

A large corporation needs to build a reporting tool containing 120 customized reports. The developers spend four weeks building a prototype that demonstrates 20 of them.

If the prototype reports use the same method that the final application will, you can estimate that building the final application will take around 6 times as long or 24 weeks.

If the prototype reports are prebuilt files that display canned output that is not tied to the database, you know little about how long the final development will take.

To make schedule estimates more accurate, a prototype might include some routines that are written nearly at production quality. You can use those to help validate your schedule.

Example

Developers take 3 weeks to build 10 reports using the final application's data gathering and presentation techniques. Building all 120 reports will take roughly 12 times as long or about 36 weeks.

Developers also spent a week building 10 other prebuilt reports that use quick-and-dirty methods. These reports do not help you predict the final schedule, but they give the customers more examples to study.

Usually, the best routines to implement in production-quality detail are those where you have the most uncertainty. If you have displayed reports in a previous project, you probably don't need to prototype reports in detail. Use the knowledge you gained from the other project to estimate how long the reports will take in the new project. Put together some simple reports to show customers how they will work.

On the other hand, if you have never written routines to transfer files to a Web server, write those routines more carefully and use them to predict how long it will take to write all the file transfer routines in the new project.

BUGGY PROTOTYPES

In a throwaway prototype, developers use quick-and-dirty methods to get something running as soon as possible. Although the developers should not spend too much time on things such as error handling, they cannot completely ignore these issues either. The prototype must work well enough for customers to experiment with it without too many distractions.

If developers get carried away with the quick-and-dirty philosophy, the prototype might be too buggy for customers to use. If the prototype crashes five times in the first hour of experimentation, your customers will not have faith in your ability to build the final application. Customers will grow frustrated and you will lose customer buy-in, enthusiasm, and loyalty.

The prototype should trap errors that will interrupt the customer and do something reasonable, even if it isn't exactly what the final application will do. The prototype might present an error message and make the user fix a data-entry error. It might blank numeric fields where the customer has typed letters. It might even have some menus grayed out if their functions do not work well enough yet to show the user. The prototype might not go to the same lengths to fix a problem as the final application will, but it should do something reasonable.

Explain any differences between the prototype's error-handling system and the one used by the final application. That will go a long way toward keeping customers happy in the face of incomplete error handling.

EVOLUTIONARY PROTOTYPES

When you build a throwaway prototype, none of the prototype's code is used in the final application. An evolutionary prototype uses the opposite approach. In an evolutionary prototype, all the prototype's code is reused in the final application.

The idea is to build a small prototype using high-quality code. You show the prototype to the customers and get feedback. You then modify the prototype, again using high-quality code, and show the new version to the customers. You continue this process, incrementally improving the prototype, until the prototype contains all the finished application's features. You then rework the code turning high-quality code into production-quality code. The final prototype becomes the finished product.

Figure 2.2 shows this process graphically. The solid spiral indicates the high-quality code the developers use to build each prototype.

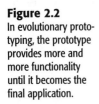

Figure 2.2
In evolutionary proto-typing, the prototype provides more and more functionality until it becomes the final application.

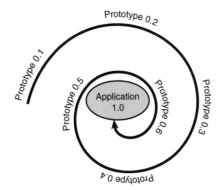

There are two differences between the throwaway prototypes shown in Figure 2.1 and the evolutionary prototypes shown in Figure 2.2. First, the throwaway prototypes use quick-and-dirty code, whereas the evolutionary prototypes use high-quality code. Second, the throwaway prototypes are used to define the application's functionality but their code is not used in the final program. The last version of an evolutionary prototype actually becomes the final application.

Using high-quality code does not mean the evolutionary prototype must be perfect, at least not initially. You can still use some of the tricks you use in a throwaway prototype: Skip some error handling, hardwire data into the code instead of loading it from a database, and so on.

This is particularly useful in the prototype's early phases when a lot of the underlying sup-port code might not have been written yet. The first prototype might consist of a fairly complete user interface in which the buttons, menus, and other interface elements don't do anything.

Although you can use shortcuts in an evolutionary prototype, you plan to come back and fix these things later. In a throwaway prototype, you don't need to replace the shortcuts because the prototype won't last very long. In an evolutionary prototype, you eventually need to replace any shortcuts you take with more maintainable code. To make finding these shortcuts easier, you should add a comment to your code whenever you take a shortcut.

Just because you can take shortcuts early on doesn't mean you can be sloppy. You can defer some tasks for later but you will have to live with any bad design decisions you make. For that reason, you need to plan more carefully before you begin writing code in an evolution-ary prototype. You need to decide how routines will interact, what code you should write now, and what you can leave for a later version of the prototype.

Evolutionary prototypes have their own advantages and disadvantages. The following sections describe some of the most important.

ADVANTAGES

Evolutionary prototypes have several advantages that make them more attractive than throwaway prototypes for many people. The following sections describe some of their most important advantages.

PROGRESS REALLY IS PROGRESS

With an evolutionary prototype, progress really is progress. If the development team implements roughly 20% of the final application's features in a particular version of the prototype, then they are roughly 20% done with development (excluding all the extra tasks like documentation). This gives customers a simple intuitive way to track progress.

Sometimes this can be misleading, however, because developers often write the easiest code first. To get the most feedback from an evolutionary prototype, the first versions usually concentrate on demonstrating the user interface. The user interface is usually easy to build so it seems as if the developers make a lot of progress initially and then slow down when they start implementing more complex features.

Usually, you can defuse any potential problems by warning customers that development will seem to slow down after the first few prototype versions.

HELPS SCHEDULING

The code in an evolutionary prototype eventually becomes part of the final application so that code should be of high quality. It should be thoroughly tested as it is written so little extra work will be needed to upgrade the code to production quality. That means it should take roughly the same amount of time to write a comparable piece of code for the final application.

Now you can compare the amount of time it actually took to write this code with the amount of time you originally scheduled for it. If the times are close, your estimates are probably reasonable.

If the amount of time to write the prototype differs greatly from what you expected, you should try to find out why. The developers might have spent extra time getting up to speed on the project and things might move faster in the future. Or the developers might have picked the easiest features to implement in the prototype and final development will take longer.

If you cannot figure out why your original time estimates were off, prototype a few more features to see whether you can get a better understanding of the problem. If the time needed to implement these tasks also differs greatly from your original estimates, you might need to revise the schedule.

EASY IN VISUAL BASIC

Building an evolutionary prototype is particularly easy in Visual Basic. Using the development environment's click-and-drag interface, wizards, and many powerful controls, you can put together a simple user interface relatively quickly and call it prototype version 0.1. This version doesn't do anything except show parts of the user interface. In fact, the entire user interface probably won't even work yet. For example, a mapping application might display a preloaded map, but it would probably not allow the user to load other maps, zoom in on parts of the map, or click objects to see what they are.

After you have some sort of user interface built, you can show it to the customers and get initial feedback. Remember that one of the important uses of a prototype is to get customer feedback as early and as often as possible. This helps prevent you from straying off track and doing a lot of unnecessary work. Testing while the program doesn't really do much lets customers make decisions about the system's overall appearance and functionality and can save you a lot of work. At this stage the customers might decide that a map is not the best way to visualize the data and they might ask you to remove the whole mapping system before you have to write all the mapping code.

You will probably need to go through a couple of cycles building new prototypes and getting customer feedback before you arrive at a reasonable overall user interface design.

As user interface features are approved, you can begin working on the code behind them. Initially, these routines might be simple stubs that present message boxes. For example, if you click the map, the program could display a message box saying "Display information about clicked object here." Later you will fill in this functionality to actually display the information.

Note that you don't need to wait until the entire user interface is approved before you begin adding features. If the customers like the mapping subsystem's proposed features, some developers can work on it while others continue refining the rest of the user interface.

ZEROS IN ON FUNCTIONALITY

Successive versions of an evolutionary prototype zero in on the features needed in the final application. The initial design should describe the program's overall capabilities, but describing all the little details can be difficult, particularly for customers who might not have a lot of experience with application development.

Showing customers steadily improving versions of the prototype helps them focus on the details. After they can perform a task with the prototype, the customers will think of consequences that they could not have before.

LESS "WASTED" CODE

When you build a throwaway prototype, you end up writing a lot of code that isn't used in the final application. Then, you need to rewrite it for the final application. Because you do not need to write this throwaway code in an evolutionary prototype, you write less code in total.

Although this seems like a clear benefit, it is a little deceptive. Usually, an evolutionary prototype explores several false paths before settling down on a final design. Some parts of the system might need to be rewritten several times before everything is finished.

In the end, evolutionary prototypes often go through as much code as a throwaway prototype, particularly because throwaway prototypes often implement only a small fraction of the application's features to be useful.

In any case, the apparent benefit of writing less code is often encouraging to the developers. They don't feel as if the code on which they spent so much time and effort is being casually discarded.

POINT RELEASES

Evolutionary prototyping lends itself naturally to point releases. After an important piece of functionality is built and thoroughly tested, you can give the prototype to the customers as a point release. Give the prototype a new version number such as 1.0 and let the customers use the features that work.

When you do this, you must be certain to deactivate every feature that is not working properly so the customers do not try to use them. If you leave an unfinished feature activated, it is certain that someone will eventually try to use it and then complain when the feature doesn't work properly. Disable or hide menu items, buttons, and other controls that activate these unfinished features.

Developers must also be certain that the released features are fully tested and debugged. On one hand, this is just another in a series of prototypes. On the other hand, customers will use this version to try to do their jobs. The features that are present must be up to production quality.

Before you start making point releases, you also need to be certain that the overall application design will work. For example, suppose later versions of the prototype require a change to your underlying database. The new database design might require changes to features you have already released. They might even destroy any work the customer has done using the previous release. Quick releases to customers make them very happy but few things make them less happy than forcing them reenter a large amount of work they have already done.

Tale from the Trenches

Back in the days before Visual Basic, I worked on a couple of projects as a toolsmith for the prototyping team. I built miscellaneous accessories and tools for them to use in building the prototype.

One of my largest tools was a screen handler. The screen handler used screen definition files to manage display, formatting, and data entry fields on a text terminal. The screen definition files determined such things as what labels were displayed and in which positions, where the data entry fields were located and what data formats they expected, and how the tab and arrow keys moved the user from one field to the next.

As the prototyping group used the screen handler, they discovered new features they needed added. I made the changes and built a new point release of the screen handler for the prototyping team.

Unfortunately these changes sometimes required modifications to the screen definition file formats. That meant the developers might have to rebuild all their screen definition files.

To avoid that, I wrote some conversion routines that translated the existing files into the new format.

It would have been nice if I could have predicted their needs in advance and avoided any inconvenience, but there wasn't time to build the entire screen handler before starting the prototype. You may not always be able to avoid this sort of problem, but you should at least think about the issue before you give your customers point releases.

EXTENSIBLE

An evolutionary prototype grows incrementally until it reaches some level of usefulness when it is released to the customers. After the customers have worked with the application for a while, they will undoubtedly think of changes and enhancements they would like. You can start building a new prototype to satisfy these requests. This is just like building one more prototype in the series. What you thought was the final application has just become a point release.

You already have the infrastructure you need in place to handle multiple prototype versions. Just start a new sequence of prototypes to test the new features. When you are ready, make another point release.

CAN TRACK CHANGING NEEDS

Today's business world changes so rapidly that, in some large projects, the final application might literally be obsolete before it is finished.

Evolutionary prototyping assumes changes come quickly so developers are already prepared to make quick changes. Source code controls should be in place so there is no confusion tracking different releases. The application architecture should be well segmented so changes to one part of the system require few modifications to other parts of the system. All the tools are present, you just need to use them.

This doesn't mean you can rush changes out hastily. Developers must still thoroughly test the code to make sure any changes work properly and that they haven't introduced problems in the rest of the application.

Tale from the Trenches

Back in its heyday, GTE had several large systems that were more than a decade old and contained more than a million lines of code. They were originally built using traditional, non-prototyping methods so they could not easily accommodate changes.

Over the years, they were extended and modified by hundreds of different programmers using a variety of development techniques. Over a few years time, the code became a Frankenstein's monster of modifications, fixes, and patches that was marginally useful and almost impossible to maintain.

The main reason these systems worked so poorly was that the developers were not set up to provide quick changes. Their development methodology required careful planning, a long study of the problem, and extremely detailed designs before developers wrote a single line of code. Any modifications had to follow the same glacial process.

DISADVANTAGES

Evolutionary prototypes have a lot of advantages. In fact, they have so many advantages that some developers argue that all applications should be built as a series of evolutionary prototypes.

Despite all their strengths, evolutionary prototypes do have some disadvantages. Most of them are easy to manage if you are aware of them.

REQUIRES A GOOD ARCHITECTURE

Sometimes you learn that the architecture you designed at the start of a project doesn't really fit the solution you eventually implement. Things change gradually as development progresses until the final pieces of code barely fit in with the overall design. The system might work, but it will probably be hard to maintain over time.

To avoid this sort of problem, you need to have a solid application architecture before you start development. The throwaway prototype provides some room for experimentation. On the other hand, changing the basic design of an evolutionary prototype can be difficult after development is underway.

Without a good framework, the first versions of the prototype might turn out to be so weak that you'll need to throw them away and start over. What you thought would be an evolutionary prototype might turn into a throwaway after all.

ALL CODE MUST BE HIGH QUALITY

In an evolutionary prototype, developers must be careful to write high-quality code from the start. Any bugs introduced early on are likely to cause other bugs and be hard to track down later.

This means developers don't have time to settle into the prototyping environment. They must already be able to write good, solid code right away without a lot of false starts. Less experienced programmers have little time to come up to speed and improve their skills in the relatively safe environment of a throwaway prototype.

INHIBITS TEAM BUILDING

When you build an evolutionary prototype, developers tend to be stuck with whatever position they are given at the start. A programmer who starts off designing the system's database is probably stuck doing that until the end, even if he has no talent for databases.

To reduce the consequences of this kind of mismatch, try to put developers to the test as soon as possible. Then reassign people if necessary before they get settled into their roles. Moving someone from one part of the project to another is a lot easier at the beginning than in the middle of development.

MIGHT DELAY RELEASES

It is sometimes tempting to put too many new features in the next version of an evolutionary prototype. One developer starts to add a new feature requested by the customers. Before that feature is fully implemented, another developer starts adding another feature. This "just one more thing" process continues with new features being added before all the previous features are implemented so the prototype never reaches a stable state again. You can show the customer prototypes, but they are buggy and filled with half-finished work.

In the extreme case, the only correctly working version of the prototype is the final version that implements everything. At that point, the customers have not properly tested many of the features so you cannot be sure they satisfy the customers' needs.

Preventing this sort of problem is just a matter of discipline. After you gather feedback on one version of the prototype, make a list of the features you will add in the next version. Then start implementing those features. Do not add anything new. When something new comes up, add it to the list for the following version.

PROTOTYPE VERSIONS TAKE LONGER

The code written for every version of an evolutionary prototype must be high quality. That means it takes longer for developers to add a feature to an evolutionary prototype than it would take to add the same feature to a throwaway prototype.

The payback comes later when the developers of a throwaway prototype need to re-implement the feature in the final application. If the developers of the evolutionary prototype do their jobs well, the prototype already contains the code that will be used in the final application. Although the evolutionary prototype takes longer, the extra time is not wasted.

Sometimes you need to explain to the customers why it seems to take so long to implement a seemingly simple feature. Tell them it will be worth it in the long run.

WASTES TIME ON UNUSED FEATURES

Sometimes developers of an evolutionary prototype waste a lot of time implementing features that are later removed from the system. An evolutionary prototype should contain only high-quality code so developers spend more effort making the new feature robust than they would in a throwaway prototype. Then the customer sees it in action and asks to have it removed.

To prevent this sort of problem, get customer feedback as soon as possible. Explain the new feature to the customers and make sure it is needed before you start writing code. You cannot predict customers' wishes every time, but the sooner you stop following unprofitable lines of research the better.

SCRAPS

Scrap refers to a quick little program that you whip out as fast as possible to test a single tool or programming technique. Scraps are barely functional programs written purely for the programmer's benefit and will never be shown to customers. Typically, they contain little or no error handling and the smallest possible user interface. The whole point is to test one or two features or ideas as quickly as possible.

Example
Suppose your application needs to draw a lot of graphs and charts. You are considering three different graphing controls. You could write one scrap using each of the controls to demonstrate the features you think you will need in your application. Based on how easily the three controls do what you want, you can decide which one to use.

After a scrap has served its purpose, it is usually thrown away and never used again. A slightly better strategy is to save the scrap in a test directory and let it gather dust. Then if you need to perform further tests, you don't need to start from scratch. Usually, scraps are so simple that you can rebuild them from scratch in an hour or two anyway.

Scraps usually are built before or during prototyping. By the time the final development starts, all the tools should be selected and any major design questions should have been answered. Occasionally, a programmer will write a scrap to test alternatives for handling some detail, but issues as fundamental as which graphing tool you will use should already be decided.

OTHER TYPES OF PROTOTYPES

Besides the two main kinds of prototypes, there are a few other useful prototyping approaches and several useful combinations. The following sections describe some of the most common.

USER INTERFACE PROTOTYPES

A user interface prototype is exactly what it sounds like: a prototype designed to test a user interface design. A user interface prototype contains buttons, menus, and lists so the customer can get a feel for how the application will work

The prototype will probably need a little code to display new forms, populate lists with fake data, and so forth, but it should contain as little other code as possible. It is like a Hollywood movie set: It looks good but there is nothing behind the facade.

After customers have had a chance to examine the prototype, you can refine it to better fit their needs. After everyone agrees that the user interface looks fine, you can begin development on the code behind the scenes.

Another approach is to refine the prototype to handle all the user interface chores and to call routines written in another language, such as C++, to do the application's bulk processing. Visual Basic makes a great front end for other languages.

THROWAWAY FOLLOWED BY EVOLUTION

You can use a throwaway prototype as a sort of preview or reality check before starting "real" development with an evolutionary prototype. The throwaway prototype lets you get something working quickly so you can gather customer feedback. Often the throwaway is a user interface prototype designed to help the customers understand how the final application will work.

After everyone agrees that the throwaway more or less defines the necessary system, you can begin application development using evolutionary prototypes. The quick feedback from the throwaway prototype helps you design a solid architecture for use in building the evolutionary prototypes.

In this kind of hybrid, the throwaway prototype is as minimal as possible. This lets you start work on the evolutionary prototype as soon as you can and reduces the amount of code that is "wasted" in the throwaway prototype. It also reduces the amount of low-quality code in the throwaway prototype that developers might otherwise be tempted to reuse.

DOWNGRADING

Sometimes you might start a project assuming you are going to build an evolutionary prototype and then downgrade it to a throwaway prototype. One reason you might do this is if someone in the company decides that the final application must be built using a different language such as C++. Another reason would be if someone decides the application must run under an operating system such as Unix that does not support Visual Basic. Ideally, these decisions should be made before development begins but sometimes they occur surprisingly late in the process.

Another reason to switch to a throwaway prototype in the middle of the process is to quickly produce something testable. For example, the customers might want to see some results before they decide whether they want to continue funding the project. You might need to slap something together quickly to show to the customers now.

In both cases, you can finish implementing the prototype's key features using quick-and-dirty throwaway techniques and gather customer feedback.

If you have been forced to abandon Visual Basic, you can then begin development with another programming language. Sometimes you can compromise and use Visual Basic for the application's user interface, and call routines written in another language for data processing. Calling routines written in other languages is relatively easy in Visual Basic.

If you can still use Visual Basic and you just need to produce a demonstration program quickly, you might be able to go back to evolutionary prototyping. Return to the earlier version of the prototype before you started using quick-and-dirty methods and start from there.

If you take this approach, you should review the dangers of throwaway prototypes. You started out focusing on an evolutionary approach so you might have forgotten some of the dangers of throwaways. In particular, you must beware of reusing code built in the quick-and-dirty style. This might not seem like a big deal, but it can ruin an otherwise fine application.

UPGRADING

Although you can downgrade from a throwaway to an evolutionary prototype, you cannot easily do the opposite. After you start writing quick-and-dirty code, it's hard to "harden" the code to production quality. Bugs often slip into that kind of code, particularly bugs that deal with how different parts of the system work together. Those are the sorts of issues that are ignored when you build a throwaway prototype.

If you must upgrade from a throwaway to an evolutionary prototype, take some time and do it right. Rewrite every routine from scratch using high-quality code. Don't leave any code unchanged unless you have thoroughly examined and tested it and you are convinced it works properly.

WHEN TO PROTOTYPE

Before you start building a prototype, you should decide whether it is even worth the effort. If you construct a prototype without knowing what you hope to gain from it, you are likely to end up wasting more time than you save.

A prototype lets you learn something about a large application by building a smaller version of that application. From your experience with the prototype, you draw conclusions about the bigger project.

A prototype will not help you much with a small application. If you think you will only need a few hours to build a program, don't bother with a prototype. Just build the application. If you don't like it, throw it away and start over.

If the main goal of the prototype is to define features, don't prototype features that have already been implemented elsewhere. If a feature is available in another application you have built or in a commercial product, show it to the customers and say, "We'll do it like this." You don't need to reinvent these features until you are certain the customers want them.

SELECTING A PROTOTYPE

Tables 2.1 and 2.2 summarize the strengths and weaknesses of throwaway and evolutionary prototypes. Use these as checklists when you decide what kind of prototype you want to use.

TABLE 2.1   STRENGTHS AND WEAKNESSES OF THROWAWAY PROTOTYPES

Strengths	Weaknesses
Ends in high-quality code	Quick changes might make customers overenthusiastic
Demonstrates many application features quickly	Temptation to reuse prototype code
Allows quick incorporation of new features	Little help in scheduling
Can make many prototype versions quickly	Prototypes might be buggy
Eases transfer to another development group	
Improves development team skills	

TABLE 2.2   STRENGTHS AND WEAKNESSES OF EVOLUTIONARY PROTOTYPES

Strengths	Weaknesses
Progress is really progress	Requires a good architecture at the beginning
Helps scheduling	All code must be high quality
Easy in Visual Basic	Inhibits team building
Zeros in on functionality	Might delay releases
Less "wasted" code	New versions of the prototype take longer
Makes point releases easy	Might waste time on unused features
Extensible	
Allows quick changes	
Can track changing needs	

Which kind of prototype you should use depends to a large extent on the personalities of your developers, customers, and organization. Developers often have a hard time starting from scratch after building a throwaway prototype, although customers like the fact that a throwaway prototype shows them something sooner. Evolutionary prototypes are easier to use in validating the project's schedule, but they take longer to give meaningful results.

Tales from the Trenches

The approach I use depends on the scope of the project. For small projects, I usually use a quick user interface prototype followed by a series of evolutionary prototypes. The user interface makes sure everyone has the same basic ideas in mind and helps determine the overall architecture. The sequence of evolutionary prototypes refines and enriches the application until it is usable, and gives the option of early point releases if they are necessary.

For larger projects, one or more throwaway prototypes built by the team leaders followed by evolutionary prototypes built by the entire development team makes sense. This combination emphasizes team building and gives the team leaders flexibility to explore different options early in development. It also gives less-experienced developers a firmly defined specification to work toward.

Throwaway, evolutionary, and other kinds of prototypes all have their strengths and weaknesses. They will all work if you make a plan and stick to it. Review your situation and each method's strengths and weaknesses. Then you can select the method best suited for your development team.

SUMMARY

There are two main kinds of prototypes: throwaway and evolutionary. Use the information in Chapter 1, "Reasons to Prototype," to determine what you hope to learn from the prototype. Use the information in this chapter to select the kind of prototyping approach you want to take.

Explicitly tell customers, developers, managers, and everyone else involved what approach you are going to take and what you hope to learn, and you should have relatively few problems. If you do not start with clearly defined goals, you will spend a lot of time and energy building a prototype that tells you far less than it could.

CHAPTER 3

PROTOTYPES IN THE LIFECYCLE

In this chapter

An application's lifecycle starts when the application is just an idea in someone's head and ends when the last version of the program is no longer used. Depending on how development proceeds, the lifecycle might last through dozens of releases that span twenty years or it might include only a single release that's used as a temporary fix while a separate, more permanent solution is built. The lifecycle can even end during application design or prototyping if the project is canceled early.

There are several different approaches to lifecycle management. The following sections describe some of the most common systems and explain how prototyping can fit into them. Some consider prototyping to be a separate lifecycle methodology, but it's not hard to apply prototyping to almost any approach.

ONE SHOT

A One Shot lifecycle assumes there will be only one version of the application and that it will be used only for a limited time. Because the program will soon be thrown away, developers skimp on the project's design and testing steps to save time. The design might be underdeveloped and missing a lot of detail. Prototyping before development and testing afterwards might be short or skipped completely. In the standard One Shot model, someone gets an idea, sits down and writes a bunch of code, and then sends the result to the user.

This sort of haphazard approach is extremely risky. Such badly planned applications often take longer than expected, don't provide the right set of features, and are declared failures before they are even used. If the application is particularly complex, the chance of failure increases tremendously.

However, if the program will be used for only a short period of time, you might not have the luxury of working through a rigorous development process. If the application is simple enough that you think it can be written in a single afternoon, it might not be worth the effort of generating detailed design documents.

In a successful One Shot development effort, there is usually no time for a prototype. Or, to think of it another way, the whole project is a prototype. It might use quick-and-dirty programming methods to get results quickly while sacrificing maintainable code.

There are two big dangers to this approach. First, if you underestimate the application's complexity, you might end up spending a lot more time and effort on the project than you thought you would be spending. In many cases, you spend more time trying to build a quick-and-dirty One Shot program than you would have spent building a more carefully planned application with a solid design. Take some time before you start a One Shot program to make at least a sketchy design. You might realize that the true scope of the problem is larger than you think. Then you have a chance to rework the design, turn the project into something more substantial, or scrap the whole thing.

The second danger of One Shots is that you might underestimate the application's lifespan. It's quite common for a program that was cranked out in a couple of hours and intended to last for a week or two to live on for years. It gets enhanced, patched, rewritten, and expanded until it becomes a Frankenstein's monster of code that bears little resemblance to the original version. Applications that grow like this are hard to understand, difficult to use, and nearly impossible to debug. Spend a little extra time thinking about the application's requirements and possible extensions. You might find that the program has more potential than you originally thought. In that case, build a solid design before you start throwing code around.

If you are really sure you can knock the code out in a couple of hours, try it. If the project turns out to be harder than you thought, step back and ask yourself if you should use a more powerful lifecycle model such as the Waterfall approach described in the next section.

WATERFALL

The One Shot approach is probably the most commonly used lifecycle model because developers build so many small, informal applications. For larger applications that use a more formal approach, the Waterfall model is undoubtedly the most common.

The Waterfall model includes a series of steps that each flow into the next. Figure 3.1 shows a Waterfall model with four steps: Analysis, Design, Development, and Testing. The results from the Analysis phase provide information to build a design in the Design phase. The design produced by the Design phase lets programmers build the application in the Development phase. The resulting program then moves into the Testing phase where testers make sure it works and satisfies the user's needs.

PART

I

CH

3

Figure 3.1
In the Waterfall model, information flows from one stage to the next.

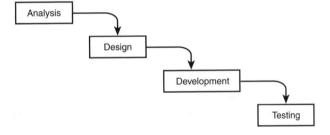

The Waterfall model is popular in large development organizations. It makes you work carefully, finishing each stage as completely as possible before moving on to the next. That makes it easy to transfer the project from one group to another during development. The project manager and the customers analyze the customers' needs. After they have determined the program's requirements, application architects and team leaders make up a program design. Development teams then move in and implement the design, with a test team verifying that the program works and that it meets the customers' needs.

Sometimes people break these four steps into smaller pieces. A more detailed model might include Information Gathering, Requirement Analysis, Architectural Design, Detailed Design, Development, and Testing.

Even these steps can be further refined. For example, you could break Development into separate subtasks for the system's different subsystems. If these subsystems are nicely segregated so they have few interactions, developers can work on the subsystems independently. All of these variations include roughly the same set of tasks; they're just presented in more or less detail.

Usually information flows from one part of the model downstream to the next. For example, information from the Detailed Design phase flows into the Development phase. However, information occasionally flows backward. During development the programmers might discover something that causes a change to the design. Testing might uncover bugs that require more development to fix. Sometimes that development uncovers larger design issues that must also be fixed. Figure 3.2 shows a more detailed view of the Waterfall model.

Figure 3.2
A more detailed Waterfall model defines more stages and allows information to flow upstream as well as downstream.

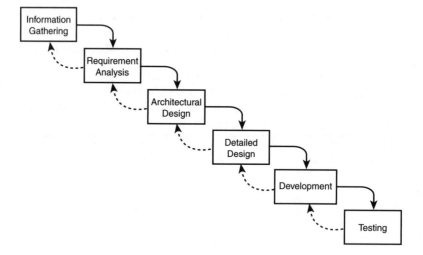

One way to add a prototype to the Waterfall model would be to include it just before the development phase, as shown in Figure 3.3. The developers would build a prototype based on the detailed design before they started on the main development tasks.

This lets the developers test new programming tools and techniques before they use them in the final application, but it doesn't take full advantage of prototyping. The whole point of prototyping is to get feedback as quickly and inexpensively as possible. By this point the requirements, architectural design, and detailed design are fixed, so changing them is difficult. If the prototype uncovers a major flaw in the architectural design, you have to step back and repeat a lot of architectural and detailed design work.

To get the most out of a prototype, you should start building it as early as possible. At each stage of development, the traditional Waterfall tasks guide you in the prototype's development. At the same time, the prototype feedback you get from the customer helps refine and improve the Waterfall development tasks.

Figure 3.3
One way to add prototyping to the Waterfall model is to build a prototype before Development.

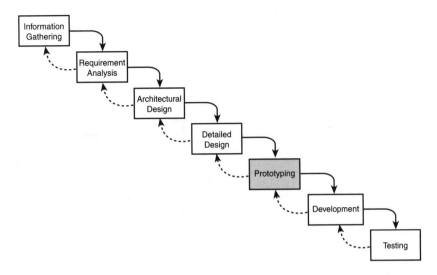

You can begin the prototype almost as soon as you start the project. During the Information Gathering stage, the prototype cannot do much because you don't have a good understanding of the application's requirements. You can still take pieces from a previous prototype to build standard amenities such as a splash screen and login features.

During the Requirement Analysis phase, you know in an informal way what the application needs to do but you have not yet written the application's requirements down precisely. During this phase, you can use the prototype to test simple alternatives and clarify the user's needs. You can also start building a user interface prototype to let the customers see what the final application will look like.

In the Architectural Design phase, you will start making serious development decisions. Now the prototype can help you test technology you have not used before. When the prototype identifies problem areas now, you can fix them before you spend a lot of time writing an incorrect detailed design and writing a lot of bad code in the Development phase.

By the time you reach the Detailed Design phase, you have completed the user interface prototype, shown it to the customers, and finished specifying the last user interface issues. You can now break the application into subsystems and design their code modules at a detailed level. As you finish specifying different subsystems, developers can get to work, using the user interface prototype as a guide to the application's behavior.

At this point, the future of the prototype depends on the prototyping approach you are using. If you are building a throwaway prototype, the prototype's job is largely done. The information you learned from the prototype now helps the programming team start over and begin building the final application in the Development phase, as shown in Figure 3.4.

Figure 3.4
A throwaway proto-
type built in parallel
with traditional
Waterfall tasks helps
define those tasks.

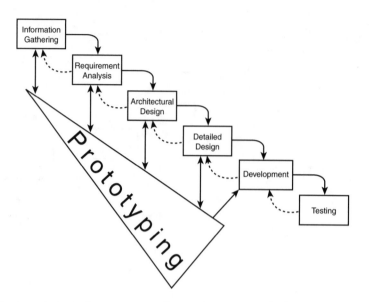

If you build an evolutionary prototype, the prototype continues to grow during the
Development phase. In fact, the Development phase doesn't really have much of a life of its
own. It simply becomes the process of refining and improving the prototype until it is ready
for testing. After testing the prototype and fixing any problems you find, the prototype
becomes the final application, as shown in Figure 3.5.

Figure 3.5
An evolutionary pro-
totype built in parallel
with traditional
Waterfall tasks even-
tually becomes the
finished application.

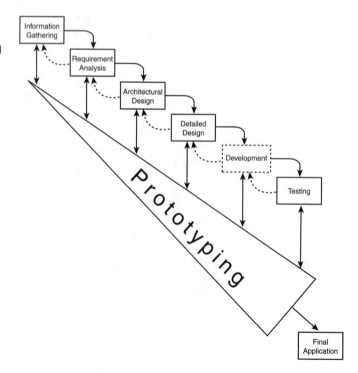

The Waterfall model is effective when the application is reasonably well defined. You start by gathering information about what the application must do. You analyze the things you learn to create a precise list of requirements. From the requirements list, you design the basic user interface and programming architecture. You refine the architectural design to form detailed designs. You build the system from those designs, test the results, and fix any problems you uncover.

This method is quite powerful and enables a team to build incredibly complex applications effectively as long as each phase works. If any one of the phases doesn't do its job properly, the system falls apart. For example, suppose you don't clearly understand what the program needs to do after you finish the Requirement Analysis phase. In that case, the architectural and detailed designs you produce could be wrong. Development then produces an application that doesn't satisfy the customers' needs. Testing does not uncover this problem because testing only verifies that the program does what it was designed to do, not what it should have been designed to do.

The prototype helps keep each of the Waterfall stages on track. Showing the prototype to the customers often helps them verify that the program will do what they need it to do. If you don't properly understand the customers' needs in the Requirements Analysis phase, the next version of the prototype will make that obvious. When the customers see the prototype, they will explain the problem and help you fix the project's requirements. The prototype sometimes lags a bit behind the development phases so the prototype may not make the problem clear until you have started some Architectural Design. At least it will help you catch the problem before you get all the way through the Testing phase.

Even with a prototype, there are situations when the Waterfall model works badly. Sometimes requirements change while development is underway. In a rapidly changing business environment, it is fairly common for the problem that the application addresses to change radically or even disappear before the application is finished. The following sections describe how some other lifecycle models can handle these cases better than the Waterfall model.

SUCCESSIVE REFINEMENT

Many people call this strategy Evolutionary Prototyping. I call it Successive Refinement to differentiate it from a prototype that evolves over time. You can use an evolutionary prototype in any development model, not just in Successive Refinement. For example, the previous section explained how to use an evolutionary prototype with the Waterfall model.

In many ways Successive Refinement is similar to the Waterfall model. Developers gather information, analyze requirements, and make architectural designs. After that point, the two methods start to diverge.

In the Waterfall model, the developers next build a detailed design for the entire project, build the application, and test it. In Successive Refinement, the developers build only part of the detailed design, implement the features they have designed, and then test those features.

They then repeat this process, designing, implementing, and testing more of the system until all of the requirements are satisfied. Figure 3.6 shows the process.

Figure 3.6
In Successive Refinement, Detailed Design, Development, and Testing repeat until the prototype satisfies all of the application's requirements.

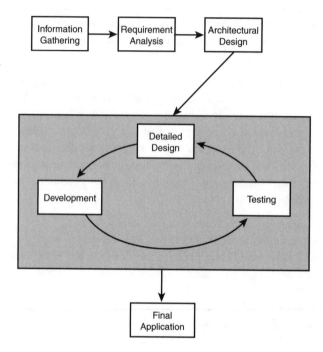

In Successive Refinement, it is common for developers to work on different iterations of the prototype. One team might have finished its tasks for version 12 and be working on the detailed design for version 13 while another team is still testing its part of version 12.

This can get a little confusing if one team gets too far ahead of the others. One way to prevent that is to not allow any team to begin coding one version until all teams are finished with the previous version. What that means in practice is the faster team spends more time designing the features they implement in the next version. That team not only anticipates more problems, it probably puts more features into the next version. Adding more features slows them down a bit and the teams stay together better in the next round.

Successive Refinement is much more flexible than the Waterfall method. If the requirements change during development, you can easily adapt. You can add new features and make modifications during the next development cycle. To reduce the chance that you have to completely scrap code, implement the features you understand the best first. As the prototype grows, your understanding of the other features increases. The customers have a chance to think about how the parts of the system fit together in the prototype, and that helps solidify the requirements.

STAGED DELIVERY

When you build an evolutionary prototype, the program slowly gains functionality until it eventually satisfies all of the customers' requirements. At some point in the middle, it does enough to actually be useful to the customers. At that point, you can release it as the first version of the application. After a few more iterations through the design, development, and test phases, the prototype contains enough new functionality to make it worth releasing a second version. This process of adding new features and then releasing a new version of the application can continue throughout the program's development until you release a final version.

Staged Delivery isn't quite as simple as this story makes it sound. Left to their own devices, the developers will probably not implement the application's features in the best order. They might implement the easiest or most interesting features first. It is unlikely that the most urgently needed features will be built first unless the development team takes some effort to make that happen.

In the worst-case scenario, missing features in the system prevent it from being useful until the last pieces are in place. For example, suppose you are building a text editor and the developers don't add features to save a modified text file until the end of the project. The program isn't very useful if you can edit a file but you cannot save the changes.

To get the most important features first, insert a Release Planning stage before each development cycle. After the requirement and architectural phases, analyze the design and pick out the features that should be implemented in the first release. The features should form a coherent set that makes sense as a group. It is easier for customers to learn new features if they are all in one subsystem rather than scattered throughout the application. Implementing most of a subsystem all at once also reduces the chance that changes to the subsystem in a future release will mess up the features you have already built.

After you have selected the features for the next release, enter a cycle of Detailed Design, Development, and Testing for those features. Work on that feature set until they all work properly. Try not to get distracted and add other features to this version of the program. If you get too carried away, you'll wind up adding everything into this release and you'll be using Successive Refinement instead of Staged Delivery. There's nothing wrong with Successive Refinement, but you should decide which strategy you are using at the beginning and stick to it.

Add to the prototype incrementally during these development cycles so you can use the prototype to validate the features. Let the users experiment with the prototype so they can decide whether the features being implemented really match those described in the requirements.

Repeat the Design, Development, Testing cycle until the first release features are working correctly. Then send version 0.1 of the program to the customers for use. Now return to the Release Planning phase, select the features you plan to implement in release 0.2, and start the development cycle again.

Repeat this whole process to create a series of point releases until the application meets all of the customers' requirements. Then release the final application version 1.0. Figure 3.7 shows this process.

Figure 3.7
Staged Delivery lets you release early versions of the application.

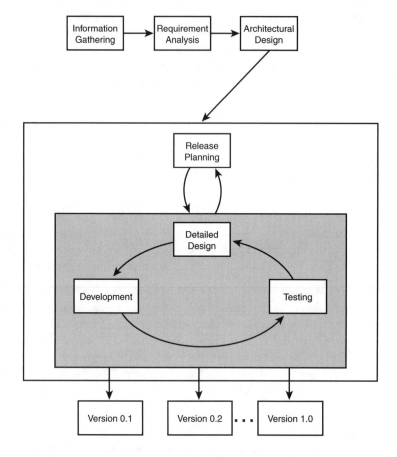

Developers tend to think most about the stages of the project where they are actually designing, writing, and testing code. After all, that's where they spend most of their time. They sometimes have a tendency to rush through the Information Gathering, Requirement Analysis, and Architectural Design phases to get to the "real" programming.

In Staged Delivery, however, the earlier stages are extremely important. They are more important when using the Staged Delivery process than they are in other approaches like Successive Refinement. When you use Successive Refinement, the growing prototype validates the requirements and architecture. If you find mistakes, you can revise the requirements or architecture and then resume development. This might force the developers to rewrite some code. That's usually inconvenient, but it's not the end of the world.

When you use Staged Delivery, however, making changes to features you have already released to the customers is much harder. The customers get used to the features provided in the version they have been using, and changing those features in even superficial ways can cause confusion. Changing the program's underlying functionality is even worse.

Tale from the Trenches

A colleague of mine once attended a two-day class describing the user interface changes to a new version of some commercial software she was using. When she got to the class, she discovered that two of the application's functions had been moved from their original function keys to new ones. That was the big change!

As soon as she was certain that was the extent of the changes, she snuck out of class and went back to work. She said that other students seemed to be having a lot of trouble with the concepts and would probably need the entire two days.

To avoid any more disruption than necessary, you should spend extra time in the Information Gathering, Requirements Analysis, and Architectural Design phases. Add extra detail to the design so you have a clear roadmap for development before you start writing code.

Probably the hardest parts of an application to change in point releases are those that deal with loading and saving data. Suppose you give the customers version 0.1 of a circuit design program. They use the application to build a few hundred circuits. Now you give them release 0.2 of the program, and it uses a different file format. Now, all of the circuits the customers have built are worthless. Few things depress customers more than learning that the hundreds of hours they spent using an early version of your program were wasted and that they need to do it all over again.

At this point, your customers may demand that you build a translation program to upgrade their circuit files from the old format to the new one. Now you are stuck building and debugging extra translation programs that you probably didn't include in the original development schedule.

Tale from the Trenches

One ongoing project I helped to build stored complex data sets in a database. Over a period of a couple of years, the application's requirements changed, so the database needed to store new types of information. Fields were dropped and some of their purposes changed and needed to be modified. These were major changes to the program requested by customers so we had some excuse for not knowing these changes would be needed in advance.

In a few cases, we were forced to write a translation program that loaded the entire database and wrote out new versions of the data. Most of the time, however, we were able to avoid this process by using a forward-compatible data structure.

Each data record included a series of named values. You can do this easily in XML. For example, the data to describe a circle might look like this:

```
<ObjectType>Circle</ObjectType>
<Radius>35</Radius>
<X>100</X>
<Y>75</Y>
...
```

Before loading a record, the program initializes the data variables to default values. For a circle object, it might set X and Y to zero, and the Radius to 10.

Next the program reads through the fields in this object's record, replacing the default values with the values it finds. When it reads the X field, it sets the value of the object's X variable to 100.

If the program reads a version 0.1 data file that doesn't include some field that was added in version 0.2, the default values let the program continue running. If an older version of the file does not include a Radius value, the circle keeps the default value of 10.

If the program finds a field that existed in version 0.1 but not in version 0.2, it either ignores that field or maps it to another field. For instance, suppose version 0.1 files give circles a LineStyle property but in version 0.2 that field was removed. When the program reads data written in the old format, it simply ignores any LineStyle values it finds.

This technique is very flexible. A version 0.2 program can read a version 0.1 data file and automatically translate the data into the new format. A version 0.1 program can even read a version 0.2 file! It might lose some data when it ignores new fields added in version 0.2, however, so you might want to warn the user, or at least not allow the user to save the data in the older format.

Spend extra time designing the application's architecture. Focus on the user interface's major features so you won't have to make big changes to the user interface after you have given your customers an early version. Also pay close attention to how the program loads and saves data so you won't have to build extra translation programs later.

LIMITED SCHEDULE

The Limited Schedule approach is very similar to Staged Delivery. The main difference is that you do not have enough time or money to get all the way to the final release. You build point releases until you run out of time or money. You declare the last point release to be the final one and you are done. The Limited Schedule process is shown in Figure 3.8.

In a Staged Delivery, you implement the most important features first so the customers get the greatest benefit as soon as possible. You might defer an important feature to a later release so you can study it more, refine its design, and see how it fits into earlier versions of the prototype. The important thing is that you eventually get around to implementing every feature.

In a Limited Schedule, however, you might not have time to implement all of the features you would like. In that case, you cannot defer important features arbitrarily. If you are certain you have time and money for at least three releases, you might defer an item until the second or third release, but you cannot put off the more important features indefinitely. In a Limited Schedule, features are typically implemented in their order of importance. Then if something takes longer than you expect or the schedule gets shortened even further, you have at least implemented the highest priority items.

Figure 3.8
In a Limited Schedule, development continues until the time or money runs out.

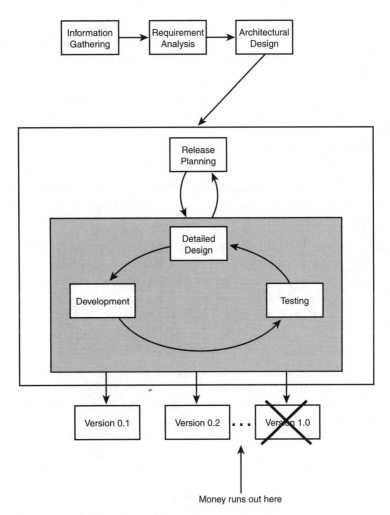

EXTENDED LIFECYCLE

All the lifecycle strategies discussed so far take an application from the idea stage through a first release. The complete lifecycle also includes future releases until the program is no longer used.

So how do you extend these models to cover future releases? The short answer is, "Do it all over again." Start with a new Information Gathering phase to identify the features you plan to provide in the next release. You can use customer feedback from the application's previous version to help pick the new features to add. Work your way through Requirements Analysis, Architectural Design, and all the other phases of application development.

Having a working version of the program when you start building the new version is a huge advantage. You can show the program to customers and ask them what changes they would like. You can also use the previous version as a starting point for the next generation of prototypes.

If you don't need to make major structural changes to the application, the basic architecture you established in the first version can guide you in building later releases. If you are lucky, fundamental items like file structure and data access methods will not change, so you don't need to worry much about them.

You don't need to use the same development approach you used in the program's first version to produce the subsequent versions. You can use whatever development model is most appropriate. For example, you might use Successive Refinement to build version 1.0 and then switch to Staged Delivery for release 2.0.

Staged Delivery is particularly well suited to applications where you have a good understanding of how the application must work. When you start from an existing version, you have a big head start on deciding how future versions will operate. The biggest danger in a Staged Delivery is that changes introduced in a later release might require changes to features included in an earlier release. If the program's core architecture won't change much in the second release, these risks are much smaller. That makes Staged Delivery a good choice for later releases.

If you are building a mass-market application, you might not want to provide intermediate releases to the customers. Instead you wait until the final version 2.0 release is ready and then you deliver the completed product. In that case it might still be helpful to use a Staged Delivery approach or a Limited Schedule model. Release dates for products are often determined by management, marketing, or some other factor that has little to do with the development team's progress. If you use a Limited Schedule approach, you are almost guaranteed to have a version ready for release when it is required.

Keep in mind that development must stop early enough to give your documentation and training groups time to prepare manuals and training materials for the customers. You can keep testing the application after the final release version is selected, but you should avoid adding new features to the program. Anything you add after that point cannot be properly documented.

SUMMARY

All of these development approaches have their strengths and weaknesses. The One Shot approach works well if the application is small and you don't plan to use it long. It produces a kind of quick-and-dirty program.

The Waterfall model works well in large development organizations. Carefully working from one stage to the next and finishing each stage before moving to the next one makes it easier to hand development from one team to another.

Successive Refinement lets a more agile team of developers accommodate changes to the requirements throughout the project. It is appropriate where the application's requirements are initially unclear or you expect them to change during development. Staged Delivery and Limited Schedule projects are special cases of Successive Refinement.

Prototypes are very useful in all of these approaches. You can begin a prototype as soon as you learn about the customers' needs. During each stage of development, the prototype grows. It gives a more and more detailed idea of what the final application will look like. Customers can give you feedback so you can adjust the requirements and design accordingly. At the same time, the prototype validates the program's architectural design so you are sure you can build the application.

If you are using a throwaway prototype, discard it after the Architectural Design phase and begin final application development. By this point, the prototype has ensured that your overall design is sound, so you can finish the project, and that the application will satisfy the user's needs.

If you are building an evolutionary prototype, you move into the more concentrated development stages. You must expand and refine the prototype until it handles all of the customers' needs.

PART

I

CH

3

PART II

THE PROTOTYPE LIFECYCLE

CHAPTER **4**

ANALYSIS

In this chapter

When you come right down to it, programming is a translation process. Someone must translate a collection of thoughts and ideas into a series of program commands that a computer can execute to do something useful. The people who perform this translation are programmers.

Unfortunately, the people with the ideas that need to be translated usually are not programmers. Customers have some idea of what they want but they have no chance of turning their ideas into a program.

The ultimate job of the programmers is to take these sometimes vague ideas and translate them into a program. The first step in this process is understanding the customers' thoughts, needs, and wishes. That is the fundamental task of analysis.

The following sections describe some of the steps you can take to analyze the customers' needs. They explain how to gather information from the customers and turn that information into concrete requirements you can use to design the application. They also describe information gathered for a fictitious software project named VB NetLab.

It's hard to build meaningful prototypes during this stage of development. Generally, you don't know enough about the system to start writing code. You might still be able to anticipate some programming needs far in advance and test alterative strategies.

For example, if you know you want to use XML to distribute data across the Internet, you might want to build some quick throwaway prototypes to gain more experience with XML. You should usually avoid building prototypes that are more directly related to the application domain, however. During the analysis phase, you want to keep your mind and options open. You shouldn't start making design decisions until you understand the whole picture.

UNDERSTAND THE CUSTOMERS' NEEDS

Before you can translate your customers' needs into an application, you need to understand those needs. Unless you have previous experience in the customers' domain, you need to spend some time familiarizing yourself with their particular universe.

Customers think in their own terms. There is no way they can translate their needs into computer architecture terms you can easily convert into a program. They cannot learn your language, so you need to learn theirs. Until you understand their terms, you can't understand their problem. This can be one of the hardest parts to building a project.

Do everything you can to learn about your customers' jobs. Learn how they perform day-to-day tasks. Read any instructional materials they have. Spend some time watching them at their jobs. Take notes and ask questions. If they will let you, take pictures, record discussions, and video tape them at work so you can review their routine later at your leisure.

You don't need to understand everything as well as your customers do. Learning their jobs as well as they know them could take years. You do, however, need to know enough about their jobs to understand the problem they are asking you to solve.

Tale From The Trenches

During the years I spent working for GTE Laboratories, our customers were often members of GTE Telephone Operations (TELOPS), the part of the company that provided actual telephone service. These people thought in terms of outside plant, class 4 switches, repeaters, cable pairs, junction boxes, channel banks, above the line and below the line, local loop, CPE, POTS, and B1 service. They worked with dozens of existing computer systems running on several different hardware platforms and operating systems. Most of them had literally spent decades working with this equipment and had no trouble rattling off acronyms faster than you could write them down.

To try to understand the customers' needs, we (the developers) started by reading, or at least thoroughly skimming, *The Dow Jones-Irwin Handbook of Telecommunications*, the best overview of telecommunications operations at the time. Next, we studied a small book TELOPS had compiled listing hundreds of acronyms commonly used in the company. We obtained copies of the manuals for the software systems used by our clients and learned what those systems were supposed to do, what they actually did, and how the customers used them.

Every year, we sent a few developers to the company's physical plant training school. Those developers got an abbreviated taste of the training that the company's repair people experienced. They got to climb into cable vaults, diagnose simulated faults in real telephone circuits, and splice fiber optic cable.

With all this as background, we descended upon our customers. We toured their facilities to get an overview of the operation. Then we sat down and watched them do their jobs for several days. Although they could describe their jobs in a few minutes, it took a while for us to uncover all of the most important facets of their jobs. We pestered them with unending questions, asking why they did things in certain ways and why they didn't do them in others.

You might think that all of these interruptions would annoy the customers. In fact, most people are willing and even eager to talk about their jobs as long as you don't keep them from being able to do their work.

By the time we finished, we understood the basics of our customers' environment and the work they did. We still couldn't come anywhere close to doing their jobs, but at least we spoke some of their language. We knew what they wanted and why they wanted it. Equally important, we knew how any solution we built would fit into their existing environment. You don't make friends by building a system that solves one problem but creates others.

If this all seems like a lot of work, you're right. It took a couple of years for developers to get a really good feel for how all the pieces of the TELOPS puzzle fit together. That experience was one of the key differences between junior and senior developers. Those who had been around the longest understood more about the company and how its systems worked.

STUDY CURRENT PRACTICES

Watch the customers at work to see how they do things now. If you are replacing an existing process, you probably need to be able to handle all of the procedures the customers already perform. It's usually quite hard to convince customers to give up features they already have.

If you are implementing a new process, think about how it will fit in with the customers' present systems and practices. You want your system to fit in as smoothly as possible without disrupting the customers any more than necessary.

Studying current practices might also show you solutions to problems the customers didn't even know they had. Your new developer's point of view might identify opportunities the customers overlooked. In that case, it sometimes makes sense to put your planned project on hold and address some other issue first.

Tale From The Trenches

In one project, we were sent to GTE's three billing centers. If we had been forced to write a mission statement, it would have been something lame like, "Wander around the billing centers looking for something useful we can do with computers." You could have silver-plated the statement by talking about synergy and leveraging existing systems, but it still wouldn't really have said anything concrete.

After only a few hours, we discovered that the billing centers were spending a huge amount of time trying to identify customers who had large outstanding account balances. They would then send out warning letters or disconnect the customers' service. We now had a concrete mission: "Write a program that identifies customers with large outstanding balances."

After a little more digging, we learned that the existing systems were already printing out a list of customers with outstanding balances every day. Unfortunately, the printout was unsorted. It included thousands of customers all mixed together. Customers who owed pennies were mixed in with those who owed the thousands of dollars. Each day, the printout consumed a stack of paper almost three feet high!

Although this huge list was being printed, no one was using it. It was just taking up space in a storage room. There was no way the clerks could sift through this mess and find the customers with the largest balances.

From there, the solution was easy. We used off-the-shelf software to write a printer emulator. To the mainframe printing this report, it looked just like a printer. The program grabbed all the printed output, sorted it, and let the user decide how many of the largest outstanding balances to print. It actually took longer to get permission to send the printout to the new computer than it did to write the program!

It turned out that only about 50–100 customers had balances big enough to worry about and the top five customers accounted for about 90 percent of the total outstanding payments. The billing center's impossible task had suddenly been reduced to the work of a few minutes each day.

This project was a success in part because we waited until we understood the customers' problem before we tried to define our mission. After we understood their existing environment and practices, an opportunity to help jumped out at us. Learning about the printout made the solution equally obvious.

(To be continued…)

When you study the customers' work environment and current practices, be sure you understand the customers' true problems rather than just the problems they think they see. Often the customers have ideas about how a computer can help solve their problems but they either don't really understand how the computer can help or they misidentify the problem. In many cases, the customers suggest solutions that only address the symptoms of a larger problem.

Tale From The Trenches (continued)

In the previous Tale From The Trenches, the billing center clerks wanted a way to look through an enormous printout and identify the customers with the largest outstanding balances. The initial solution did just that. It gave the clerks a brief, sorted summary of those customers. The clerks then used their other computer systems to check each of those accounts for recent payments and other extenuating circumstances before sending the customer a warning letter or disconnecting their service.

As we studied the situation, we realized that the real problem wasn't the gigantic unsorted printout. The problem was really the fact that the system generating the printout didn't take action itself. It made the billing center clerks manually disconnect accounts with large outstanding balances.

Version two of our program collected the printout's information as before. It then logged onto the other system and looked for things like recent payments and notes that might indicate special circumstances. Based on rules given to us by the billing center, the program then automatically printed out warning letters or disconnected service as appropriate.

Be sure you understand the whole picture before you start making changes. If you address the situation's symptoms instead of the real problem, you might make your customers' jobs harder in the long run.

Mission Statement

After you have a good understanding of the customers' needs, you can write a one or two sentence mission statement describing the project. The intent is to give a little bit of motivation. Someone who reads only the mission statement should be able to understand more or less what the application is for without knowing any of the details. It should tell managers and executives what problem is being solved. It should also tell developers what system they are going to build.

Example
For the fictitious VB NetLab application, the mission statement might look like this:

VB NetLab is an application that demonstrates fundamental networking concepts and algorithms for Visual Basic programming students. The students can easily add their own code to the program to build network algorithms of their own.

After you write the mission statement, ask yourself if a corporate executive could understand it. If the executive would need a degree in computer science to know what you are going to do, the statement needs work.

Also ask yourself if a junior level programmer who read it would know what sort of application you are going to build. Avoid statements that are vague and non-specific. These might be useful in executive overviews and might be your higher-level goal, but they are not clear enough to keep a software project on track.

A statement like, "Improve customer service by reducing product defects," is not specific enough to give programmers an idea about what they should do. The statement, "Build an application that tracks product defects throughout all phases of production to identify the places that introduce the most defects," is much better. It tells what problem you are solving (finding the places that introduce the most defects) and it describes a concrete system you can build (a defect tracker).

PART
II

CH
4

WISH LIST

The wish list contains notes jotted down as they come up during early meetings with the customers. At this stage, don't try to organize these notes much. Don't tell the customers something cannot be done. Just jot down whatever the customers think is important. The idea is to capture as many of the customers' needs and desires as possible.

Try to keep the discussion focused on the customers' abstract requirements. Avoid specific implementation and user interface details whenever possible. Let the customers daydream about the ideal application they would build if anything were possible. There will be time to refine the ideas and weed out the less useful ones later. If the customers start asking for telepathic interfaces and artificial intelligence that can guess what they want to do, gently nudge them back into reality. Otherwise, try to keep the creative juices flowing.

Think about features provided by similar applications. Many programs allow you to save and load data in a variety of different formats created by other programs. Do you need that feature? Many programs provide printing and print previewing. Do you need that, too?

The VB NetLab wish list might include these items:

- A single desktop program.
- Load, edit, and save networks.
- Operations to perform massive edits. For example, select the links in an area and then set all their costs at once. The same applies with nodes.
- Allow the user to select specific nodes or links.
- Graphical editor.
- Ability to resize and rescale.
- Zoom in and out. Scroll.
- Support directed and undirected networks.
- One-way links.
- Turn penalties and prohibitions.
- Link costs, node costs.
- Students should be able to easily add their own modules to the program to test new algorithms. Extensible.
- Algorithms to support:
  - Label correcting shortest path.
  - Label setting shortest path.
  - Max flow.
  - Minimal spanning tree.
- Features to let the students easily display the results of their calculations.
- Commands to automatically create grid and random networks. Other network topologies.

- Graphically display the workings of an algorithm.

- Network algorithms as Web services.

- Concrete examples. For example, you can work allocation using max flow, identify critical paths, and so on.

- Save network in forward star format. Other formats?

- A master program should be able to test the students' algorithms. It should check correctness, programming style, comments, variable naming conventions, etc. Everything that makes up good code.

- Printing.

- Export an image of the network in bitmap, WMF (Windows Metafile), and EMF (Enhanced Metafile) formats.

It's worth taking a little while to think at the highest level possible, but it is often hard to separate this step with the next one where you get more specific about application requirements. Try working at the higher level. If your customers can't work at a high level, don't try to force them. Take notes on whatever requirements they think are important at the level of detail they want to give. Later you can flesh out the less thoroughly described requirements so all of the requirements have the same level of detail.

When you build a wish list, and when you take the next step of converting the wish list into an initial requirements list, the number of items the customers want often grows quickly. Keep the customers focused on the end goal, but don't rule anything out yet. There's plenty of time for that later when you build a requirements specification.

PART

II

CH

4

INITIAL REQUIREMENTS LIST

Eventually the customers start to run out of ideas. At that point, start refining the requirements, define the items listed in the requirement notes more precisely, and describe each requirement in enough detail that you can be sure everyone agrees on what it means. At this point you can also start grouping related requirements.

You don't need to eliminate anything yet, though as you define things carefully, the customers often decide something is not really all that important or that it can be deferred to a later release. They will also think of new items to add. Just add them in the same level of detail as everything else.

The slightly refined VB NetLab wish list now looks like this:

Program Architecture:

- A single desktop program.
  - One user will use the program. It is not a multi-user application.
  - No password is required.

- No network interface is required.
- Let the user edit more than one network at a time using an MDI (multiple document interface).
    - The Windows menu lets the user:
        - Select among the networks that are loaded.
        - Tile the child windows.
        - Cascade the child windows.
        - Arrange the child windows' icons.

Network algorithms as Web services (Is this really necessary?):

Network files:

- Load, edit, and save networks.
- Files are saved with .net extension.
- Save network in forward star format. Other formats?
- Program will warn the user before exiting or loading a new network if changes have not been saved.
- Loading and saving commands:
    - Open.
    - New.
    - Save.
    - Save As.
    - Save All.
    - Close.
    - Export to:
        - CorelDRAW!
        - WMF.
        - EMF.
- Printing commands:
    - Print.
    - Print preview.
    - Select printer.
    - Print to file.

Network Structure:

- Support directed and undirected networks.
- One-way links.

- Turn penalties and prohibitions.
- Link properties:
  - Label.
  - Cost.
  - Capacity for max flow algorithms.
- Node properties:
  - Label.
  - Cost.
  - Distance to root for label setting algorithms.
  - Selected link for shortest path algorithms.
  - Shape.
  - Foreground and background color.

Algorithms to support:

- Label correcting shortest path.
- Label setting shortest path.
- Max flow.
- Minimal spanning tree.
- Others.
- Concrete examples. For example, work allocation using max flow, identify critical paths, and so on.

Graphical editor.

- Zoom in and out. Scroll.
- Ability to resize and rescale.
- Menus and a toolbar provides access to different editing modes (select, add node, delete node, etc.) and different algorithm modes (select nodes for shortest path, select nodes for max flow, etc.).
- Operations to perform massive edits. For example, select the links in an area and then set all their costs at once. The same applies with nodes.
  - Select nodes and links by clicking and dragging a region. Links that are partially in the selected rectangle are selected.
  - Holding down the Shift key adds the selected objects to the selection set.
  - Holding down the Control key toggles the selected objects' selection state.
  - Allow selection using an irregular area rather than just a rectangle.
  - Selected items are identified visibly.

PART

II

CH

4

- Operations apply only to a specific kind of object. For example, if you set Speed to 10, this applies only to selected links because nodes do not have speeds. If the item is ambiguous (like cost, label, and so on), the program should have separate entries for the node and link items (for example, Node Cost and Link Cost).
- Setting a link's speed makes its cost equal to its length divided by the speed.
- Right clicking on a selected object presents the appropriate popup menu for the selected objects.
- Right-clicking on an unselected object selects that object and presents the appropriate popup menu for it.
  - Operations include:
  - Setting properties for objects (link costs, speeds, and so on).
  - Delete selected objects.
  - Copy, cut, paste.
  - Paste into other applications like CorelDRAW, Paint, Word, Excel.
  - Undo and redo.

- Commands to automatically create test networks:
  - Grid with specified number of express links.
  - Random with specified number of express links.
  - Other topologies.
- Allow the user to select specific nodes or links.
  - Select nodes or links by clicking on them.

Extensibility:

- Students should be able to easily add their own modules to the program to test new algorithms. Extensible.
- Allow students to add validation routines that validate their results.
- Features to let the students easily display the results of their calculations:
  - Draw shortest paths.
  - Draw flows.
  - Display total flow.
  - Display elapsed time.
- Graphically display the workings of an algorithm.

Instructor extensions:

- The instructor should be able to check each student's:
  - Correctness.
  - Programming style.
  - Comments.

- Variable naming conventions.
- Indentation.
- Everything else that makes up good code.

Asking that the program use an MDI interface is a user interface decision, so it might not really belong here. In this case, the customers want to be able to edit more than one network at a time and they specifically want an MDI application to do that. During this step, the goal is to record all of the customers' desires, not to argue over whether this is the right time to decide on user interface features.

REQUIREMENTS SPECIFICATION

Now it is time to organize the requirements and look them over thoroughly. Clarify any items that are vague or inconsistent. When the requirements specification is finished, everyone should have the same idea of what the program will and will not do.

This is also the time to decide which features will actually be part of the program. During the wish list and initial requirements gathering steps, the list of requirements can become huge. Now is the time to pare things down to a manageable size.

Decisions you make about which features to include help determine the first version's scope and thus the amount of work required. Decide which features are most important and which are least important. See if any are redundant and can be eliminated. Find out if any can be deferred until a later release.

If you decide to defer a requirement, don't delete it from the specification. Instead, add it to a new Deferred section so you won't forget about it later.

Prioritize the items scheduled for releases 1.0 and 2.0. If you run out of time building release 1.0, know which items you can push back into release 2.0. If you start running far ahead of schedule, know which items you can move from release 2.0 to release 1.0.

This is also the time to question underlying assumptions. Ask if there are other ways you might accomplish the same thing. By generalizing one requirement, you might be able to remove others. Consolidate and simplify requirements where that is possible.

Think about the main purpose of the application and ask yourself which features work towards that purpose. Look for features that were tacked on because they seemed cool and remove them. Refer back to your mission statement to help stay focused on what is and is not important.

Take a moment to review VB NetLab's mission statement:

> *VB NetLab is an application that demonstrates fundamental networking concepts and algorithms for Visual Basic programming students. The students can easily add their own code to the program to build network algorithms of their own.*

PART

II

CH

4

Using this statement as a guideline, you can create rules for deciding which features belong in release 1.0, which should be deferred until release 2.0, and which should be deferred indefinitely. Release 1.0 should include the smallest set of features necessary for students to use the program to learn about network algorithms. If it's not absolutely essential, it's not part of release 1.0.

Release 2.0 should contain features that make using the program easier but that the student can live without if necessary. If the release 1.0 features do not use up all of the available time, some of these items may slide back into release 1.0.

Anything that does not directly contribute to learning about network algorithms and that doesn't make the program easier to use should be deferred indefinitely.

Now look again at the initial requirements list. The list contains several features that are cool and might even be occasionally useful, but that are not central to the task of helping students learn about network algorithms. Printing a picture of a network might sometimes be useful, but it is something students can live without in release 1.0, so it belongs in release 2.0.

Exporting networks into graphic files (CorelDRAW!, bmp, WMF, EMF, and so on) or other applications (Word, Excel, others) are even less critical. This might help with reports, but it doesn't address the main goal of learning to implement algorithms. These features can wait until release 3.0 or later.

Copy, cut, paste, undo, and redo capabilities would help you build complex networks like street networks, but the focus of the application is on algorithms, not building realistic networks. These features make the program easier to use but are not absolutely necessary, so they belong in release 2.0.

For the same reasons, the program can be an SDI (single document interface) application instead of an MDI application. The student does not need to edit more than one network at a time so there's no need to complicate the program with this feature. In fact, the user rarely needs to copy and paste nodes and links from one network to another, so an MDI isn't very important. It can wait until release 3.0 or later.

The program's Windows menu and a Save All command help manage the MDI child windows, so they aren't needed until the program uses MDI.

Different node colors and shapes (rectangles, ovals, and so on) might be nice. You could also extend the idea to make links of different color, thickness, and style. None of these things would help students learn to write network algorithms, however. In fact, nodes and links don't really need to display a label at all. These are definitely things the students can do without in release 1.0. It's even questionable whether they are useful enough to be in release 2.0.

Concrete examples that use network algorithms lie just a little outside the scope of this project. You can think of these examples as word problems that demonstrate the network algorithms. Although they would certainly help give students a better understanding of the algorithms, they tend to need their own customized user interfaces. Trying to build a system that handles arbitrary examples might be possible, but it would make this project a lot bigger. In this example, this requirement is deferred to control the size of release 1.0. This requirement will be reevaluated while planning for release 2.0.

Many of the graphical editing features (scale, zoom in and out, scroll, menus, and so on) are relatively complicated and are not critical to the main goal of learning about network algorithms. They are more editing convenience features, so they belong in release 2.0.

Some graphical editing features, like popup menus that allow you to create new nodes and links, are necessary to create a network. Those must go into release 1.0. Where you draw the line is a bit unclear. It might depend on the amount of time left in the schedule after you decide which other features to include. If prototypes show that some of the other requirements are easier or harder than you thought, you might move some of these in or out of release 1.0.

Systematically letting students add validation routines sounds hard and is not absolutely essential, so it's part of release 2.0. Validating results is good programming practice, however, so it might be moved into release 1.0 if time permits.

Graphically displaying the inner workings of algorithms in general sounds next to impossible, so it is deferred indefinitely.

The instructor extensions also sound like wishful thinking. You might be able to write a program to see if the students are indenting properly and using comments, but judging overall clarity of style would be hard. Besides, those features deal with grading solutions, not with the students' implementing them, so they don't fit the mission statement. These features are deferred indefinitely.

With these changes, VB NetLab's new prioritized feature list looks like this:

Release 1.0:

Program Architecture:

- A single desktop program.
  - One user will use the program. It is not a multi-user application.
  - No password is required.
  - No network interface is required.

Network files:

- Load, edit, and save networks.
- Files are saved with .net extension.
- Save network in forward star format.
- Program will warn the user before exiting or loading a new network if changes have not been saved.

- Loading and saving commands:
  - Open.
  - New.
  - Save.
  - Save As.
  - Close.

Network Structure:

- Support directed and undirected networks.
- One-way links.
- Turn penalties and prohibitions.
- Link properties:
  - Cost.
  - Capacity for max flow algorithms.
- Node properties:
  - Cost.
  - Distance to root for label setting algorithms.
  - Selected link for shortest path algorithms.

Algorithms to support:

- Label correcting shortest path.
- Label setting shortest path.
- Max flow.
- Minimal spanning tree.
- Others.

Graphical editor:

- Menus and a toolbar provides access to different editing modes (select, add node, delete node, and so on) and different algorithm modes (select nodes for shortest path, select nodes for max flow, and so on).
- Operations to perform massive edits. For example, select the links in an area and then set all their costs at once. The same applies with nodes.
  - Holding down the Shift key adds the selected objects to the selection set.
  - Holding down the Control key toggles the selected objects' selection state.
  - Selected items are identified visibly.

- Operations apply only to a specific kind of object. For example, if you set Speed to 10, this applies only to selected links because nodes do not have speeds. If the item is ambiguous (like cost, label, and so on), the program will have separate entries for the node and link items (for example, Node Cost and Link Cost).
- Setting a link's "speed" makes its cost equal to its length divided by the speed.
- Right-clicking a selected object presents the appropriate popup menu for the selected objects.
- Right-clicking an unselected object selects that object and presents the appropriate popup menu for it.
- Operations include:
    - Setting properties for objects (link costs, speeds, and so on).
    - Delete selected objects.

- Commands to automatically create test networks:
    - Grid with specified number of express links.
    - Random with specified number of express links.
- Allow the user to select specific nodes or links.
    - Select nodes or links by clicking on them.

Extensibility:

- Students should be able to easily add their own modules to the program to test new algorithms. Extensible.
- Features to let the students easily display the results of their calculations:
    - Draw shortest paths.
    - Draw flows.
    - Display total flow.
    - Display elapsed time.

Release 2.0:

Extensibility:

- Allow students to add validation routines that validate their results.

Network files:

- Printing commands:
    - Print.
    - Print preview.
    - Select printer.
    - Print to file.

Graphical editor:

- Zoom in and out. Scroll.
- Ability to resize and rescale.
- Operations to perform massive edits. For example, to select the links in an area and then set all their costs at once. The same applies with nodes.
  - Select nodes and links by clicking and dragging a region. Links that are partially in the selected rectangle are selected.
  - Holding down the Shift key adds the selected objects to the selection set.
  - Holding down the Control key toggles the selected objects' selection state.
  - Allow selection using an irregular area rather than just a rectangle.
  - Copy, cut, paste.
  - Paste into other applications like CorelDRAW, Paint, Word, Excel.
  - Undo and redo.
- Commands to automatically create test networks:
  - Other topologies.

Extensibility:

- Allow students to add validation routines that validate their results.

Algorithms to support:

- Concrete examples. For example work allocation using max flow, identify critical paths, and so on.

Network Structure:

- Link properties:
  - Label.
- Node properties:
  - Label.
  - Shape.
  - Foreground and background color.

Release 3.0:

A single desktop program:

- Enables the user to edit more than one network at a time using an MDI (multiple document interface).
  - The Windows menu lets the user:
    - Select among the networks that are loaded.
    - Tile the child windows.

- Cascade the child windows.
- Arrange the child windows' icons.

Network algorithms as Web services.

Network files:

- Save network in formats other than forward star.
- Loading and saving commands:
  - Save All.
  - Export to:
    - CorelDRAW!
    - WMF.
    - EMF.

Extensibility:

- Graphically display the workings of an algorithm.

Instructor extensions:

- The instructor should be able to check each students':
  - Correctness.
  - Programming style.
  - Comments.
  - Variable naming conventions.
  - Indentation.
  - Everything else that makes up good code.

VB NetLab is a relatively simple application, so it is easy to use as an example. A full-blown business system might require interfaces to dozens of other corporate systems and databases, a powerful multi-user database system, hundreds of reports, redundant hardware, systematic backups, and all sorts of other elaborate features. The specification for a full-featured system could easily be hundreds of pages long.

Tale From The Trenches
A proposal often includes at least a high-level specification detailing what the proposed system will do. Our proposal for an emergency police dispatch system was about 60 pages long.

A *request for proposal* (RFP) or *request for technical proposal* (RFTP) is a document written by customers to describe an application they want to have built. The RFP is a requirements document. Depending on how detail-oriented the customer is, an RFP might give you a big head start in writing a detailed requirements specification.

To turn an RFP into a detailed specification, you might only need to add a section explaining the differences between what you intend to do and what the RFP says. You might also need to add a bit of high-level design to show how different parts of the system will fit together.

Some formal RFPs even have checklists listing mandatory and desired features. In evaluating your proposal, the customers might look primarily at how you fill out this checklist. In that case, your specification might be little more than a cover letter, a page or two of discussion, and a bunch of check marks.

Tale From The Trenches

During my tenure at GTE Laboratories, we dealt with some gargantuan specifications. An RFP for a police dispatch system was roughly 170 pages long. Our preliminary proposal was only about 25 pages long because the RFP did a good job of specifying what the system needed to do.

An RFP that spanned many telephone company operations came in two thick ring binders holding roughly 1,000 pages! Our proposal for that project basically listed the parts of the huge RFP that we were going to address. It also gave some high-level detail explaining how different pieces would fit together and how they would relate to other parts of the RFP in case someone else built them.

Yet another RFP for version 3 of an existing application filled a ring binder with about 500 pages. The technical specification, functional specification, and detailed module requirements for this monster filled another ring binder with about 600 pages. This tribute to documentation prowess grew in large part because it was based on an existing product. Every document that was ever written about how version 2 worked was included in the specification for version 3.

SUMMARY

The first step in any project is understanding the customers' needs. Because they don't speak your language, you need to learn to speak theirs. This might not seem like programming, but it's an important part of producing a useful system. Unless you understand the customers' needs, how can you possibly satisfy them?

CHAPTER 5

DESIGN

In this chapter

Design is often the most neglected part of application development. In their haste to begin writing code, programmers rush through the design and make only incomplete plans for how the application's components fit together. They assume they can figure out the details as they go along.

For all but the tiniest projects, this is a huge mistake. It's extremely hard to retrofit a good design onto a project after you begin writing code. As you build the different parts of the system, you make countless small decisions. Although each decision might make sense locally in the context of the routine you are writing at the moment, the decisions you make in different parts of the system will not necessarily work well together globally.

At best, you might need to rewrite a lot of code to make different parts of the system work together. In the worst case, slightly different assumptions in different parts of the application can cause subtle bugs that take a huge amount of effort to find and fix.

This chapter describes some of the issues you should keep in mind while designing your application. It doesn't try to cover everything there is to know about application design. Software design in general is a huge topic, and you can and should read several good books about it. You should read books on user interface design, object-oriented design, database design, and good programming practices in general. You can see some of the design and software engineering books I like www.vb-helper.com/mustread.htm.

This chapter focuses on issues related to prototyping. It explains how to use prototypes to improve your design and how to build a design that makes prototyping easier.

THE PERFECT DESIGN

From an application development point of view, the perfect design works like this. You review the requirements from the analysis phase. You decide how the program will satisfy the requirements and you build a design for the system. The design is a blueprint that specifies exactly how each piece of the system works and how the pieces fit together.

The pieces are disconnected, so the implementation details of one piece do not affect the implementation details of any other piece. You make no mistakes in the design, so it describes a system that really works.

Next, you assign the different pieces described by the design to different developers. They each build their separate pieces, using the design documents as a guide. If the design contains enough detail, this should be an almost mechanical process. The developers need to figure out how to implement these different pieces, but they do not need to make any global decisions.

EXAMPLE

Suppose a program uses an array named m_Players holding 50 strings with lengths between 5 and 20. At some point, the program needs to sort this list so one developer writes a routine that sorts the array. Later, someone realizes that the array should really be called m_Users and that it should hold up to 75 strings. This requires changes to the code that sorts the array. Still later, someone else discovers that a routine is needed to sort an array named `m_AdvancedUsers` that also holds strings. Someone needs to write a new routine to sort that array.

In this example, the `m_Users` array and the sorting routine are tightly coupled. Changes to one require changes to the other. Because the sorting routine is linked to the `m_Users` array, that routine cannot help sort other arrays.

Contrast this with a design that calls for a more generic routine that sorts an array of strings passed to it as a parameter. Now one developer can work on the sorting routine while the other developers work on other tasks. The main program calls the routine, passing it the `m_Players` array as a parameter. When the name of the array is changed to `m_Users`, the main program only needs to change the subroutine call. The routine itself remains the same. Another developer who needs to sort a new `m_AdvancedUsers` array can invoke the same routine, passing it the new array.

In this case, the design separates the sorting routine from the data it sorts. That lets work on the routine and data progress simultaneously.

When the developers are finished, each piece works perfectly and satisfies the design requirements to the letter. Because the design is perfect, the assembled pieces fit together perfectly and the system is a success.

If the different pieces of the system are completely decoupled, developers can work on them in parallel. You can assign a different developer to each piece and the developers can all work at the same time without interfering with each other. That enables the developers to build the whole system in the least possible time.

Of course few things ever work perfectly, and design is certainly one of them. No one anticipates every interaction among the different parts of a complex system. If the project uses new hardware or software that the developers have not tried before, you might discover unexpected interactions during development. Often the requirements guiding the design are imperfect, so they must be modified during the design or development phases.

Even with the uncertainty these factors can add, a good design is important. Every decision made by the design eliminates a possible source of conflict for developers. Even if the decision ultimately needs to be changed, at least it gives developers a consistent point of view for making decisions.

DESIGN APPROACHES

Designers can tackle design in many ways. Probably the most common approaches are

- User interface design
- Database design
- Object-oriented design
- Procedural design

You can think of these approaches as using a different point of view. User interface design looks at the application from the user's point of view. It studies how the user will do different things using the system.

A database design approach thinks about the application from the data's point of view. It focuses on how and where the data is stored, and on how it is loaded, edited, and saved by the application.

Object-oriented and procedural designs focus on the programmer's point of view. They think about the code the programmers will build to make the application work.

Each of these approaches has its advantages and disadvantages. Each method captures part of the system's behavior, though none of them captures everything. In practice, it is usually worthwhile to combine several of these design approaches to gain the benefits of each.

For example, a user interface architect starts building a user interface design to show what the system will look like to the user. Meanwhile, the lead database developer designs the application's database. Other team leaders use object-oriented or procedural methods to make a design describing how the system works behind the scenes. These designs connect the user interface and database designs, telling how the program takes data from the database, processes it, and displays it to the user.

In many cases, it makes sense to build a high level object-oriented design describing the main objects in the system. Then for each of those objects, you build a more detailed procedural design showing how each object will do its job.

An application's different designs often interact closely. In this example, the database design and object-oriented design identify almost the same data objects. The object-oriented or procedural design ties the user interface and database designs together. Until both the user interface and data designs are finished, the object-oriented or procedural design of the code behind-the-scenes cannot be complete.

To help the designs progress smoothly, each designer needs to be aware of what the other designers are doing. Designers can keep their designs as independent as possible for as long as possible, but eventually they must all come together to describe the same application.

The following sections describe these different design approaches. They explain the strengths and weaknesses of each approach and demonstrate them using the VB NetLab example. They also explain how you can use prototypes to test each of these kinds of designs. User interface prototypes are one of the most common kinds of prototype, but you can build prototypes for other designs, as well.

USER INTERFACE DESIGN

User interface design focuses on what the user sees in the finished program. It does not address the way the code works to produce the results the user sees. Ideally it deals exclusively with the end results from the user's point of view with no inside knowledge of what's going on behind the scenes.

In actual practice, user interface design often bows to practical considerations; the distinction between the user interface design and the program's internal workings blurs slightly. Fight this trend for as long as possible. Concentrate on what should be rather than on what is easy to implement.

EASIER SAID THAN DONE

User interface design is not as easy as it looks. A user interface is a lot like a movie soundtrack. If the production team does a good job, you don't even notice it's there. If they do a bad job, you are constantly distracted from the main plot.

In a well-designed application, the user interface is simple and intuitive. It seems so natural that it's hard to imagine the application having been designed in any other way. Of course, the application *could* have been built in some other way, probably for the worse. Because the interface appears simple, many programmers get the false impression that making the interface was easy.

Building a good user interface is a lot of work. It takes study and experience to figure out the best types of controls to use for a particular task and how those controls should be arranged to seem as natural as possible.

Before you start dropping text boxes on a form, read a few books on user interface design. Look at the applications you use and try to figure out what you like and dislike about them. Use the good ideas and avoid the bad ones in your own application.

User Interface Books

Some of the books I've used to study user interface design include

- *The Art of Human-Computer Interface Design* edited by Brenda Laurel (Addison-Wesley, 1990)
- *About Face: The Essentials of User Interface Design* by Alan Cooper (IDG Books, 1995)
- *GUI Bloopers: Don'ts and Do's for Software Developers and Web Designers* by Jeff Johnson (Morgan Kaufmann, 2000)
- *The Design of Everyday Things* by Donald Norman (Currency/Doubleday, 1990)

As you probably guess from its title, *The Design of Everyday Things* discusses the design of ordinary objects such as telephones and door handles. While these are not part of computer interfaces, the book's thought-provoking discussions can help you think about user-interface design from a new perspective.

PART

II

CH

5

A style guide is a reference for designing applications in a particular environment. It explains in detail what standard menus look like, what shortcut keys to use, how you should group buttons, and so forth. Style guide rules are necessary but not sufficient because they cannot address your specific application directly. A Windows style guide will say the leftmost menu should be the File menu. It cannot tell you how to graphically display work-flow through a machine shop because that is not a standard feature of most Windows applications.

Different programming environments have different standard user interface styles and different style guides. For example, programs running on Windows, Mac OS, XWindows, and Motif have slightly different conventions. Web applications run on systems using different operating systems so they have their own set of conventions. Because you are probably writing Visual Basic programs to run in Windows, you should focus on Windows styles.

Books that focus on other user interface styles can give you a useful perspective. They can also sometimes give you ideas you would not think of if looking only at other Windows applications. However, you should usually make your application perform standard operations in the same way other Windows applications do. That lets experienced Windows users learn to use your program as quickly as possible.

For example, applications in the Motif windowing system use the key combinations Control-Insert, Shift-Del, and Shift-Insert to perform the copy, cut, and paste operations. Most Windows applications use Control-C, Control-X, and Control-V for these tasks. Although you can use either set of shortcuts in your application, Windows users will have a lot less trouble running your application if you stick with Control-C, Control-X, and Control-V.

In addition to books, you can learn about user interface design by studying other Windows applications. Experiment with them and see which features work well and which are awkward. Use established products because first releases often contain awkward user interface features that are fixed in later releases. If you can, compare versions 1.0 and 2.0 to see what the developers changed.

You might even want to hire a professional graphic artist or user interface designer to help with your project. Keep this person involved throughout the design phase. Don't expect a professional to come in at the last moment with a few minor suggestions that magically fix the 132 poorly designed forms you already have tightly linked together.

Tale from the Trenches

The Human Factors group was down the hall from my office at GTE Laboratories. Human Factors was full of psychologists and behavioral scientists. Their specialty was studying how users interact with systems such as software applications and telephone systems to figure out what worked and what didn't. Unfortunately, GTE project teams often didn't consult them for advice or waited until a project was finished and then asked their opinion.

In one case, GTE Airphone was trying to define a rate scheme for telephones on airplanes. A focus group found out the current length of phone calls using this service. Then they made all calls a fixed rate. Customers who made a call of the average length or longer saved money using the new fixed rate scheme.

Sadly, customers don't think that way. They start a phone call believing they can keep it short and then they end up talking longer than they expect. When they start the phone call, they think the fixed rate is a rip-off because they're only going to talk for a minute or two. Because of this perception, people stopped making phone calls. Even though most would have saved money, they wouldn't begin the phone call.

If Airphone had consulted the Human Factors group before hand, would they have foreseen this problem? Possibly. By the time Human Factors was asked to figure out what was going wrong, however, it was too late. Several employees had bet their careers on the project, so they couldn't back down. After a period of decimated revenue, the appropriate people were disciplined and a rate system charging by the minute was restored.

The moral is to consult user interface experts early, while it's not too late to benefit from their expertise.

USER INTERFACE PROTOTYPES

When you first have an idea of what the user interface might look like, show the customers paper sketches of what you have in mind. Be sure you are on the right track before you build any forms.

When you think you have a reasonable idea of what the customers want, make a quick non-functional prototype by building some simple Visual Basic forms. The forms can display frames, labels, fields, buttons, and other visible controls, but the controls shouldn't do anything yet.

Tale from the Trenches

One project I worked on was a programming environment for telephone switch programs. A switch engineer would write a program in our scripting language and then use the environment to execute it on the switch. This let the engineer perform such tasks as assigning phone numbers, changing customers' services, blocking certain kinds of service, and so forth.

The developer assigned to build the environment's user interface did a great job. The environment provided a lot of useful features such as setting breakpoints, stepping through one switch command at a time, modifying the switch code on the fly, and saving the programming changes or backing them out of the switch database.

However, he made several non-standard user interface decisions. These were immediately obvious to the more experienced developers as soon as they saw the first demonstration of the environment. He was a bit overwhelmed by the number of changes that were requested, but after the shock wore off he reworked the user interface and built a better product. These issues were addressed in the first prototype *before* the customer had a chance to see it.

If this developer had studied user interface design a bit more, he would have caught most of these things himself. As it was, he learned from more senior developers in a sort of apprenticeship under fire.

You do not need to demonstrate every form. If the application calls for 25 nearly identical reporting screens, just build one and tell the customers that all the others look similar. If the customers want some forms to be different from the others, break those forms out of the group and build simple examples.

Stick to simple forms for now. If a part of the interface will take a lot of work, keep it in the paper sketch stage until you are positive you know what the customers want. Then you can build a prototype of this form without wasting a lot of effort on incomplete ideas.

EXAMPLE

Suppose you are building a customer management system with mapping capabilities. You want a map of your area with icons showing each customer's location. If you double-click an icon, the customer's information pops up in a new window.

Building this map would be a lot harder than just positioning some labels and text boxes on a form. Wait until you are certain the customers like what you have in mind. Then start by building a form that displays a sample map. This version of the prototype will not let the user load new maps. In fact, the program probably won't implement scrolling and zooming either. It might simply display a scanned image on the form's background.

Show this version to the customers and get feedback. Don't start writing code for scrolling, zooming, locating customers, positioning customers, and so on until you are sure you are still on the right track. You might also need to wait for other design efforts before you know how maps and the customer positions will be stored in the database.

Use the customers' feedback on the different sample forms to refine the design. After the customers like the basic forms, add the application's toolbars, menus, and popup menus. Initially give the commands code that just displays a message box when they are invoked.

When all the menus are in place, start adding the navigation code that glues all the forms together. This code may be in buttons, toolbars, menus, context menus, or other control event handlers. Often you will have to cheat to display a particular form. For example, you might hardcode values into lists that should be loaded from a database. You might display a specific account's data in a form instead of using values entered by the user to select the account data. The idea now is to show how the user will navigate between the program's forms, not to display perfectly correct data.

EXAMPLE

Suppose the program's main form lets the user search a customer database and displays a list of customer names. The user double-clicks one to see the complete record for that customer on a separate form.

Initially, you won't know the database layout. You will probably be pretty sure that there will be a Customer table, but you can't be sure it won't be broken into a master record connected to detail tables until you have finished the database design. In that case, you cannot really query the database to get a list of customers. You also cannot display a real customer record when the user double-clicks a customer's name.

Although you cannot really implement these features yet, you can fake it. When the user tries to search the database, make the prototype display a fixed list of customer names. You can code these names directly into the ListBox at design time.

When the user double-clicks an entry, make the prototype display a customer detail form with fixed values filled in. Enter the values directly in the TextBoxes and other controls on the customer detail form.

If you have time and want to get fancy, the detail form could show different values for different customers but that isn't really necessary at this point. The idea in this version of the prototype is to give the customers an idea of what you envision the final application doing rather than actually viewing customer data.

When the navigation code is more or less working, so the customer can see how all the forms fit together, you are ready to start implementing more substantial application features. At that point, you need to have some idea of the program's database and internal designs. Wait for those designs. Don't just start writing code. If you strike out on your own without guidance, you will probably have to rewrite a lot of code when you finally know how the pieces of the application really fit together. This not only wastes your time, but it also usually produces code of a lower quality. Code written once after careful planning generally has better quality than code that has been written and rewritten.

VB NETLAB VERSION 0.01

The purpose of user interface design is to specify what the application looks like to the user. The first version shows what the development team thinks the interface will look like. Prototype versions let the developers take feedback from the customers and refine the design.

The VB NetLab UI 0.01 program shown in Figure 5.1 is the first version of VB NetLab's user interface prototype. It includes the program's basic menus and toolbar buttons. The toolbar buttons allow quick selection of the editing modes available in the Edit menu.

Figure 5.1
The first version of VB NetLab's user interface prototype demonstrates its basic menus and toolbar buttons.

FILE MENU

VB NetLab lets the user load, modify, and save network files. Those are the same features provided by other editing programs such as word processors and drawing programs. Those programs already have a common set of file manipulation functions, so VB NetLab should imitate them. A user who is familiar with any of those programs immediately understands the purposes of these functions in VB NetLab.

The File menu contains these standard file manipulation commands:

- **New (Ctrl+N)**—Closes the current network file and starts a new one
- **Open (Ctrl+O)**—Opens an existing network file
- **Close**—Closes the current network file
- **Save (Ctrl+S)**—Saves changes to the current network file
- **Save As (Ctrl+A)**—Saves the current network file with a new name
- **MRU File 1**—Reopens the most recently edited network file
- **MRU File 2**—Reopens the second most recently edited network file
- **MRU File 3**—Reopens the third most recently edited network file
- **MRU File 4**—Reopens the fourth most recently edited network file
- **Exit**—Exits the program

If the current network has been modified, the New, Open, Close, and Exit commands ask the user whether the program should save the changes before continuing.

Whenever the program has a name for the current network file, it displays the file title (the file name without the complete path) in its form caption inside brackets. When the network is modified, the program adds an asterisk before the name so the user can easily tell the network has been changed. For example, if the user loads the network file `C:\Tests\Streets1.net` and then modifies it, the program's caption is VB NetLab*[Streets1.net].

The Save command is available at all times. If the user selects this command and the program does not have a file name for the current network, the program treats the command as it would Save As.

The MRU file list displays the program's four most recently used files. If the user selects one of these commands, the program opens the corresponding file. If the MRU list does not include four files, the menu items for any missing files are hidden. If there are no files in the list, the separator between these commands and the Exit command is also hidden.

The program stores the MRU list in the Registry and updates it whenever a file is opened or saved. It also updates the list if the user tries to open a file that no longer exists. For example, if the user tries to open MRU file 1 but that file no longer exists, the program removes it from the MRU list.

EDIT MENU

VB NetLab includes several commands for editing networks. These commands are contained in the Edit menu and most are repeated in the toolbar. When the user selects a command from the menu, the corresponding toolbar button depresses and vice versa. The network editing commands include

- **Add Nodes**—Puts the program in Add Nodes mode. While in this mode, the program creates a new mode wherever the user clicks.

- **Delete Nodes**—Puts the program in Delete Nodes mode. While in this mode, the program deletes any node the user clicks. It also deletes any links connected to that node.

- **Add Links**—Puts the program in Add Links mode. While in this mode, the user can click and drag from one node to another to create a new link connecting those nodes.

- **Delete Links**—Puts the program in Delete Links mode. While in this mode, the program deletes any link the user clicks.

- **Edit Node**—Puts the program in Edit Node mode. If the user clicks a node while the program is in this mode, the program displays a dialog through which the user can edit the node's properties.

- **Edit Link**—Puts the program in Edit Link mode. If the user clicks a link while the program is in this mode, the program displays a dialog through which the user can edit the link's properties.

DATA MENU

VB NetLab includes commands for generating simple test networks. In version 0.01, these include grid networks and random networks. The Data menu contains two commands for generating test networks:

- **Grid Network**—Presents a dialog through which the user can specify parameters for creating a test grid network

- **Random Network**—Presents a dialog through which the user can specify parameters for creating a random test network

HELP MENU

VB NetLab uses standard help menu commands. By using standard commands, the program makes it easier for users to find the help they need. Anyone who has used Windows help before knows that the Index command displays the help index and that the About command displays program copyright and version information. The help menu includes these standard items:

- **Contents**—Displays the help table of contents
- **Index**—Displays the help Index page
- **Search**—Displays the help search page
- **About**—Displays an About dialog giving the program's copyright and version information

The program also displays the About dialog as a splash screen when it first starts. When the program begins, it displays the About dialog with no buttons. After two seconds, the dialog automatically unloads itself.

When the user selects About from the Help menu, the program displays the About dialog with an Ok button that gives the user the option to close it at any time.

VB NETLAB VERSION 0.02

Version 0.02 of the VB NetLab user interface prototype contains no code. The customers can display the menus and click the buttons, but the program just sits there doing nothing. Although this version of the program doesn't do anything, the customers can look at it and think about how it would work. The descriptive text in the previous section helps fill in some of the details.

Even with this minimal prototype, consulting with the customers and a user interface specialist uncovered several problems with the toolbar buttons.

- **Inconsistent**—The Add Nodes button uses a plus sign inside a circle but the Add Links button uses a plus sign to the side.
- **Hard to understand**—None of the customers could guess the buttons' purposes. The buttons have ToolTips that help, but using the ToolTips slows the users down.
- **Modality**—Each button puts the program into a different mode. The depressed button shows the mode the program is in, so at least the modality is not hidden. Users often find modes confusing, however. For example, it is likely that users will forget they are in Delete Nodes mode and accidentally delete a node while trying to do something else. This would be less of a problem if the program provided Undo and Redo features, but those have been deferred until release 2.0.
- **Grouping**—The buttons are not grouped logically. The node buttons and link buttons should be grouped separately.
- **Missing menu**—The Select button on the far left has no corresponding item in the Edit menu. To be consistent, all of the toolbar buttons should have corresponding menu items.

The customers also noticed that there was no method for moving nodes or clicking and dragging to select many nodes and links at a time. They were told that these features were outside the scope of this initial prototype and that they should wait until the next version.

With this initial feedback, the developers went away and brainstormed. They looked at how other programs handled these issues. They paid particular attention to drawing applications. Users of those programs tend to spend most of their time in a normal editing mode. In that mode, the user can click, shift-click, and click and drag to select one or more objects. That seems like it should also work for VB NetLab. The code needed to demonstrate this selection model was somewhat complicated, however. To avoid spending a lot of time writing code that might get thrown away, the concept was described to the customers before work on writing code began.

When other drawing programs enter a special mode, they often use the mouse pointer to indicate the mode. For example, when VB NetLab enters Delete Node mode, the mouse pointer could change to a small circle with an X through it.

To edit objects, some other drawing programs display a bewildering assortment of menu items depending on the items selected. Translating this idea into VB NetLab's terms, if nodes are selected the Edit menu displays commands appropriate for nodes. If links are selected, the menu displays commands appropriate for links. If nodes and links are selected, the menu displays commands appropriate to both, such as Delete.

All of this seems a little complicated. It also doesn't provide a method for creating new nodes and links. The user would still need to enter some sort of Add Node and Add Link modes.

An alternative strategy is to display context menus when the user right-clicks an object. If the user selects one or more nodes and right-clicks one, the program displays a popup menu holding commands for manipulating the nodes. These commands include Edit, Delete, and Add Link.

Similarly, if the user selects links and right-clicks one, the context menu contains the link commands Edit and Delete.

If the user right-clicks an empty part of the program's drawing surface, the context menu displays the Add Node command. The new node is added at the position the user clicked.

With this new design, the toolbar is no longer needed. That avoids all the issues of confusing and badly grouped buttons.

Figure 5.2 shows version 0.02 of the user interface prototype. This version's File, Data, and Help menus are the same as the first version's. Its Edit menu now contains Select All Nodes, Select All Links, and Delete commands.

Figure 5.2
VB NetLab's user
interface prototype
version 0.02 uses con-
text menus instead of
a toolbar.

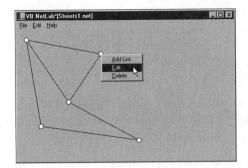

This version of the prototype still doesn't do very much. It doesn't let the user select nodes and links. When the user invokes commands in the main menu or the context menus, the program just displays message boxes describing what it will eventually do.

The customers liked the Data menu in version 0.01, so this version demonstrates that menu's features a little further. If the user invokes the menu's Grid Network command, the program displays the dialog shown in Figure 5.3.

Because the Grid Network dialog will replace the current network if the user clicks its Ok button, the final application should prompt the user to save any changes to the current net-work before displaying the dialog. The prototype displays the dialog without any warning.

Figure 5.3
VB NetLab's Grid
Network dialog lets
the user select para-
meters for creating a
test grid network.

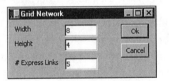

Figure 5.4 shows a sample grid network created by the Grid Network dialog. Notice that the prototype resets the filename displayed in the form's title bar because the new network has not been saved in a file yet.

Figure 5.4
Grid networks like this
one let the student
test network algo-
rithms on a standard
network configuration.

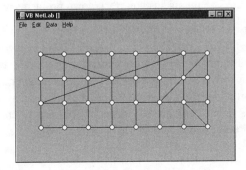

The Data menu's Random Network command works much as the Grid Network command does. It displays a dialog where the user can enter test network parameters. If the user clicks Ok, the dialog creates a random network. Because this feature is so similar to the Grid Network function, it is easy to explain to the customers and it doesn't need to be included in the prototype.

Listing 5.1 shows the most interesting code used by this version of the prototype. Node data is stored in an array of standard Visual Basic Point objects called m_Nodes. Each Point's X and Y fields give the position of its node on the drawing surface.

Link information is stored in an array of Link objects called m_Links. Each Link object contains pointers to the link's start and end nodes.

The program's MakeTestData subroutine generates a small fixed network of nodes and links. The DrawNetwork subroutine uses that data to draw the sample network. This network gives the customers something to look at and the program uses it to determine which context menu it should display when the user right-clicks the drawing surface. The form's Paint event handler calls DrawNetwork to refresh the display whenever the form is exposed.

If the user clicks the Grid Network dialog's Ok button, the dialog's code invokes the MakeGridNetwork subroutine. This routine takes as parameters the width and height of the grid of nodes, and the number of express or shortcut links it should create. It creates the right number of nodes and then adds links so each node is connected to those that are next to it vertically and horizontally. It then creates express links that connect two randomly selected nodes. This is a standard type of network used to test network algorithms.

When MakeGridNetwork picks random nodes to connect with express links, it sets two variables node1 and node2 to the indexes of the nodes it has selected. It then makes a link connecting the nodes. The program could perform both of these steps in one long statement, including the code that selects random node numbers in the New Link statement. But, it keeps these tasks separate for two reasons. First, this makes the code easier to understand.

Second, keeping these statements separate makes the node numbers selected easy to see in the debugger. Suppose there was a problem creating the new link and the debugger stopped on the New Link statement. At that point, you cannot see the values generated by the NextDouble method. Those values are used up, and if you call NextDouble again, you get new values instead of the ones that caused the problem. That makes debugging this piece of code difficult. Breaking the code into separate statements lets you track down problems more easily.

The form's MouseDown event handler first verifies that the user pressed the right mouse button. It uses the MouseIsOver function to get a pointer to the object beneath the mouse. Next, the event handler hides all of the commands in the context menu. Then, depending on the kind of object under the mouse, the routine makes some of the context menu commands visible. For example, if the item under the mouse is a node, the routine makes the Edit, Add Link, and Delete commands visible. The event handler finishes by presenting the context menu. The menu command event handlers perform their tasks when the user selects them.

The `MouseIsOver` function first examines the nodes stored in the `m_Nodes` array. It calculates the distance from each node to the point of interest. If the distance between these points is less than the radius of a node, the node is at this point so `MouseIsOver` returns it.

If the mouse is not over a node, the `MouseIsOver` function examines the links. For each link, it calls the `DistToSegment` function to see how far the point is from the link. If the distance is less than the value `LINK_DISTANCE`, the link is at this point so `MouseIsOver` returns it.

The `DistToSegment` function calculates the distance between a point and a line segment. This is the most complicated piece of code in this version of the prototype. It is also the only piece of code that might be reused in the final application. The rest of the code that stores node and link information, initializes the sample network, and processes `MouseDown` events will almost certainly be rewritten.

The `DistToSegment` function is interesting but not really central to the discussion of prototypes so you can skip to the next section, "Further VB NetLab Versions," if your calculus is a little rusty.

`DistToSegment` considers the link as a parameterized line segment starting at the point (X1, Y1) and running to the point (X2, Y2). Let dx = X2 – X1 and dy = Y2 – Y1. Then, if you let the variable t go from 0.0 to 1.0, the following equations define the points on the segment.

```
X(t) = X1 + dx * t
Y(t) = Y1 + dy * t
```

If dx and dy are both zero, the segment is actually a point, so `DistToSegment` returns the normal distance between the segment's single point and the target point (px, py).

If dx and dy are not both zero, then the distance between the point (X(t), Y(t)) and (px, py) is:

```
Dist = Sqrt((X(t) - px) ^ 2 + (Y(t) - py) ^ 2)
```

Plugging in the values of X(t) and Y(t) gives:

```
Dist = Sqrt((X1 + dx * t - px) ^ 2 + (Y1 + dy * t - py) ^ 2)
```

The goal is to find the value of t that minimizes this distance. That gives the value of t where the line segment is closest to the point (px, py). From there, you can find the point (X(t), Y(t)) and calculate the distance from there to (px, py).

The value of t that minimizes the distance also minimizes the square of the distance, so you can make the equation a little simpler by squaring it.

```
Dist2 = (X1 + dx * t - px) ^ 2 + (Y1 + dy * t - py) ^ 2
```

To find the minimum distance using calculus, take the derivative of the equation with respect to t and set the result equal to zero. Then simplify the equation and solve it for t.

```
2 * (X1 + dx * t - px) * dx + 2 * (Y1 + dy * t - py) * dy = 0
```

If you divide both sides of the equation by 2 you get:

```
(X1 + dx * t - px) * dx + (Y1 + dy * t - py) * dy = 0
```

Rearranging a bit gives:

```
t * (dx + dy) + (X1 - px) + (Y1 - py) = 0
```

Solving for t makes this:

```
t = (px + py - X1 - Y1) / (dx + dy)
```

This equation may seem intimidating but all of the values px, py, X1, Y1, dx, and dy are known so you can plug them into the equation.

This value of t gives the coordinates of the point on the line between (X1, Y1) and (X2, Y2) that lies closest to the target point (px, py). If t < 0.0, then the point (X(t), Y(t)) lies off the end of the segment and (X1, Y1) is the point on the segment that is closest to (px, py). Similarly if t > 1.0, then the point (X(t), Y(t)) lies off the other end of the segment and (X2, Y2) is the point on the segment closest to (px, py).

After the DistToSegment function knows the coordinates of the point on the segment that lies closest to the target point (px, py), it can easily calculate that distance.

Listing 5.1 shows the most interesting pieces of the VB NetLab 0.02 prototype's code including the DistToSegment function.

LISTING 5.1   MOST OF THIS CODE, USED BY VB NETLAB PROTOTYPE VERSION 0.02, WILL BE REWRITTEN IN THE FINAL APPLICATION.

```
Private Class Link
    Public Node1 As Point
    Public Node2 As Point
    Public Sub New(ByVal from_node As Point, ByVal to_node As Point)
        Node1 = from_node
        Node2 = to_node
    End Sub
End Class

' Node and link data.
Private m_Nodes() As Point
Private m_Links() As Link

' Make some test data.
Private Sub MakeTestData()
    ' Make some nodes.
    m_Nodes = New Point() { _
        New Point(20, 20), _
        New Point(180, 50), _
        New Point(110, 150), _
        New Point(50, 200), _
        New Point(260, 230), _
        New Point(370, 40), _
        New Point(300, 120), _
        New Point(350, 200) _
    }

    ' Make some links.
    m_Links = New Link() { _
```

LISTING 5.1 CONTINUED

```
            New Link(m_Nodes(0), m_Nodes(1)), _
            New Link(m_Nodes(0), m_Nodes(2)), _
            New Link(m_Nodes(0), m_Nodes(3)), _
            New Link(m_Nodes(1), m_Nodes(2)), _
            New Link(m_Nodes(2), m_Nodes(4)), _
            New Link(m_Nodes(3), m_Nodes(4)), _
            New Link(m_Nodes(1), m_Nodes(5)), _
            New Link(m_Nodes(1), m_Nodes(6)), _
            New Link(m_Nodes(5), m_Nodes(7)), _
            New Link(m_Nodes(6), m_Nodes(7)), _
            New Link(m_Nodes(4), m_Nodes(6)), _
            New Link(m_Nodes(4), m_Nodes(7)) _
        }
End Sub

Public Sub MakeGridNetwork(ByVal wid As Integer, ByVal hgt As Integer, _
    ByVal express_links As Integer)
    Dim r As Integer
    Dim c As Integer
    Dim dist As Integer
    Dim link_num As Integer
    Dim node1 As Integer
    Dim node2 As Integer
    Dim rnd As New System.Random()
    Dim num_nodes As Integer

    ' Calculate a good distance between nodes.
    If ClientRectangle.Width / wid < ClientRectangle.Height / hgt Then
        dist = ClientRectangle.Width \ (wid + 1)
    Else
        dist = ClientRectangle.Height \ (hgt + 1)
    End If

    ' Make the nodes.
    num_nodes = wid * hgt
    ReDim m_Nodes(num_nodes)
    For r = 0 To hgt - 1
        For c = 0 To wid - 1
            m_Nodes(r * wid + c) = New Point((c + 1) * dist, (r + 1) * dist)
        Next c
    Next r

    ' Make the links.
    ReDim m_Links(express_links + hgt * (wid - 1) + wid * (hgt - 1))
    link_num = 0
    ' Horizontal links.
    For r = 0 To hgt - 1
        For c = 0 To wid - 2
            node1 = r * wid + c
            m_Links(link_num) = New Link(m_Nodes(node1), m_Nodes(node1 + 1))
            link_num = link_num + 1
        Next c
    Next r
    ' Vertical links.
    For c = 0 To wid - 1
```

LISTING 5.1 CONTINUED

```vb
            For r = 0 To hgt - 2
                node1 = r * wid + c
                m_Links(link_num) = New Link(m_Nodes(node1), m_Nodes(node1 + wid))
                link_num = link_num + 1
            Next r
        Next c
        ' Express links.
        For r = 1 To express_links
            node1 = CInt(Int(rnd.NextDouble * num_nodes))
            node2 = CInt(Int(rnd.NextDouble * num_nodes))
            m_Links(link_num) = New Link(m_Nodes(node1), m_Nodes(node2))
            link_num = link_num + 1
        Next r

        ' Redraw the network.
        DrawNetwork()

        ' Reset the caption because this is a new network.
        Me.Text = "VB NetLab []"
End Sub

' Draw the network.
Private Sub DrawNetwork()
    Dim i As Integer

    ' Clear the drawing area.
    m_Canvas.Clear(Me.BackColor)

    ' Draw the links.
    For i = 0 To UBound(m_Links)
        m_Canvas.DrawLine(m_LinkPen, _
            m_Links(i).Node1.X, m_Links(i).Node1.Y, _
            m_Links(i).Node2.X, m_Links(i).Node2.Y)
    Next i

    ' Draw the nodes.
    For i = 0 To UBound(m_Nodes)
        m_Canvas.FillEllipse(m_NodeBrush, _
            m_Nodes(i).X - NODE_RADIUS, m_Nodes(i).Y - NODE_RADIUS, _
            NODE_RADIUS * 2, NODE_RADIUS * 2)
        m_Canvas.DrawEllipse(m_NodePen, _
            m_Nodes(i).X - NODE_RADIUS, m_Nodes(i).Y - NODE_RADIUS, _
            NODE_RADIUS * 2, NODE_RADIUS * 2)
    Next i

End Sub

' Redraw the network.
Public Sub Form1_Paint(ByVal sender As Object, _
  ByVal e As System.WinForms.PaintEventArgs) Handles Form1.Paint
    DrawNetwork()
End Sub

' Display an appropriate context menu.
Public Sub Form1_MouseDown(ByVal sender As Object, _
```

LISTING 5.1   CONTINUED

```
ByVal e As System.WinForms.MouseEventArgs) Handles Form1.MouseDown
    Dim over_object As Object
    Dim menu_item As MenuItem

    ' Do nothing if this isn't a right click.
    If e.Button <> MouseButtons.Right Then Exit Sub

    ' See what the mouse is over.
    over_object = MouseIsOver(e.X, e.Y)

    ' Hide all the popup menu items.
    For Each menu_item In Me.mnuPopup.MenuItems
        menu_item.Visible = False
    Next menu_item

    ' See what kind of thing this is.
    If over_object Is Nothing Then
        ' Over nothing. Allow:
        '    Add Node
        mnuPopupAddNode.Visible = True
    ElseIf TypeOf over_object Is Point Then
        ' Over a node. Allow:
        '    Edit
        '    Add Link
        '    Delete
        mnuPopupEditObjects.Visible = True
        mnuPopupAddLink.Visible = True
        mnuPopupDeleteObjects.Visible = True
    ElseIf TypeOf over_object Is Link Then
        ' Over a link. Allow:
        '    Edit
        '    Delete
        mnuPopupEditObjects.Visible = True
        mnuPopupDeleteObjects.Visible = True
    End If

    mnuPopup.Show(Me, New Point(e.X, e.Y))
End Sub

' Return the object the mouse is over.
Private Function MouseIsOver(ByVal X As Single, ByVal Y As Single) As Object
    Dim i As Integer
    Dim dx As Single
    Dim dy As Single
    Dim dist As Single

    ' See if the mouse is over a node.
    For i = 0 To UBound(m_Nodes)
        dx = X - m_Nodes(i).X
        dy = Y - m_Nodes(i).Y
        If Math.Sqrt(dx * dx + dy * dy) <= NODE_RADIUS Then
            Return m_Nodes(i)
        End If
    Next i
```

LISTING 5.1 CONTINUED

```
    ' See if the mouse is over a link.
    For i = 0 To UBound(m_Links)
        If DistToSegment(X, Y, _
            m_Links(i).Node1.X, m_Links(i).Node1.Y, _
            m_Links(i).Node2.X, m_Links(i).Node2.Y) _
                <= LINK_DISTANCE _
        Then
            Return m_Links(i)
        End If
    Next i

    Return Nothing
End Function

' Return the distance from the point (px, py) to the segment
' (X1, Y1) —> (X2, Y2).
Private Function DistToSegment( _
  ByVal px As Double, ByVal py As Double, _
  ByVal X1 As Double, ByVal Y1 As Double, _
  ByVal X2 As Double, ByVal Y2 As Double) As Double
    Dim dx As Double
    Dim dy As Double
    Dim t As Double

    dx = X2 - X1
    dy = Y2 - Y1
    If dx = 0 And dy = 0 Then
        ' It's a point not a line segment.
        dx = px - X1
        dy = py - Y1
        Return Math.Sqrt(dx * dx + dy * dy)
    End If

    t = (dx * (px - X1) + dy * (py - Y1)) / (dx * dx + dy * dy)
    If t < 0 Then
        dx = px - X1
        dy = py - Y1
    ElseIf t > 1 Then
        dx = px - X2
        dy = py - Y2
    Else
        X2 = X1 + t * dx
        Y2 = Y1 + t * dy
        dx = px - X2
        dy = py - Y2
    End If
    Return Math.Sqrt(dx * dx + dy * dy)
End Function
```

FURTHER VB NETLAB VERSIONS

Version 0.02 of the VB NetLab prototype, together with some explanation, describes most of the program's fundamental user interface features. The prototype shows how the user can right-click on different objects in the drawing area to display an appropriate context menu.

It shows where the user can find the program's different menu commands. None of these features do anything, but some explanation can help the customers understand how everything will fit together.

So far this all seems reasonable. The user can load a network or create a new one, edit the network by adding and removing nodes and links, and save the results.

VB NetLab must also let the Visual Basic programming students who are the users add network code of their own to the application. For example, an assignment might ask the students to implement an algorithm that finds the shortest path between two nodes. The students must be able to add this kind of algorithm to the program. The students must also be able to add an interface so the program's user can execute the algorithm at runtime.

You could add a toolbar and buttons to let students manage their algorithms. Unfortunately, that would complicate the interface. Buttons for every implemented algorithm would take up room no matter which algorithm the student uses. Toolbars are also somewhat confusing and might sidetrack the students when they should be concentrating on network algorithms.

After some discussion, the customers and development team agreed to add an Algorithm menu to the program. Students will add a new submenu for each algorithm and add items inside the submenus as needed. For example, the student will add a Label Correcting Shortest Path menu with items Set Start Node and Set Stop Node.

You could add the Algorithms menu to make version 0.03 of the prototype, but that menu wouldn't do anything. Seeing it wouldn't tell the customers anything they don't already know.

You could also add more features to the prototype. You could start writing code to show how the program will load, edit, and save networks.

However, demonstrating these features would require a lot of nontrivial code. Remember, the point of the user interface prototype is to gather feedback and make sure the development team and customers agree on what the program will look like without writing a lot of code. The prototype version 0.02, together with some explanation, describes the application's features well enough. There's little point in writing a lot of difficult code to further describe something that the customers already understand. That code will come later.

The prototype also doesn't use the methods and data structures that the final application will use. For example, the final application will certainly not use Point objects to represent nodes. Writing complicated code to make the prototype data structures work better is a waste of time. The developers will throw all that code away when they implement the final data structures anyway.

Rather than trying to improve code that will be discarded anyway, you should end the user interface prototyping here. The program is not very complete and doesn't demonstrate many features, but it is good enough to verify that development is on the right track.

After you finish the other forms of program design, particularly the procedural design, you can rebuild prototype version 0.02 using the application's final data structures and methods.

Then you can use that version as the beginning of an evolutionary prototype that eventually turns into the final application.

DATABASE DESIGN

Database design focuses on the data and how it is stored. Database design has been around as long as databases, and a lot has been written about it. This section describes some basic techniques you can use to design a simple database. There isn't enough room in this book for me to cover everything there is to know about databases. You should probably read a good database programming book or two before you start building more complex databases. A couple of books that provide good introductions to database programming in Visual Basic are *Beginning Visual Basic 6 Database Programming* by John Connell (Wrox, 1998) and *Professional Visual Basic 6 Databases* by Charles Williams (Wrox, 1999). While these books were written for Visual Basic 6, much of their advice for programming with ADO transfers easily to ADO.NET.

Database design is often a useful exercise even if the application will not use a database. It helps you understand the system's most important objects and how they interact. Usually a database design maps easily into an object-oriented design. Viewing the data from both the database and object-oriented perspective sometimes helps fill out the object-oriented design.

Database design usually assumes the application uses a relational database, but the particular brand of database is unimportant. The data can be stored in Access, Oracle, or XML files. As long as the database supports the concept of tables holding records made up of fields, this kind of design is useful.

VB NetLab saves and restores network data in XML files, although it manipulates network data at runtime using objects that do not have exactly the same structure.

Tale from the Trenches

I usually find database design a bit tedious. There are always a couple of valid ways to design a particular system, and it doesn't matter much which one you use. For some reason I have never completely understood, however, many (though not all) database designers are willing to defend their designs to the bitter end. I think they correctly realize that their design is an extremely important part of the application and they think changes to their design are an affront to their authority.

I have worked on several projects with other companies (or with other divisions inside the same company) who had these database maniacs. Head-to-head confrontation doesn't work with these fanatics. I have found two successful strategies. First, you can surrender. Often their designs are good enough that you can accept them, perhaps with a few minor changes, and move on to something more interesting.

The second strategy is to devote a full-time developer to gently steering this person towards the right result. With enough patience, you can often convince the troublesome designer that the changes you want were his idea.

In any case, starting the database design early is probably your best defense. If the difficult designer gets a head start, you're in trouble. If his design is more complete than yours, he can reasonably claim it is better.

RECORDS AND TABLES

Relational databases are the most common form of database used by Visual Basic programs. Relational databases group related data into tables. A table may contain many records holding similar data for different instances of the objects it describes.

For example, a Customer table contains data that describes customers. Each record includes fields describing that customer: name, address, phone number, account balance, and so on. Each record contains the same kinds of data for different customers.

The first step in designing the database is defining the tables. These usually correspond naturally to objects in the system. For example, if you are writing a point-of-sales system, you might want objects to represent customers, orders, and items on orders. To hold these kinds of data, you need tables for customers, orders, and order items. To keep things easy to understand, give the tables simple names like Customer, Order, and OrderItem.

After you identify the system's objects, it is usually obvious what pieces of data go with each kind of object. Customer records have names, addresses, phone numbers, and so forth. An order contains a shipping address, billing address, payment method, sales tax, and a list of order items. An order item has a description, unit cost, and quantity in the order.

You also need to add fields to tie these records together. One way to do that is to give the Customer and Order tables a CustomerId field. This field is an arbitrary value that ties Customer and Order records together. The orders for a customer with a given CustomerId have the same CustomerId. You could select the Order information for the customer with CustomerId 326 using the SQL statement:

```
SELECT * FROM Orders WHERE CustomerId = 326
```

Similarly, you could give Order and OrderItem records an OrderId field. To find the OrderItems that go with an Order record, you would search for OrderItem records with the same OrderId.

Figure 5.5 shows the relationships among these tables graphically. The lines connecting the tables indicate the number of records that match in each. For example, the line connecting the Customer table to the Order table has one branch on the Customer end and three branches at the Order end. That means one Customer record corresponds to many Order records. This connection starts at the Customer record's CustomerId field and ends at the Order record's CustomerId field to indicate that those are the fields that tie the two tables together.

Similarly, one Order record corresponds to many OrderItem records. This link starts at the Order tables OrderId fields and ends at the OrderItem table's OrderId field to indicate that those are the fields that tie these tables together.

Figure 5.5
Database design starts with the basic objects the system manipulates. In this example, those are Customers, Orders, and OrderItems.

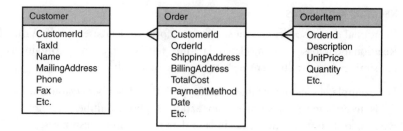

FIRST NORMAL FORM

After you have defined the application's main table structure, you should *normalize* the data. When you normalize the data, you refine the table definitions to ensure that they have certain standard properties that are described shortly. These properties guarantee that the database has a certain level of flexibility.

The database is in *first normal form* (1NF) if the tables do not contain repeated fields. The example shown in Figure 5.5 includes a couple of repeated fields. The Customer record's Phone and Fax fields represent different values but they represent the same kind of values: phone numbers.

That's not a big deal, but what if you later decide that customers need an additional AfterHoursPhone field? You would need to modify the Customer table to add another kind of phone number. You would also need to modify the program's user interface and the code that loads, validates, edits, and saves the new values in the database. When you decide to add yet another AccountsPayablePhone field, you need to do it all over again.

Instead of repeating this kind of data several times, you can pull out the phone numbers and give them their own table. Give the PhoneNumber table a Type field to indicate the type of each phone number record: Phone, Fax, AfterHoursPhone, AccountsPayablePhone, and so on. Also give this table a CustomerId field to tie it to the Customer table.

Now the user interface can display a Customer's phone numbers in a list. When you add a new phone number, the list displays it automatically. When you write the code that loads and saves phone numbers to deal generally with the list instead of with specific phone number types, you don't have to change it to accommodate new phone number types either.

Similarly, the Order table contains two address fields: ShippingAddress and BillingAddress. For the same reasons, you can pull these out into a new Address table. If you design the user interface and code behind the scenes properly, you don't have to change them to add new addresses to Order records.

As long as you're creating a new Address table, you should also pull the MailingAddress field out of the Customer table. There is currently only one address in that table, but you're already creating an Address table, and this saves trouble if you later add more address fields to the Customer table.

If you are going to use the Address table for both Customer and Order addresses, you cannot tie the Address table directly to the others using the CustomerId field because that would tie every Address for a Customer to every one of its Order records. You also cannot use the OrderId field because the Customer table doesn't have an OrderId field.

To tie these three tables together, give the Address table an AddressId field. To link the Customer table with the Address table, add a new CustomerAddress table. This table contains a CustomerId field and an AddressId field. To find the addresses for a Customer record, the program locates the CustomerAddress records with the corresponding CustomerId value. It then uses the AddressId field to locate the right Address records.

Similarly, build an OrderAddress table to tie the Order and Address tables together using OrderId and AddressId fields. Figure 5.6 shows this database design.

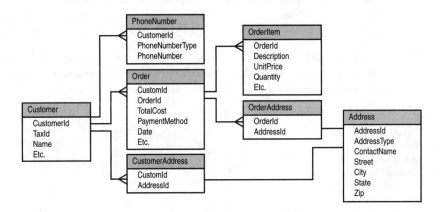

Figure 5.6
To convert the initial design into first normal form, addresses and phone numbers move into their own tables.

At this point, you might wonder if you need separate PhoneNumber and Address tables. Many phone numbers correspond to addresses and vice versa. For example, a billing address might correspond to a phone number to call if there are questions about the bill.

You could add a couple more tables to allow the program to link phone numbers and addresses to each other. This would give you the greatest flexibility, but it would also make things more complicated. The user interface and the code managing the data would need to be able to manipulate a phone number with or without an associated address, and an address with or without an associated phone number.

An easier solution is to replace the two tables with a new Contact table. This table contains both address and phone number information. In some cases, a Contact record might include address information but no phone number, or a phone number with no address. That would waste a little space, but it would be much simpler.

SECOND NORMAL FORM

A database is in *second normal form* (2NF) if it is in first normal form and every field in each record is directly related to the record's key. Another way to think about this is that every field in a record should add new information to that record.

In this example, the Customer table's Name field adds new information to its record. It gives the name for the corresponding customer. The name field is a function of its particular customer record.

On the other hand, the OrderItem table contains a couple of pieces of information that are not unique to each OrderItem record. Different customers could buy the same products in different orders. For instance, they might both buy the same model of computer. In that case, the OrderItem records would contain the same values for those items' Description and UnitPrice fields. That means the Description and UnitPrice are not a function of the primary key OrderId because different OrderId values can give the same Description and UnitPrice. These items are related more to themselves than to the OrderId.

To continue normalizing the database, you can pull these repeated values out into their own Product table. Give this table a ProductId field and use it to connect the Product records to the OrderItem table. Figure 5.7 shows the new database design.

Figure 5.7
To put the database in second normal form, the product data moves into its own table.

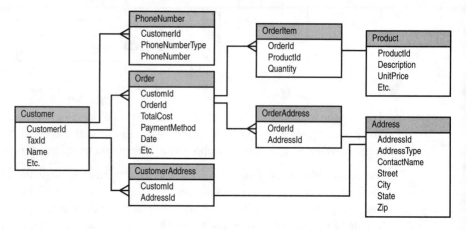

In this new version of the database, the OrderItem table plays a role similar to the CustomerAddress and OrderAddress tables. It serves to link one record in one table to several records in another table. It also adds one piece of information of its own: Quantity. That is the only piece of information that is unique to a particular OrderItem record.

THIRD NORMAL FORM

A database is in *third normal form* (3NF) if it is in second normal form and the fields in the table do not depend on each other. Another way to think about this is that no field gives information that is also contained in another field.

One consequence of this is that a table should not contain a field that is a simple function of other fields. In this example, the Order table contains a TotalCost field that is the sum of the costs of the items in the order. To calculate those costs, the program can multiply the Quantity from each OrderItem record by the UnitPrice in the corresponding Product record. It can then add up all these values to get the order's total cost. That means the Order table's TotalCost field is unnecessary.

A subtler example of this arises in the Address table. If you know the Zip code for an address, you can look up the city and state. That means, in theory at least, you could remove the City and State fields and rely on the Zip code.

In practice, this level of normalization is usually not worth the trouble. You should probably eliminate fields like TotalCost that are easy to calculate when needed, but removing City and State adds extra complication for the programmers without gaining much. Figure 5.8 shows the database without the TotalCost field but keeping City and State.

Figure 5.8
To put the database in third normal form, TotalCost is removed because it can be recalculated as needed.

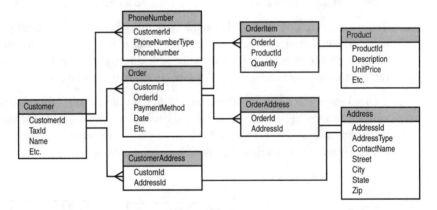

THE PURPOSE OF NORMALIZATION

The whole point of normalization is to make the database more flexible. Look again at the original tables in Figure 5.5. If you decided to add a new address or phone number to the Customer or Order tables, you would need to do extensive user interface remodeling and rewrite a lot of code. If you decided to change the name of a product item, you would need to change it in every OrderItem record. If you changed an item's UnitPrice, all of the TotalCost values would be incorrect.

When you look at the database design in Figure 5.7, you'll see that it handles these changes more gracefully. You can add as many new addresses and phone numbers as you like without changing the user interface or source code. To change a product's description or price, you only need to modify that product's record. The program picks up the new values when it uses that record to display an order.

Of course, some of these changes might not make a lot of sense. If you change an item's price after you've sold it, you will get some strange results. It would probably be better to create a new Product record with the new information and use it when you create orders in the future.

DENORMALIZATION

You can definitely carry normalization too far. Normalizing a database tends to make it take up less space. It also makes it more flexible and makes locating some kinds of data easier.

On the other hand, when you split a table into pieces you need to perform a join to put the information back together. To find a customer's addresses in this example, the program would need to join the Customer table with the CustomerAddress table and then with the Address table.

```
SELECT * FROM Customer, CustomerAddress, Address
WHERE Customer.CustomerId = CustomerAddress.CustomerId
  AND CustomerAddress.AddressId = Address.AddressId
```

Performing this kind of join takes some extra time. You might get slightly better performance if you denormalize the database and either pull the address information back into the Customer table or connect the Customer table directly to the Address table. The first idea removes all of your flexibility, so it's probably not a good solution.

To implement the second idea, you could add CustomerId and OrderId fields to the Address table. A customer's address records would have valid CustomerId fields and null OrderId fields. An order's address records would have valid OrderId fields and null CustomerId fields. Figure 5.9 shows this version of the database design.

Figure 5.9
Sometimes, denormalizing the database slightly improves performance.

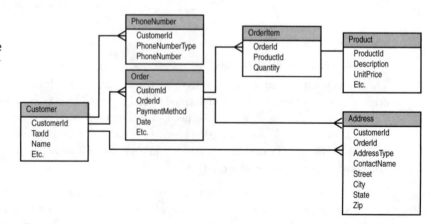

This removes one level from the join, though it creates its own set of problems. It means one of these fields is unused in every Address record so it wastes a little space. It also means customers and orders cannot easily share Address records. If a Customer record and an

Order record were linked to the same address data in different Address records, you would need to modify both to make any changes and still keep the record synchronized.

Tale from the Trenches

In one project, I worked with another company. We were both working for a third company who was acting as prime contractor for someone else, but that's another story. We had all agreed that the other company would do the project's database design and I would build the user interface.

For some reason, their design hyper-normalized the database. Instead of putting data in a single table, the design put each piece of data in a separate table linked to the first with a record ID.

For example, I wanted to use a single Address table containing all of the address fields:

LastName

FirstName

Street

City

State

Zip

and so forth

Their design called for an Address table containing only an address ID. The AddressDetail table linked to the Address table with the same ID. It also contained ItemName and ItemValue fields to hold the address values.

AddressId

ItemName

ItemValue

The AddressDetail records for a typical address might look like:

12090	"FirstName"	"Nick"
12090	"City"	"Nuisance"
12090	"Street"	"128 Dead Programmer Gulch"
12090	"City"	"Bugsville"
12090	"State"	"CO"
12090	"Zip"	"80217"

and so forth

This design was unbelievably flexible. You could add new Title, SecondaryPhone, and FavoriteFood fields to the AddressDetail table without changing the Address table at all.

Unfortunately, this design made the user interface a nightmare. The address information would need to be stored in some sort of grid so the user could view and modify the arbitrarily long list of address fields. The program would also need some way to order the fields so the address displayed in the right order: FirstName, LastName, Street, City, State, and Zip. The user interface could do all this, but it would be very awkward for the user.

This design also added an extra join whenever the application needed to load or save address data. Although the added flexibility is interesting, we didn't really need it. We didn't plan to add SecondaryPhone or FavoriteFoods fields to the address information.

In the ensuing war over this issue, the other company's database designer refused to back down (see the previous Tale From The Trenches). Eventually, the project manager from the prime contractor had to step in and declare that the database would not be hyper-normalized, but that wasn't before we had wasted a week or so bickering.

PART

II

CH

5

Think carefully before you decide to denormalize a database. Sometimes developers denormalize to make the database more closely match Visual Basic classes they have already defined. Sometimes they think denormalization will make a query faster. In some cases, however, this provides only a marginal improvement in speed. If denormalizing a table reduces a query's time from 0.5 seconds to 0.4 seconds, the user won't notice the difference.

Rather than modifying the database to match the programmer's objects or to improve queries that may not need it, focus on the database's flexibility. If denormalization prevents you from adding new kinds of addresses that you think you will need later, it's not worth the trouble.

LOOKUP TABLES

Many applications need simple lookup tables. These tables map one set of values to another. Lookup tables are very straightforward and don't interact much with other tables in the database design.

For example, you might have a States table that has two fields: StateAbbreviation and StateName. You could use that table to look up a state's abbreviation and find out what its name is. Other lookup tables might map warehouse names to codes, vehicle type codes to names and descriptions, account statuses to abbreviations, and part numbers to descriptions.

A lookup table is also called a *domain table* because it defines a domain from which certain values must be selected. For instance, the States table defines the domain of state names that are allowed in state name fields.

Lookup tables are intended to hold data that changes infrequently. A lookup table might map part numbers to descriptions if the parts you work with change only rarely. Parts inventories that change daily belong in some other part of the database.

If you don't know whether a table should be a lookup table, think about who will modify it and how often. If the table will be updated by the system administrator every few months, it might be a lookup table. If the program modifies the table entries frequently while the users do their work, it is definitely not a lookup table.

Because lookup tables change so rarely, a prototype can load all of the table's values when it starts. It can then refer to the table's values in memory instead of performing a database query. The ADOTools program described in Chapter 11, "Database Tips and Tools," demonstrates a lookup table. When it starts, the program loads a lookup table that maps account status codes to account status names. Look in the "ADO Tools" section of Chapter 11 for this program's details.

USER ACCESS TABLES

If your program will have different levels of user privilege, you probably want to include tables that define privileges for the users. Chapter 11 describes a user privilege system in which a UserPrivileges table contains two fields: UserName and Privilege. A typical entry that says the user Rod is allowed to view employee information might have UserName = Rod and Privilege = VIEW_EMPLOYEES.

The program can use this table as a type of lookup table. When the user logs in, the program loads the UserPrivileges records for the user, saving the Privilege values in some sort of collection or array. The program can then use this lookup data to see if the user has particular privileges.

For example, when a form containing a List Employees button loads, the program can see if the lookup data includes the value VIEW_EMPLOYEES. If the value is not present, the program can disable or hide the List Employees button. See the "User Privileges" section in Chapter 11 for more details on user privileges in a prototype.

VB NetLab Database Design

VB NetLab has a relatively simple database design. The program is not password protected, so it doesn't need a UserPrivileges table. It doesn't work with states, part numbers, or anything else concrete enough to require a lookup table.

The only data VB NetLab needs to save and restore is the network data. Figure 5.10 shows a sample directed network. The circles are nodes. The lines are links. The numbers on top of the links are the links' costs.

Figure 5.10
VB NetLab saves and restores networks consisting of nodes connected by links.

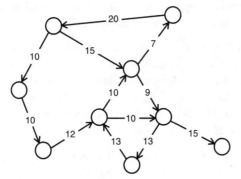

VB NetLab's networks contain two kinds of objects: Nodes and Links. The program stores these objects in the Nodes and Links tables.

The Nodes table contains the fields NodeId, X, and Y. The X and Y fields give the node's location. The NodeId identifies the node.

The Links table contains the fields NodeFrom, NodeTo, and Cost. The NodeIdFrom and NodeIdTo fields give the NodeIds in the Nodes table for the nodes that this link connects. The Cost field gives the node's cost.

Figure 5.11 shows this database design. Here the Nodes table's NodeId field links to both the NodeIdFrom and NodeIdTo fields in the Links table.

In a network, each node may be the start or end point of many links. That means each NodeId may appear in either the NodeIdFrom or NodeIdTo fields in many Links records. That's why the links between the tables are drawn with forked ends in Figure 5.11.

Figure 5.11
The VB NetLab database design uses two tables: Nodes and Links.

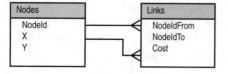

This design is not in first normal form because the NodeIdFrom and NodeIdTo fields in the Links table are both references to node IDs. You could give the database greater flexibility by creating a new LinkNodes table and moving those fields there. You would link the new table to the Links table by giving them both new LinkId fields.

The new design would allow you to add mode nodes to a link, but that doesn't make any sense in this context. A network link always connects exactly two nodes. Pulling the NodeIdFrom and NodeIdTo fields into their own table would allow greater flexibility that would never be used and would complicate the design. For VB NetLab, it's better to stick with the original non-normalized design shown in Figure 5.11.

In the final version of the VB NetLab program, the node and link objects will probably have additional properties. Nodes might include their own costs, colors, and labels. Links might include flows and restrictions to let you simulate prohibitions on certain vehicles over the links. These extra properties will add new fields to the Nodes and Links tables but they won't change the basic design. The fields listed in Figure 5.11 should be enough to demonstrate the fundamental concepts in the prototype.

VB NetLab does not need to allow users to easily share network files, so the network information does not need to be stored in a centralized shared database. To keep things simple from the user's point of view, VB NetLab will save and restore different databases in separate files.

It doesn't matter too much which kind of database the final application uses to store the network files. It could use Access database files, XML files, or any other type of relational database. During prototyping, however, it is often useful to be able to manually read and edit the files so you can build test data sets and see that the prototype is working correctly. To make that easier, the VB NetLab prototype stores its network data in XML files. The following code shows the structure of a typical network XML file.

```
<Node>
    <NodeId>1</NodeId>
    <X>100</X>
    <Y>20</Y>
</Node>
<Node>
    <NodeId>2</NodeId>
```

```
      <X>120</X>
      <Y>20</Y>
</Node>
...
<Link>
    <NodeIdFrom>1</NodeIdFrom>
    <NodeIdTo>3</NodeIdTo>
    <Cost>10</Cost>
</Link>
<Link>
    <NodeIdFrom>2</NodeIdFrom>
    <NodeIdTo>1</NodeIdTo>
    <Cost>20</Cost>
</Link>
...
```

OBJECT-ORIENTED DESIGN

Object-oriented design focuses on the objects in the application that do all the work. It works to define the application's most important classes and their relationships.

The first step in object-oriented analysis is identifying the application's major classes. After you know what classes you will use, you can refine the definitions to determine how the classes work together to implement the application's features.

IDENTIFYING CLASSES

The first step in object-oriented design is identifying the main object classes the program will use. Often these are similar to the tables you identify in a database design. That makes some sense because both database tables and classes include data. Classes also capture functionality, so they do not always map directly to database tables.

If you look back at Figure 5.11, you'll see that VB NetLab's data structure is very simple. The program uses only two tables: Nodes and Links. Those tables map naturally into Node and Link classes, but Node and Link are names that are a bit too common in Visual Basic for comfort. To avoid confusion, VB NetLab will call its classes NetlabNode and NetlabLink.

The highest level description of these classes is straightforward.

- **NetlabNode**—Stores information about a node
- **NetlabLink**—Stores information about a link

In the database, the Nodes and Links tables use numeric values to determine which nodes are connected by which links. To find the nodes that a link connects, you find the Nodes records with NodeId field matching the NodeIdFrom and NodeIdTo fields in the Links table.

Objects from the NetlabNode and NetlabLinks classes can refer to each other directly instead of using a node ID number. In addition to X and Y fields that give a node's position, the NetlabNode class can include a Links collection containing references to the NetlabLink objects that leave it.

The NetlabLink class can include a Cost field, and fields NodeFrom and NodeTo that contain references to the nodes at the link's endpoints.

NOUN PHRASES

One trick for identifying a program's classes is to read through the requirements specification and pull out all the noun phrases that represent something within the program. Find the words that represent people, places, and things, and highlight them.

Be sure to include abstract things such as commands, schedules, and billing systems. You may not be able to take a photograph of a billing system, but it might make a useful object in your application.

Do not include phrases that describe the program itself. For example, in the final VB NetLab release 1.0 specification listed at the end of Chapter 4, "Analysis," the noun phrase "A single desktop program" describes the program itself. There is no single desktop program within the application so that phrase is not very promising as an object candidate.

The most promising noun phrases in the release 1.0 specification are

- Network structure
- Network files
- Directed and undirected networks
- One-way links
- Turn penalties and prohibitions
- Algorithms
- Operations to perform massive edits
- Commands to automatically create test networks

STUDYING NOUN PHRASES

After you make a list of noun phrases, study the phrases more closely to see which would make good classes. In this example, the phrase "Network structure" really means the network itself. The network is the central item to this program, so it makes sense to create a NetlabNetwork class to represent network data structures.

Because VB NetLab program is a single document interface (SDI) application, it will only load one network at a time. That means it will only use one instance of the NetlabNetwork class at a time, so you could store the network data structure in program variables instead of in a class of its own. There are at least three reasons why it is better to use a class. First, if you later want to convert VB NetLab into a multiple document interface (MDI) program, being able to store multiple networks in different instances of the NetlabNetwork class will help.

Second, if you ever decide to build another program that uses networks, it will be easier to reuse this program's code if the network is stored in its own class. The new application will be able to immediately take advantage of all the network functionality you build into the class. The class will also let you build a new program that uses more than one network at a time.

The third reason for putting the network data structures in their own class is that it makes loading new data files safer. Suppose you load a network and work on it for a while. You save the changes and then try to open a new network file. The program reads half of the file and then encounters a file format error. What should the program do? If it has already destroyed the data for the first network, it cannot redisplay that network. It can display no network at all.

On the other hand, suppose the program tries to load the new network file into a new NetlabNetwork object. If it fails, the original NetlabNetwork object is still around so it can redisplay that network. Only after it successfully reads the new file does the program destroy the old network's data and display the new data.

The next noun phrase in the list is "Network files." Network files don't really do anything in this program except get read and written. One way to handle this would be to build a class that loads a network file and creates the corresponding internal data structures. The class would also take a network data structure and write it into a file. This class could help insulate the data structures from the data file structures. If you created a new data file structure, you could insert a new network file class that knew how to read it into the existing internal data structures. This flexibility is unlikely to be very helpful, however, because you will probably want to modify the internal data structures to take into account the new file structure. There would be little point in changing the data file structure if you didn't want to do something new with the network.

Rather than giving the network data file its own class, I'm going to pull the file loading and saving routines into the NetlabNetwork class.

The phrases "Directed and undirected networks," "One-way links," and "Turn penalties and prohibitions" really describe details contained within a network, not new objects in their own rights. We might want them back later, but for now let's assume they are part of the "Network structure" phrase.

The "Algorithms" phrase makes a tempting class. A standard NetlabAlgorithm class would include a Title property giving a title for the program to display in its Algorithm menu. The class would define an Apply method that acts on a NetlabNetwork object.

To add a new algorithm to the program, the student would derive a new class from the NetlabAlgorithm class and override the Apply method. The student then only needs to instantiate the new class and tell the program to add it to the Algorithm menu.

Unfortunately, different algorithms take different inputs. A shortest path algorithm finds a path between two selected nodes in a network. A minimal spanning tree algorithm only needs the network itself. A Hamiltonian path algorithm needs a network and a collection of nodes that it should connect with a circuit. A single NetlabAlgorithm class cannot allow for all of these different possibilities. Trying to allow for all of these cases would make the program complicated and might prevent it from handling other algorithms with different needs in the future. The goal of this application is to let students learn about network algorithms, not to teach them about elaborate object-oriented techniques.

Instead of creating a NetlabAlgorithm class, the program will keep algorithm code in simple subroutines. To add a new algorithm, a student will add new items to the Algorithm menu and give those items event handlers that do whatever the new algorithm needs. These subroutines could lie in the main program, but it probably makes more sense to include them in the NetlabNetwork class so the algorithm can operate on its own network data. That will make the NetlabNetwork class more useful if it is ever included in other applications.

The phrase "Operations to perform massive edits" is similarly tempting. You can imagine a NetlabMassEdit class defining an Apply method that acts on the selected nodes and links in a network. To create a specific edit, you would derive a child class and override its Apply method. Each class would have an entry in the Edit menu. When the user invoked the menu item, the program would call the corresponding object's Apply method. This class does not have the same problem as the NetlabAlgorithm class because all mass edits need the same inputs. They all act on the nodes and links currently selected in a network.

One indication that NetlabMassEdit is not a great class candidate is the fact that the program will only ever use one instantiation of each subclass. The program will never have more than one network loaded at a time so there's no need to have more than one instance of a particular class of mass edit object. In fact, the Apply method could take a NetLabNetwork object as a parameter so a single mass edit object could service any number of networks.

One possible reason for making a NetlabMassEdit class would be if that class included a lot of code that is shared by its derived classes. Then deriving child classes would save a lot of duplicated code. That is not the case, however. The parent class would only define the Apply method and the child classes override it, providing their own code. This isn't a good reason to make this class, either.

After considering all these arguments, it makes more sense to implement mass edit features in subroutines rather than in classes. As is the case for algorithms, you can put these routines inside the NetlabNetwork class so the mass edit routines can operate on their own network data. That increases the ability of the NetlabNetwork class to manage its own data and will make it more useful if it is ever included in another program.

The last phrase to consider is "Commands to automatically create test networks." Again you could make a class to do this, but this class would have the same problems as the NetlabMassEdit class. The program would only make one instance of each random network class and the derived classes would share very little common code. As is the case with mass edits, it's probably better to put these random network features in methods inside the NetlabNetwork class.

Now the list of noun phrases has been narrowed to the single class NetlabNetwork. That class should include code to provide the following:

- Store the network data
- Load and save network files
- Directed and undirected networks
- One-way links
- Turn penalties and prohibitions
- Algorithms
- Mass edits
- Test networks

It might seem like I've gone to a lot of work to talk myself out of a bunch of classes. This analysis did uncover one new class not included in the database design: NetlabNetwork.

After you've done a few analyses like this one, the process is much faster. You can read through the detailed specification and quickly pick out the noun phrases that are mostly likely to be useful. You might need a few minutes of more careful thought to decide against some classes such as the algorithm and mass edit classes, but the whole process should only take a few minutes for a small project such as VB NetLab.

STANDARD CLASSES

There are several standard kinds of classes you should consider when you look for an application's classes. In applications that require user security, you might want a User object to represent the user and the user's privileges. You might also want classes to represent different parts of the application. They might represent different screens or reports and the privileges a user needs to access them.

Sometimes it is convenient to have classes that manage specific user interface elements. For example, a class might manage the interactions among fields on a form. Often, you can do without these classes if you put the code to manage the interactions inside the controls' event handlers. If you need to use a similar interaction in several places, however, it is more convenient to create a class that can do the work for you.

VB NetLab doesn't need user security and has a very simple user interface, so it doesn't really need any of these classes. You could force these kinds of classes into the program but it would only complicate things for little purpose.

PART

II

CH

5

REFINING CLASSES

After you have identified the program's main classes, you can refine their definitions. Figure 5.12 shows a more detailed diagram of the NetlabNetwork, NetlabNode, and NetlabLink classes. The NetlabNetwork object's Nodes and Links arrays hold references to the NetlabNode and NetlabLink objects that make up the network.

The NetlabNode class contains a Links array that holds references to the links leaving this node. Notice that the database design held this information only implicitly. To find the links leaving a node, you must search the Links table for records where the NodeIdFrom field matches the NodeId field in the corresponding Nodes record. That search is reasonable for a relational database, but it is very inefficient for a network algorithm. Providing an explicit Links array in the NetlabNode class in some sense denormalizes the data structure. It makes most network algorithms much easier, though.

The NetlabLinks class includes two fields, NodeFrom and NodeTo, which give references to the nodes the link connects.

Figure 5.12
A detailed class diagram shows relationships among the VB NetLab classes.

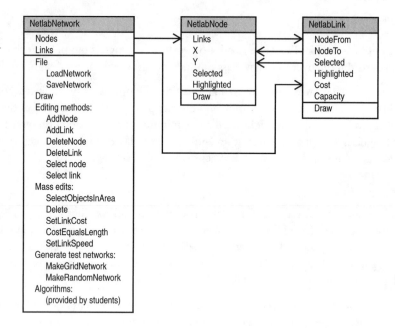

This high-level object-oriented design should be enough to get developers started. As the developers start to implement these classes, they define additional properties and methods. They might even discover new classes that can make development easier. However, the overall design using three main classes, NetlabNetwork, NetlabNode, and NetlabLink, should work.

PROCEDURAL DESIGN

Procedural design focuses on how things get done. In a purely procedural design, you look closely at the program's specification and convert it into a list of things that the program needs to do. Next you refine this list of tasks to provide some detail about how each task will be accomplished. Then you refine the descriptions some more, adding new detail that explains how the steps you have already identified will be done. You continue refining the task descriptions, explaining how more and more of the details will work, until you have a very detailed specification of the tasks. When it would be easier to just write out the code than it would be to provide any more detail, you write the code.

In a large project, the process of refining task descriptions stops at a point where the implementation teams understand the tasks well enough that they can finish refining them. Then the implementation teams break up and continue refining their subsystems separately.

In an object-oriented language such as Visual Basic, an approach that combines object-oriented and procedural design usually seems to work best. With this method, you start by creating an object-oriented design that identifies the application's main classes and their interactions. The previous section shows how to do that.

For each task identified in the object-oriented design, you make a procedural design. You begin by stating each object's tasks. You refine the task definitions, giving details about how each task will be accomplished. You add more detail and continue to refine the task descriptions until you reach the point where it would be easier to just write the code than to continue adding more detail. At that point, you start writing code.

Don't forget to consider the tasks performed by the application itself. Most development efforts do not think of the application as a separate class, but it usually performs a lot of tasks such as managing the MRU list, keeping track of file names, knowing whether data has been modified, giving the user a chance to save changes before exiting, and so forth.

In a large project, the break between object-oriented design and procedural design is a natural place to handoff work. The system architects can develop the object-oriented design at a high level. They can then transfer the class structure to development teams who begin procedural design of their own classes. At this stage, the different teams still need a lot of coordination to ensure that the different classes work together. After the procedural design is finished at a high level, the interactions among classes should be well defined. The development teams can continue refining their procedural designs on their own and eventually implement those designs.

VB NetLab Design Level 1

VB NetLab's object-oriented design identified three main classes: NetlabNetwork, NetlabNode, and NetlabLink. At this level, the NetlabNode and NetlabLink classes are quite simple. They just need to hold data to define the network. The students will add procedures that manipulate these objects to perform network algorithms. The classes need a few other features like the ability to draw themselves and translate themselves to a from an XML data format, but they are not very interesting compared to the NetlabNetwork class.

The NetlabNetwork class is more interesting from a design point of view. It needs to manage operations at a network level. To do that, this class must coordinate operations that span multiple nodes and links. For example, to find the node closest to a particular point, the NetlabNetwork class must examine many nodes. The node class cannot handle this operation at its own level because each NetlabNode object knows only about its own node. It doesn't know where the other nodes are.

A real development effort would need to prepare designs for the NetlabNetwork, NetlabNode, and NetlabLink classes. It would also need to include a design for the features provided by the application code itself. The NetlabLink class is more interesting than the others, so the following sections focus on it to provide a design example.

According to the NetlabNetwork object's object-oriented design earlier in this chapter, this class should do the following:

- Store the network data
- Load and save network files
- Include directed and undirected networks
- Include one-way links
- Handle turn penalties and prohibitions
- Let the students implement algorithms
- Perform mass edits
- Build test networks

This list serves as the highest-level design for the NetlabNetwork class.

VB NETLAB DESIGN LEVEL 2

The next step in the procedural design of this class is to expand each of these items to provide more detail:

- Store the network data. This includes methods to manipulate the network data structure.
  - The class must have its own method for accessing the network's node and link objects. In contrast, if the data structure were a tree, the network would only need a reference to the tree's root node. Then it could find the other nodes by following the root node's links. A network, on the other hand, does not need to be connected, so there might not be a path from any node to every other node.
  - The class will provide access to the network in the form of functions that return the node or link nearest to a given point.
  - The class will provide a Draw method that draws the entire network.
  - The class will provide methods to edit the network: AddNode, AddLink, DeleteNode, DeleteLink.
- Load and save network files.
  - The class will provide methods for loading and saving network data structures in XML files.
- Include directed and undirected networks.
  - You can treat undirected networks as a special case of directed networks where every link from node A to node B has a corresponding backward link from node B to node A. This doesn't really make the network any more complex, so the program will work only with directed networks.
  - Include one-way links.
  - A one-way link is just a link where its associated backward link has infinite cost and zero capacity. The program will do nothing special to handle one-way links.

- Handle turn penalties and prohibitions.
  - Turn penalties and prohibitions are quite complicated, so they are not described here. In a real development project, designers might decide to defer these items until release 2 after they discover how complicated they are.
- Let the students implement algorithms.
  - The program doesn't need to do anything more than provide the support functions described earlier (find neatest node, find nodes in an area, and so forth) so students can implement the algorithms.
- Perform mass edits.
  - The class will provide a method that returns two collections holding references to the nodes and links within a rectangular area.
- Build test networks.
  - The class will provide methods for generating grid and random networks.

Review this more detailed list of tasks to make sure they all make sense. In this example, the program can handle directed and undirected networks, one-way links, and algorithms without taking any special action, so those tasks are already described at a sufficient level of detail. Turn penalties and prohibitions are complicated enough that they are deferred until release 2.

VB NetLab Design Level 3

After you are satisfied that the remaining tasks should not be dropped or deferred, rewrite their descriptions in even more detail. At this point, you might start making programming decisions. For example, in this version of the design you can specify that the NetlabNetwork class will store its NetlabNode and NetlabLink objects in collections. The class can remove an object from the middle of the collection more easily than it can remove an object from the middle of an array.

As you provide details for one task, you might discover that you need other features you didn't think of before. For example, while describing a typical mass edit operation, I decided that the FindObjectsInRectangle, SelectObjectsInRectangle, SelectedNodes, and SelectedLinks methods would be useful.

Store the network data. This includes methods to manipulate the network data structure.

- The class must have its own method for accessing the network's node and link objects. In contrast, if the data structure were a tree, the network would only need a reference to the tree's root node. Then it could find the other nodes by following the root node's links. A network, on the other hand, does not need to be connected so there might not be a path from any node to every other node.
- The class will store nodes and links in the private m_Nodes and m_Links collections so it is easy to remove nodes and links from the middle of the collections.
- The class will provide access to the network in the form of functions that return the node or link nearest to a given point.

- The FindNearestNode function loops through the m_Nodes collection calculating the distance from the target point to each node.

- The FindNearestLink function loops through the m_Links collection calculating the distance from the target point to each link. See the DistToSegment function in prototype version 0.02 for code that calculates the distance between a point and a line segment.

- The class will provide a Draw method that draws the entire network.

- The Draw method clears the drawing surface and then loops through the m_Links collection drawing the links. It then loops through m_Nodes and draws the nodes. That makes the nodes drawn on top of the links.

- The NetlabNetwork class provides these drawing attribute properties:

Property	Default Value
BackColor	Light gray
LinkColor	Black
HighlightedLinkColor	Yellow
SelectedLinkColor	Red
NodeOutlineColor	Black
NodeFillColor	White
HighlightedNodeOutlineColor	Black
HighlightedNodeFillColor	White
SelectedNodeOutlineColor	Black
SelectedNodeFillColor	White
NodeRadius	5

- The node and link classes have their own properties to indicate whether they are selected or highlighted.

- The class will provide methods to edit the network: AddNode, AddLink, DeleteNode, DeleteLink.

- AddNode(X, Y) creates a new node, adds it to the m_Nodes collection, and returns a reference to the new node.

- AddLink(node1, node2) creates a new link, adds it to the m_Links collection, and returns a reference to the new link.

- DeleteNode(node) removes the node from the m_Nodes collection. It also removes the links that start or end at the node.

- DeleteLink(link) removes the link from the m_Links collection.

- DeleteLinkBetween(node1, node2) removes all links between these two nodes from the m_Links collection.

- None of these methods automatically redraws the network.

Load and save network files.

- The class will provide methods for loading and saving network data structures in XML files.

- The XMLText property procedures convert the network to and from an XML representation.

- The basic structure of the file will be

```
<NETWORK>
  <NODES>
    [node information]
    [node information]
    ...
  </NODES>
  <LINKS>
    [link information]
    [link information]
    ...
  </LINKS>
<NETWORK>
```

- The NetlabNetwork object will call methods provided by the NetlabNode and NetlabLink objects to write node and link information. How the nodes and links are stored is irrelevant to the NetlabNetwork class.

- To allow references between objects in the XML file, nodes and links will have ID numbers in the file. For example, a link will have NodeId1 and NodeId2 values giving the indices of the nodes it connects in the XML file. Those IDs might not be needed in the network data structure as long as they can be created when the XML text is generated.

Include directed and undirected networks.

- You can treat undirected networks as a special case of directed networks where every link from node A to node B has a corresponding backward link from node B to node A. This doesn't really make the network any more complex, so the program will work only with directed networks.

Include one-way links.

- A one-way link is just a link where its associated backward link has infinite cost and zero capacity. The program will do nothing special to handle one-way links.

Let the students implement algorithms.

- These are added by the students. The program doesn't need to do anything more than provide the support functions described earlier (find neatest node, find nodes in an area, and so forth) so students can implement the algorithms.

Perform mass edits.

- The class will provide a method that returns two collections holding references to the nodes and links within a rectangular area.

- The FindObjectsInRectangle routine returns these collections.

- The SelectObjectsInRectangle routine selects the objects within the rectangle. The routine loops through the nodes and links in the m_Nodes and m_Links collections, setting the Selected property to True for any objects that lie at least partially inside the rectangle. For nodes that means the center of the node is within distance NodeRadius of the rectangle. For links that means the link intersects the rectangle.

- The SelectedNodes function returns a collection holding references to the nodes that are currently selected. This function builds the collection by looping through the m_Nodes collection and copying references to the nodes with a true Selected property value.

- The SelectedLinks function returns a collection holding references to the links that are currently selected. This function builds the collection by looping through the m_Links collection and copying references to the links with a true Selected property value.

- A typical mass edit operation works like this.
  1. The user clicks and drags to select a rectangle.
  2. The user interface part of the program calls SelectObjectsInRectangle to select the objects.
  3. The user invokes the Delete command.
  4. The user interface uses the SelectedLinks function to find the selected links. For each selected link, it calls DeleteLink to remove the link.
  5. The user interface uses the SelectedNodes function to find the selected nodes. For each selected node, it calls DeleteNode to remove the node.

- Note that some of these operations might not be performed as efficiently as possible. For example, it might be faster to keep updated m_SelectedNodes and m_SelectedLinks collections at all times. Also, locating nodes and links near a point or within a rectangle would be faster using a quadtree data structure. For the small networks this program will manipulate (under 1,000 nodes or so), these methods should be fine. For information on quadtrees, see a graphics book such as my book *Visual Basic Graphics Programming* by Rod Stephens (Wiley, 2000).

Build test networks.

- The class will provide methods for generating grid and random networks.
- See the MakeGridNetwork routine in prototype version 0.02.
- The MakeRandomNetwork routine will arrange nodes in a circle so as many links as possible are visible.

In this version of the NetlabNetwork class procedural design, most of the functionality has been defined in enough detail that a reasonably experienced programmer could start writing code. If some of the tasks were still unclear, you would continue refining the design, adding more detail to the tasks, until a programmer could take over with little trouble.

You can adjust the level of detail in the design to fit the individual developers who will be writing the code for a specific piece of the application. If an experienced developer was assigned to implement the NetlabNetwork object's mass editing features, this design might be more than enough.

On the other hand, suppose a relatively inexperienced developer was assigned to build the XMLText property procedures. In that case, you might need to provide even more detail for that part of the system. That developer might also need to do some extra reading about XML files to understand how to get the job done. There's nothing wrong with assigning someone to a task that they cannot instantly solve. That's how good programmers become great ones. Just be certain to specify the problem precisely so the developer understands the goal.

Tale from the Trenches

A telephony provisioning application I worked on included a design module where the user could build a circuit by dragging and dropping components onto a drawing area and connecting them. Unfortunately, the design for that part of the system gave only about as much information as the previous sentence. That might have been okay, but the task was assigned to a less experienced developer who didn't really know how to approach the problem and who was afraid to ask for help. The result was a module that was buggy, hard to extend, and didn't really do it's job. That module became the limiting part of the system. If the task had been designed in more detail or assigned to a more experienced developer, there probably would have been no trouble.

A different project that managed telephone switch software allowed the user to build simple programs in a special scripting language. For example, a script could loop through a series of phone numbers and assign a particular type of service to each of the numbers. The scripting part of this application was also under-designed and assigned to a less experienced developer. Fortunately this developer knew he was in over his head and asked for help. I sat down with him and we evaluated a couple of different approaches to building a scripting language. He selected one, did some homework to learn about parsing this kind of script, and wrote a great scripting module.

It's not always easy to ask for help, particularly when you want to show everyone you know how to do this stuff. To make matters worse, the senior developers who can help the most are usually already stretched thin with their own tasks and the random emergencies that always pop up in software projects. Interrupting their work to get help with your problems is never easy. You can help minimize the need for this by making sure every part of the application is specified at a level of detail that satisfies the needs of the developer assigned to it.

On a large project, it is natural to transfer the design to the programming teams after this level of design is complete. Ideally, the design is already detailed enough that interactions among different parts of the system have been specified. That lets each team take over its own module design and work independently. The teams can each add more detail to their module's design without interfering with the designs of other modules.

DESIGN TIPS

The following sections describe some quick tips for application design. These are things you should keep in mind while you design an application.

PART
II

CH
5

TAKE YOUR TIME

Most projects spend too little time on design and too much time resolving problems that arise because different developers make conflicting decisions on issues that should have been addressed in the design. Mistakes in the design are much easier to fix during the design phase than they are after they're built into the code.

Don't rush into the development phase before the design is complete. It might be tempting to start building some pieces of the system before the entire design is complete, but that can be dangerous. If other parts of the system interact with the ones you start building early, you might wind up rewriting parts of the system. Even worse, you might end up with a lot of very subtle bugs.

TRY DIFFERENT ARCHITECTURES

Don't be afraid to try different application architectures. Think about multi-tier systems, Web services, shared databases, ADI versus MDI, ADO versus ADO.NET, and other factors that can change the application's overall design.

If you really cannot decide on these architectural issues, make some quick prototypes and see which works best. Show them to your customers and get their opinions.

These things are much easier to change in the design phase than they are after you start writing code. Be sure you make the right decision now so you don't have to rewrite a lot of code later.

TRY DIFFERENT DESIGN APPROACHES

The section "Design Approaches" earlier in this chapter explains user interface, database, object-oriented, and procedural design approaches. For the best results, see what each of these approaches says about the system.

See which design elements make sense when you use all four methods. Those are elements you probably want to keep in the final design.

Spend some extra time studying any design elements that make sense in only one design approach. Those elements might be unnecessary.

KEEP THINGS MODULAR

Keep the pieces of the system modular. Each form, object, subroutine, and other distinct piece of the system should be as independent as possible. Ideally, the programmer implementing a routine should not need to know anything about how the application's other routines are implemented.

ENCAPSULATE INFORMATION

Encapsulation is an important concept in keeping parts of the system modular. The idea is that any information that is not needed outside of an object should be encapsulated within that object. Code outside of that object should not be aware that this information exists. If other routines don't know that this information exists, they cannot tie themselves to that information either accidentally or intentionally. Then, if the information changes, these other routines will not break.

EXAMPLE

Suppose you are writing a sales program for a company in Colorado. You want a function that takes as parameters a dollar amount and a location. It returns the Colorado sales tax for that amount sold at that location.

In Colorado, the sales tax depends on the state, county, and city sales tax rates for that location. It also depends on whether the location must pay additional tax for rapid transit or sports stadium development.

The sales tax function needs to know the current tax rates for all of the relevant jurisdictions to calculate the tax. Other routines that call this function should not know about all these rates and should not know the calculation's details. All that information should be encapsulated in the sales tax function.

You can encapsulate complexity in a project at several levels. At the lowest level, subroutines and functions should encapsulate their behavior as much as possible. Another part of the system calling a routine should know the routine's inputs and outputs but not how it works.

Classes and modules add a higher layer of encapsulation. For example, if a module includes variables declared with the Private keyword, those variables are available within the module but cannot be seen by other parts of the program. That encapsulates their data.

ActiveX controls, programs, servers, and other compiled program units add still another level of encapsulation. For instance, an ActiveX control project might include several modules that provide helper routines for the control. Those routines are available to the control but not to the program that uses it.

Use encapsulation as much as possible. It hides unnecessary complexity from other parts of the application so developers can use routines without needing to know every last detail of how they are implemented.

KEEP CODE FOCUSED

Each piece of the system should be tightly focused. An object or subroutine should do one clearly defined thing. That makes it easier for other programmers to understand what the object or routine does without needing to understand all the details.

EXAMPLE

In Visual Basic 6, a PictureBox's Line method draws a line. Depending on the parameters you pass it, the line might have absolute starting and ending positions, the first position might be relative to the current drawing position, and the second point might be relative to the first point. If you want the line to start at the current drawing position, you can omit the starting point's coordinates entirely. You can override the PictureBox's current drawing color by specifying the color the line should use. You cannot override the line thickness or style, however. By adding the B parameter, you can specify that the line should actually be a box instead of a line. If you add the F parameter, you can indicate that the rectangle should be filled, possibly overriding the PictureBox's FillStyle property. The Line statement certainly doesn't do one clearly defined thing.

PART
II

CH
5

In Visual Basic.NET, this mess has been replaced by two simple commands: DrawLine and DrawRectangle. To draw a line, you pass DrawLine the coordinates of the line's end points and a Pen object describing the line's drawing style. To draw a rectangle, you pass DrawRectangle the coordinates of the rectangle's upper left corner, the rectangle's width and height, and a Pen object describing the rectangle's drawing style. That's it. No confusing B and F parameters. No messing around with absolute or relative coordinates. No omitted first coordinates to start from the current drawing position. These routines are focused and easy to understand.

After you get used to it, you can use Visual Basic 6's Line statement without too much trouble. With a little practice, you learn all its quirks and you forget how strange it is.

In your application, however, many routines will not be used often enough for the developers to get thoroughly used to their quirks. A developer might use a particular subroutine a few times, but might not use it often enough to become comfortable with any strange behavior.

Keep the parts of the system focused so it's easy to understand what they do. Don't make the developers struggle to understand what an object or subroutine does.

CLEARLY DEFINE INTERFACES

Clearly define the interfaces for every function, subroutine, class, control, and so on. Make it obvious how to use the public methods provided by these objects. Define every method's inputs and outputs unambiguously so developers can use them easily without wasting a lot of extra time deciphering the meanings of obscure parameter names. Developers should be able to concentrate on getting their pieces of code to work rather than on how to use their tools.

One way to help ensure that your interfaces are clearly defined is to write *interface contracts*. An interface contract is a document that specifies exactly what a routine does, what its inputs are, and what its outputs are. Ideally, the system's detailed design can specify interface contracts for routines before they are implemented. Then developers can write routines that implement the contracts without worrying that some other routine's interface might change.

Another technique is to imagine that you are writing tools that you will sell commercially. Would other developers want to buy a confusing tool like Visual Basic 6's Line statement? Would you want to write the documentation?

AVOID DEEP INHERITANCE

True inheritance is one of the most over-hyped features in Visual Basic.NET. It lets you derive one class from another by adding or overriding behavior in the original base class.

Inheritance is certainly useful, but it is also easy to abuse. A designer who gets carried away can build a complex hierarchy of objects that describes a particular system to a meaningless level of detail.

EXAMPLE

Suppose you are building an application to simulate traffic flow through a street network. You design classes to represent roads, parking lots, streetlights, stop signs, and cars.

Then you realize that cars and 18-wheeled big rig trucks behave differently. Big rigs accelerate, turn, and stop more slowly than cars. They also cannot fit under some bridges. So you create a new Vehicle class and make Car and BigRig subclasses.

That gets you thinking about other kinds of vehicles. You build a Trailer class. Then you add subclasses of cars to represent compact and subcompact cars. You add on a Truck class and its subclasses Pickup and SUV. Soon you have dozens of different Vehicle subclasses when all you really needed were a few restrictions on a basic vehicle class.

One major clue that this hierarchy is needlessly complicated is that the classes don't really add any new information to the system. All the program really needs from each of these classes is speed, maximum acceleration and deceleration, and possibly size. Every one of these classes must support these same properties for the vehicle simulation. If you move these properties into the parent class Vehicle, you are left with a whole bunch of subclasses that differ only in their names. It is simpler to just use one Vehicle class.

Use the fewest number of classes you can to get the job done. Extra classes just add unnecessary complexity and confusion.

USE MODULES AND CLASSES APPROPRIATELY

Many programmers, particularly those who are relatively inexperienced, have trouble deciding whether they should implement a routine as a separate subroutine in a module or as a method in a class. When development is well underway, they discover they made the wrong choice and need to convert the routine from a module subroutine to a class method or vice versa. That not only takes extra time and effort, it can also introduce new bugs to find and fix later.

Decide whether a piece of code should be a module routine or a class method during the design phase. Give the matter some extra thought so developers won't have to switch approaches later.

To determine whether you need a module or a class, think about the routine's data needs. Subroutines provide functionality. Classes provide functionality together with related data. If you need to write a routine that performs some calculation or acts upon data owned by some other part of the system, use a subroutine in a module. If you need to tie functionality to related data, build a class.

EXAMPLE

Suppose your program needs to know if floppy drive A: is ready. You could build a FloppyDrive class and give it an IsReady method. The program would instantiate the class, call IsReady, and then destroy the object.

This is a lot of work for such a simple purpose. Unless your computer needs to work with more than one floppy drive, you'll never need to create more than one instance of the class.

You could just as easily build a public FloppyDriveIsReady function in a source code module. Then any part of your program could invoke it without creating an object, calling IsReady, and then immediately destroying the object.

Contrast the previous example with the following one.

EXAMPLE

Suppose you need to keep an array of integers in sorted order. You could try to implement this in a code module. You would give the module a private array of values and public subroutines to add, access, and remove items. The AddValue routine would update the array so the new item was inserted in the right position.

Now suppose you wanted to give the program another sorted integer array. You would have to create a new module with its own array of values and its own routines to manipulate them. Now you have to maintain two sets of almost identical code without making any mistakes. Next, someone will want to add a third sorted list and you'll really start to regret not having created a SortedArray class.

Some reasons to pick a subroutine instead of a class include

- The routine is a pure calculation that doesn't use any data.
- The routine looks at data but does not modify or rearrange it.
- You know you will never need more than one instance of any data being manipulated.

Some reasons to pick a class instead of a subroutine include

- You want to tie routines closely to some related data.
- You might want more than one instance of the data either now or in the future.
- You want to use class methods to encapsulate the routines and data in one tight package.
- The routine you are considering is naturally related to other subroutines that you would like to package all in one place.

Both modules and classes encapsulate a group of related routines and data. In the end, which technique you use often comes down to what feels right to you.

ANALYZE USE CASES

A *use case* is a scenario that the user needs to perform using the finished application. For example, a VB NetLab user case might state that the student must

1. Implement a specific algorithm for the current assignment and installs it in the program.
2. Load a standard network for this assignment.
3. Execute the algorithm on the network.
4. Compare the solution given by the algorithm with the posted correct solution.

After you have defined use cases, you can compare them to your program design to see if you have included the capabilities needed to satisfy the use cases. The result should be a set of scripts that explain how the user executes each step of the scenario. For this example the result might indicate that the student:

1. Implement a specific algorithm for the current assignment and installs it in the program:

   The student enters the algorithm code in the application and makes appropriate menus in the Algorithm menu.

   The code accesses the program's m_Network object from the NetlabNetwork class to manipulate the network. It sets the Highlighted properties of the nodes and links in its solution and redraws the network.

2. Load a standard network for this assignment:

   The student selects the File, Open command. In the file selection dialog, the student selects the standard network file and clicks Ok.

   Standard network files are stored on a shared folder so all students can find them. Alternatively, the students can each receive a floppy disk or CD containing the standard networks and their solutions.

3. Execute the algorithm on the network.

   The student selects the appropriate items from the new menu in the Algorithms menu. For example, in a shortest path algorithm, the user would:

   - Select the Set Start Node command and click the start node.
   - Select the Set Finish Node command and click the finish node.
   - Select the Find Path command to execute the algorithm.

4. Compare the solution given by the algorithm with the posted correct solution.

   The student uses Paint or some other drawing program to look at a screen capture of the program displaying the correct solution.

You can begin writing use cases as soon as you understand what the customers need to do. As you work on the design, you can work through the use cases to see if the design can handle them all. If it cannot, you need to adjust the design accordingly.

When you have finished developing the application, you can try to follow the steps listed in the use case scripts. If you cannot perform each of the use case tasks, there is something wrong with the design or the implementation.

After the program can satisfy all of the use case scenarios, you can use the use cases to help produce documentation and training materials.

PART

II

CH

5

Tale from the Trenches

Some of the larger business applications I worked on had more than one hundred use cases. These were written by some of the customers who were assigned specifically to work with us. They even had their own offices in our building. They stayed with us throughout the entire development process, helping with the requirements, design, and testing.

MAKE SURE EVERYTHING IS NECESSARY

Be certain everything that goes into the design really needs to be there. The design stage gives you a great opportunity to fight feature creep. Don't let developers or customers add unnecessary features to the application, even if they are really cool or seem easy to implement.

Even if you know a feature would be useful, ask yourself if it is essential. Although something might be handy under certain unusual circumstances, you might get a better application if you leave it out to preserve a cleaner design.

BE CONSISTENT

Try to make different parts of the application work as consistently as possible. This rule applies to every kind of design. In the user interface, don't have one part of the program ask if the user wants to save changes while another part of the program asks if the user wants to discard changes. During database design, don't pull state codes into a lookup table in one case and not in another. During procedural design, don't store items in an array in one routine and in a linked list in another.

If your designs are consistent, the users and developers will be less confused and make fewer mistakes.

MINIMIZE INTERACTIONS

Keep interactions between different parts of the application to a minimum. The more interaction there is between two pieces of code, the harder it is for developers to correctly implement the code. Every developer will need to think about how every change affects other parts of the system.

Interactions also result in changes rippling through the system. Changing one piece of code might force you to modify another related piece of code and that might require changes to still another piece of code. All this makes enhancing and maintaining the code over time difficult.

Tale from the Trenches

One system I worked on at GTE Laboratories contained an equipment request server. One part of the application described a piece of equipment it wanted reserved and then sent the description to a request server via a remote procedure call (RPC).

The request server performed a series of steps to find the right equipment. For example, it began by checking an inventory database for exactly the right piece of equipment at the right telephone office. If it didn't find the right equipment, it looked for an existing assembly that combined other parts to perform the same job as the needed piece of equipment. If that failed, it looked for pieces that could be assembled into an assembly that would work. If nothing else worked, the request server would order a new piece of equipment and have it sent to the right location.

After all this was finished, the equipment request server was supposed to send information about the action it had taken back to the requesting application.

This was a reasonable design. The interaction between the application and the equipment request server was clearly defined, so work could progress on both halves of the system simultaneously. Or so we thought.

After we reached a certain point in development, it came time to test the two subsystems together. The RPC layer didn't work properly. While we fixed that, the equipment request server developer made a couple changes. When we got the RPC layer working, the equipment server didn't process the request correctly. While the equipment server developer fixed that, the developer working on the main application made a couple changes of his own. When we tried to get them to work together again, there was another mismatch caused by the fact that the main application used a newer and more complete version of the argument-passing scheme. Now the server had to be modified to catch up.

By now, you can probably see where this was leading. While we tried to get these two pieces of the system to cooperate, the developers of neither were free to move forward with their own subsystems.

At that point I stepped in and told the main application developers to write their requests into a text file. I told the equipment server developers to read their requests and write their responses in text files. Then everyone could move ahead independently again. After both teams had their code working properly, we could synchronize their file formats and finally move the communications back into the RPC layer.

SUMMARY

In a mad rush to produce working code, developers often skimp on design or omit it entirely. This is a terrible mistake. Code that's slapped together without planning is almost never as good as code that has had even minimal planning. For a project large enough to justify prototyping techniques, holding back on design makes the resulting application hard to maintain, modify, and extend in the future. It increases the number of bugs in the system and might even result in enough conflict among different subsystems that the application never works.

I suppose it's possible that an over-designed project could get stuck in the design phase as developers rehash every subsystem again and again, never actually producing any code. I've never seen this happen, however. On the other hand, I have seen several under-designed projects that needed extensive revisions before they worked.

A popular complaint among programmers is, "We never have time to do it right the first time, but we always have time to do it over again." Another version of this idea would be, "We never have time to do it right the first time, but we always have time to spend a few hundred thousand dollars developing a system that never quite works and doesn't get used."

Spend some extra time building a good detailed design. Your time will be repaid many times over during development.

PART

II

CH

5

CHAPTER

6

DEVELOPMENT

In this chapter

When they think of application development, most programmers think of the development phase. This is where programmers write the actual source code that produces the application. It's the part that most programmers find the most interesting, challenging, and fun.

This chapter describes some tips and techniques you might find useful while building prototypes during the application's development phase. Some of these ideas apply to any development effort. Many, however, are meant specifically for working with throwaway prototypes. They describe shortcuts for performing common programming tasks in a prototype with a minimum of programming effort. In some cases, you will need to rewrite the code using more robust techniques before you move the code into the final application.

Some of the sections that follow describe simplifications that make building a prototype easier. Sometimes the technique being simplified is an important part of the application and you need to demonstrate it in the prototype.

For example, one of the following sections recommends that you avoid remote procedure calls. Moving remote server code inside the main program makes it easier to develop and debug. However, if one of the purposes of the prototype is to demonstrate a Web service, you need to invoke the service remotely at some point.

In cases like this one, it is usually easier to build the feature in a simplified prototype first. After you have the basic framework running, you can complicate things. In this example, you would start by integrating the server code into the main program. After the program was correctly calling the server routines and those routines were returning the proper results, you would pull the server code out and put it in a Web service.

VERSION CONTROL

At its highest level, a version control system manages the different versions of an application released to customers. At a more detailed level, it also manages all of the different versions of all of the files associated with the project. That includes compiled executables, source code, documentation, and proposals. It can include anything you want to keep records of over time. It can even include weekly archives of memos and email.

Version control lets you keep track of everything that has happened during development. A version control system lets you go back in time and recover an earlier version of a document or program. For example, you could retrieve an old version of a prototype to see how the program has changed. You could also look at older versions of a program to see when a bug was introduced. By looking at the changes between that version and the previous one, you can often narrow down the bug's location.

Ideally, you should start working with a version control system as soon as you start gathering user requirements. Then you can store requirements lists, memos, and other background information in the version control system so nothing is accidentally lost.

Before you start writing any code, be sure you are completely satisfied with your version control system. During development, you need to keep track of different prototype versions.

You might need to go back to a previous version of a prototype to see what you have changed since then. If you don't use a version control system, you might not be able to recover the version you need.

Like many other development tasks, version control isn't terribly difficult. It's just one more thing you need to sit down and think about. You need to develop a version control strategy before you begin development so you can keep track of all of the pieces in a rapidly developing prototype.

After you start development, it becomes harder to retrofit version control to the existing project. You quickly lose the ability to go back to previous versions of the code and other documents.

Some version control systems let you split document versions into multiple branches and let them evolve separately. For example, you might add changes to a document's version 1.0 to form version 1.0A. You could add different changes to version 1.0 to form version 1.0B. Versions 1.0A and 1.0B could then continue to change independently.

This kind of version splitting can be confusing, and it's usually not necessary. It can be handy, however, if you need to fix a bug in an older version of an application.

EXAMPLE

Suppose you are working on version 3.2.1 of your product. When you finish with this round of development, you will release the result to your customers as version 3.3.

Now a customer reports a bug in version 3.2, the most current version the customers have. Depending on the bug's importance and whether there is a workaround, you might not be able to wait and fix the bug in version 3.3. In that case, you can split version 3.2 and form version 3.2A. You include the bug fix in that version and release it to customers. You should also apply the changes to the latest version (3.2.1) so the bug is fixed in the next release.

Figure 6.1 shows this series of program versions.

Figure 6.1
To fix a bug in an older version, this projects splits into two branches: 3.2A and 3.2.1.

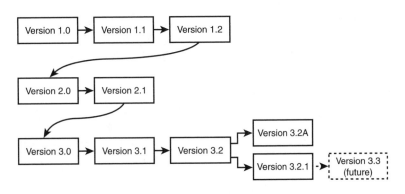

In some cases you might need to branch off of older versions of the program. If you are still supporting version 3.0 and a customer reports a high-priority bug, you might need to create a new 3.0A branch.

In other cases, fixing one bug might either cause another bug or make an existing bug obvious. In that case, you might need to extend the new branch with new versions 3.0A.1, 3.0A.2, etc.

To avoid all this extra work, many companies provide no support for older versions. In this example, they would fix the reported bugs in version 3.3 and then require customers to upgrade to the latest version for the bug fix.

Some change control systems are optimized for text documents like plain ASCII text files and source code. To conserve space, they might store only a document's original version. For new versions, they store a list of changes to the previous version. The list would hold a series of lines added, removed, and modified.

This sort of system works well with text files, but it might have trouble with binary files like bitmaps, compiled programs, and Microsoft Word documents. The system might waste a lot of time trying to figure out what part of these files has changed from one version to the next. In the end, it probably needs to store a complete new version of the file anyway.

Visual SourceSafe is one of the more popular source code control systems used with Visual Basic. As soon as you start a project, install Visual SourceSafe (or some other version control system) and start using it. You can use the early project phases to practice using its features. When you reach the development phase, you should know how to use it properly.

DEFINING VERSIONS

Most Windows applications display their version number when they start. They also display version information if the user selects **Help**, **About**. You can make displaying version information easier by storing that information in the project's properties.

Double-click the file AssemblyInfo.vb in Solution Explorer. Find the statement that assigns the assembly Version and set it to the program's current version. As long as you're editing the assembly's attributes, you can also set the company and product names as shown in the following code.

```
<Assembly: AssemblyCompany("VB Helper")>
<Assembly: AssemblyProduct("CoolWare")>
<Assembly: AssemblyVersion("1.4.9.16")>
```

At runtime the program can use these values to display information about itself in an About Dialog or in its caption as shown in the following code.

```
Private Sub Form1_Load(ByVal sender As System.Object, _
  ByVal e As System.EventArgs) Handles MyBase.Load
    Me.Text = Application.ProductName & " " & Application.ProductVersion
    lblCompanyName.Text = "by " & Application.CompanyName
End Sub
```

DEFINE A DIRECTORY STRUCTURE

Different developers should work with their own copies of the application; doing so enables them to make changes without fear of breaking other developers' code. After making a complete and consistent set of changes and testing them, a developer can check all of the changes back into the version control system so other developers can use the new code.

To minimize confusion, define the application's directory structure before anyone starts writing code. Then have all of the developers use that same directory structure when they work on the project files.

For example, you might decide that a complete version of the application will begin in a directory named after its current major and minor version. Inside that directory, you could have a Source directory to hold Visual Basic source code and a Data directory to hold databases, XML, and other data files. Inside those directories, you might define other subdirectories for different classes or application subsystems.

The RelatedProjects example contains five subdirectories: Data, Doc, DataLoader, DataReader, and ProjectSolution.

The Data directory holds data files used by the application. The programs included in this project solution read and write the files in this directory. For this example, the Data directory just contains the file Test.xml.

The Doc directory contains documents related to the project. In this example, those are the files Info.doc and Proposal.doc. These would contain information about the application and the application proposal. In a real application, this directory would also contain specifications, memos, and any other documentation related to the application.

The DataLoader directory holds a Visual Basic project that opens the file Data\Test.xml and writes records into it. The DataReader directory contains another Visual Basic project that reads this file and displays its contents in a data grid control.

Finally, the ProjectSolution directory contains a single Visual Basic project solution that includes all of the other application files. It contains references to the DataLoader and DataReader projects. From this single solution, you can edit both projects. If you right-click one of the projects in the Solution Explorer and select the Set As StartUp Project command, you can run that project.

The project solution also contains references to the files Info.doc and Proposal.doc in the Doc directory. If you double-click one of these files in the Solution Explorer, the system opens the file in the editor your system uses for .doc files, which is probably Microsoft Word.

The solution does not contain a reference to the data file Test.xml. When the DataLoader program writes this file, the solution does not automatically update its view of the file. If the solution contained a reference to the file, it might keep an outdated view of the file and that would be confusing.

PART

II

CH

6

Using a collection of related subdirectories and a project solution containing references to all of the application's important files, you can easily keep track of the files and modify them all from one place.

CONTROL CHANGES

During the early part of the requirements analysis phase, you should let the customers freely add to the list of things they want the application to do. As the requirements solidify, you need to help the customers prioritize these items and determine which will be included in the application's first release.

The customers should request fewer changes during application design. They had plenty of opportunity to tell you what they want during the requirements analysis phase; now they should only be thinking of things they forgot before.

During the development phase, you need to take firm control of any changes to the requirements. Form a change committee that must approve any requirements changes before they are passed to the developers. This will help ensure that only changes that are really necessary make it into the project. That protects the developers and the system architecture from constant changes. Too many changes at this stage will force the programmers to rewrite a lot of code and might require a completely new application design.

DON'T RUSH INTO DEVELOPMENT

Although most programmers enjoy development more than the other phases of application development, you must not let them rush into writing code too quickly. Development is the third phase in building an application. You must complete the requirements analysis and application design phases before you can confidently write production-quality code.

Many programming studies have shown that the later a bug is detected, the harder is it to find and correct. When programmers rush into the development phase, the program might contain bugs that should have been avoided by careful requirements analysis and design. If those bugs are not found until the development or testing phases, they can be very hard to correct.

In the worst case, the application works correctly but does not satisfy the customers' needs. In that case, the problem might not be discovered until after the testing phase and the customers see the final product. At that point, it might be impossible to fix the problem. The application might be so far off target that it can only be saved by a total rewrite. Studies have shown that a large percentage of the applications written each year fail because they do not correctly meet their customers' needs.

Even if the developers have a good set of requirements, the application is still unlikely to work properly unless it has a solid design. Even the best programmers need a roadmap to ensure that the code written for different parts of the system fit together properly. If different parts of the system make different assumptions, programmers might have to rewrite a lot of code to make the pieces work together.

EXAMPLE

Suppose an application uses a set of system parameter values to determine such things as form layout, network connection characteristics, and the location of files. Suppose Amy builds the main user interface assuming those values are stored in an Access database. However, suppose Bill makes the forms that the system administrator uses to maintain those configuration values assuming the values are stored in the system registry.

If the application design doesn't spell out which method should be used, Amy and Bill might not realize they are using different assumptions until they try to test the system as a whole. They might even have built separate prototypes that show their separate approaches work. In fact, the integrated application might even seem to work because Amy's code can read system parameters and Bill's code can maintain system parameters. It might take a while to notice that these pieces of code don't work with the same parameters.

When they finally do see the problem, either Amy, Bill, or both need to do a lot of rewriting. Because both of these methods has its advantages and disadvantages, neither is clearly better, so Amy and Bill might have a big fight over who has to do all the rewriting. All this could have been prevented by a reasonably complete application design.

Although developers cannot be certain of producing high-quality code until the requirements analysis and application design are complete, that doesn't mean they cannot build prototypes. As soon as part of the system has been specified, developers can build simple prototypes to test the design and get customer feedback. You can then use the information you learn from the prototypes to refine the requirements and design.

When you build this kind of early prototype, you should assume that it is a throwaway prototype, unless you are certain that the piece of the application being demonstrated has already been fully designed. Don't waste a lot of time writing a perfect prototype if you are only going to use it to validate part of a shifting requirements list.

EVOLUTIONARY VERSUS THROWAWAY PROTOTYPES

The difference between evolutionary and throwaway prototypes is greatest during development. The code in an evolutionary prototype is eventually incorporated into the final application. To build a high-quality application, you must ensure that the prototype contains only high-quality code. Although you might rewrite some pieces of the prototype to fix problems, counting on fixing problems later is dangerous. In a rush to implement other features and high-priority changes to the application, it is very easy to forget to go back and fix code that was written hastily. Write good code the first time through. Test the code while it is still fresh in your mind and then move on to another part of the program.

When you build a throwaway prototype, you expect to discard the prototype's code before final application development. You hope to learn something from the prototype but then not reuse its code later. In this case, you only need the code to work well enough to let you run the prototype. It does not need to be reusable or maintainable in the long run because, for the prototype, there is no long run.

PART

II

CH

6

Before the application's final design is set, it is common to use throwaway prototypes to test pieces of the system. Because there is a good chance the final design will not match what you are building, it doesn't make much sense to spend extra time writing bulletproof code at this point. Building a quick prototype to refine the requirements list and test the design makes sense. Wasting time writing code that will be scrapped anyway does not.

FOLLOW THE DESIGN

Stick to the design in whatever form it exists while you build the prototype. If you find that you need to stray from the design to fix a problem, don't just start writing code. You might be able to solve your particular problem, but you might also write a bunch of code that doesn't work well with the rest of the application.

Before you start violating the initial design, think about the new information you have and how it fits in with the rest of the system. Then revise the design so it solves the new problem. Consider how the changes will affect other parts of the application so the new design doesn't break anything. Taking some time to step back and reevaluate the design often gives you a more consistent and maintainable application in the end.

Be particularly careful when you revise the design to accommodate changes requested by the customers. Those changes often make sense individually but over time add up to make the application inconsistent and confusing to the user. Consider the changes together. See where they are similar and where they differ. Try to make one comprehensive change to the design instead of a series of small changes.

Sometimes developers use prototyping as an excuse for poor design. They believe the different prototype versions can converge on a proper application architecture without a formal design. That's generally not true. During prototyping and development, programmers focus too narrowly on implementing specific features. They tend not to see the bigger picture. Start with a solid design and stick with it to make the best possible application and prototypes.

STANDARDIZE EXCEPTION HANDLING

Define a standard error handling scheme for all developers to use. This keeps your error handling consistent and it saves the developers time creating their own systems. See Chapter 13, "Error Handling," for specific error handling suggestions.

If you build a single set of error handling routines, you can afford to spend a little more time on them than developers would if they were building their own. You can add extra features to give you much better tracking of errors as the prototype is tested. For example, you can make the standard error handlers write error information into a log file and send an email to you describing the problem. Few developers would go to that much trouble. It is likely that they would use `On Error Resume Next` statements to hide errors instead of using error handlers to pinpoint problems.

Standardized error handlers also make it more likely that developers will actually use some error handling. Many developers assume their code works and they provide little or no error handling. If you get the developers to help build a set of standard error handling routines, they are more likely to use them. After a while, using the routines becomes a habit.

DEFINE CODING STANDARDS

Define coding standards for all of the developers to follow. Many developers get lazy about following coding standards while building prototypes, particularly throwaway prototypes. But coding standards can speed up development even in a throwaway prototype. By making the code more consistent, they make it easier for developers to read and understand the program. By increasing the developers' understanding, coding standards help developers know how the different parts of the application work together. They can write code more quickly and with fewer bugs. Using coding standards during prototyping is also good practice for final application development, when coding standards are even more important.

DEFINE STANDARD HEADER COMMENTS

Define standard header comments programmers should use at the beginning of modules, classes, and routines. These comments should describe such things as:

- The purpose of the code
- How the code works
- References to articles or books that explain the techniques used by the code
- Data structures used by the code
- Input and output variables and parameters
- Potential interactions with other parts of the application
- Anything else the developer thinks would help someone else understand the code
- Possible future changes or enhancements
- The name of the original author

Header comments in final applications also often include a list of changes made to the code, the dates the changes were made, and the names of the programmers who made the changes. This information is less useful in a quickly developing prototype. Often the code changes so quickly that the list of changes is too long to be meaningful. However, a programmer who modifies the code should at least revise the header comments to make sure they describe the code in its latest form.

PART
II

CH
6

DEFINE NAMING CONVENTIONS

Create naming conventions for classes, routines, and variables. Hungarian notation is one common system that uses prefixes to make a variable's scope and data type clear. For example, many programmers start module-level variables with the letter "m" and global variables with the letter "g."

The variable's next three letters define its data type. For instance, gintNumUsers would be a global integer variable.

Note that it's still up to developers to add meaningful names to the scope and data type prefix. The prefix in mlngNUES tells you the variable is a module-level long integer, but it doesn't tell you what the variable means. A variable named mlngNumUnknownErrorSources is much easier to understand even if it takes a little longer to type.

The exact system of abbreviations you use to define variable names is unimportant. It doesn't matter whether you represent a command button with btn or cmd as long as all of the developers are consistent. Go to Microsoft's Web site and search for "Hungarian notation" to get several articles describing Hungarian notation in detail and giving lists of suggested abbreviations. Pick the system that you think makes the most sense and write it up so all of the developers can use the same system.

USE COMMENTS

Make sure the programmers use plenty of comments in their code. Some programmers skimp on comments when they build a throwaway prototype. They believe no one will read the code again so there's no point taking any extra time to make the code easier to read.

That might be true if no one ever read the code, but even in a throwaway prototype the code is often rewritten. Writing comments also helps clarify the code in the developer's mind, and sometimes the act of writing comments uncovers a bug.

Tale from the Trenches
In one of the first large prototypes I helped build, all of the developers provided two levels of commenting. We included a normal set of comments explaining key lines of code. We provided another set of comments starting in the code's 80th column. Normally when you looked at the code or printed it, the second set of comments was chopped off so you saw only the first set of comments. If you were confused by a piece of code, you could always reduce your display font size or print the code on extra wide paper to see the more detailed second level of comments.

For some reason, the final development group that took over the prototype after us believed that these comments were excessive and distracting. They had an official policy that prohibited all comments that were not absolutely necessary to understanding the code. After we gave them the prototype code, they removed our second-level comments.

About a month later, they discarded a large part of the prototype's code and replaced it with an off-the-shelf tool. They then spent another couple of months learning how to use the tool and re-implementing the prototype's features with it. The reason they discarded the prototype code was that they couldn't understand it. They couldn't understand it because they had removed 80 percent of the comments.

DON'T INTERNATIONALIZE

Building a good multilingual application can take a long time. To do the job properly, you need to enlist the help of native speakers of the languages you want to support. You need to load and display different versions of the application's text and icons. You might also need to rearrange the application's controls to make the layout look good in languages that say the same things with strings of different sizes.

All this trouble is usually unjustified in a prototype. Build the prototype in a single language and then worry about supporting other languages later when you build the final application.

IGNORE PORTABILITY

Visual Basic.NET automatically makes your application portable to a wide variety of different hardware platforms. If a computer runs any of the more recent Windows operating systems, chances are good that your program will work on it.

There are times, however, when you might want to support several different configurations that are not hidden by VB.NET. For instance, you might want your application to rearrange its controls to fit 15-, 17-, or 21-inch monitors.

There are several third-party resizing controls that you can use to do this automatically. These controls don't necessarily take best advantage of the monitor's surface, however. They usually just make a form's controls proportionally bigger or smaller so they fill the available area. You can usually do better with some custom arrangements. For example, you might leave most of the controls unchanged but stretch a grid control so it fills as much of the form as possible. That lets you display more data on larger monitors.

VB.NET itself includes controls that can stretch to fit an area. Using these controls, you can achieve better results.

In a prototype, it usually isn't worth the effort to perform more than the simplest customized programming to ensure portability to more than one hardware platform. Just build a prototype that works on the computer you will use to provide demonstrations. You can worry about other platforms later when you build the final application.

SIMPLIFY I/O

Input and output are a large part of many programs. Often the input, output, and user interface code make up the bulk of the application. I've worked on projects that contained 3,000–4,000 lines of code to process data and 25,000–35,000 lines of code to load, format, display, and save the data.

By not building the entire application, you are already restricting the user interface code in your prototype. If you can simplify the input and output code as much as possible, you can reduce the number of lines of code you need to write to create a useful prototype.

You can load and save data in many ways. You can store data in text files, binary files, INI files, XML, or databases. Some of these, text and binary files for example, are relatively easy to use but provide few features for manipulating data. Others, including databases, are a bit harder to use but provide features to select, merge, and sort information.

To keep the prototype as simple as possible, pick a single input/output technique and use it whenever possible. Even if the final application will read and write data in delimited text files, HTML, XML, and binary files, demonstrate only one of those methods in the proto-type. Use the simplest method if at all possible. Of the options listed for this example, delimited text files are probably easiest.

Plain text files are even simpler. Visual Basic's Write statement saves a delimited value into a text file. The Input statement reads a value written by Write. You can easily build input and output routines by using Input to read values in the same order in which Write saved them into the file.

To ensure that you read and write the fields in the same order, build the output routine using Write. Copy that routine and change the file mode from Output to Input. Then replace the calls to Write with calls to Input.

The TextFile program described in Chapter 9, "Loading Data," uses this technique to load and save data when the program starts and stops. See the "Text Files" section in Chapter 9 for further details.

This method is not very robust. Every field must be present and in the correct order. The Write statement surrounds strings with double quotes so the text should not include any double quotes. If a string does contain quotes, the Input function gets confused.

Still, this method is extremely simple, so it is a reasonable choice for a prototype. If you need more elaborate data processing features, you should probably use a database or XML file. Chapter 9 describes these methods in detail.

Do not use binary files unless absolutely necessary. Binary files are hard to examine and modify, so it is harder to tell if they contain errors. It is also difficult to edit binary files manually so you might have trouble fixing them if they become corrupted. It's interesting that Visual Basic 3 allowed you to save project files in a space-saving binary format, but now all Visual Basic projects are saved in text files. Microsoft realized the minimal space saving wasn't worth the extra trouble of dealing with binary files.

SIMPLIFY SUBSYSTEM COMMUNICATIONS

In larger programs, different subsystems within the application must communicate with each other. For example, a server application invokes subroutines in a client subsystem to retrieve information, process data, or perform some specialized action.

Two subsystems might communicate in many ways, depending on the application's needs. One subsystem's code might simply call a subroutine or function provided by the other. The second subsystem might provide a class with methods that the first uses. Both of these approaches are easy to implement and the interaction between the two subsystems is easy to understand.

Subsystems that have more elaborate communications needs can exchange data through databases, files, or remote procedure calls. The Web Services introduced in Visual Studio.NET make it relatively easy to invoke a remote Web Service.

Although these more complicated techniques might be necessary in the final application, they are usually overkill in a prototype. The fact that the two subsystems might be running in separate processes on different computers makes testing and debugging the communication harder.

If you can, build the subsystems so they can communicate using simple subroutine or method calls. Build the server subsystem so you can include its code directly within the main application. Then the client subsystem can invoke its methods directly. You can use this version of the prototype to test the subsystems together. When you build the final application, you can break the subsystems apart. Figure 6.2 shows this process.

Figure 6.2
Simplify communications by placing server subsystems in the main prototype application.

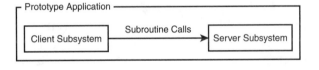

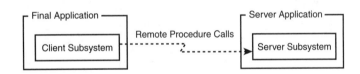

If it is impractical to include the server subsystem directly within the prototype, you can use text files to simulate the communication. The client writes a request into a text file. The server reads that file, performs some action, and writes the result into a new text file. The client then reads the new file to see what happened.

You can make the server application process the text file in several ways. It can run continuously, examining the request file's modification time until the file changes. The server then reads and processes the file, and writes the result file. The client subsystem watches the result file in a similar way to tell when the response is ready. If you want to cut the server out of the loop, you can have the client read a pre-built response file as soon as it has finished writing the request file. This lets you test the client code before the server has been built.

Using text files helps keep the two processes separated. If you have a problem with one, you can manually create text files to test it. Even if the server subsystem doesn't work, you can still demonstrate the client part of the prototype using a pre-built text file to simulate the server's response. Figure 6.3 shows this idea.

Figure 6.3
Simplify complex com-
munications with
intermediate text files.

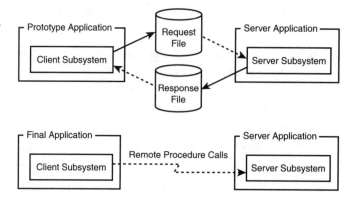

If you keep the client and server subsystems separated like this, work can proceed on both independently. After you have them both working, you can remove the intermediate file and connect them directly to each other.

SIMPLIFY SYNCHRONIZATION

Visual Basic.NET provides better tools for multi-threading than previous versions of Visual Basic. The Thread class lets a program start and control an asynchronous process. The program can pause, resume, or stop the thread, and can synchronize with it using the SyncLock statement.

Although using threads is much easier in Visual Basic.NET than in previous versions, asynchronous programming can be very confusing. It's hard to keep track of what each thread is doing, and debugging multiple threads can be bewildering.

Many programs use multi-threading to allow the user interface to react to the user while the program performs some long calculation. If you do not correctly disable user interface features that should not be available during the calculation, the user might start other threads that perform the same or a different task. At best, that slows the program down while it tries to perform several complex tasks at once. In the worst case, those tasks can interfere with each other.

Tale from the Trenches
In one application, we had set up a testing center where the customers could experiment with our prototype. The user interface system we used was inherently multi-threading so buttons and menus could respond to the user even when the program was performing long calculations.

One of the customers discovered that he could make two duplicate message boxes appear at the same time if he double-clicked a button. The program received the first click and presented the message box. Before the message box appeared, it received the second click and ran the code to display the message box again. The result was two message boxes.

The customer showed us this error and we told him we would fix it. He then went on to try the exact same thing with every other button in the system. With some, he could produce the same error. Then he noticed that if he clicked fast enough, he could display three, four, or even more message boxes at the same time. Despite our repeatedly telling him that these bugs were all part of the same problem, he spent the rest of the afternoon merrily clicking away and writing bug reports for a button clicked twice, the same button clicked three times, four times, and so forth.

This might not have been the most constructive use of his time, but he certainly enjoyed himself. He also looked productive to his management because he generated a lot of bug reports.

From our point of view, it was annoying that this one issue made the project appear buggier than it really was. On the other hand, by fixing this one issue we cleared out a large percentage of our bug reports.

Avoid using timers for the same reason. A timer executes a piece of code that is independent of the rest of the application. Trying to debug a piece of code when a timer fires and starts executing another piece of code can be confusing.

Resuming execution after stepping through the code in the debugger can also make the sequence of events hard to understand. If a timer fires while you are stepping through the code, its event is queued for later delivery. When you remove any breakpoints and restart the program, the timer event handling code executes immediately.

This situation can be even more puzzling if you are trying to debug the timer's event handler itself. As soon as you finish stepping through the event handler, the event handler starts running again because it is time for the next Timer event.

You can escape these annoyances by avoiding multi-threading in the prototype. Multi-threading only complicates what is probably already a difficult enough project. After you have the basic features working, you can move specific subroutines into separate threads if necessary.

AVOID UNFAMILIAR TECHNOLOGY

Testing new technology is one of the more important uses of a prototype, but you should try not to use too many unfamiliar technologies at the same time. If something goes wrong, you might have a lot of trouble figuring out which tool is at fault. When you call the tool vendors, they often blame each other, the operating system, Visual Basic, and even your code. It's much easier for them to let you eliminate every other possibility before they take a look at their own product.

Test each new technology separately. After you are familiar with your new tools individually, you can try to make them work together.

MINIMIZE TOOL USE

Even if you have tools that work correctly, using too many tools together can cause problems in the long run. When a new version of one tool is available, you might want to upgrade. However, the new version might be incompatible with one of the other tools. If that's the case, you have to wait until an upgrade of that tool is available. That upgrade might break some other tool, and you might be stuck waiting for upgrades until all of the tools reach another point of compatibility.

In the worst case, one tool is always incompatible with another and you never find a stable combination again. You might be stuck forever with the configuration you originally used to build the application. If one of the vendors does release a new version of a tool that you would really like to use, you might be out of luck. I've worked in several environments where the customers had outdated hardware and ancient operating systems because some of the tools they used only worked with those configurations.

Microsoft has gone out of its way to ensure that Visual Basic.NET will peacefully coexist with Visual Basic 6. You should be able to run older applications written in Visual Basic 6 on the same computer as newer programs written with Visual Basic.NET.

Reduce the chances of version chaos by minimizing your use of complex tools. Every unusual database tool, special purpose ActiveX control, and exotic piece of hardware you add to the system makes version mismatches more likely.

REUSE EXISTING CODE

If you have code from a previous project that can help with the prototype, reuse it. Copy and paste the code into the new prototype and modify it as needed. In the long run, you can consider generalizing the code and building a library that other projects can reuse. For now, just modify the code for the prototype's current needs. You can rewrite the code to make it more elegant later when you build the final application. At that point, you can decide whether you should make a more general library or not. Having used the code in the prototype also helps give you another perspective on the code so you better understand how you might need to generalize the code to make it useful in other projects.

If someone else has written a project that contains features you need, see if you can reuse their code. You can make this kind of reuse easier if you keep an index of routines that might make good candidates for reuse.

Often, developers suffer from the Not Invented Here Syndrome. This is the tendency for programmers to prefer to write code rather than using someone else's. Writing code is more fun than trying to figure out how someone else's code works, so developers often reinvent code that has already been written.

Developers might tell themselves that they can write better code than the code already written. That might or might not be true. In a prototype, however, it is less important that the code be perfect than that it works. You are usually better off copying existing code and modifying it for the prototype. If there really is a better way to write the code, it can be rewritten it when the final application is built.

Developers also sometimes tell themselves that it will take less time to rewrite the code than to figure out how the existing code works. If that's true, there is a serious problem in your software development organization. All code, even the code used in throwaway prototypes, should be documented well enough that it can be understood without a lot of effort.

You need to be vigilant if you are to avoid falling victim to the Not Invented Here Syndrome. Before you write new code, ask yourself if someone else has already done it for you. At staff meetings, remind other developers to look for opportunities to reuse. Use recycled code to finish boring parts of the application faster so you can move on to something no one has done before.

BUY THIRD-PARTY TOOLS

The Not Invented Here Syndrome also applies to commercial software products. Developers would often rather build a tool than buy a product that does the same thing. This is almost always a big mistake. Building even a simple tool can take hundreds of hours. Multiply that effort by a typical programmer's hourly wage and it's extremely unlikely you will save money. When you add in debugging and maintenance costs, you are guaranteed to lose when you build the tool yourself. Management also sometimes falls into this trap. A manager thinks the project's programmers should develop the tool rather than spending money to buy it. After all, building tools is what the programmers are for, right? Wrong! Programmers are for building tools that do not already exist.

This problem can be magnified if the manager has separate software and personnel budgets. A manager who has used up his software budget might be tempted to waste thousands of dollars' worth of programmer time to avoid purchasing a few hundreds dollars' worth of software. If you are caught in this situation, ask upper management for a special budget extension. The payback in increased productivity will justify the cost of most tools.

The only reason to build a tool when you can buy something similar is if the commercial product doesn't do exactly what you need it to do. If the tool is at all close to what you need, see if you can get by with it, at least in the prototype. After you and your customers have used the tool for a while in the prototype, you might decide that its functionality is good enough. In that case, you will have saved yourself a lot of time and trouble. Even if you decide the tool is not good enough, you will have a better understanding of the features you need to build.

Tale from the Trenches

The first really big project I worked on was a shipping application for Gillette. My assignment was to build the screen output routines. Those included a mapping system and a screen handler.

The screen handler drew text and simple line graphics on a monitor. The user could tab from field to field, entering data. Building a form like this is easy in Visual Basic, but the application was not running on a Windows operating system and we weren't using Visual Basic.

The second large system I worked on was for GTE. At this time, commercial products were available for doing this sort of screen handling. We evaluated the products available and decided that they did not provide the features we needed, so I made another screen handler. I had learned a lot during the previous project; but this application had much more complex needs, so it was still a lot of work.

I caught Not Invented Here Syndrome. Although I made use of the things I learned in the previous project, it would have been even easier to buy a commercial screen handler. It would not have done everything exactly the way we wanted, but it would have been good enough to use effectively, and I would have been free to work on more interesting parts of the project.

After we transferred the prototype to GTE Data Services, the company's software maintenance organization, they pulled out all of the screen handler code and rewrote the user interface using a commercial package.

This was mostly a case of Not Invented Here Syndrome on their part. They thought they could rebuild all of the screens from scratch more quickly than they could understand the existing screen handler code. It turned out they were wrong and several developers spent months re-implementing the screens using the commercial package.

In the end, the application wound up using a commercial package so the programmers with GTE Data Services didn't need to do as much maintenance work as they would have with the customized system. We got the correct outcome despite our best efforts.

There are two morals to this story. First, don't succumb to Not Invented Here Syndrome. It will waste your time and be more expensive in the long run.

Second, if you do reinvent a tool that is available commercially, someone might later replace your code with the commercial product and all your work will have been wasted. Wouldn't it be better to start with the product and then replace it with customized code later if that proves absolutely necessary?

BUILD A TOOL LIBRARY

A well-stocked tool library can make code reuse easier. When one developer builds a tool to perform some generic task, he should add the tool to the library and tell the other developers what it does.

Other developers should use that tool instead of building their own. This lets you get more use out of less code. If the tool performs a particularly complex task, sharing the same tool can save a lot of time. You can reinvest some of the time you save in perfecting the tool. If every programmer builds their own version of the tool, some will work better than others. If everyone shares the same tool, it is worth a little extra work to make sure the tool works well.

In addition to the rather obvious benefit of code reuse, building a generic tool helps separate the tool from the code that uses it. When a subroutine is written for general use, it must have a more precisely defined interface than it might if only one programmer is going to use it in a specific piece of code.

A tool library is even more effective if you can afford to assign a programmer to be the toolsmith for the whole project. When developers need a tool, they ask the toolsmith. The toolsmith knows if the necessary tool already exists or if an existing tool can be modified to solve the new problem.

Sometimes generalizing a tool makes it harder to use in specific instances. A programmer building a tool for his own use tends to make the tool as easy as possible for his specific situation. Because a specialized toolsmith is less closely involved with the code that uses the tools, he can have a more objective view of how the tool should work.

KEEP IT SIMPLE...BUT NOT TOO SIMPLE

Ideally, a prototype should be as simple as possible while still showing the features you want to demonstrate. Do not implement complex algorithms where simpler ones will work adequately for the prototype. Start with a simple algorithm. If you later discover that the simple algorithm won't work, you can implement a more complex scheme.

Example

Suppose the prototype needs to sort some numbers and you already have a working sorting routine that uses the insertionsort algorithm. Insertionsort is simple and fast for small lists but it is extremely slow for large lists. If you think the prototype only needs to sort a hundred or so items, use the routine you already have written.

Later, if the customers start loading data sets so large that the prototype must sort thousands of items, you can build a new sorting routine that uses a faster sorting algorithm such as quicksort.

This doesn't mean you need to be intentionally stupid. If you have a good reason to believe a simple algorithm will be insufficient, you don't need to use it. This is one of the areas where an experienced developer has an advantage.

If you don't know whether or not you need a complex algorithm, start with the simpler version. You usually waste less time building a simple routine that you later replace than you would building a routine that is more complicated than necessary.

Getting the simpler version running quickly also lets other parts of development continue. If you build the complicated version first, parts of the prototype that need to use the routine must wait until it is finished.

DON'T GENERALIZE

To keep code as simple as possible, do not generalize it unnecessarily. If the prototype doesn't need a more general routine, don't write one. Just build the features the prototype actually needs now.

PART

II

CH

6

This might seem like it contradicts some of the earlier advice for reusing code and building a tool library. If a subroutine is not reasonably general, it is hard to reuse and doesn't make a good addition to the tool library.

However, during prototype development is not the best time to generalize code. If you see a routine that would make a good candidate for generalization, insert a comment next to it saying so. Then after the prototype is complete and you have some free time between projects, you can go back and rewrite the routine for your tool library.

VB NETLAB 0.03

Version 0.01 and 0.02 of VB NetLab are user interface prototypes. Version 0.03 begins to show some of the application's features.

In version 0.02, all of the menu items are stubbed out so they display message boxes. For example, the following code shows how the program responds to the File menu's Save command. The program simply displays a message box telling the user that it will save the file some day.

```
Public Sub mnuFileSave_Click(ByVal sender As Object, _
  ByVal e As System.EventArgs) Handles mnuFileSave.Click
    MsgBox("Save the current file here", _
        Microsoft.VisualBasic.MsgBoxStyle.OKOnly, _
        "Not Yet Implemented")
End Sub
```

Version 0.03 starts adding functionality to these commands. As more functionality is added, the new features are shown to the customers in controlled demonstrations. This gives the developers more feedback so they can adjust the prototype as they build it.

The following sections describe the most interesting features demonstrated by VB NetLab version 0.03. The complete code listing is quite long, so it is not shown here. You can download the whole project from the book's Web site.

DESIGN CHANGES

VB NetLab versions 0.01 and 0.02 are throwaway user interface prototypes. With version 0.03, the program becomes an evolutionary prototype. That means the quick-and-dirty design used in the earlier versions must be replaced. Version 0.03 needs a more stable architecture that can handle changes to the prototype as it evolves in later versions.

VB NetLab version 0.02 displays only a single example network to give the customers some idea of what a network will look like in the final application. To display this network, version 0.02 uses a lot of shortcuts. It stores Node data using Point objects. These objects include a point's X and Y position but no other information. Network algorithms need to attach other information to nodes to process them. Similarly, version 0.02's Link class is too simple for complicated network algorithms. VB NetLab version 0.03 uses more sophisticated Node and Link classes stored in their own modules.

The new `NetlabNetwork` class represents a whole network of Nodes and Links. The `NetlabNetwork`, `Node`, and `Link` classes separate the main user interface from the network data structure. That makes these networks more useful for applications that need to manipulate but not display a network.

EXAMPLE

For example, consider a work assignment problem. You have a collection of jobs that can only be performed by people with certain skills. You also have a collection of people who have their own sets of skills. You need to assign people to jobs so each person has the skills needed to do the assigned job. The goal is to have people assigned to as many jobs as possible.

You can model this problem with a network. Build nodes for each job and each person. Build a one-way link between each person node and the job nodes where the person has the skill needed to complete the job. Add a source node and a sink node. Connect the source node to each person node and connect each job node to the sink node.

You can solve the problem of assigning people to jobs by solving the network flow problem. If you allow only one unit of flow along each link, the goal is to find the link flows that make the most flow from the source node to the sink node. The links that are used between people and jobs give the assignments.

Figure 6.4 shows a small work assignment network. In this example, person 1 is assigned to job A, person 2 to job C, person 3 to job B, and person 4 to job D. For more information on maximal flow calculations and other network algorithms, see my book *Ready-to-Run Visual Basic Algorithms* (Rod Stephens, 1998, John Wiley & Sons).

By separating the network operations from the user interface, VB NetLab 0.03 makes it easier for a program to use this network structure. It can use the `NetlabNetwork` class to solve problems like the assignment problem without including VB NetLab's forms.

Figure 6.4
You can solve the work assignment problem with a network flow calculation.

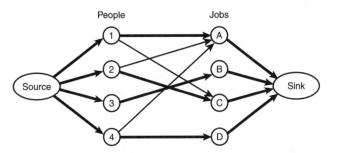

Although it makes sense to separate the user interface from the network classes, the two must come together at some point. When the user interacts with the program, the code must somehow translate that action into the `NetlabNetwork`, `Node`, and `Link` objects that make up the current network.

For example, when the user clicks the application, it must somehow figure out which Node in the network was clicked. The main program could look through all of the Node objects to see which one was clicked, but that would make the main program more complicated than necessary.

VB NetLab 0.03 moves this sort of operation into the `NetlabNetwork`, `Node`, and `Link` classes. The program asks a `NetlabNetwork` object to locate the `Node` at the clicked point. The `NetlabNetwork` object iterates through its loaded `Node` objects asking them how far each is from the point. The `Node` objects each know their own positions so they can determine how far they are from the point.

Moving this kind of operation down into the lower level objects that make up the network keeps the main program's job easier. Information is stored as locally as possible. The `Node`s contain their position information. The `NetlabNetwork` object coordinates the efforts of the `Node` objects to decide which is closest to the point. This is the lowest level at which the objects can determine which `Node` is closest, because the `Node`s themselves do not have access to each other's data.

Moving this `Node` location task into the `NetlabNetwork` and `Node` classes makes sense and doesn't really move the program's user interface responsibilities too far away from the main program. You also can argue that locating a node is a geometric operation rather than a pure user interface operation.

VB NetLab version 0.03 also moves several obviously graphical operations into the classes. To draw the network, the program calls its `NetlabNetwork` object's `Draw` method. That method loops through the `NetlabNetwork`'s `Link` objects, calling their `Draw` methods. It then repeats the process with its `Node` objects, calling their `Draw` methods.

Although this architecture pushes a purely user interface task deeply into the network objects, it makes the program easier to manage because it localizes information. `Node` locations are stored in the `Node` class. The `Node`s that make up a `Link` are stored in the `Link` class. The `NetlabNetwork` class coordinates so the `Node`s draw on top of the `Link`s. The main program only needs to invoke the `NetlabNetwork`'s `Draw` method.

MAKING A SPLASH

The most interesting part of the main form's constructor creates a new `frmSplash` object. It then invokes that form's `ShowSplash` method to display the form as a splash screen.

When the user invokes the Help menu's About command, the program creates another instance of the `frmSplash` form. This time it invokes the form's `ShowAbout` method. The following code shows how the main program uses this form.

```
Public Sub New()
    MyBase.New()
    Form1 = Me
    'This call is required by the Win Form Designer.
    InitializeComponent()
    ' Display the splash screen.
    Dim dlgSplash As New frmSplash()
    dlgSplash.ShowSplash()
    ' Make an initial NetlabNetwork object.
    m_Network = New NetlabNetwork()
    ' Start the file dialog in the project directory.
    dlgFileSave.InitialDirectory = ProjectDirectory()
    dlgFileOpen.InitialDirectory = dlgFileSave.InitialDirectory
```

```
End Sub
' Display the about dialog.
Public Sub mnuHelpAbout_Click(ByVal sender As Object, _
  ByVal e As System.EventArgs) Handles mnuHelpAbout.Click
    Dim dlgAbout As New frmSplash()

    dlgAbout.ShowAbout()
End Sub
```

The `frmSplash` form displays an About dialog or a splash screen like the one shown in Figure 6.5. This form contains a PictureBox and two labels that display basic information about the program. The Ok button simply closes the form.

Figure 6.5
The `frmSplash` form displays both splash screens and About dialogs such as the one shown here.

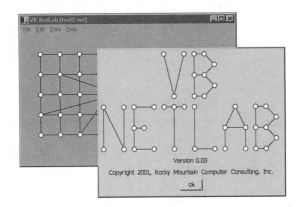

The form also contains a `Timer` with its `Interval` property set to 3000 milliseconds or three seconds. When the timer event executes, it unloads the form.

A few of this form's properties were set at design time to make the form behave like a splash screen or About dialog. Its `Text` property is blank, `BorderStyle` is set to `FixedDialog`, and `ControlBox` is set to `False`. That makes the form non-resizable, immovable, and without a title bar. The form's `StartPosition` property is set to `CenterScreen` so the form appears in the middle of the screen, and its `TopMost` property is true, so the form appears above all other forms.

The most interesting parts of `frmSplash`'s code are the methods that display the form. The `ShowAbout` method displays the form modally so the user must close it before interacting with the rest of the application.

The `ShowSplash` method hides the form's Ok button and resizes the form to fit. It then enables the Timer that will unload the form and displays the form non-modally. That lets the rest of the program continue to run while this form is displayed. After the time expires, the Timer closes the form and the program works normally.

```
' Show the form as an About dialog.
Public Sub ShowAbout()
    ' Display the form modally.
    Me.ShowDialog()
```

```
End Sub
' Show the form as a splash screen.
Public Sub ShowSplash()
    ' Hide the Ok button and resize the form to fit.
    btnOk.Visible = False
    Me.Height = btnOk.Top + Me.Height - Me.ClientSize.Height

    ' Enable the timer.
    tmrUnload.Enabled = True

    ' Display the form non-modally.
    Me.Show()
    Me.Refresh()
End Sub
```

The Splash example program is a less interesting application than VB NetLab, but it displays the more interesting splash screen shown in Figure 6.6. When the splash screen loads, it calls the `ShapeFormToBitmap` subroutine shown in Listing 6.1 to fit itself to an irregular image.

`ShapeFormToBitmap` begins by creating a Windows region that fits the image. It then examines the pixels along each row in the image. When it finds a series of pixels that match the image's mask color, the subroutine makes a rectangle that includes those pixels and then excludes the rectangle from the region. When it is finished, the region contains only the pixels that did not match the mask color.

The routine finishes by setting the form's `Region` property to the region it has constructed. That restricts the form to the region giving it a cutout appearance.

Figure 6.6
The `frmSplash` form displays both splash screens and About dialogs such as the one shown here.

LISTING 6.1   PROGRAM SPLASH USES THE `ShapeFormToBitmap` ROUTINE TO MAKE AN INTERESTING SPLASH SCREEN

```vb
' Restrict the form to the image where it doesn't match
' the mask color.
Public Sub ShapeFormToBitmap(ByVal frm As System.WinForms.Form, _
  ByVal mask_image As System.Drawing.Bitmap, _
  ByVal mask_color As System.Drawing.Color)
    Dim rgn As System.Drawing.Region
    Dim rect As Rectangle
    Dim Y As Integer
    Dim X As Integer
    Dim X1 As Integer

    ' Remove the form's decorations.
    frm.ControlBox = False
    frm.Text = ""
    frm.BorderStyle = FormBorderStyle.None

    ' Load the mask picture.
    frm.BackgroundImage = mask_image

    ' Make the form fit the picture.
    frm.Width = mask_image.Width
    frm.Height = mask_image.Height

    ' Make a region that covers the whole image.
    rect = New Rectangle(0, 0, mask_image.Width, mask_image.Height)
    rgn = New System.Drawing.Region(rect)

    ' Examine each row of pixels.
    For Y = 0 To mask_image.Height - 1
        ' Start at the leftmost pixel.
        X = 0
        X1 = 0

        Do
            ' Move to the right until we find a pixel
            ' that is not the mask color.
            Do While X < mask_image.Width
                If Not (mask_image.GetPixel(X, Y).Equals(mask_color)) _
                    Then Exit Do
                X = X + 1
            Loop

            ' Exclude pixels X1 to X from the region.
            If X > X1 Then
                rect = New Rectangle(X1, Y, X - X1, 1)
                rgn.Exclude(rect)
            End If

            ' Skip pixels until we find one that is the
            ' mask color.
            Do While X < mask_image.Width
                If mask_image.GetPixel(X, Y).Equals(mask_color) Then Exit Do
                X = X + 1
```

PART

II

CH

6

LISTING 6.1 CONTINUED

```
            Loop
            X1 = X

            If x >= mask_image.Width Then Exit Do
        Loop
    Next y

    ' Restrict the form to the region.
    frm.Region = rgn
End Sub
```

`ShapeFormToBitmap` is not blindingly fast because it examines every pixel in the image one at a time. Its performance is good enough for small images on fast computers, however. It's certainly impressive enough to make a good impression in a prototype. If the splash screen is too slow for the final application, you can replace it with a simpler screen.

With a little extra effort, you can make a region defined by a `GraphicsPath` object. You can pre-compute the points along the edges of the image and use those points to create the `GraphicsPath`. This makes the splash screen appear more quickly, but it takes a lot more effort than using the `ShapeFormToBitmap` subroutine. It might be necessary in the final application, but `ShapeFormToBitmap` is good enough for a prototype.

SAFEGUARDING DATA

The main program's form is in charge of ensuring that any changes to the data are saved. It uses the variable `m_DataModified` to keep track of whether the current network has been modified since it was loaded or last saved. The `SetDataModified` routine clears or sets `m_DataModified`. If the program is trying to set `m_DataModified` to True and it is already True, the routine does nothing. Otherwise, `SetDataModified` sets `m_DataModified` to True.

Then `SetDataModified` updates the program's caption. If the data has been modified, it displays an asterisk between the application's name and the form's name so the user can tell the data has not been saved. If `m_DataModified` is False, `SetDataModified` removes the asterisk in the caption so the user can tell the data is safe.

Whenever the data is safe, the program calls `SetDataModified(False)` to indicate that the data has not been modified. The program does this after it creates a new network, loads a network file, or saves the current network data.

Whenever the data is modified, the program calls `SetDataModified(True)` to indicate that the data has been modified. The only way VB NetLab version 0.03 can modify its data is to create a grid network so that this is the only time version 0.03 does this. Version 0.04 can also add or delete nodes and links so it calls `SetDataModified(True)` in those cases, as well.

Whenever the user does something that will close the current network, the program calls the `DataSafe` function to make sure that it is safe. For example, if the user tries to open a new network file, start a new network from scratch, or close the application, the program calls `DataSafe`.

DataSafe first checks the `m_DataModified` variable. If `m_DataModified` is False, then the current network has not been changed since it was loaded or last saved. In that case, it is safe to discard the current data so DataSafe returns True.

If `m_DataModified` is True, DataSafe tells the user that the data has been modified and asks if it should save the changes. If the user clicks Yes, DataSafe calls the Save routine to save the data. If the current network was originally loaded from a file, the program saves the data back into that file. If the network was newly created so it doesn't have a file name, the program lets the user select a file for the data. Note that the user might cancel the file selection dialog at this point and prevent Save from saving the data.

When the call to Save returns, the data might or might not have been saved. DataSafe checks the `m_DataModified` variable to see if Save successfully saved the data. If the data was saved, DataSafe returns True. If the data was not saved, DataSafe returns False so the calling routine does not discard the current network data.

When DataSafe asks if it should save the data, the user might click No. In that case, the user does not care if the program discards the current network data. DataSafe returns True to tell the calling routine that it is ok to discard the data.

Finally, when DataSafe asks if it should save the data, the user might click Cancel. In that case, the user does not want to discard the current data or to save it. DataSafe returns False so the calling routine does not discard the data.

Listing 6.2 shows the most interesting pieces of code that deal with protecting the data. The `mnuFileNew_Click` event handler at the end shows how the program uses these routines. It first calls DataSafe and exits if the data is not safe. The event handler then creates a new NetlabNetwork object, resets the file name and title, and calls SetDataModified to flag the data as unmodified and to set the form's caption. It finishes by calling the new network's Draw method to display the empty network.

LISTING 6.2   VB NETLAB USES THIS CODE TO ENSURE ITS DATA IS SAFE.

```
' The currently loaded network.
Private m_Network As NetlabNetwork
' The file name for the currently loaded network.
Private m_FileName As String = ""
Private m_FileTitle As String = ""
' True when the data has been modified.
Private m_DataModified As Boolean
' Set or clear the m_DataModified flag.
Private Sub SetDataModified(ByVal data_modified As Boolean)
    ' Do nothing if we are setting m_DataModified
    ' to True and it is already True.
    If data_modified And m_DataModified Then Exit Sub

    ' Save the new value.
    m_DataModified = data_modified

    ' Display the correct caption.
    If m_DataModified Then
```

LISTING 6.2   CONTINUED

```
            Me.Text = "VB NetLab*[" & m_FileTitle & "]"
        Else
            Me.Text = "VB NetLab [" & m_FileTitle & "]"
        End If
End Sub
' Return True if it is safe to discard the current data.
Private Function DataSafe() As Boolean
        ' It's safe if the data has not been modified.
        If Not m_DataModified Then Return True

        ' The data has been modified.
        ' Ask the user if we should save the data.
        Select Case MsgBox("The data has been modified. Do you want to save it?", _
                Microsoft.VisualBasic.MsgBoxStyle.YesNoCancel, "Data Modified")
            Case Microsoft.VisualBasic.MsgBoxResult.Yes
                ' Try to save the data.
                Save()

                ' If the data is still modified,
                ' we did not save the data.
                Return (Not m_DataModified)

            Case Microsoft.VisualBasic.MsgBoxResult.No
                ' Don't save the data.
                Return True

            Case Microsoft.VisualBasic.MsgBoxResult.Cancel
                ' Cancel the data discard.
                Return False
        End Select
End Function
' Start a new network.
Public Sub mnuFileNew_Click(ByVal sender As Object, _
    ByVal e As System.EventArgs) Handles mnuFileNew.Click
        ' Make sure the data is safe.
        If Not DataSafe() Then Exit Sub

        ' Create the new network.
        m_Network = New NetlabNetwork()

        ' Set the new caption.
        m_FileName = ""
        m_FileTitle = ""
        SetDataModified(False)
        ' Redraw.
        m_Network.Draw(picNetwork.CreateGraphics())
End Sub
```

LOADING AND SAVING NETWORKS

VB NetLab saves and loads network data in XML files. The main program doesn't know anything about how networks are stored; it just uses file dialogs to let the user pick the files to save or load. It then calls the `NetlabNetwork` object's `Save` and `Load` methods and lets them do all the real work.

The `NetlabNetwork` class stores references to `Nodes` and `Links` in its `m_Nodes` and `m_Links` collections. The `Save` method loops through these collections, saving `Node` and `Link` information into an XML file. The `Load` method reads the entries in an XML file to build these collections.

The `Save` method creates a new `XmlDocument` object and gives it a standard XML version 1.0 declaration. It adds comments saying the file was written using VB NetLab 0.03 and giving the current date and time.

Next, the `Save` method creates an XML root node named `VBNetLab_Network`. It gives this node a `Version` attribute with value 0.03. When the program later loads a network file, it uses the `Version` to determine whether it can understand the file's network structure.

`Save` then makes an XML subnode named `Nodes`. It loops through the `m_Nodes` collection adding XML nodes inside the `Nodes` element. For each `Node` in the `m_Nodes` collection, the program creates an XML element named `Node`. It gives the element two attributes (X and Y) and sets their values to hold the coordinates of the `Node` in the network.

After adding each `Node`'s information to the `XmlDocument`, the routine sets the Node's XmlId property. This is just the index of the `Node` in the `m_Nodes` collection. The program uses this index to save and restore Links.

After it has added all of the `Nodes` to the `XmlDocument`, `Save` creates a `Links` subnode inside the `XmlDocument`'s root node. It then loops through the `m_Links` collection adding the `Link` information. For each `Link`, the routine creates an XML element named `Link`. It gives this element two attributes (`Node1` and `Node2`) and sets their values to the indexes of the `Nodes` that this `Link` connects.

After it has saved all the `Node` and `Link` information into the `XmlDocument`, `Save` calls the document's `Save` method to write the data into an XML file.

Listing 6.3 shows the XML file representing the network shown in Figure 6.7.

LISTING 6.3   AN XML FILE REPRESENTING THE NETWORK.

```
<?xml version="1.0" standalone="yes"?>
<!--Network data created by VB NetLab 0.03-->
<!--2001-05-18T16:16:55-->
<VBNetLab_Network Version="0.03">
  <Nodes>
    <Node X="91" Y="91"/>
    <Node X="182" Y="91"/>
    <Node X="91" Y="182"/>
    <Node X="182" Y="182"/>
  </Nodes>
  <Links>
    <Link Node1="1" Node2="2" Cost="91"/>
    <Link Node1="3" Node2="4" Cost="91"/>
```

LISTING 6.3   CONTINUED

```
      <Link Node1="1" Node2="3" Cost="91"/>
      <Link Node1="2" Node2="4" Cost="91"/>
      <Link Node1="1" Node2="4" Cost="128.69343417595164"/>
   </Links>
</VBNetLab_Network>
```

Figure 6.7
VB NetLab saves networks in XML files.

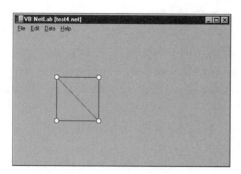

The NetlabNetwork's Load method reads network data from an XML file saved by the Save method. Load begins by reading the XML file into an XmlDocument object. It finds the document's root node and verifies that its Version attribute is 0.03. If the file has some other version, Load gives the user a chance to cancel loading the file.

Load allocates new m_Nodes and m_Links collections to hold the network's new links. It then loops through the XML nodes inside the document's Node element. For each entry, Load creates a new Node object using the element's X and Y attributes as the Node's coordinates.

Next the Load method loops through the elements inside the XmlDocument's Links element. For each element, Load reads the element's Node1 and Node2 attributes to get the indexes of the Nodes that the Link should connect. It locates the Nodes in the m_Nodes collection and uses them to create the new link.

Listing 6.4 shows the NetlabNetwork object's Save and Load methods.

LISTING 6.4   THE Save AND Load METHODS PROVIDED BY THE NetlabNetwork CLASS SAVE AND LOAD NETWORK DATA FROM XML FILES.

```
' Node and link data.
Private m_Nodes As New Collection()
Private m_Links As New Collection()
' Save the network data into the indicated file.
Public Sub Save(ByVal file_name As String)
    Dim xml_document As New Xml.XmlDocument()
    Dim xml_declaration As Xml.XmlDeclaration
    Dim xml_comment As Xml.XmlComment
    Dim root_node As Xml.XmlNode
    Dim node_attribute As Xml.XmlAttribute
```

LISTING 6.4   CONTINUED

```
Dim parent_node As Xml.XmlNode
Dim child_node As Xml.XmlNode
Dim i As Integer
Dim test_node As Node
Dim test_link As Link

' Convert the network data into an XML document.
' Create an empty document.
xml_declaration = xml_document.CreateXmlDeclaration("1.0", "", "yes")
xml_document.AppendChild(xml_declaration)

xml_comment = xml_document.CreateComment( _
    "Network data created by VB NetLab 0.03")
xml_document.AppendChild(xml_comment)

xml_comment = xml_document.CreateComment(Now().ToString())
xml_document.AppendChild(xml_comment)

' Create the root node.
root_node = xml_document.CreateElement("VBNetLab_Network")
node_attribute = xml_document.CreateAttribute("Version")
node_attribute.Value = "0.03"
root_node.Attributes.Append(node_attribute)
xml_document.AppendChild(root_node)

' Make entries for the nodes.
parent_node = xml_document.CreateElement("Nodes")
root_node.AppendChild(parent_node)
i = 1
For Each test_node In m_Nodes
    ' Make the Node's XML node.
    child_node = xml_document.CreateElement("Node")
    parent_node.AppendChild(child_node)

    ' Save the node's X and Y values as attributes.
    node_attribute = xml_document.CreateAttribute("X")
    node_attribute.Value = test_node.X.ToString()
    child_node.Attributes.Append(node_attribute)

    node_attribute = xml_document.CreateAttribute("Y")
    node_attribute.Value = test_node.Y.ToString()
    child_node.Attributes.Append(node_attribute)

    ' Set the node's index.
    test_node.XmlId = i
    i = i + 1
Next test_node

' Make entries for the links.
parent_node = xml_document.CreateElement("Links")
root_node.AppendChild(parent_node)
For Each test_link In m_Links
    ' Make the Link's XML node.
```

PART

II

CH

6

LISTING 6.4 CONTINUED

```
        child_node = xml_document.CreateElement("Link")
        parent_node.AppendChild(child_node)

        ' Save the indexes of the Nodes that
        ' this Link connects.
        node_attribute = xml_document.CreateAttribute("Node1")
        node_attribute.Value = test_link.Node1.XmlId.ToString()
        child_node.Attributes.Append(node_attribute)

        node_attribute = xml_document.CreateAttribute("Node2")
        node_attribute.Value = test_link.Node2.XmlId.ToString()
        child_node.Attributes.Append(node_attribute)

        node_attribute = xml_document.CreateAttribute("Cost")
        node_attribute.Value = test_link.Cost.ToString()
        child_node.Attributes.Append(node_attribute)
    Next test_link

    xml_document.Save(file_name)
End Sub
' Load the network data from the indicated file.
' Return True if there is a problem, False otherwise.
Public Function Load(ByVal file_name As String) As Boolean
    Dim xml_document As New Xml.XmlDocument()
    Dim xml_attributes As Xml.XmlAttributeCollection
    Dim root_node As Xml.XmlNode
    Dim node_attribute As Xml.XmlAttribute
    Dim parent_node As Xml.XmlNode
    Dim child_node As Xml.XmlNode
    Dim children As Xml.XmlNodeList
    Dim i As Integer
    Dim new_node As Node
    Dim new_link As Link
    Dim new_node1 As Node
    Dim new_node2 As Node
    Dim new_cost As Double

    ' Load the document.
    xml_document.Load(file_name)

    ' Verify that the file was written by VB NetLab 0.03.
    root_node = xml_document.DocumentElement()
    xml_attributes = root_node.Attributes()
    If xml_attributes.Item("Version").Value <> "0.03" Then
        If MsgBox("This file was written with VB NetLab " & _
            xml_attributes("Version").Value & _
            ". Some data might be read incorrectly." & _
            CrLf & CrLf & "Continue anyway?", _
            Microsoft.VisualBasic.MsgBoxStyle.YesNo, _
            "Warning") = MsgBoxResult.No _
        Then
            ' Return a failure code.
            Return False
```

LISTING 6.4   CONTINUED

```
        End If
    End If

    ' Empty the m_Nodes and m_Links collections.
    m_Nodes = New Collection()
    m_Links = New Collection()

    ' Load the nodes.
    parent_node = root_node.ChildNodes(0)
    children = parent_node.ChildNodes()
    i = 1
    For Each child_node In children
        new_node = New Node( _
            CInt(child_node.Attributes.Item("X").Value), _
            CInt(child_node.Attributes.Item("Y").Value))
        m_Nodes.Add(new_node)
    Next child_node

    ' Load the links.
    parent_node = root_node.ChildNodes(1)
    children = parent_node.ChildNodes()
    For Each child_node In children
        new_node1 = _
CType(m_Nodes(CInt(child_node.Attributes.Item("Node1").Value)), Node)
        new_node2 = _
CType(m_Nodes(CInt(child_node.Attributes.Item("Node2").Value)), Node)
        new_cost = CDbl(child_node.Attributes.Item("Cost").Value)
        new_link = New Link(new_node1, new_node2, new_cost)
        m_Links.Add(new_link)
    Next child_node

    ' Return a success code.
    Return False
End Function
```

DRAWING AND FINDING NODES AND LINKS

The NetlabNetwork class delegates many of its other methods to the Node and Link objects that make up the network. For example, its Draw method takes a Graphics object as a parameter. It clears the Graphics object and then loops through the m_Links collection invoking each Link's Draw method so it draws itself. It then loops through the m_Nodes collection calling each Node's Draw method. By drawing the links first, the Draw method makes the Nodes appear on top.

The NetlabNetwork object's MouseIsOver function returns the object that lies at a specific point. The routine first loops through the m_Nodes collection. It calls each Nodes' IsAt function to see if the Node is at the target point. If the routine finds a Node that contains the point, MouseIsOver returns that Node. If no Node contains the point, MouseIsOver uses a similar method to loop through the m_Links collection. It invokes each Link's IsAt method to see if the Link is at the point.

Listing 6.5 shows the Draw and MouseIsOver routines.

PART

II

CH

6

LISTING 6.5 **THE** NetlabNetwork **CLASS DELEGATES ITS** Draw **AND** MouseIsOver **ROUTINES TO THE** NodeS **AND** LinkS **IT CONTAINS**

```
' Clears the drawing surface and then loops through the
' m_Links collection drawing the links. It then loops through
' m_Nodes draws the nodes.
Public Sub Draw(ByVal canvas As System.Drawing.Graphics)
    Dim test_link As Link
    Dim test_node As Node

    ' Clear the drawing area.
    canvas.Clear(SystemColors.Control)

    ' Make the links draw themselves.
    For Each test_link In m_Links
        test_link.Draw(canvas)
    Next test_link

    ' Make the nodes draw themselves.
    For Each test_node In m_Nodes
        test_node.Draw(canvas)
    Next test_node
End Sub
' Return the object the mouse is over.
Public Function MouseIsOver(ByVal X As Integer, ByVal Y As Integer) _
  As Object
    Dim test_node As Node
    Dim test_link As Link

    ' See if the mouse is over a node.
    For Each test_node In m_Nodes
        If test_node.IsAt(X, Y) Then Return test_node
    Next test_node

    ' See if the mouse is over a link.
    For Each test_link In m_Links
        If test_link.IsAt(X, Y) Then Return test_link
    Next test_link

    Return Nothing
End Function
```

The program uses the MouseIsOver method to decide which items belong in the popup menu it displays when the user right-clicks the network. The picNetwork_MouseDown event handler shown in Listing 6.6 executes when the user clicks the network. If the user does not press the right mouse button, the routine just exits.

If the user presses the right button, the event handler uses the m_Network object's MouseIsOver method to get a reference to the object the user is clicking. The routine hides all of the items in the form's popup menu mnuPopup. The program then restores the menu items that are appropriate for the type of object under the mouse and displays the popup menu.

LISTING 6.6   THE `picNetwork_MouseDown` EVENT HANDLER DISPLAYS THE POPUP MENU
ITEMS THAT ARE APPROPRIATE FOR THE OBJECT CLICKED

```
' Display an appropriate context menu.
Public Sub picNetwork_MouseDown(ByVal sender As Object, _
   ByVal e As System.WinForms.MouseEventArgs) Handles picNetwork.MouseDown
    Dim over_object As Object
    Dim menu_item As MenuItem

    ' Do nothing if this isn't a right click.
    If e.Button <> MouseButtons.Right Then Exit Sub

    ' See what the mouse is over.
    over_object = m_Network.MouseIsOver(e.X, e.Y)

    ' Hide all the popup menu items.
    For Each menu_item In Me.mnuPopup.MenuItems
        menu_item.Visible = False
    Next menu_item

    ' See what kind of thing this is.
    If over_object Is Nothing Then
        ' Over nothing. Allow:
        '     Add Node
        mnuPopupAddNode.Visible = True
    ElseIf TypeOf over_object Is Node Then
        ' Over a node. Allow:
        '     Edit
        '     Add Link
        '     Delete
        mnuPopupEditObjects.Visible = True
        mnuPopupAddLink.Visible = True
        mnuPopupDeleteObjects.Visible = True
    ElseIf TypeOf over_object Is Link Then
        ' Over a link. Allow:
        '     Edit
        '     Delete
        mnuPopupEditObjects.Visible = True
        mnuPopupDeleteObjects.Visible = True
    End If

    mnuPopup.Show(Me, New Point(e.X, e.Y))
End Sub
```

The mnuPopup menu contains items to add and remove Nodes and Links. When the user
selects one of those commands, the corresponding event handler does whatever is appropriate.

THE Node CLASS

The Node class represents a network node. In addition to X and Y properties, this class
includes several shared variables that determine how nodes are drawn. For instance, the

PART

II

CH

6

PenNormal and BrushNormal properties determine how Nodes are normally drawn. Because these properties are shared, all Node objects share the same values. They are initialized so the pen is black and the brush is white. That makes normal Nodes appear as black circles with white centers.

```
Private Shared m_PenNormal As Pen = New Pen(System.Drawing.Color.Black)
Private Shared m_BrushNormal As Brush = Brushes.White
```

The Node class has a similarly shared m_NodeRadius variable that determines a Node's size.

Listing 6.7 shows how a Node object draws itself. The Draw method checks the Node's SelectStatus variable to see if it should be drawn normally, highlighted, or selected. It selects the correct pen and brush, draws a circle filled with the brush, and then draws a hollow circle with the pen. This version of the program fills the circle with white and then outlines it in black.

The previous section explains how the NetlabNetwork class calls the Node's Draw method to draw the network's nodes.

LISTING 6.7   THE Node OBJECT'S Draw METHOD DRAWS THE Node USING THE APPROPRIATE PEN AND BRUSH.

```
' Determines whether the link is drawn normally,
' highlighted, or selected.
Public Enum NodeSelectStatus
    Normal
    Highlighted
    Selected
End Enum
Public SelectStatus As NodeSelectStatus
' Draw the node on the indicated canvas.
Public Sub Draw(ByVal canvas As Graphics)
    Dim the_pen As Pen
    Dim the_brush As Brush

    ' See which pen and brush we should use.
    Select Case SelectStatus
       Case NodeSelectStatus.Normal
            the_pen = m_PenNormal
            the_brush = m_BrushNormal
       Case NodeSelectStatus.Highlighted
            the_pen = m_PenHighlighted
            the_brush = m_BrushHighlighted
       Case NodeSelectStatus.Selected
            the_pen = m_PenSelected
            the_brush = m_BrushSelected
    End Select

    ' Draw the node.
    With canvas
        .FillEllipse(the_brush, _
            X - m_NodeRadius, Y - m_NodeRadius, _
```

LISTING 6.7   CONTINUED

```
                m_NodeRadius * 2, m_NodeRadius * 2)
        .DrawEllipse(the_pen, _
            X - m_NodeRadius, Y - m_NodeRadius, _
            m_NodeRadius * 2, m_NodeRadius * 2)
    End With
End Sub
```

The rest of the Node's source code is straightforward, so it is not shown here. You can download the whole project from the book's Web site.

THE Link CLASS

The Link class is very similar to the Node class. Its Draw method follows the same approach as the Node's Draw method. The Link class uses shared private variables to store the pens it uses to draw the links. The Draw method examines the Link's SelectStatus variable to decide which pen to use. It then draws a line between the Link's Nodes. Listing 6.8 shows how Link objects draw themselves.

```
' Pens for drawing the link.
Private Shared m_PenNormal As Pen = New Pen(System.Drawing.Color.Black)
Private Shared m_PenHighlighted As Pen = New Pen(System.Drawing.Color.Red)
Private Shared m_PenSelected As Pen = New Pen(System.Drawing.Color.Yellow)
' Determines whether the link is drawn normally,
' highlighted, or selected.
Public Enum LinkSelectStatus
    Normal
    Highlighted
    Selected
End Enum
Public SelectStatus As LinkSelectStatus
' Draw the link on the indicated canvas.
Public Sub Draw(ByVal canvas As Graphics)
    Dim the_pen As Pen

    ' See which pen we should use.
    Select Case SelectStatus
        Case LinkSelectStatus.Normal
            the_pen = m_PenNormal
        Case LinkSelectStatus.Highlighted
            the_pen = m_PenHighlighted
        Case LinkSelectStatus.Selected
            the_pen = m_PenSelected
    End Select

    ' Draw the link.
    With canvas
```

PART

II

CH

6

LISTING 6.8   CONTINUED

```
        .DrawLine(the_pen, _
            Node1.X, Node1.Y, _
            Node2.X, Node2.Y)
    End With
End Sub
```

The rest of the Link's source code is long and less interesting, so it is not shown here.

FEEDBACK

One of the main purposes of building prototypes is to get feedback from the customers early and often. Even in a simple project like this one, where I play the roles of developer and customer, experimenting with the prototype can give unexpected insights.

VB NetLab 0.03 doesn't do much more than open and save files. Even with such limited functionality, a few minutes of testing made it obvious that the File menu's Close command was unnecessary. All it did was create a new, blank network, and the New command already does that.

The program could be modified to hide the network drawing area completely, but that adds extra work to the project without providing much benefit. This might make more sense in programs such as Microsoft Word and the Visual Basic development environment where open documents take up significant resources and lock files on the disk.

VB NetLab, however, is more similar to programs such as Notepad where an open document doesn't take up many resources. Keeping this in mind, I decided to remove the Close menu command.

As my customer (me) experimented with version 0.03, the prototype's deadline grew closer, so I reprioritized and looked for features to defer until a later release. The code that lets the user select Nodes and Links is fairly involved, so I pushed it out of version 0.04. The Edit menu's Select All Nodes and Select All Links commands go with the Node and Link selection code, so I deferred those as well.

The Edit menu's Delete command also assumes you have selected some Nodes and Links. Because object selection will not be part of version 0.04, the Delete command should not either.

Finally, as I worked with the program, I realized that it would sometimes be useful to have a Clear command that removed all of the network's Nodes and Links. That would allow the user to start over easily.

With these modifications to the design, I started work on version 0.04.

VB NetLab 0.04

The two biggest changes to VB NetLab in version 0.04 are the ability to edit the current network and the MRU list. The most interesting code that implements these two features is described in the following sections.

Editing Networks

VB NetLab Version 0.03 uses the NetlabNetwork object's MouseIsOver function to tell when the user right clicks an object. It then displays a popup menu with entries that depend on the type of object. See the section "Drawing and Finding Nodes and Links" earlier in this chapter for more information. Table 6.1 shows the menu items allowed when the user right-clicks different items.

TABLE 6.1   WHEN THE USER RIGHT-CLICKS AN OBJECT, VB NETLAB DISPLAYS THE APPROPRIATE POPUP MENU CHOICES.

Item Clicked	Popup Commands
Node	Add Link Edit Node… Delete Node
Link	Edit Link… Delete Link
Nothing	Add Node

Version 0.03 of the program displayed this popup menu, but the menu's commands only presented message boxes telling what they were for rather than actually doing anything. Version 0.04 of the prototype includes code to add and delete Links and Nodes. It still doesn't include code for editing Nodes or Links.

Listing 6.9 shows how the program's main form adds and deletes Nodes and Links. When the user selects the Add Node popup menu item, the program creates a new node. The MouseDown event handler saves the mouse's coordinates in the variables m_RightClickX and m_RightClickY. The mnuPopupAddNode_Click event handler places the new node at that position. It calls SetDataModified to flag the network data as changed and then redraws the network.

The mnuPopupAddLink_Click event handler begins the process of adding a new Link to the network. First it saves a reference to the Node that the user clicked in the variable m_AddLinkNode1. It sets that Node's SelectStatus property to Highlighted and redraws the Node so it appears highlighted on the screen.

The event handler then uses a trick for managing complicated mouse events. It saves a reference to the network drawing area in the variable m_picAddLink. This PictureBox variable was declared using the WithEvents keyword so the program now receives events for that control. In this case, that means the program receives m_picAddLink_MouseMove and m_picAddLink_MouseDown events.

When the program receives an m_picAddLink_MouseMove event, it uses the current network's FindNearestNode method to find the Node closest to the mouse. It then highlights that Node so the user can see which nodes would be connected with the new link.

When the user clicks the mouse, the m_picAddLink_MouseDown event handler creates the new Link and calls SetDataModified to flag the data as changed. Then it resets the SelectStatus of the Link's Nodes so they are no longer highlighted. The event handler then sets m_picAddLink to Nothing. That prevents these event handlers from receiving events until the next time m_picAddLink is set. Finally, the event handler redraws the network.

Deleting Nodes and Links is easier than creating a new Link. The mnuPopupDeleteNode_Click event handler uses the m_Network object's MouseIsOver method to get a reference to the Node the user clicked. It then uses an Assert statement to verify that the object is really a Node. If it is not, the program contains a bug that made the popup menu display the Delete Node command even though the user did not click a Node.

If the event handler survives the Assert statement, it uses the m_Network object's DeleteNode method to delete the Node. It then redraws the network and uses SetDataModified to flag the data as changed.

The mnuDeleteLink_Click event handler works in a similar manner. It uses the m_Network object's MouseIsOver method to get a reference to the Link the user clicked. It uses Assert to verify that the object really is a Link, uses the m_Network object's DeleteLink method to remove the Link from the network, redraws the network, and calls SetDataModified.

LISTING 6.9   VB NETLAB 0.04 INCLUDES CODE TO ADD AND DELETE NODES AND LINKS

```
Private WithEvents m_picAddLink As System.WinForms.PictureBox
' Add a new node.
Protected Sub mnuPopupAddNode_Click(ByVal sender As Object, _
  ByVal e As System.EventArgs)
    ' Create the new node.
    m_Network.AddNode(m_RightClickX, m_RightClickY)
    SetDataModified(True)

    ' Redraw.
    m_Network.Draw(picNetwork.CreateGraphics())
End Sub
Protected Sub mnuPopupAddLink_Click(ByVal sender As Object, _
  ByVal e As System.EventArgs)
    ' See what node the user clicked.
    m_AddLinkNode1 = m_Network.FindNearestNode(m_RightClickX, m_RightClickY)

    ' Redraw this node selected.
    m_AddLinkNode1.SelectStatus = Node.NodeSelectStatus.Highlighted
    m_AddLinkNode1.Draw(picNetwork.CreateGraphics())

    ' Set m_picAddLink so it gets events.
    m_picAddLink = picNetwork
```

LISTING 6.9 CONTINUED

```
End Sub
' Draw the link we would be adding.
Public Sub m_picAddLink_MouseMove(ByVal sender As Object, _
   ByVal e As System.WinForms.MouseEventArgs) Handles m_picAddLink.MouseMove
    Dim new_node As Node

    ' See what node is nearest.
    new_node = m_Network.FindNearestNode(e.X, e.Y)

    ' If new_node and m_AddLinkNode2 are the same, then this Link
    ' is unchanged since the last time. Do nothing more.
    If new_node = m_AddLinkNode2 Then Exit Sub

    ' Unhighlight the previous m_AddLinkNode2.
    If Not m_AddLinkNode2 Is Nothing Then
        m_AddLinkNode2.SelectStatus = Node.NodeSelectStatus.Normal
        m_AddLinkNode2.Draw(picNetwork.CreateGraphics())
        m_AddLinkNode2 = Nothing
    End If

    ' If new_node and m_AddLinkNode1 are the same, then the two
    ' nodes are the same and do not define a link.
    If new_node = m_AddLinkNode1 Then Exit Sub

    ' Save the new m_AddLinkNode2.
    m_AddLinkNode2 = new_node
    m_AddLinkNode2.SelectStatus = Node.NodeSelectStatus.Highlighted
    m_AddLinkNode2.Draw(picNetwork.CreateGraphics())
End Sub
' Stop selecting a new link.
Public Sub m_picAddLink_MouseDown(ByVal sender As Object, _
   ByVal e As System.WinForms.MouseEventArgs) Handles m_picAddLink.MouseDown
        ' Reset the first node's SelectionStatus.
        m_AddLinkNode1.SelectStatus = Node.NodeSelectStatus.Normal

        ' See if the second node is Nothing.
        If Not m_AddLinkNode2 Is Nothing Then
            ' We have a second node.
            ' Reset its SelectionStatus.
            m_AddLinkNode2.SelectStatus = Node.NodeSelectStatus.Normal

            ' Create the new link.
            m_Network.AddLink(m_AddLinkNode1, m_AddLinkNode2)
            SetDataModified(True)
        End If

        ' We are done with these nodes.
        m_AddLinkNode1 = Nothing
        m_AddLinkNode2 = Nothing

        ' Don't track events for this any more.
        m_picAddLink = Nothing

        ' Redraw the whole network.
        m_Network.Draw(picNetwork.CreateGraphics())
```

PART

II

CH

6

LISTING 6.9   CONTINUED

```
End Sub
' Delete the node.
Protected Sub mnuPopupDeleteNode_Click(ByVal sender As Object, _
  ByVal e As System.EventArgs)
    Dim over_object As Object

    ' See what object the user clicked.
    over_object = m_Network.MouseIsOver(m_RightClickX, m_RightClickY)

    ' Make sure we got a Node.
    Debug.Assert(TypeOf over_object Is Node)

    ' Delete the node.
    m_Network.DeleteNode(CType(over_object, Node))

    ' Redraw.
    m_Network.Draw(picNetwork.CreateGraphics())

    ' The data has been modified.
    SetDataModified(True)
End Sub
' Delete the link.
Protected Sub mnuPopupDeleteLink_Click(ByVal sender As Object, _
  ByVal e As System.EventArgs)
    Dim over_object As Object

    ' See what object the user clicked.
    over_object = m_Network.MouseIsOver(m_RightClickX, m_RightClickY)

    ' Make sure we got a Link.
    Debug.Assert(TypeOf over_object Is Link)

    ' Delete the link.
    m_Network.DeleteLink(CType(over_object, Link))

    ' Redraw.
    m_Network.Draw(picNetwork.CreateGraphics())

    ' The data has been modified.
    SetDataModified(True)
End Sub
```

Editing Nodes and Links is not much harder than adding and deleting them. These routines use the m_Network object's MouseIsOver function to find the object the user clicked. They then copy that object's properties onto an editing form. When the user finishes modifying the values, the program copies the results back into the clicked object.

Right now, the Node and Link classes don't have many properties that are worth editing, so this feature is postponed for a later version.

MRU LIST

VB NetLab manages its MRU list with the help of the routines `LoadMRUList`, `DisplayMRUList`, `AddMRUFile`, `SaveMRUList`, and `RemoveFromMRUList` shown in Listing 6.10.

The program stores its MRU filenames and titles in the Registry. The `LoadMRUList` routine uses the `GetSetting` function to load these values from the Registry and save them in the `m_MRUNames` and `m_MRNUTitles` collections. It uses the index of each item to locate its entry in the Registry. For example, the first file's name is stored with application VBNetLab, section MRUList, and key name Name0.

After it loads the file names and titles, `LoadMRUList` saves references to the MRU menu items in the `m_MRUMenus` array. This makes it a little easier to manipulate the menus later. `LoadMRUList` then calls `DisplayMRUList` to make the File menu show the correct menu entries.

`DisplayMRUList` loops through the `m_MRUNames` collection. For each entry, it sets the Text of the corresponding MRU item in the File menu to the file's title. It also makes these menu items visible. After it has set the menu items for the MRU files, it hides the remaining MRU menu items. For example, if there are currently only three files in the MRU list, the fourth MRU menu item is hidden. Finally, `DisplayMRUList` displays a menu separator above the MRU menu items if any of the items are visible. If all of the items are invisible, the routine hides this separator so the File menu does not display two separators in a row.

The `AddMRUFile` subroutine adds a new file to the MRU list. The routine starts by calling `RemoveFromMRUList` to remove the new file from the MRU list if it is already there. It then adds the new filename and title to the top of the `m_MRUNames` and `m_MRUTitles` collections. If the collections now have more than four items, the routine removes the files at the end of the list. `AddMRUFile` then calls subroutine `SaveMRUList` to save the list to the Registry and calls `DisplayMRUList` to update the program's menus.

Subroutine `SaveMRUList` uses the `DeleteSetting` statement to delete the whole Registry section MRUList for the VBNetLab application. `DeleteSetting` throws an exception if the section does not exist, so the routine protects itself with a `Try...Catch` block. After if has cleaned out any old entries, `SaveMRUList` uses `SaveSetting` to write the current MRU file names and titles into the registry.

`RemoveFromMRUList` removes a file from the MRU list. This routine loops through the `m_MRUNames` collection comparing the entries to the target filename. When it finds a match, the routine removes the filename and corresponding title from the MRU collections.

The end of Listing 6.10 shows the `mnuFileMRU0_Click` event handler. When the user clicks the first MRU item in the File menu, this event handler uses `DataSafe` to see if the data is safe. If the data is safe, the routine calls subroutine `LoadFile`, passing it the name of the MRU file selected and `LoadFile` reloads the selected file.

PART

II

CH

6

LISTING 6.10 VB NETLAB USES THESE ROUTINES TO MANAGE ITS MRU LIST

```
' MRU list variables.
Private m_MRUNames As Collection
Private m_MRUTitles As Collection
Private m_MRUMenus() As MenuItem
' Load the MRU list from the Registry.
Private Sub LoadMRUList()
    Dim i As Integer
    Dim file_title As String
    Dim file_name As String

    ' Load the saved entries.
    m_MRUNames = New Collection()
    m_MRUTitles = New Collection()
    For i = 0 To 3
        file_name = GetSetting( _
            "VBNetLab", "MRUList", "Name" & i.ToString(), "")
        If file_name.Length > 0 Then
            file_title = GetSetting( _
                "VBNetLab", "MRUList", "Title" & i.ToString(), "")
            m_MRUNames.Add(file_name)
            m_MRUTitles.Add(file_title)
        End If
    Next i

    ' Initialize the MRU menu entries.
    ReDim m_MRUMenus(4)
    m_MRUMenus(0) = Me.mnuFileMRU0
    m_MRUMenus(1) = Me.mnuFileMRU1
    m_MRUMenus(2) = Me.mnuFileMRU2
    m_MRUMenus(3) = Me.mnuFileMRU3

    ' Display the MRU list.
    DisplayMRUList()
End Sub
' Display the MRU list entries.
Private Sub DisplayMRUList()
    Dim i As Integer

    ' Load the used entries.
    For i = 1 To m_MRUNames.Count
        m_MRUMenus(i - 1).Text = CType(m_MRUTitles.Item(i), String)
        m_MRUMenus(i - 1).Visible = True
    Next i

    ' Hide unneeded entries.
    For i = m_MRUNames.Count + 1 To 4
        m_MRUMenus(i - 1).Text = "&" & i.ToString & " " & _
            CType(m_MRUTitles.Item(i), String)
    Next i

    ' Show the separator if necessary.
    Me.mnuFileExitSep.Visible = m_MRUMenus(0).Visible
End Sub
' Add a file name to the MRU list.
Private Sub AddMRUFile(ByVal file_name As String, ByVal file_title As String)
```

LISTING 6.10   CONTINUED

```
    ' Remove the file from the MRU list if it
    ' is already there.
    RemoveFromMRUList(file_name)

    ' Add the new file to the top of the list.
    If m_MRUNames.Count > 0 Then
        m_MRUNames.Add(file_name, , 1)
        m_MRUTitles.Add(file_title, , 1)
    Else
        m_MRUNames.Add(file_name)
        m_MRUTitles.Add(file_title)
    End If

    ' If there are more than 4 files, remove the last ones.
    Do While m_MRUNames.Count > 4
        m_MRUNames.Remove(m_MRUNames.Count)
        m_MRUTitles.Remove(m_MRUTitles.Count)
    Loop

    ' Save the new MRU list.
    SaveMRUList()

    ' Display the new MRU list.
    DisplayMRUList()
End Sub
' Save the MRU list.
Private Sub SaveMRUList()
    Dim i As Integer

    ' Delete any current Registry entries.
    Try
        DeleteSetting("VBNetLab", "MRUList")
    Catch e As Exception
        ' Ignore the error that occurs if the section
        ' does not already exist.
    End Try

    ' Save the current file names and titles.
    For i = 1 To m_MRUNames.Count
        SaveSetting("VBNetLab", "MRUList", "Name" & (i - 1).ToString(), _
            CType(m_MRUNames.Item(i), String))
        SaveSetting("VBNetLab", "MRUList", "Title" & (i - 1).ToString(), _
            CType(m_MRUTitles.Item(i), String))
    Next i
End Sub
' Remove this file from the MRU list.
Private Sub RemoveFromMRUList(ByVal file_name As String)
    Dim i As Integer

    ' See if the name is already in the list.
    For i = m_MRUNames.Count To 1 Step -1
        If String.Compare(file_name, _
            CType(m_MRUNames.Item(i), String), True) = 0 _
        Then
            ' The name is here. Remove it.
```

```
            m_MRUNames.Remove(i)
            m_MRUTitles.Remove(i)
        End If
    Next i
End Sub
' Reload MRU file number 0.
' The other MRU menu items are similar
' so they are not shown here.
Public Sub mnuFileMRU0_Click(ByVal sender As Object, _
    ByVal e As System.EventArgs) Handles mnuFileMRU0.Click
    If Not DataSafe() Then Exit Sub
    LoadFile(CType(m_MRUNames.Item(1), String))
End Sub
```

The main program uses these routines in several ways to manage its MRU list. When the program starts, it calls LoadMRUList to load the MRU list from the registry.

Subroutine LoadFile loads a network file. If this routine encounters an error loading the file, it calls RemoveFromMRUList to remove the file from the MRU list. If LoadFile loads the file successfully, it calls AddMRUFile to add the newly opened file to the MRU list. If the file was already on the list, AddMRUFile moves it to the top of the list.

Subroutine SaveAs saves the network in a new file. If it succeeds, SaveAs calls subroutine AddMRUFile to add the new filename to the MRU list. If the filename was already on the list, AddMRUFile moves it to the top.

SUMMARY

This chapter describes several tips for building prototypes, particularly throwaway prototypes. These tips let you implement features quickly so you can show them to customers and get feedback. Although the application's requirements and architectural design should be reasonably solid at this point, you should keep your mind open to change. The sooner you show customers a prototype, the sooner they can spot flaws, and the sooner you can correct them. The longer you wait to make changes, the harder they become and the more likely it is that you will be stuck with an application that doesn't fill the customers' needs.

CHAPTER

7

TESTING

In this chapter

Many developers spend little or no time testing their prototypes. They just write a bunch of code and hope it works. Then they run through various demonstration scenarios and fix any problems they encounter.

This unplanned testing strategy might work for some simple prototypes, but it usually makes development more difficult than it needs to be. This chapter describes some testing issues that you should understand when you build a prototype. Although you probably won't spend as much time testing the prototype as you spend testing the final application, you need to perform some testing to build a useful prototype as quickly as possible.

TEST

Whenever you write any non-trivial piece of code, there is a good chance it contains a few bugs. When you work with other developers on an application complex enough to justify prototyping, you are guaranteed to have some bugs.

It is a well-known fact that bugs are easier to remove if they are found soon after they are created. If you find a bug in a subroutine the first time you run it, fixing the bug is usually relatively painless. On the other hand, if you don't notice there is a problem until your routine is used in a complicated series of subroutine calls, it might take you a while to find the problem. The problem might be in your routine, in one of the routines that called it, or in the data those routines are using.

Despite the fact that bugs are easiest to fix when they are caught right away, many developers write code and never test it. They plug the new code into the application and expect it to run. If a problem arises, they step through the code trying to find the bug. Often the bug is in the most recently modified code, but it takes a while to step through all of the other routines trying to pin the bug down.

Tale from the Trenches

I know of a programmer who works in exactly this way. He maintains a suite of programs that control precision test equipment. He makes major modifications to an important application and then assumes the changes will work flawlessly. After all, if he knew he had introduced a bug, he would fix it. Because he doesn't know about any bugs, he assumes they aren't there.

A few days later when a technician needs to perform an important test and runs the program, it doesn't work. Now instead of being a simple debugging session, it's become an emergency. The programmer and his manager get pulled in, sometimes late in the evening, to get the code working as quickly as possible. It's been a while since the programmer has worked on the code, so he doesn't remember exactly what changes he made. Together with the increased time pressure, that makes the debugging process even slower than it would usually be.

Meanwhile, the technician is standing there with nothing to do until the test is complete. The program is tying up an expensive heavily used piece of test equipment that could be doing something more useful than debugging code. The component that the technician needs to test is probably almost ready for shipping, so delaying the test might actually affect the customer.

All of this trouble could have been avoided if the programmer had spent a few minutes testing his changes on the development computer before installing them on the computer that controls the test equipment.

Tale from the Trenches

Glenn, a good friend of mine, recently finished a project where the development team used an interesting strategy to encourage developers to test their code. If you checked in code that broke the system build, you got a rubber chicken tacked beside your door. You kept the chicken until the next developer got careless and broke the build.

I'm sure outsiders who walked past their offices and saw a rubber chicken tacked to the wall wrote the experience off as just another of those weird things programmers do. This way, peer pressure is used to persuade developers to test their code. It's more fun than—and probably just as effective as—progress reviews and complaints by management.

At the end of this project, the chicken retired; and Glenn, who happened to be its last recipient, got to keep it. Knowing Glenn, I half suspect he made the last error on purpose so he could keep the chicken.

Now a new project is starting. Instead of a chicken, its mascot is a skunk.

In a way, Visual Basic's development environment is partly to blame for this laziness. Its excellent interactive debugging features make programmers think it's easy to find bugs. Even with breakpoints, watches, and the ability to examine variable values while the program is running, it is still easier to correct bugs if you find them before you plug the new code into an application.

The best time to test a routine is right after you write it and it is fresh in your mind. After you finish writing a subroutine, test it to make sure it works. Usually a few minutes of testing is all it takes to flush the majority of the bugs out of a subroutine. When even a simple bug can take hours to fix later, it's well worth investing a little time at the start to find as many bugs as possible.

WRITE TEST ROUTINES

Sometimes testing a single subroutine isn't easy. You might need a big part of the application to create data for the routine to use and to interpret the results.

Build test routines to simulate the program's actions. Have the test routines build the test data and pass it into the subroutine you want to test. If it's particularly difficult to generate test data, write some into a text file by hand and then build a test routine to load the text file. This might take a few minutes, but it's worth it if you find a single bug. Even if you don't find any bugs, the extra confidence it gives you in the code is worth it.

When you have finished testing the subroutine, save the test routines. Comment out their source code but keep them in case you need them later. You can make this a little easier by putting test routines in separate modules. For example, if you build a Customer class, create a TestCustomer code module that contains subroutines that test the Customer class methods. When you are ready to use the prototype code to start building the final application, you can easily exclude these test modules.

USE BLACK BOX TESTING

In *black box testing*, you pretend you know nothing about how a routine works internally and you focus on the routine's inputs and output. You generate as many different inputs as you can and you send them into the routine. If the actual results don't match those you expected, you have found a bug. Then you can step through the code in the debugger running the test data to see where the routine goes astray.

If you can write routines to generate random inputs and then verify the results, you can test a huge number of inputs very quickly. It might even be possible to test every conceivable input. Then you can be absolutely certain that the routine works.

You should pay particular attention to unusual input values. Try to think of the strangest, most unlikely inputs you can and see how the routine handles them. Try passing the routine the largest and smallest inputs it can accept, as well as no inputs at all. If there are illegal inputs, document them in the comments at the beginning of the routine. Then make sure the routines that invoke this one are guaranteed to filter out those illegal values.

EXAMPLE

Suppose you write a subroutine that arranges up to five numbers in sorted order. It would be easy to write a routine that randomly selects five numbers, passes them into the routine, and then verifies that the results are sorted. If you run this test routine a few dozen times successfully, you can have some confidence that the routine works correctly. Because this test should be extremely fast, you can run it a few million times to gain even more confidence.

If you also know that the numbers being sorted are always between 1 and 50, you can write a routine to generate all of the possible combinations. It will take a few minutes for the test routine to run through all 37 billion or so combinations, but when it is finished you can rest assured that the routine works.

Almost. There are still a couple of strange things to consider. The routine is intended to sort up to five numbers. The test programs described so far only check cases where the routine tests exactly five items. You still need to test the routine with four, three, two, one, and zero inputs. You should also see what the routine does if two or more of its inputs are the same, or if some of the inputs lie outside the range 1 to 50.

It will take some extra time to build these tests, but if the routine passes all of these tests you can have some confidence that it works properly. Then you can move on the next piece of the prototype that you need to build without looking back.

Black box testing is sometimes easiest if the person testing the code is not the person who wrote it. The developer who wrote the routine knows how it works and understands the sort of inputs it expects. For that reason, the writer might unconsciously avoid passing the routine values that don't make sense. Those values are more likely to uncover bugs than typical inputs, so it is important that they are included.

USE WHITE BOX TESTING

In *white box testing*, you know the internal structure of the routine you want to study. You carefully pick the test inputs to exercise every part of the routine's code. Then you feed the inputs into the routine and verify the results much as you do with black box testing.

It is a good idea to step through the code a few times in the debugger to verify that the test cases really have executed all of the routine's code. If a piece of code is never tested, it might still cause problems when it finally executes. In most applications, the users exercise the code far more than developers do during testing. Eventually, the users stumble across all of the weird combinations that execute this untested code and cause problems.

Tale from the Trenches

A repair dispatching application I worked on proves that the users eventually discover every bizarre combination of inputs you can imagine, and even those that you can't. The program assigned a few thousand jobs to a hundred or so employees each day. The trick was matching each job with someone who had the skills and equipment to do the job while meeting as many customer appointments as possible.

This project used an evolutionary prototype. After the prototype was finished to the point where we thought it was ready for testing, we installed it at the dispatch center and let the customers use it to assign jobs for a couple weeks. We found a few bugs early on and fixed them. By the end of the first week, the program was running smoothly.

However, in two different instances during the test period, the program assigned a repairman to work at his ex-wife's house. Never in our wildest dreams had we thought this problem might occur.

Even if we had thought about it, we would probably have dismissed this as ludicrously unlikely. What are the odds that the program would assign someone to work at an ex-spouse's house? The answer is that this had to happen eventually. The amazing thing is that it happened not once but twice during the prototyping period.

Fortunately, this application was designed to keep human beings in the loop. The repair people recognized their former spouses' addresses and called the dispatch center to ask for different assignments.

One of the best ways to test a routine is white box testing followed by black box testing. Using what you know about the routine's internal structure, you can design a series of tests to exercise all of the code and to check the strange cases. Then you can throw a large number of random inputs at the routine to see if you can find any completely unexpected problems.

TEST PERFORMANCE

Performance testing is not as important in a prototype as it is in a final application. The prototype should demonstrate the features that the application will implement. It doesn't need to run at the same speed as the final application.

On the other hand, you can use the prototype to make some predictions about the final application's performance. If the prototype takes 35 seconds to perform a complex database query with one user connected to the database, you should be worried if the final application needs to support 150 users.

Think about the environments in which the prototype and the final application will be used and determine how any differences in the environments will affect performance. For example, suppose the developers build the prototype using 1GHz Pentium 4 processors but the customers will be running the application on 60MHz 486-based PCs. Unless the prototype runs with blinding speed, you could be in trouble. Even if the prototype is incredibly fast, the final application might be too slow on the customers' computers. You might all be in for an unpleasant surprise and some painful rewriting when you install the final application.

Tale from the Trenches

In several of the applications I helped develop, we knew the customer would buy new hardware to run our application. We bought the fastest computers currently available for our prototype development.

A year or so later, when the application was finished, the customers bought their computers. In the intervening year, the speed of computer hardware had greatly increased. If we got acceptable performance out of our development machines, our customers were just fine. Even with a greater number of users, the customers got better response times than we had during development.

You can prevent this sort of disaster by working on computers comparable to the customers'. You should at least have a demonstration system set up where you can perform some simple performance tests.

Tale from the Trenches

Once in a while, the differences between the developers' and customers' computers works in your favor. If you build the prototype on computers that are slower than your customers', the developers will always have a good appreciation for the performance the customers will see.

Even this strategy can backfire, however. On one project, we purchased new computers that were much faster than those used by the company that built our database tools. The output of the reporting facility scrolled off the screen so quickly that you couldn't read any of it.

Our database administrator went to a user's group meeting and asked the company spokesmen how to solve this problem. His jaw dropped and everyone else at the meeting was amazed. All of the other customers were using older computers. They were so frustrated at how slow the reports ran that it had never occurred to anyone to make the reporting utility pause between pages.

Sometimes the prototyping techniques developers use affect performance. For example, suppose the prototype uses slow file operations and simplified algorithms, but the final application will use much faster database operations and optimized algorithms. In that case, you might not have any trouble, even if the prototype seems unacceptably slow. Tell your customers that the prototype is not optimized for speed and you expect the final application to run faster.

Tale from the Trenches

The Visual Basic.NET Beta version 1 was not optimized for speed. Even on state-of-the-art hardware, building an application takes orders of magnitude longer than it does in Visual Basic 6.

Microsoft told its customers that Beta 1 was not optimized for speed. This version is intended to demonstrate features that are new in the language and the development environment, and to gather feedback. Its speed is not intended to reflect that of the final release.

TEST WITH REALISTIC DATA

Perform tests with the most realistic data possible. If you cannot easily make the data by hand, write a program to generate it. For example, many large applications are designed to work with hundreds or thousands of records. If you test a prototype using a database that contains only a dozen records, you might not be able to make any useful guesses about the performance of the application. In this case, you should write a program to generate the hundreds or thousands of records you expect to see in the final application.

Make the records as realistic as possible. If a field should contain a name, pick random names from a list. Or at least use random strings of letters. If you give the field the values VALUE1, VALUE2, and so on, the data will not have the distribution you would normally expect in a list of names. A random selection of letters will not have the right distribution either, but it will be closer than the sorted list VALUE1, VALUE2, and so forth.

EXAMPLE

Sorting algorithms provide a good example of routines that are sensitive to data type and distribution. There are many different sorting algorithms that give good performance under different circumstances. The bubble-sort algorithm is extremely fast for lists that are almost sorted. If the values are VALUE1, VALUE2, and so on with one or two items out of place, bubblesort will be about as fast as you can hope.

On the other hand, bubblesort relies on the data being initially almost sorted. If the list of items is randomly arranged, bubblesort is one of the slowest algorithms you can use. In that case, quicksort would be a much better choice.

Quicksort works with integer, real, or string data, and has very good performance if the data is initially randomly arranged. It can have some problems if the data is initially sorted, however.

If the data you are sorting consists of integers, countingsort might work for you. Depending on the number of items and the range they span, countingsort can be so much faster than quicksort that it almost seems to sort by magic. It doesn't do as well with a few values spread over a wide range and it doesn't work with strings.

As you can see, the nature of the data has a huge impact on the sorting algorithm you should choose. Unless you understand the nature of the data, you cannot make the right decision. Similarly, if the prototype does not use data that is similar to the data the final application will use, you cannot expect to get reliable performance results by testing the prototype.

PERFORM STRESS TESTS

Stress tests determine how an application stands up under heavy usage. Stress tests are particularly important for applications that must handle a large number of users. In a typical stress test, you either have a bunch of users exercise the application at the same time or you use software to simulate the actions of a bunch of users.

As is the case with other kinds of performance testing, you need to make sure the tests are as realistic as possible. If you don't have realistic data and the testers don't perform realistic actions, you won't learn anything reliable about the application's performance.

Tale from the Trenches

One GTE application I worked on was supposed to allow several dozen users to work simultaneously on a large, centralized database. After we installed about a dozen prototype workstations, the customers performed their version of stress tests.

They had written a script that all of the test users would follow. A lead tester stood at the front of the room and told everyone to enter a certain record ID. Then on the count of three, all of the testers pressed Enter to load the record. Much to our customers' annoyance, the system did not always respond within the five-second time limit they had set.

In the next test, all of the testers opened the same system administrator and configuration screens at the same time. Time after time, the prototype failed to meet their time requirements.

When we heard about the tests, we realized that their tests were not realistic. To improve performance, the database was distributed over several disk drives. When the testers all tried to open the same record at the same time, however, all of their computers tried to access the same record in the database. That meant they all sent requests to the same disk. The resulting disk contention slowed the database far more than normal usage would.

It was extremely unlikely that all of the users would try to open any record at the same time. There was practically no chance whatsoever of them all trying to open the exact same record at the same time.

When the testers tried to access the system administrator screens at the same time, they performed an even less realistic test. This test caused disk contention just as the previous test did. Unlike the previous test, however, it was not even theoretically possible. Only two users would have system administrator privileges in the final application, so no more than two users could try to open those screens at the same time.

We rewrote the tests so users tried to open randomly selected records, work with them for a brief period of time, and then close them. After an hour or so, this less synchronized testing showed there was nothing wrong with the application's performance. As long as the users didn't try to do anything too unusual, there was no problem.

As an interesting postscript, the first set of tests did have a big impact on training. When the customers designed their training materials, they made sure that each student got a slightly different set of instructions so they didn't all try to work on the same records at the same time.

Visual Studio.NET is designed to make it easier to build widely distributed scalable applications. If you build an application out of a collection of independent Web Services, you can study the performance of each separately. If a particular Web Service is a bottleneck, you can move it to a faster computer. You might also be able to distribute multiple copies of the service on more than one computer.

Similarly, if a centralized database is the bottleneck, you might be able to move it to a faster computer. Depending on the type of database, you might be able to distribute it across multiple hard disks or make copies of it with replication. The loosely coupled servers envisioned by Microsoft give you greater opportunities for optimizing performance.

TEST FOR SCRIPTED DEMOS

An application's early prototypes are often demonstrated to the customers under carefully controlled circumstances. A developer follows a prepared script to demonstrate the prototype's key features.

To prepare for this kind of demonstration, you should make a copy of the database and any files the program will use. Then walk through the steps you want to demonstrate taking careful notes of everything you do. When you find bugs, fix them. Reset the database and any files you saved and try again until you can demonstrate all of the prototype's key features without any bugs.

When you are finished, convert your notes into a script. You can add comments to remind yourself about features you want to point out to the customers.

Restore the database and any files you saved and repeat the steps following the script. If you deviate from the script, update it so it is correct. At this point, you might discover more data that you did not properly save and restore. Add any new files or database tables to your list of things to reset before starting the demonstration.

Repeat this process, resetting the data and running through the script, until you can follow the script exactly without any surprises. Then save the current version of the prototype along with the initial database and any files you need to restore in a safe place. If you need to run the application on a computer that does not have Visual Basic installed, be sure to include the application setup kit.

If you stick to the script, you probably don't need to do any more testing on the prototype before the demonstration. But there are still some weird ways the prototype might fail. For example, if the application uses the name of the computer, other computers on the local network, or date-sensitive data, it might fail on a demonstration machine. If you can think of anything along those lines, you might have to do some extra testing. You might also need to write some setup routines that reset the application's data for the current system and date.

Tale from the Trenches

A tax software project I helped build for the State of Minnesota had lots of date dependencies. For example, if a customer filed a tax return more than a certain number of days late, the program charged the customer a late filing penalty. Whenever we tested the application, we had to be aware of the current date and of the dates stored in the database.

For example, we might have created mileage data for a particular trucking company during the fourth quarter of a specific year. If we created a tax return for that company during the following January, the return would not include a late penalty. If we tried to run the same demonstration a few months later, the return would include a late penalty.

To solve this problem, we used a word processor to manually edit the scripts we used to populate the database. Another approach would have been to reset the demonstration computer's system clock. That might have confused the database and other parts of the system, so we decided against it.

Before a demonstration, I save the prototype's source code, database, files, slides, notes, and other documentation I want to bring to the demonstration on a write-once CD-ROM. That way I know I have a working demonstration system from which nothing can be accidentally deleted.

If you install the prototype and its files on a laptop in your office and verify that it works before you go to the customer's site, you don't have to worry about installing the prototype on the customers' computer right before the demonstration. Even if you do install the prototype on your own laptop, bring the source code and documentation on a CD-ROM in case the files on your laptop somehow get corrupted.

PART

II

CH

7

If you cannot bring your own computer to the demonstration, try to install the prototype as far ahead of time as possible. If you do not have access to the demonstration computer, mail a CD-ROM to your customers and ask them to have their system administrator install it. You don't want to find out that the prototype won't run at the last second with your customers staring over your shoulder.

When the time for the demonstration finally arrives, be careful not to stray even a little bit from the script. You only tested the scripted parts of the prototype so you might find bugs if you try something new.

Tale from the Trenches

When I was about to give the first demonstration of the Minnesota tax software prototype, one of the database developers claimed there was nothing I could do to hurt the database. I foolishly believed him and used the prototype to view some data that was not part of my demonstration script. That crashed the database and it took almost three hours for the database developers to put things back together.

Fortunately, I made this mistake before the customers arrived, and we had a couple hours of design discussions to work through before the demonstration, so the prototype was working again when we needed it. It was a very close call, though.

Don't let the customers force you out of your script. If they ask to see something else, tell them that the prototype isn't ready for that yet.

After the main demonstration is completely finished, you can consider letting the customers experiment with other parts of the prototype. Don't do this unless you have a good working relationship with your customers and you think the prototype is unlikely to crash. You don't want to make a bad impression, particularly at an early demonstration of one of the prototype's first versions. Be sure to warn the customers that this is only a prototype and that it has not been thoroughly tested. Also warn them not to invoke any features you think are dangerous.

TEST FOR CUSTOMER USE

To get the most out of your prototypes, you should let your customers experiment with them. Descriptions, slide shows, and carefully scripted walkthroughs don't give the customer the same appreciation for a product as actually sitting down and experimenting with it. After the customers have experimented with the program for a while, they become comfortable with the prototype's main ideas. Then they start to realize the kinds of things that are possible.

Tale from the Trenches

In many of the projects I've helped build, we got the most productive feedback only after the customers had spent an hour or two working with the prototype. When we demonstrated a new version of a prototype, we typically spent one half to a full day discussing the application's architecture, database design, interactions with other systems, network requirements, and other high-level topics.

Then we would spend an hour or two showing the customers the prototype in a carefully scripted demonstration. After that, we let them ask questions about how to do specific things using the prototype. We demonstrated how to do these things if the necessary features were ready in the prototype.

At this point we let the customers take over and experiment on their own. This is when they really started understanding the prototype and all of its potential. When they tried to do the tasks they normally handle on a day-to-day basis, they found the places where the prototype made things easier or more difficult. That led them to think about new ways of doing things and really got the questions and suggestions flowing.

When you plan to let your customers use the prototype, you need to test the code much more thoroughly than you do before you show them a scripted demonstration. You cannot tell ahead of time what the customers will try to do, so you must ensure that every feature that the customers can access works correctly. Use the black box, white box, and other testing methods to ensure that the features the customer can access do not crash the prototype.

If you know a feature doesn't work, disable the menu item or button that activates it. If the feature is activated in some other way, for example by a timer, comment out its code. Don't let the customers use a feature that you know will crash the prototype.

If a feature can work under some circumstances but not others, make the prototype disable the feature when the customers run it. If you use the user privilege techniques described in Chapter 11, "Database Tips and Tools," you can assign different privileges to yourself and the customers. The prototype can check the privileges of the username entered on the logon form to determine whether it should disable these features. Have the customers log on using one username and use another for yourself.

LISTEN TO THE CUSTOMERS

If you let the customers experiment with the prototype, listen to what they have to say. Fix any bugs they find and consider any changes they request. Do not dismiss the customers' concerns, no matter how strange they might seem. Sometimes customers describe real problems in ways you have trouble understanding. You might need to watch the customer use the prototype to understand what it is they don't like.

Believe the customers if they say they have seen a bug even if you cannot reproduce it. Sometimes users don't know what they did to cause a problem or they might be unable to explain the steps they took to make the program crash. If they cannot tell you how to reproduce the error, you might have a lot of trouble fixing it. Once again, you might need to watch the customers using the application to see how they made an error occur before you can attack the problem.

Tale from the Trenches
While testing the prototype for a telephone switching application, one of our customers found a way to crash the application. She resized a particular form several times and after a while it crashed, bringing down the whole application. She didn't know what was special about what she was doing; no particular data needed to be displayed on the form, and there was no way to predictably reproduce the error.

This is a developer's worst nightmare: an irreproducible bug that crashes the system every now and then for no obvious reason. If you cannot reproduce an error, it is very hard to find and fix the code. It is even harder to be sure the code is fixed afterwards because you cannot repeat the steps that make the error occur if it is not fixed.

I tried resizing the form on my system and couldn't get the program to crash. My initial thought was that the bug was some sort of memory leak that used up more and more memory every time you resized the form. I resized the form literally hundreds of times but still couldn't make the program crash so that possibility seemed unlikely. I asked the customer for more details and she said that sometimes the program failed after an hour or two of testing and sometimes after only a few minutes.

With no other ideas in mind, I flew from Boston to Dallas to watch the customer crash the program. After several minutes of trying, she couldn't do it. Just as she was starting to doubt her own sanity, the program died. She had done exactly what she said she had: started the program and resized the form a bunch of times.

I sat down and tried to reproduce the steps she had taken. After fifteen minutes, I still couldn't get the program to crash and we were starting to wonder if the system somehow recognized her fingertips and crashed just for her. Finally, I got the program to fail. I experimented with the screen for several more minutes and got it to crash a couple more times.

I stared at the screen for a while and then realized what the critical piece of information was. It wasn't how many times you resized the form, what data was on the form, or even what size you gave the form. It was the size of a particular control on the form. When you resized the form, the program rearranged its controls to fit the new size. There was a scrolled window control on the form holding a list of values. If you resized the form in just such a way that this scrolled window control was exactly 1 pixel tall, it crashed.

After I figured this out, it was easy to build a small test program that demonstrated this fact. It took only a few minutes more to modify the code so it always made that particular control at least two pixels tall.

The moral is to listen to the customers even if they seem crazy. The customers are probably not trying to mislead you. If you can't understand what they are saying, it's because you don't have enough information, not because they are imagining things.

Pay particular attention to complaints about features the customers do not want. If the prototype does something the wrong way or does something the customers don't need, fix or remove that feature before you spend a lot of time building it the wrong way.

If the customers ask for new features, write them up and send them to your change control committee. If the customers really need to modify the application, you should let them. However, you cannot let the customers make indiscriminate changes that might not fit in with the system's overall design. See if they can live without some enhancements until the next release.

If the customers absolutely insist that they need a huge number of changes, you should start over at the project's specification stage. You will end up with a better application if you start from scratch with a new set of requirements and a new architectural design instead of forcing too many changes onto the existing design.

VB NETLAB 0.05

VB NetLab 0.05 includes several subroutines designed to test the program's code. This version of the program includes a Test menu that provides access to the test routines. Each of the Test menu's items put the program in a special testing mode to verify one of the program's routines.

These test modes are for testing only and are not necessarily compatible with the application's normal functions. After you run a test mode, the program might be left in an unusual state. For example, these modes might delete the currently loaded network without flagging the data as modified. To avoid damaging the data, quit without saving changes after you run a test routine.

Before you give the prototype to the customers for testing, you can quickly make the Test menu invisible. That hides all of these possibly dangerous functions from the customers.

It is difficult to test all of the program's code automatically, so VB NetLab was also tested using use cases. *Use cases* walk a tester through a series of operations to verify that the program behaves as expected.

The following sections describe the test routines and uses cases used to test VB NetLab 0.05.

POINT TO LINE DISTANCES

One of the prototype's trickiest pieces of code is the Link object's `DistancePointToSegment` method. This function determines the distance from a point to the link. The `Link` class uses this function in its `DistanceToPoint` method to see how far the *Link* is from a point.

The following code shows how the program tests the `DistanceToPoint` method and thus the `DistancePointToSegment` function. When the user selects the Point-to-Line Distance Test menu item, the program calls `DataSafe` to make sure the current network has been saved. It then creates a new network containing two nodes and one link. The menu's event handler sets the `m_TestDistanceToPointPic` variable, so it refers to the program's network drawing area. This variable is declared using the `WithEvents` keyword so the program can catch its `MouseDown` events in a separate event handler.

The new `MouseDown` event handler fires when the user clicks the network drawing area. The routine calls the test link's `DistanceToPoint` function to see how far the clicked point is from the link. It then draws a circle of that radius around the point. If the function is correct, the circle should just touch the link.

```
' Variables used to test the Link object's
' DistanceToPoint function.
Private m_TestDistanceToPointNode1 As Node
Private m_TestDistanceToPointNode2 As Node
Private m_TestDistanceToPointLink As Link
Private WithEvents m_TestDistanceToPointPic As System.WinForms.PictureBox
' Test the Link object's DistanceToPoint function.
Public Sub mnuTestPointToLineDistance_Click(ByVal sender As Object, _
  ByVal e As System.EventArgs) Handles mnuTestPointToLineDistance.Click
      ' Make sure the data is safe.
    If Not DataSafe() Then Exit Sub

    ' Create the new network.
```

```
    m_Network = New NetlabNetwork()

    ' Set the new caption.
    m_FileName = ""
    m_FileTitle = ""
    SetDataModified(False)
    ' Create two nodes and one link.
    m_TestDistanceToPointNode1 = m_Network.AddNode(50, 50)
    m_TestDistanceToPointNode2 = m_Network.AddNode(300, 200)
    m_TestDistanceToPointLink = m_Network.AddLink( _
        m_TestDistanceToPointNode1, _
        m_TestDistanceToPointNode2)
    ' Set the m_TestDistanceToPointPic reference so we can
        ' process events more easily.
    m_TestDistanceToPointPic = Me.picNetwork

    ' Redraw.
    m_Network.Draw(picNetwork.CreateGraphics())
End Sub
' When the user clicks on the network, see how far away the link is.
' Then draw a circle with that radius around the point clicked.
' If all is well, the circle should just touch the link.
Public Sub m_TestDistanceToPointPic_MouseDown(ByVal sender As Object, _
  ByVal e As System.WinForms.MouseEventArgs) _
  Handles m_TestDistanceToPointPic.MouseDown
    Dim distance As Integer
    ' See how far the point is from the link.
    distance = CInt(m_TestDistanceToPointLink.DistanceToPoint(e.X, e.Y))
    ' Draw the circle.
    picNetwork.CreateGraphics().DrawEllipse( _
        New Pen(System.Drawing.Color.Black), _
        e.X - distance, e.Y - distance, 2 * distance, 2 * distance)
End Sub
```

Figure 7.1 shows the results after clicking the form several times. Notice how circles near the ends of the Link touch the Link's end points and are not tangent to the Link.

Figure 7.1
Circles that just touch the link verify that the DistancePointTo Segment function works.

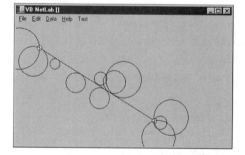

FILE SAVE AND RESTORE

The Link object's DistancePointToSegment function might be the trickiest piece of code in the VB NetLab prototype, but the code that saves and restores network files is arguably the most important piece of code. If the program did not correctly save and restore files, the users couldn't build and save test networks. The users also couldn't run standard test networks provided by the instructor. Because these routines are so important, they deserve extra testing.

The first step in verifying that the program can save and restore files is to build a test file by hand, load it into the program, and verify that the network looks like it should. Figure 7.2 shows VB NetLab displaying the following handmade network file LoadTest.net.

```
<?xml version="1.0" standalone="yes"?>
<!--Handmade network to see if VB NetLab 0.05 loads correctly-->
<!--2001-05-19T10:57:13-->
<VBNetLab_Network Version="0.05">
  <Nodes>
    <Node X="20" Y="20"/>
    <Node X="60" Y="40"/>
    <Node X="100" Y="20"/>
    <Node X="80" Y="60"/>
    <Node X="100" Y="100"/>
    <Node X="60" Y="80"/>
    <Node X="20" Y="100"/>
    <Node X="40" Y="60"/>
  </Nodes>
  <Links>
    <Link Node1="1" Node2="2" Cost="1"/>
    <Link Node1="2" Node2="3" Cost="2"/>
    <Link Node1="3" Node2="4" Cost="3"/>
    <Link Node1="4" Node2="5" Cost="4"/>
    <Link Node1="5" Node2="6" Cost="5"/>
    <Link Node1="6" Node2="7" Cost="6"/>
    <Link Node1="7" Node2="8" Cost="7"/>
    <Link Node1="8" Node2="1" Cost="8"/>
  </Links>
</VBNetLab_Network>
```

To build this network file, I first drew a small network on graph paper. I then wrote the file using the syntax VB NetLab is supposed to expect. I changed the first comment to say the file was handmade. VB NetLab doesn't read that comment, so that change made no difference.

Figure 7.2
VB NetLab must be able to open handmade network files to display networks like this one.

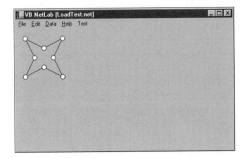

The second step in validating the file save and restore routines is to save a network and manually verify that it makes sense. For this test, I saved the network shown in Figure 7.2 into the new file SaveTest.net. I then compared the new and original files line by line. As I expected, the first comment was different because I had not followed VB NetLab's standard procedure for filling in that comment in the handmade file. The second comment was also different because the files were created at different times.

The rest of the files were identical except all of the Cost values for the Links were wrong. This identified a bug in the way the program was initializing the Link objects. I fixed that bug, tried again, and the files matched.

These two load and save tests give a little assurance that the program can load and save network files. The save test even uncovered a bug. There's a limit to the number and complexity of the network files you can write and validate by hand, however.

An automated testing routine can further guarantee that the network reading and writing routines work. Writing a routine that generates a random network, saves it to a file, and then verifies that the file is correct would be difficult. One method is to write a routine that saves the network into a file in a different way and then verifies that the files are the same. That routine would use Visual Basic's standard file output routines to write an XML file that looks like VB NetLab's standard network format.

A simpler option is to have the program generate a random network, save it to a file, reload the saved network, and save it into another file. The program then compares the two network files to see if they are identical. If the program's file saving routines and its file loading routines do not use exactly the same format, it is unlikely that the files will be the same.

The code shown in Listing 7.1 demonstrates this approach. When the user selects the Test menu's File Save and Restore command, this event handler executes. The routine begins by calling DataSafe to let the user save the current network. It then repeats 20 trials of its test.

For each trial, the routine creates a new network and gives it a random number of new Nodes positioned randomly on the program's drawing area. Then, for a random number of links, the program picks two of the new nodes at random and uses them to make a new link. The routine assigns the new Link a random Cost.

After it has built this random network, the program saves it into a file. It loads the file into a new NetlabNetwork object and saves the new network into another file.

Next the routine loads the two network files into XmlDocument objects. It removes the comment containing the time the files were written and compares the two document's OuterXml values. If the values are the same, then the two network files are identical (aside from the date and time comment).

Listing 7.1   VB NetLab's tests its network saving and restoring routines by saving and restoring a random network.

```vb
' Verify that the form can save and restore a network correctly.
Public Sub mnuTestFileSaveAndRestore_Click(ByVal sender As Object, _
  ByVal e As System.EventArgs) Handles mnuTestFileSaveAndRestore.Click
    Dim base_name As String = _
        Application.StartupPath & "/SaveAndRestoreTest.net"
    Dim trial As Integer
    Dim max_x As Integer
    Dim max_y As Integer
    Dim rand As New Random()
    Dim xml_document1 As New Xml.XmlDocument()
    Dim xml_document2 As New Xml.XmlDocument()
    Dim new_nodes As Collection
    Dim num_nodes As Integer
    Dim node_num As Integer
    Dim num_links As Integer
    Dim link_num As Integer
    Dim new_node As Node
    Dim new_link As Link
    Dim node_num1 As Integer
    Dim node_num2 As Integer

    ' Make sure the data is safe.
    If Not DataSafe() Then Exit Sub
    max_x = Me.ClientRectangle.Width - 20
    max_y = Me.ClientRectangle.Height - 20
    For trial = 1 To 20
        ' Create a random network.
        m_Network = New NetlabNetwork()
        new_nodes = New Collection()

        ' Make random nodes.
        num_nodes = CInt(1 + rand.NextDouble() * 100)
        For node_num = 1 To num_nodes
            new_node = m_Network.AddNode( _
                CInt(10 + rand.NextDouble() * max_x), _
                CInt(10 + rand.NextDouble() * max_y))
            new_nodes.Add(new_node)
        Next node_num

        ' Make random links.
        num_links = CInt(1 + rand.NextDouble() * 100)
        For link_num = 1 To num_links
            node_num1 = CInt(Int(1 + rand.NextDouble() * num_nodes))
            node_num2 = CInt(Int(1 + rand.NextDouble() * num_nodes))
            new_link = m_Network.AddLink( _
                CType(new_nodes.Item(node_num1), Node), _
                CType(new_nodes.Item(node_num2), Node))
            new_link.Cost = 10 + rand.NextDouble() * 300
        Next link_num

        ' Save the network.
        m_Network.Save(base_name & "1")

        ' Reload the network.
```

LISTING 7.1 CONTINUED

```
        m_Network.Load(base_name & "1")

        ' Save the network again.
        m_Network.Save(base_name & "2")

        ' Load the two network XML documents.
        xml_document1.Load(base_name & "1")
        xml_document2.Load(base_name & "2")

        ' Remove the date and time comments.
        xml_document1.RemoveChild(xml_document1.ChildNodes.Item(2))
        xml_document2.RemoveChild(xml_document2.ChildNodes.Item(2))

        ' Verify that the two documents are identical.
        If xml_document1.OuterXml <> xml_document2.OuterXml Then
            MsgBox("Test failed")
            Stop
        End If

        m_DataModified = False
        m_Network.Draw(picNetwork.CreateGraphics())
    Next trial

    ' Delete the test files.
    Kill(base_name & "1")
    Kill(base_name & "2")

    ' Let the user know we are done.
    MsgBox("Done")
End Sub
```

This test might seem a little silly. After all, the program is basically writing the same network twice and verifying that the two network files are the same. Although it is possible that the file saving and loading routines contain complementary mistakes, it is more likely that they work in the same way. This test would have caught the Link Cost initialization bug if it had not already been discovered by the manual tests described earlier in this section.

USE CASES

Much of VB NetLab deals with the user interface. User interfaces are hard to test automatically. It's difficult to write a routine that moves the mouse to different parts of the screen, right-clicks, selects the Add Node command, and then verifies that a new Node was correctly added at the position clicked.

You can buy tools that perform this kind of test. You walk through a test while the tool records the application's actions. Later the tool can play back the steps you took. The tool can then examine various application properties to see if it got the same result you did. For example, it can see if a text box contains the right value, if an image matches the image you got, and so forth.

This kind of tool is useful for regression testing. In *regression testing*, you perform a series of tests to make sure that recent changes to the code have not broken the application. Although regression testing is an important part of application development and maintenance, it plays a smaller role in prototyping. When you build a prototype, changes are frequent and they often alter the application's previous behavior. With a rapidly changing prototype, automated regression testing often finds error when the change in behavior is intentional. These kinds of tests are more useful later when the application is more stable.

One way to test user interfaces is to use a long series of use cases that describe a series of tasks that the user must perform using the final application, together with the expected results.

EXAMPLE

A typical use case for VB NetLab might look like this:

Title: Make new network

Purpose: Verify data safe features and caption changes when creating a new network.

1. Select the File menu's **New** command to start a new network. Verify that the form is blank and that its caption is VB NetLab [].
2. Right-click the empty form. Verify that the popup menu contains the Add Node item and nothing else.
3. Select **Add Node**. Verify that a node appears. Verify that the form's caption changes to VB NetLab*[].
4. Click the form's **Close** button (the little X in the upper right corner). Verify that the program warns you that the data has been modified and asks if you want to save the changes. Verify that your choices are Yes, No, and Cancel. Click **Cancel**.
5. Select the File menu's **Exit** command. Verify that the program gives you the same warning as in step 4. Again, click **Cancel**.
6. Press **Ctrl+S**. Verify that the program displays a File Save dialog. Click **Cancel**.
7. Repeat tests 4 and 5.
8. Press **Ctrl+S** again. Enter the filename Test.net in the File Save dialog and click **Save**. Verify that the form's caption changes to VB NetLab [Test]. Use Windows Explorer to verify that the file is created.
9. Select the File menu's **Exit** command. Verify that the program closes immediately.

You can see that this use case is very detailed. It explains exactly what the user should do and what the program should do in response. In a formal project, the use cases would be printed out and testers would run through each one, checking off the tests and noting any that fail. A large project might have hundreds of use cases.

Designing and executing use cases can be slow, tedious work. It's also quite important, particularly for testing user interfaces and other parts of the system that are hard to test automatically.

You might be able to get help from your customers in both writing and testing use cases. Writing use cases lets them further specify the system's behavior. Executing the use cases lets them see for themselves that the prototype is following the specification. It also gives the customers more experience with the prototype, and that might help them think of new issues you need to discuss.

PART

II

CH

7

SUMMARY

The best time to test code is right after you write it and it is still fresh in your mind. The longer you wait, the harder it is to understand the code. If you wait too long, any bugs you do find will be harder to fix than they would have been had you caught them right away.

Unfortunately, many developers don't test their code at all. Others test only a few expected situations and do not consider less typical situations that are more likely to make the code fail.

Although a prototype doesn't need to be absolutely perfect to be useful, it should not crash as soon as the customers see it. A prototype is like a facade that shows what the final application will look like. When the customers see a bug, they see the emptiness behind the facade. Instead of focusing on the prototype's features so they can provide meaningful feedback, the customers are distracted by bugs and crashes. Worst of all, a buggy prototype reduces your customers' faith in your ability to finish the application. Do at least some testing to make sure the prototype gives your customers a positive experience.

PART III

PROTOTYPING TECHNIQUES

CHAPTER **8**

WIZARDS

In this chapter

In the context of application development, wizards are not men with funny beards who work at all hours of the night on mysterious projects that only they can understand. Those are programmers.

In this context, a *wizard* is a program that presents you with a series of tabs or forms to ask questions and gather information. When it has collected all the facts it needs, the wizard generates some sort of useful output. Most commercial software packages use a wizard to gather information before installing the program. These wizards ask for such information as your name, company name, the product ID, where the software should be installed, and whether the wizard should make an icon in your startup menu and on the desktop.

VB.NET comes with a variety of wizards that help automate common programming tasks such as displaying Add-Ins, selecting data sources, and connecting to a database. Some can build most of a complete application for you.

The Data Form Wizard provided by VB.NET is particularly useful for building prototypes. By selecting a few options and filling in a few blanks, it lets you quickly build a fully functional data-manipulation program.

The following sections explain some of the biggest dangers of using wizards. The rest of the chapter describes some wizards that can help you quickly build prototypes.

THE TROUBLE WITH WIZARDS

The Data Form Wizard can save you a lot of time and trouble. It can generate code to load data from a database, build classes to represent database records, and bind controls to the data so it is displayed automatically.

Although the Data Form Wizard can save you a lot of work, it has some serious drawbacks. The following sections describe some of the most important Data Form Wizard drawbacks. Actually, these same drawbacks apply to most wizards.

ONE-WAY TRANSFORMATION

The Data Form Wizard combines information about a database with information you enter to generate a form that manipulates the database. This is a one-time, one-way process much like scrambling an egg: After you've done it, you can't go back. You can't present the wizard with a data form and have it back up to recreate the database that produced it.

More importantly, if you change the database, the data form does not change to match. If you add a new field, the automatically generated form will not show it. If you remove a field from the database, the form will probably crash when it tries to load data.

If you make changes to the underlying database, you must either run the wizard again to produce a completely new form or modify the form and its associated code yourself. If the wizard produces exactly the result you want, great. Rerun the wizard and you are finished.

Unfortunately wizards often do almost, but not exactly, what you want. That is the next big problem with wizards.

CLOSE BUT NOT PERFECT

A wizard does what it does and nothing else. If it doesn't do exactly what you want, you're out of luck. You cannot cajole the wizard into making a few changes no matter how small they are. If you really need some changes, you'll have to make them yourself.

Changing the wizard's code is like breaking the seal marked "Warranty void if broken" on the bottom of your toaster. After you modify the wizard's output, you're on your own. If you break the wizard's code, you'll have to fix it yourself. The wizard cannot help you.

Even worse, if you make changes to the database or other underlying data the wizard used to write the code, you cannot easily rerun the wizard. If you do, you'll lose any changes you made and you'll need to make them again. Unless you take very careful notes, you are likely to forget to make the changes or to make them incorrectly the next time.

The alternative is to modify the wizard's original output to take the new changes into account. For example, if you add a new field to a database table, you can add code to load and display the new field. That's possible if you can figure out how the wizard's code works, but it means making even more changes that you will have to maintain in the future.

Example

Suppose you build a prototype database to hold employee data. You enter some test records and use the Data Form Wizard to build a form displaying the records in a grid. Unfortunately, the grid initially displays the table's columns in alphabetical order so you do some work to rearrange the columns so they make more sense. You also change the grid's appearance a little, remove the Load button created by default, and add code to load the data automatically when the form loads (you'll see how later in this chapter). The result is shown in Figure 8.1.

After you work with this version of the prototype for a while, the customer decides the table should contain an additional Fax field to hold employees' fax extensions. You have to make a tough decision. You can modify the database and then use the Data Form Wizard to make a new form. In that case, you'll need to reapply all the changes you made to modify the grid's appearance, rearrange its columns, and display the data automatically.

Alternatively, you can pull open the code written by the Data Form Wizard and try to figure out how it works. You could then add code to load the new field and display it with the others. Either way, you're in for a lot of work.

Figure 8.1

This form was created by the Data Form Wizard and then modified.

LastName	FirstName	EmployeeId	Office	Extension	Grade	HomeStreet	HomeCity
Appledorf	Angela	2716	8-2761	4526	7	21435 Programmer Ln	Bugsville
Balentine	Bernard	673	2-3279	3878	6	3762 Debugger Wy	Bugsville
Chandery	Cindy	3767	8-3277	4766	8	746 Manager Pl	Bugsville
Danvers	Darleene	5476	6-3876	6435	7	7326 Hacker Ave	Bugsville
Edwards	Evan	5786	2-1897	0436	7	435 Rundown Ct #32B	Cityburg
Frederickson	Francine	7598	7-1001	2767	9	47 Executive Glen	Posh Acres
Glenarsdale	Giovani	7367	3-9287	0000	4	746 Secretary St	Abend

The Data Form Wizard lets you specify several options so it can build a wide variety of different data forms. Hopefully one of those will be close enough to what you want that you can live with it. Then, you can regenerate the form whenever you need to and you won't have to worry about reapplying modifications.

UGLY CODE

Wizards often produce code that is easy for them to generate but hard for you to understand. The code might include few or no comments, the indentation might be sloppy, and variables and methods might not follow your naming conventions. The code usually includes no explanation of its general approach, so the code seems to do things for no apparent reason.

Listing 8.1 shows some of the EmployeeClass generated by the Data Form Wizard to create the form shown in Figure 8.1. Note the lack of comments and seemingly random values pulled out of the air. For example, why does the code use http://www.tempuri.org/EmplopyeeClass.xsd for the Namespace of the class? What is Namespace anyway?

These things are hidden behind the scenes and are used to load data into a grid control using ADO.NET. If you know enough about ADO.NET, you can figure this out. If you just wanted to display data from a local database in a grid, you might have no idea how this all works. In that case, modifying the code in Listing 8.1 is a certain path to disaster.

LISTING 8.1 THIS IS A SMALL PART OF THE CODE GENERATED BY THE DATA FORM WIZARD GENERATED FOR THE FORM SHOWN IN FIGURE 8.1.

```
Public Class EmplopyeeClass
    Inherits System.Data.DataSet

    Private tableCount As Integer
    Private relationCount As Integer
    Private tableEmployeesTable As EmployeesTable

    Public Sub New()
        MyBase.New
        Me.InitClass
    End Sub

    Public Overridable ReadOnly Property
<System.ComponentModel.PersistContentsAttribute(true)> Employees As EmployeesTable
        Get
            Return Me.tableEmployeesTable
        End Get
    End Property

    Private Sub InitClass()
        Me.DataSetName = "EmplopyeeClass"
        Me.Namespace = "http://www.tempuri.org/EmplopyeeClass.xsd"
        Me.tableCount = 1
        Me.relationCount = 0
        Me.tableEmployeesTable = New EmployeesTable("Employees")
```

LISTING 8.1   CONTINUED

```
        Me.Tables.Add(Me.tableEmployeesTable)
    End Sub
    Protected Overrides Function HasSchemaChanged() As Boolean
        Return (((Me.tableCount) <> (Me.Tables.Count))) Or (((Me.relationCount)
<> (Me.Relations.Count))))
    End Function
    Public Overrides Function ShouldPersistTables() As Boolean
        Return ((Me.tableCount) <> (Me.Tables.Count))
    End Function
    Public Overrides Function ShouldPersistRelations() As Boolean
        Return ((Me.relationCount) <> (Me.Relations.Count))
    End Function
    Public Overrides Sub ResetTables()
        Dim i As Integer = 0
        Do While ((i) < (Me.Tables.Count))
            If ((Me.Tables(i)) = (Me.tableEmployeesTable)) Then
            Else
                Me.Tables.Remove(Me.Tables(i))
            End If
            i = ((i) + (1))
        Loop
    End Sub
    Public Overrides Sub ResetRelations()
        Dim i As Integer = 0
        Do While ((i) < (Me.Relations.Count))
            Me.Relations.Remove(Me.Relations(i))
            i = ((i) + (1))
        Loop
    End Sub


    Public Delegate Sub EmployeesRowChangeEventHandler(ByVal sender As [object],
ByVal e As EmployeesRowChangeEvent)

    Public Class EmployeesTable
        Inherits DataTable
        Implements System.Collections.ICollection

        Private columnCount As Integer
        Private constraintCount As Integer
        Private columnLastName As Employees_LastName
        Private columnFirstName As Employees_FirstName
        Private columnEmployeeId As Employees_EmployeeId
        Private columnExtension As Employees_Extension
        Private columnGrade As Employees_Grade
        Private columnHomeCity As Employees_HomeCity
        Private columnHomeState As Employees_HomeState
        Private columnHomeStreet As Employees_HomeStreet
        Private columnHomeZip As Employees_HomeZip
        Private columnOffice As Employees_Office
        Public EmployeesRowChanged As EmployeesRowChangeEventHandler
        Public EmployeesRowChanging As EmployeesRowChangeEventHandler
        Public EmployeeIdColumnChanging As DataColumnChangeEventHandler
        Public ExtensionColumnChanging As DataColumnChangeEventHandler
        Public FirstNameColumnChanging As DataColumnChangeEventHandler
```

LISTING 8.1 CONTINUED

```
    Public GradeColumnChanging As DataColumnChangeEventHandler
    Public HomeCityColumnChanging As DataColumnChangeEventHandler
    Public HomeStateColumnChanging As DataColumnChangeEventHandler
    Public HomeStreetColumnChanging As DataColumnChangeEventHandler
    Public HomeZipColumnChanging As DataColumnChangeEventHandler
    Public LastNameColumnChanging As DataColumnChangeEventHandler
    Public OfficeColumnChanging As DataColumnChangeEventHandler


        Public Default ReadOnly Property Item(ByVal index As Integer) As
EmployeesRow
        Get
            return CType(Me.Rows(index), EmployeesRow)
        End Get
    End Property
        Public Overloads Sub New(ByVal name As [string])
            MyBase.New(name)
            Me.InitClass
        End Sub
        Public Overloads Sub New()
            MyBase.New("Employees")
            Me.InitClass
        End Sub


        Public Overridable ReadOnly Property Count As Integer Implements
System.Collections.ICollection.Count
            Get
                Return Me.Rows.Count
            End Get
        End Property
        Public Overridable ReadOnly Property
System_Collections_ICollection_IsReadOnly As Boolean Implements
System.Collections.ICollection.IsReadOnly
            Get
                Return false
            End Get
        End Property
```

Code generated by wizards is usually hard to understand so it's hard to modify safely. If you make changes without fully understanding the code, you are just as likely to create new bugs as you are to make things better.

WIZARD TROUBLE CONCLUSIONS

The code generated by a wizard can save you a lot of time, but it can also make a lot of trouble. If a wizard does exactly what you need, you are in luck. Use the wizard and do not modify the code it produces.

If the wizard does almost what you want, see if you can live with what it can do. It might be worth a little inconvenience not to have to worry about keeping modifications to the code up to date.

If you really need to make changes to the wizard's output, see whether you can live with the wizard's raw output during prototyping and describe how the final application will be different. Then if you make changes to the underlying database during prototype development, you can rerun the wizard without losing any modifications you have made. When you start building the final application, the database design should be fairly complete so you won't need to change it later. You can run the wizard one last time and then make your modifications with less chance that you will need to rerun the wizard later.

Although wizards have their drawbacks, they are great for building prototypes. You might want to make changes in the final application, but they can often put together something reasonable with little effort on your part.

THE DATA FORM WIZARD

The Data Form Wizard lets you build several different kinds of data forms quickly and easily. These forms can display all the records in a database table in a grid, in multiple grids showing master/detail relationships, or separately one record at a time.

There are five basic steps to using the Data Form Wizard:

1. Create the database.
2. Create a new form.
3. Create an `ADODataSetCommand` object.
4. Invoke the `Generate DataSet` and `Generate DataSetCommand` Methods.
5. Invoke the Data Form Wizard.

These steps are described in the following sections. Some are rather complicated.

CREATE THE DATABASE

Use your favorite database tool to build the database you will use. It is important that the database you build is as close to correct as possible. If you make changes to the database, the code generated by the Data Form Wizard will not automatically take the changes into account. If you must change the database, you will need to either rerun the wizard or modify the code yourself to take the changes into account. In the first case, you will destroy any changes you have made manually. In the second case, you might add bugs to the code and you will need to maintain any changes you make later.

CREATE A NEW PROJECT

To create a new project to hold the new data form, choose File, New, Project. Click the Visual Basic Projects project type and select Windows Application. Enter the project's name and location in the text boxes. Do this now so the project is placed in a reasonable location. If you don't enter the name and location now, Visual Basic gives the project a default name such as WindowsApplication1 and places it in whatever directory you happened to be using last. After you pick an application name and location, click OK.

To add a new data form to an existing project, choose Project, Add Windows Form. Select the Local Project Items category and click Windows Form. Give the new form a name and click Open.

CREATE AN ADODataSetCommand OBJECT

Open the Windows form that you want to make into the new data form. In the Toolbox, click the Data tab. Click the ADODataSetCommand object, drag it onto the form, and drop it there. This starts the DataSetCommand Configuration Wizard. The wizard walks you through the process of creating a new ADODataSetCommand object and adding it to the form.

Figure 8.2 shows the steps you take to work through the DataSetCommand Configuration Wizard. The following sections describe these steps in detail and show what the wizard looks like during the process. This seems like a lot of steps but they are easy enough if you take them one at a time.

Figure 8.2
You can use this diagram to navigate the DataSetCommand Configuration Wizard.

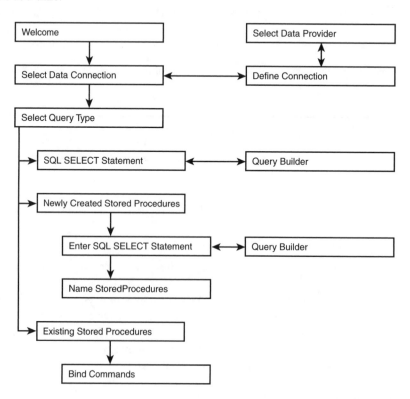

Tip

You can use the DataSetCommand Configuration Wizard later to reconfigure the DataSetCommand object. Open the form and click the DataSetCommand object. The Properties window lists several commands under the last property. Click the command labeled Configure DataSetCommand to restart the DataSetCommand Configuration Wizard.

WELCOME

The DataSetCommand Configuration Wizard begins with the welcome screen shown in Figure 8.3. This screen just introduces the wizard. Click Next.

Figure 8.3
The DataSetCommand Configuration Wizard's welcome screen introduces the wizard.

SELECT DATA CONNECTION

The next screen, shown in Figure 8.4, lets you select the database connection the form will use to display data. If you have data connections already configured, you can select one from the drop-down list.

Figure 8.4
Use this screen to select a data connection.

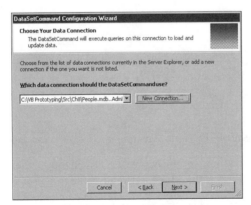

If you have no data connections configured, click the New Connection button to make the Data Link Properties dialog box shown in Figure 8.5 appear. VB.NET assumes you will be using SQL Server so this dialog box begins with SQL Server selected as the data provider.

If you do not want to use SQL Server, click the Provider tab and select the data provider you want. In Figure 8.6, the Jet 4.0 OLE DB Provider is selected. This provider works with Access (.mdb) databases.

Figure 8.5
If you want to use an SQL Server data provider, specify its connection information.

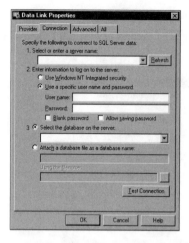

Figure 8.6
Select a data provider. Here the Jet 4.0 OLE DB Provider is selected.

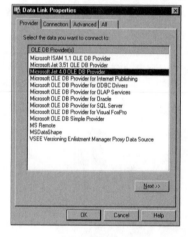

After you chose a provider, click the Next button or the Connection tab.

Fill in the connection information for whichever data provider you selected. Figure 8.7 shows the Connection tab filled in for a Jet 4.0 data provider.

After you have selected a data provider and filled in the necessary connection information, click the Test Connection button. The dialog box tries to open the database to make sure you have specified valid connection information. If the test fails, fix the connection information and try again.

After you successfully test the database connection, click the OK button to finish specifying the connection.

Figure 8.7
Specify connection
information for the
Jet 4.0 data provider.

SELECT QUERY TYPE

After you have selected a data connection, the DataSetCommand Configuration Wizard
displays the form shown in Figure 8.8. Here you can decide which method the new
DataSetCommand will use to access the database. The three options are using an SQL statement, using new stored procedures, and using existing stored procedures. Pick the method
you want to use and click Next. The three options are described in the following sections.

Figure 8.8
Pick a query type
from this wizard
dialog box.

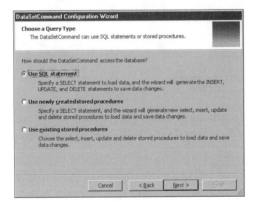

SQL STATEMENT

If you decide to use an SQL statement, the DataSetCommand Configuration Wizard displays the form shown in Figure 8.9. Enter an SQL SELECT statement that picks the records
you want to display.

Figure 8.9
Define the SQL state-
ment that selects
records for the
DataSetCommand.

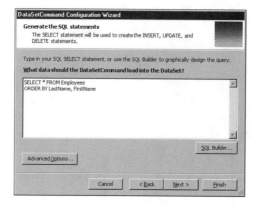

If you like, you can use the Query Builder to help compose the SELECT statement. Click the SQL Builder button on the form shown in Figure 8.9 to see the Query Builder (see Figure 8.10).

Figure 8.10
Use SQL Builder to
define an SQL
SELECT statement.

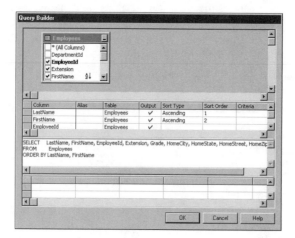

If no tables appear at the top of Query Builder, right click in the upper area and select the Add Table command. Select the table you want to use and click Add.

Check the boxes next to the fields you want to display.

> **Tip**
>
> Select the fields in the order in which you want them displayed. Query Builder adds them to the query in that order.

For each field you want to use in sorting the returned records, click the Sort Order column and enter the field's sort order. The query in Figure 8.10 specifies that the records should be sorted first by LastName and then by FirstName.

When you have finished building the query, click OK.

> **Tip**
>
> If you want to modify the SELECT statement later, open the form and click the DataSetCommand object. In the Properties window, find the SelectCommand property and click the plus sign to its left to expand it. Enter the new SELECT statement in the CommandText field.
>
> If you want to use the Query Builder to modify the statement, click the ellipsis (...) to the right of the CommandText field.

After you have entered the SQL SELECT statement you want to use, click Next to see the screen shown in Figure 8.11. When you click the Finish button, the wizard makes an ADODataSetCommand object configured using the settings you entered. It also creates an ADOConnection object to connect the ADODataSetCommand to the database you selected.

Figure 8.11
Finish up with the DataSetCommand Configuration Wizard.

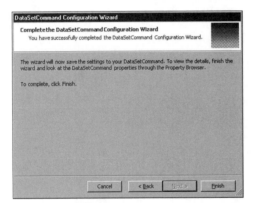

Connecting the DataSetCommand object to the database using an SQL SELECT statement is relatively easy. Using stored procedures as described in the next two sections has its advantages, but entering in an SQL statement is a bit simpler.

NEW STORED PROCEDURES

When you attach a DataSetCommand object to a database using an SQL SELECT statement, the SELECT statement is coded into the DataSetCommand object's properties. If you decide to change the statement later, you need to open the program in the development environment and modify the properties. Initially creating the DataSetCommand object is easy. Unfortunately you need to recompile the application to change the connection information.

Instead of placing the SELECT statement inside the DataSetCommand object's properties, you can have the DataSetCommand invoke stored procedures contained in the database to access the data. The stored procedures contain code that selects, adds, updates, and deletes records. Now the `DataSetCommand` object does not need to know all the details of working with the data, it just needs to know the names of the stored procedures.

To make changes to the way records are selected, you only need to change the definition of the stored procedures in the database. You don't need to recompile the application because the `DataSetCommand` object uses the same stored procedures.

This can be handy if the details of how the records are selected will change frequently. On the other hand, this is not a perfect solution either. Although you can change the stored procedure's internal details, you can't really change their inputs and outputs. The `DataSetCommand` object includes information telling it which parameters in the stored procedures correspond to which fields it should display. If you change the stored procedures' parameters, the `DataSetCommand` object might not display the right values.

If you decide to connect the `DataSetCommand` to the database using new stored procedures, the DataSetCommand Configuration Wizard displays the form shown in Figure 8.12. Enter an SQL SELECT statement that selects the records you want to display. The wizard will use that statement to build the stored procedures it uses to display, add, modify, and delete records.

Figure 8.12
Enter a SELECT statement for use in new stored procedures.

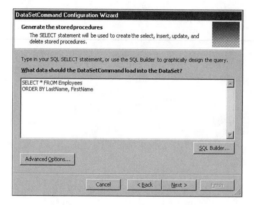

If you want, you can use the Query Builder to compose the SELECT statement just as you can when you attach the `DataSetCommand` object to the database using an SQL statement. (See the earlier "SQL Statement" section in this chapter for details.)

After you have entered the SELECT statement, click Next to see the screen shown in Figure 8.13.

After you enter the names for the stored procedures, click the Preview SQL Script button to see the SQL statements the wizard will use to create the procedures. Click the Next button to make the wizard continue. If you check the Yes, Create Them in the Database for Me check box, the wizard automatically adds the stored procedures to the database.

Figure 8.13
Enter the names
you want the wizard
to give the stored
procedures.

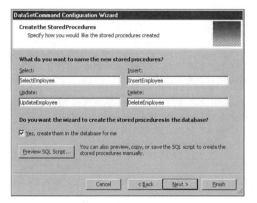

After the wizard creates the stored procedures, the screen shown in Figure 8.11 appears to indicate that the wizard has finished collecting data. When you click the Finish button, the wizard makes an ADODataSetCommand object configured using the settings you entered. It also creates an ADOConnection object to connect the ADODataSetCommand to the database you selected.

EXISTING STORED PROCEDURES

If you have already written stored procedures for selecting, adding, updating, and deleting records, you can tell the wizard to connect the DataSetCommand object to the database using them. When you tell the wizard to use existing stored procedures, you see the screen shown in Figure 8.14.

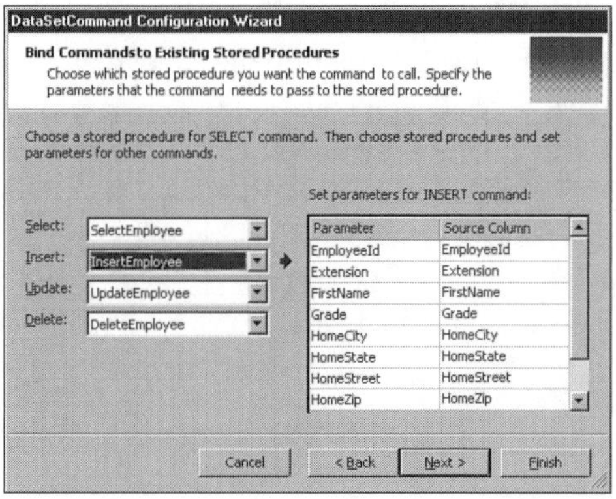

Figure 8.14
You can bind com-
mands to stored
procedures.

Use the Select drop-down list to pick the stored procedure the wizard should use to select records. Similarly use the Insert, Update, and Delete drop-down lists to pick stored procedures for the other commands.

After you have assigned one of these commands, you need to tell the wizard which stored procedure parameters correspond to which database columns. If you give the stored procedure parameters the same names as the corresponding database columns, the wizard is smart enough to guess that they should match. For example, the following code shows the text used to define the InsertEmployee stored procedure:

```
CREATE PROCEDURE InsertEmployee(@LastName VARCHAR, @FirstName VARCHAR,
  @EmployeeId VARCHAR, @Office VARCHAR, @Extension VARCHAR, @Grade VARCHAR,
  @HomeStreet VARCHAR, @HomeCity VARCHAR, @HomeState VARCHAR, @HomeZip VARCHAR)
AS
  INSERT INTO Employees (LastName, FirstName, EmployeeId, Office, Extension,
    Grade, HomeStreet, HomeCity, HomeState, HomeZip)
  VALUES (@LastName, @FirstName, @EmployeeId, @Office, @Extension, @Grade,
    @HomeStreet, @HomeCity, @HomeState, @HomeZip)
```

In this procedure, the LastName parameter corresponds to the LastName database column, the FirstName parameter corresponds to the FirstName column, and so on.

If the parameter names do not match, you need to help the wizard make the association. Click the Source Column entry for each parameter and select the corresponding database column from the drop-down list.

After you define the stored procedures the wizard should use, click Next to see the final wizard's screen shown in Figure 8.11. Click the Finish button to finish initializing the ADOConnection and ADODataSetCommand objects.

INVOKE THE GENERATE DATASET AND GENERATE DATASETCOMMAND METHODS

Open the form that contains the ADOConnection and ADODataSetCommand objects you created. Choose DataClass, Generate DataSet. Give the new DataSet a name like dsEmployees and check the box indicating you want an instance of the class added to the designer.

Then from the same menu, select Generate DataSetCommand Methods. You can also find both of these commands in the Properties window below the last property.

These commands make a DataSet class representing the data you have selected. The class includes all the methods needed to load, add, update, and delete records from the DataSet. You should see an .xsd file in the Solution Explorer. This file is an XML schema that defines the DataSet's format. If you click the Show All Files tool at the top of the Solution Explorer, you will see that this file has a subitem. Click the plus sign to the left of the .xsd file to expand it and you will see the DataSet class. Select the class and click the View Code tool to see the code that the wizard generated. You probably shouldn't modify the code, but it's interesting to look at.

INVOKE THE DATA FORM WIZARD

Finally you can invoke the Data Form Wizard itself. Open the form containing the DataSetCommand. Select the Data tab in the Toolbox, and then click and drag the DataFormWizard tool onto the form.

The Data Form Wizard leads you through a series of steps much like the DataSetCommand Configuration Wizard does. The basic steps are

1. The Welcome screen appears.

2. Select DataSet.

3. Select Data Load Method.

4. Select Fields To Display.

5. Select Display Style.

These steps are described in the following sections.

THE WELCOME SCREEN APPEARS

Like the DataSetCommand Configuration Wizard, the Data Form Wizard begins with a Welcome screen (see Figure 8.15). Click Next to start configuring the data form.

Figure 8.15
The Data Form Wizard starts by showing the Welcome screen.

SELECT DATASET

In the Data Form Wizard's next screen, shown in Figure 8.16, select the DataSet you want to display on the form. If you followed the steps in the earlier sections in this chapter, you will have only one DataSet named dsEmployees. The "DFWQuery1" in the DataSet name shown in Figure 8.16 is the name of the application.

Figure 8.16
Select the DataSet to display on the form.

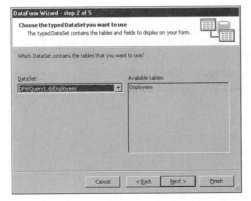

After you select the DataSet to display, click Next.

SELECT DATA LOAD METHOD

The Data Form Wizard's next screen, shown in Figure 8.17, lets you specify the method the form should use to load data from the DataSet. Select the FillDataSet method. This method was created when you executed the Generate DataSetCommand Methods command described earlier in this chapter.

Figure 8.17
Select the form's data load method.

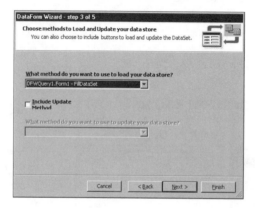

If you check the Include Update Method check box, the Data Form Wizard will include code to allow the user to save changes to the data. By default, this box is not checked and the database is not updated with any changes the user makes to the DataSet. If you check this box, you must also specify the method the program should use to save the modified data. In this example, you would select the UpdateDataSource method that was created at the same time as the FillDataSet method.

SELECT FIELDS TO DISPLAY

After you have specified the data load and update methods, the wizard displays the screen shown in Figure 8.18. Select the fields you want displayed on the form and click the Next button.

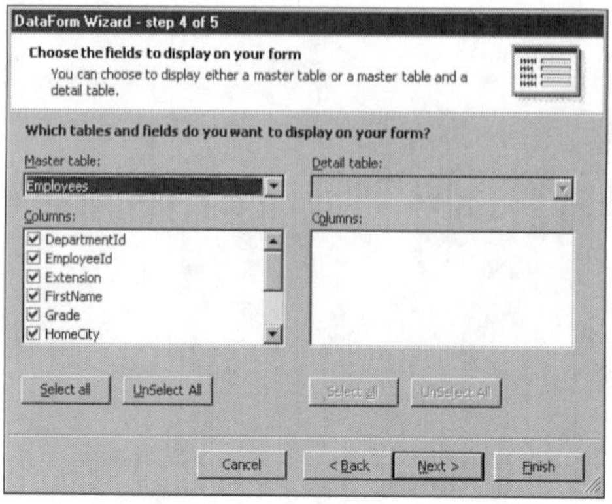

Figure 8.18
Select the fields to display on the form.

SELECT DISPLAY STYLE

The Data Form Wizard's next screen, shown in Figure 8.19, lets you decide between a grid display that shows all the records in the DataSet at once, and a single record display that shows one record at a time.

Figure 8.19
Select the display style.

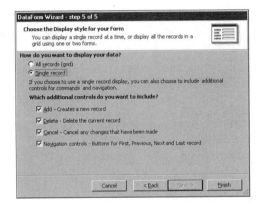

GRID DISPLAY

If you select a grid display and click the Finish button, the wizard creates a form similar to the one shown in Figure 8.20. In this example, the Data Form Wizard did not include an update method so any changes to the DataSet are not copied back to the database.

Figure 8.20
You can display all records in a single grid.

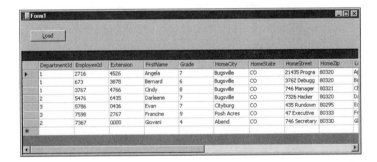

Click the Load button to make the program load the DataSet into the grid. Click a column header to make the grid sort the records using the corresponding field. Click the header again to reverse the sort. A little arrow to the right of the header's text shows the sort order.

To modify a field, click the field's cell and type in the new value. To delete a record, click the leftmost column to select that record. Then press the Delete key.

To add a new record, click one of the fields in the bottommost row (the one with the asterisk in the leftmost column). The program creates a new row that initially contains all null values. Click the fields to fill in the new values.

The grid display provides a simple, intuitive method for the user to view and manipulate a lot of data at once. It works well when the user wants to compare fields for different records. It works best when the records contain few enough fields that they can all fit on the screen at one time.

SINGLE RECORD DISPLAY

If you select a single record display and click the Finish button, the wizard creates a form similar to the one shown in Figure 8.21.

Figure 8.21
You also can display records one at a time.

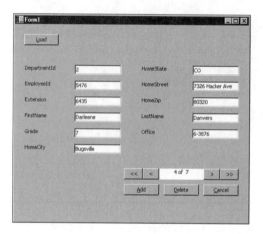

Click the Load button to load the DataSet. In this example, the Data Form Wizard included an update method. After you have made changes to the DataSet, click the Update button to transfer the changes to the underlying database.

After you have loaded the DataSet, you can use the navigation buttons <<, <, >, and >> to move through the DataSet.

To modify a field, type the new value in the corresponding text box. To delete the current record, click the Delete button. To add a new record, click the Add button.

While you are editing a record, you can cancel your changes by clicking the Cancel button. If you move to another record without canceling the changes, the changes become permanent.

The form produced by the Data Form Wizard takes a few silent actions. For example, if you enter invalid data in a field, the program will not let you move the focus out of that field. In particular, if you enter letters in a numeric field, focus stays trapped in that field.

The single-record display works well if the user wants to see all the fields for a single record at one time. It is particularly handy when there are too many fields in each record to fit on the screen in a grid.

CUSTOMIZING GRID DISPLAYS

The initial layout of the grid display leaves something to be desired. The columns are all the same width no matter how big the data in each field is, the fields are arranged alphabetically rather than in some more meaningful order, and the user must click the Load button to load the data. You can easily customize the form to make a few improvements.

To make the form size its columns to fit the data, set the control's `PreferredColumnWidth` property equal to `AutoColumnSize`. To automatically load and update the DataSet, move the code in the Load and Update buttons into the form's `New` and `Dispose` methods:

```
Public Sub New()
    MyBase.New

    Form1 = Me

    ' This call is required by the Win Form Designer.
    InitializeComponent

    ' Load the DataSet.
    Me.LoadDataSet()

    ' Size the columns to fit the data.
    grdEmployees.PreferredColumnWidth = grdEmployees.AutoColumnSize
End Sub

'Form overrides dispose to clean up the component list.
Public Overrides Sub Dispose()
    ' Try to save the data.
    Try
        Me.UpdateDataSet()
    Catch eUpdate As System.Exception
        System.WinForms.MessageBox.Show(eUpdate.Message)
    End Try

    MyBase.Dispose()
    components.Dispose()
End Sub
```

To change the grid's column order, open the form and click the grid control to select it. In the Properties window, select the `GridTables` property and click the ellipsis on the right to display the DataGridTable Collection Editor shown in Figure 8.22.

Select the `GridColumns` property and click the ellipsis on the right to display the DataGridColumn Collection Editor shown in Figure 8.23.

Click the members of the collection and look at their Header properties to see which fields they are. For example, in Figure 8.23 the selected column is the EmployeeId field. Use the up- and down-arrow buttons to arrange the fields in the order you want. When you have finished, click the OK button. Figure 8.24 shows the result.

Figure 8.22
Open the DataGridTable Collection Editor to modify the grid's column ordering.

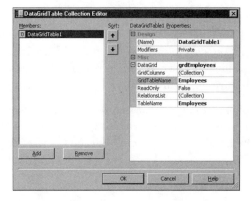

Figure 8.23
The DataGridColumn Collection Editor lets you change the ordering of the grid columns.

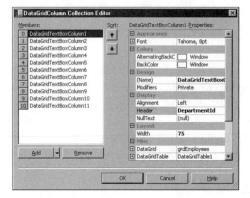

Figure 8.24
This grid display lists the database fields in a more natural order.

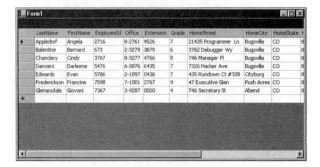

These changes are not difficult to make but they can take some time. If you change the underlying database, you might want to rerun the Data Form Wizard to rebuild the form. In that case, you will lose the changes and you will have to make them again. If you decide to customize the form like this, keep notes on what you changed so you can make the changes again quickly if necessary.

CUSTOMIZING SINGLE-RECORD DISPLAYS

The initial single-record display also has a few problems. All the fields have the same width regardless of the width of the data, the fields are arranged alphabetically and in somewhat arbitrary positions, and the form requires the user to click the Load and Update buttons to load and save the data.

These problems are even easier to fix than they are for the grid display. Move the data loading and updating code into the form's New and Dispose methods as before. The following code also adds a statement to update the record number displayed after the data is first loaded:

```
Public Sub New()
    MyBase.New()

    Form1 = Me

    ' This call is required by the Win Form Designer.
    InitializeComponent()

    ' Load the DataSet.
    Me.LoadDataSet()

    ' Update the record number display.
    Me.mfp_lblNavLocation.Text = _
        (((((Me.BindingManager(objdsEmployees, "Employees").Position) + _
            (1)).ToString) + (" of  "))) + _
            (Me.objdsEmployees.Tables("Employees").Rows.Count.ToString))
End Sub

'Form overrides dispose to clean up the component list.
Public Overrides Sub Dispose()
    ' Try to save the data.
    Try
        Me.UpdateDataSet()
    Catch eUpdate As System.Exception
        System.WinForms.MessageBox.Show(eUpdate.Message)
    End Try

    MyBase.Dispose()
    components.Dispose()
End Sub
```

Rearrange the controls on the form to give the appearance you want. Be sure to change the controls' TabIndex properties so the user can tab between them in a natural order. Figure 8.25 shows one possible version of the form.

Figure 8.25
This single-record display shows its fields in a more natural order.

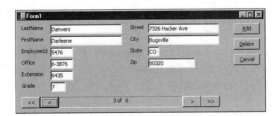

These changes are mostly straightforward but they can be time consuming. If you change the underlying database, you might need to rerun the Data Form Wizard to rebuild the form. In that case, these changes are lost and you will have to apply them again. If you decide to customize the generated form like this, be sure to keep notes on what you changed so you can make the changes again as quickly as possible.

MASTER/DETAIL DATA

You can use the Data Form Wizard to display master/detail data. One table—the master—defines a group of records. A different table provides corresponding detail for each master record.

Example
Suppose a database contains a Departments table with the fields DepartmentName and DepartmentId. The Employees table includes a DepartmentId field giving each employee's department. For each record in the Departments table, the Employees table lists the employees that belong to the department.

Building a master/detail display using the Data Form Wizard uses many of the same techniques described in earlier sections in this chapter.

First, start a new project. From the Data tab in the Toolbox, drag an ADODataSetCommand object onto the form. Configure the object as described in the "Create an ADODataSetCommand" section earlier in this chapter. Select or create a new data connection as before. Use an SQL statement to define the records selected by the DataSetCommand. Make the statement select the master records. Be sure to include the DepartmentId field that will link the master and detail records together, as in the following example:

```
SELECT DepartmentName, DepartmentId
FROM Departments
ORDER BY DepartmentName
```

After you have created this ADODataSetCommand to select the master records, create another one to select the detail records. Select the same data connection. Use an SQL statement that selects the detail records. Be sure to include the DepartmentId field that will link the master and detail records:

```
SELECT LastName, FirstName, Office, Extension, EmployeeId, DepartmentId
FROM Employees
ORDER BY LastName, FirstName
```

Make sure the form is open and select DataClass, Generate DataSet. Give the DataSet a meaningful name such as dsDepartmentsEmployees, check the Add an Instance of This Class to the Designer check box, and click OK.

At this point, VB.NET creates an xsd file that defines the DataSets generated by the ADODataSetCommand objects you created. Double-click the xsd file to open the XML Designer. The display should look something like Figure 8.26.

Figure 8.26
The XML Designer displays the structure of the two DataSets you created.

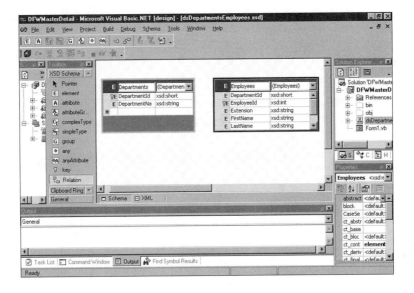

Open the XSD Schema tab in the Toolbox and drag a `Relationship` object onto the detail DataSet. In this example, that is the Employees DataSet. This opens the Relation Editor shown in Figure 8.27. The editor should be smart enough to guess that the DepartmentId field in the Departments DataSet links to the DepartmentId field in the Employees DataSet.

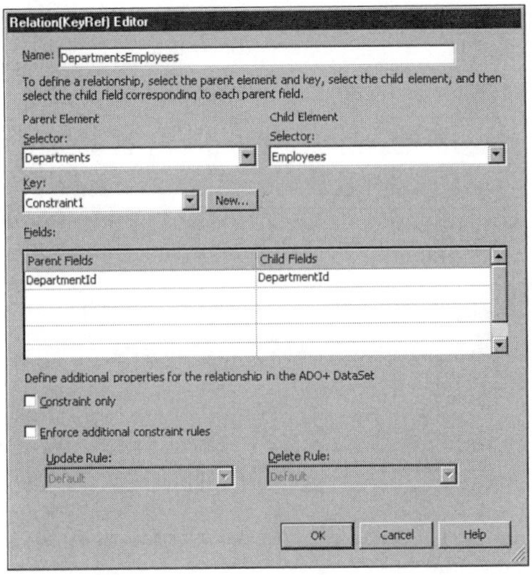

Figure 8.27
The Relation Editor defines the relationship between the master and detail DataSets.

When you click OK, the Relation Editor adds a relationship icon with lines connecting the two tables to the XML Designer as shown in Figure 8.28.

Figure 8.28
The XML Designer shows a `Relationship` object connecting the master and detail DataSets.

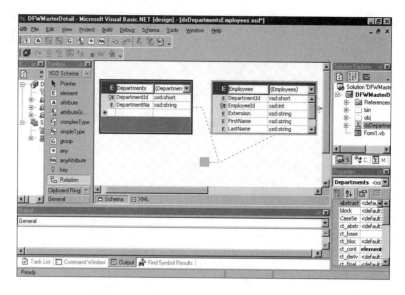

If you need to modify the `Relationship` object later, right-click it in the XML Designer and select the Edit Relationship command.

After you have defined the master and detail DataSets and the relationship between them, reopen the form. Choose DataClass, Generate DataSetCommand Methods. From the Build menu, select the Build command to compile the project and resolve any internal references.

Now you are finally ready to use the Data Form Wizard. Make sure the form is still open and click the Data tab in the Toolbox. Drag the DataFormWizard tool from the Toolbox onto the form. The wizard will run much as it is described in the "Invoke the Data Form Wizard" section earlier in this chapter.

When the wizard asks you to select a DataSet in step 2, pick the DataSet you created. In this example, the DataSet is called `DFWMasterDetail.dsDepartmentsEmployees`. Here `DFWMasterDetail` is the name of the project.

The wizard lists two tables available in the DataSet. These are the results of the two `DataSetCommand` objects you created. They represent the master and detail records.

Click Next and select the method the form should use to load data. Pick the `FillDataSet` method as in the previous examples.

When you click Next again, the wizard displays the screen shown in Figure 8.29. When this screen first appears, all the master fields are selected but none of the detail fields are selected. Select the master and detail fields you want the form to display.

Figure 8.29
Select the master and
detail fields to display.

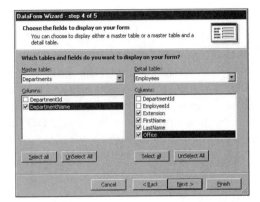

In many applications, you might not want to display the field that links the master and details records. Like the DepartmentId field in this example, these fields are often just used to link tables together and they are not meaningful to the user.

Continue working through the wizard's screens. Select a grid display and finish building the form. The final result is shown in Figure 8.30.

Figure 8.30
The Data Form
Wizard generates this
kind of form to dis-
play master/detail
relationships.

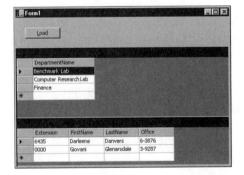

Like other automatically generated forms, this one has some problems. You can customize it to make it look better, automatically load and save data, and so on.

OTHER WIZARDS

VB.NET includes several other useful wizards, including the Add-In Wizard, Deploy Wizard, and Migration Wizard. These are more general programming wizards that are less useful for quickly building a prototype. For example, the Add-In Wizard helps you build add-ins that extend the Visual Basic development environment. Building new development tools like this can be useful but the topic is outside the scope of this book.

The Migration Wizard helps translate programs written in previous versions of Visual Basic into VB.NET applications. Simply open the existing project and the wizard will help you update the project. In some cases, at least until you get used to VB.NET, you might be able to build a prototype faster using Visual Basic 6. Then, you can use the Migration Wizard to upgrade the project to VB.NET later.

One wizard-like tool that has an unexpected use is the Data Link Properties dialog box. Some database programs open their databases at runtime using a connection string. The connection string format is complex, so composing one from scratch can be difficult. For example, the following code shows how a program might set an ADO connection string for an Access database with the location stored in the db_name variable:

```
conn.ConnectionString = _
    "Provider=Microsoft.Jet.OLEDB.4.0;" & _
    "Data Source=" & db_name & ";" & _
    "Persist Security Info=False"
```

To use the Data Link Properties dialog box to compose a connection string, go to the Server Explorer window and double-click the Add Connection item. This opens the Data Link Properties dialog box shown earlier in Figures 8.5, 8.6, and 8.7. Use the dialog box to link to the database and click OK.

In Server Explorer, find the new database link and click it. The ConnectString property shown in the Properties window gives you the information you need to set a connection string at runtime.

For example, the Data Link Properties dialog box generates the following ConnectString (all on one line). If you want to add this string to your source code as a quoted string, you should replace the double quotes with single quotes so Visual Basic doesn't get confused by quotes within a quoted string. You can also remove fields that you do not need to set explicitly. This string is roughly equivalent to the previous three-line version:

```
Provider=Microsoft.Jet.OLEDB.4.0;
Password="";
User ID=Admin;
Data Source=C:\VB Prototyping\Src\Ch8\People.mdb;
Mode=Share Deny None;
Extended Properties="";
Jet OLEDB:System database="";
Jet OLEDB:Registry Path="";
Jet OLEDB:Database Password="";
Jet OLEDB:Engine Type=4;
Jet OLEDB:Database Locking Mode=0;
Jet OLEDB:Global Partial Bulk Ops=2;
Jet OLEDB:Global Bulk Transactions=1;
Jet OLEDB:New Database Password="";
Jet OLEDB:Create System Database=False;
Jet OLEDB:Encrypt Database=False;
Jet OLEDB:Don't Copy Locale on Compact=False;
Jet OLEDB:Compact Without Replica Repair=False;
Jet OLEDB:SFP=False
```

After you have copied the ConnectString from the database connection, you can use Server Explorer to remove the link if you like.

SUMMARY

Wizards have their drawbacks. They usually produce code that is difficult to understand, modify, and maintain. If you do modify a wizard's code, you cannot rerun the wizard without destroying your changes.

Even with these drawbacks, wizards can be very useful, particularly for building quick-and-dirty prototypes. Because you don't plan to maintain this kind of prototype over a long period of time, the fact that a wizard produces confusing code isn't very important. As long as it generates something close to what you want so you can demonstrate it to your customers, wizards can be extremely helpful.

CHAPTER 9

LOADING DATA

In this chapter

Most nontrivial programs store and load some sort of data. It's unusual for a program to get all its data from the user.

Visual Basic provides several different methods you can use to save and restore data under different circumstances. The following list shows some of the more common methods in increasing order of difficulty:

- Compiled-in data
- The Registry
- Resource files
- Text files
- INI files
- XML files
- Databases

This chapter describes some of the ways you can use these methods for storing data, including when each method is most useful and which is most effective in a prototype.

Keep in mind that the prototype does not need to handle data the same way the final application will. Even if the final application will use a database, the prototype could use XML files or even compiled-in data to simulate the final application.

A prototype also does not necessarily need to update the database. It is common for a prototype to act as if it is saving changes to a database when it isn't. The prototype would be more impressive if it really did update its database, but even without that feature, it should give customers a good idea of what the final application will look like.

COMPILED-IN DATA

Compiled-in data is data that is stored in the program's source code or in the control and form properties that make up the program. The following code shows how a program might initialize values on a dialog box that lets the user enter a name and address:

```
Private Sub LoadValues()
    ' Load the State ComboBox.
    cboState.Items.Clear()
    cboState.Items.Add("CO")
    cboState.Items.Add("WY")
    cboState.Items.Add("KS")
    cboState.Items.Add("AZ")
    cboState.Items.Add("NE")

    ' Initialize the values for the demonstration record.
    txtName.Text = "Bob Programmer"
    txtStreet.Text = "314159 Calculator Way"
    txtCity.Text = "Bugsville"
    txtZip.Text = "12345-6789"
    cboState.Text = "AZ"
End Sub
```

The CompiledIn1 example program, pictured in Figure 9.1, shows what the dialog box might look like in the final application. It does not save the entered data as the real application would.

Figure 9.1
CompiledIn1 uses compiled-in data to display a name and address dialog box.

A program can also use control and form properties to include compiled-in data. In this example, you could open the dialog box in the development environment and use the Properties window to set the values that the TextBoxes and ComboBox should display.

There is a slight advantage to setting these values in code. If you set the values in code, you can print the code and use it to document the values you have used.

If you set the values in the Properties window, Visual Basic creates the code that initializes the properties at runtime. This code is normally hidden in the code window but you can view it by clicking the plus sign to the left of the text "Windows Form Designer generated code" in the code window. Then you can print the property initialization code. Like other automatically generated code, this code is not nicely formatted, commented, and ordered so it won't be as easy to read as code you organize yourself.

Another drawback to this method is that loading large amounts of data is cumbersome. If you wanted to load the abbreviations for all 50 states into the cboState ComboBox, you would need 50 lines of code. Visual Basic's arrays make loading large amounts of data like this a little easier, but it's still a lot of typing.

The CompiledIn2 example program uses the following code to load the abbreviations for the 50 states plus the District of Columbia into a ComboBox. First it declares a string array named states. At the same time, it allocates the array using the New statement and initializes the array with the list of values enclosed in braces:

```
Dim states() As String = New String() { _
    "AK", "AL", "AR", "AZ", "CA", "CO", "CT", "DC", "DE", "FL", _
    "GA", "HI", "IA", "ID", "IL", "IN", "KS", "KY", "LA", "MA", _
    "MD", "ME", "MI", "MN", "MO", "MS", "MT", "NC", "ND", "NE", _
    "NH", "NJ", "NM", "NV", "NY", "OH", "OK", "OR", "PA", "RI", _
    "SC", "SD", "TN", "TX", "UT", "VA", "VT", "WA", "WI", "WV", _
    "WY"}
Dim i As Integer

    ' Load the state abbreviations into cboStates.
    cboState.Items.Clear()
    For i = 0 To UBound(states)
        cboState.Items.Add(states(i))
    Next i
```

Using similar techniques, you can build complex data structures using data values built into the code.

Although these techniques are simple, they have some disadvantages. One of the largest is that you cannot change the value of the data without editing and recompiling the program. That makes it harder to implement changes quickly. It also prevents the program from saving any modifications the user makes at runtime.

For lists such as state abbreviations that do not change during the life of the prototype, building the data into the program is possible. For data that might change frequently or data that must be updated as the program runs, compiled-in code won't work. In those cases, the methods described in the following sections would be much better.

THE REGISTRY

The system Registry contains configuration information such as user account information, user preferences, network information, and program settings. Visual Basic provides four functions that make saving and restoring program settings in the Registry easy: SaveSetting, DeleteSetting, GetSetting, and GetAllSettings.

SaveSetting

The SaveSetting function has the following syntax:

```
SaveSetting(appname, section, key, setting)
```

The *appname* parameter identifies your program in the Registry. You should set this to your program's name.

Every call your program makes to the Registry functions should use the same name. One way to guarantee that is to define a constant giving the name. Then, use that constant in all the calls to the Registry functions. Later, if you need to change the program's name for some reason, you can update this constant:

```
' Define the program's name for Registry functions.
Private Const APP_NAME As String = "RegistryTest"
...
' Save a Registry setting.
SaveSetting(APP_NAME, section, key, setting)
```

Another approach is to use the Application object's ProductName. To set the product name, click the project in the Solution Explorer. Then choose Project, Properties. In the Common Properties folder, select the Version item. Enter the product name in the Product text box. After you have defined the product name, you can use it in the Registry functions as in this code:

```
' Save a Registry setting.
SaveSetting(Application.ProductName, section, key, setting)
```

The SaveSetting function's *section* parameter gives the section within your program's Registry entries where the setting should be stored. Use different section names for different groups of related settings. For example, you might use a "Layout" section to store the positions of forms in your program. You could use an "MRUList" section to store the program's list of most recently used files.

The *key* and *value* parameters give the name of the item you want to store and its value. The following code stores the position of the form Form1 in the program's Positions section. The next time the program runs, it could use the GetSetting function to read this position information and put the form back where it was before.

```
' Save the form's position.
SaveSetting(APP_NAME, "Positions", "Form1_Left", Form1.Left.ToString)
SaveSetting(APP_NAME, "Positions", "Form1_Top", Form1.Top.ToString)
SaveSetting(APP_NAME, "Positions", "Form1_Width", Form1.Width.ToString)
SaveSetting(APP_NAME, "Positions", "Form1_Height", Form1.Height.ToString)
```

SaveSetting places values in the "HKEY_CURRENT_USER\Software\VB and VBA Program Settings" part of the Registry. For example, if a program named "ReRun" used the previous code, its values would be placed under the key:

```
HKEY_CURRENT_USER\Software\VB and VBA Program Settings\ReRun\Positions
```

DeleteSetting

The DeleteSetting function has this syntax:

```
DeleteSetting(appname, section[, key])
```

If you include the *appname*, *section*, and *key* parameters, DeleteSetting removes the key from the section you specified. If you omit the *key* parameter, DeleteSetting removes the entire section and all the keys it contains.

DeleteSetting will never delete the whole application area in the Registry. If you want to delete the whole area, you can use the Registry Editor. Open the system's Start menu and select Run. Enter the program named "regedit" and click OK. You can make any changes you want to the Registry using the Registry Editor.

Note that the Registry Editor can be extremely dangerous. If you don't know what you're doing, you can really mess up your system and even make it unbootable. Stick to the "HKEY_CURRENT_USER\Software\VB and VBA Program Settings" part of the Registry unless you have a really good reason to make changes elsewhere.

GetSetting

The GetSetting function has this syntax:

```
GetSetting(appname, section, key[, default])
```

GetSetting returns the value of the specified key in the section you indicate. If you include the *default* parameter, GetSetting returns that value if the setting does not exist where you say it should. GetSetting returns the default value if the setting isn't in the section, if the section doesn't exist, or if *appname* doesn't exist.

If you omit the *default* value, GetSetting uses the empty string "" as the default.

GetAllSettings

The GetAllSettings function has the following syntax:

```
GetAllSettings(appname, section)
```

GetAllSettings returns a two-dimensional array of strings containing the key names and values in the section you specify. The following code shows how a program might list all the settings in its Configuration section:

```
' Get all the settings in this section.
Protected Sub btnGetAllSettings_Click(ByVal sender As Object, _
  ByVal e As System.EventArgs)
    Dim settings(,) As String
    Dim i As Integer
    Dim txt As String

    ' Get the settings.
    settings = GetAllSettings(APP_NAME, "Configuration")

    ' Make sure you got something.
    If Not (settings Is Nothing) Then
        ' You got something. Make a string listing the settings
        ' separated by carriage return/line feeds.
        txt = settings(0, 0) & " = " & settings(0, 1)
        For i = 1 To UBound(settings, 1)
            txt = txt & CrLf & settings(i, 0) & " = " & settings(i, 1)
        Next i
    End If

    ' Display the settings.
    txtAllSettings.Text = txt
    Beep()
End Sub
```

GetAllSettings is useful when there are many settings in the section and the program needs to do something uniform with them. For example, a program might display a list of values in a ComboBox. In that case, it could use GetAllSettings and loop through the array of returned values adding each to the ComboBox.

GetAllSettings is less useful when the program needs to perform very different actions with each value. For instance, a program can use the following code to position a form:

```
Form1.Left = GetSetting(APP_NAME, "Positions", "Form1_Left", "0")
Form1.Top = GetSetting(APP_NAME, "Positions", "Form1_Top", "0")
Form1.Width = GetSetting(APP_NAME, "Positions", "Form1_Width", "400")
Form1.Height = GetSetting(APP_NAME, "Positions", "Form1_Height", "300")
```

In this case, reading all the values into a string array would not be very helpful because the program still needs to set the form's properties individually.

Although GetAllSettings makes loading a list of values easy, there is no corresponding function for saving a list of values. You need to use SaveSetting to save them one at a time. You can do this in a loop, however, so it's not difficult, just different. The following code shows how a program might save the values displayed in a ListBox. This code creates keys named Item0, Item1, Item2, and so on:

```
Dim i As Integer

' Save ListBox1's items.
For i = 0 To ListBox1.Items.Count - 1
    SaveSetting(APP_NAME, "ListItems", "Item" & i.ToString, _
        ListBox1.Items.Item(i).ToString)
Next i
```

You can use this technique to save more than one array of values in the same section, but it might be easier to save each in its own section. Then you can read each array in a single call to GetAllSettings. You can also delete an array's whole section in one call to DeleteSetting by omitting the key value. This is particularly handy when you want to delete the current values and replace them with new ones.

SHARING SETTINGS

A computer's Registry is stored locally on that computer. If you run your program on another computer, you will not see the settings you saved on the first computer. That means the Registry is not the best place to store settings you want available throughout a network. That is not a problem for single user programs, but can be a little confusing for multi-seat applications.

Example

Suppose you build an order-placement system that has 20 users all sharing the same database. The program could store user preferences such as startup forms, form positions, and colors in the Registry. Each user would have his own preferences stored on his computer.

If a user runs the program on another computer, the settings would be those of the person who normally uses that computer. This can sometimes be a little confusing, but is usually not a big problem if the users understand that the settings reside on the computer, not in the database.

If you want settings to be shared or available to each user on any computer in your network, you need to save them with some other method. Two methods for doing this are to store values in a text file on a file system that is shared among all the computers, or to save values in a database accessible to all the computers.

For example, you could save user preferences in a UserPreferences table in the database using the username as a key. Then no matter where the program is running, it can load the preferences for the user who has logged on.

Whether you choose to address this issue in your prototype is up to you. If you will be running the prototype on a single computer, it's not an issue. If you can run the prototype on more than one computer, however, it's not too hard to move user configuration settings into a shared database. Then you can demonstrate some relatively fancy configuration features without too much extra work. That might not make or break your project, but it shows customers you understand their needs and can help win customer buy-in.

UPDATING SETTINGS

Most programs load settings when they start. Many also load settings for a form when that form loads. When a program should save settings is a little less clear.

Many programs save their settings when the program exits. One of the most common items to save at that time is the list of most recently used (MRU) files displayed in the program's File menu.

This works well if the program ends normally. If it crashes, however, the settings are not saved. This wouldn't be an issue if the program always exited normally, but these days it is rare to find a program that never crashes. Even if the program is flawless, the system might crash, other programs might use up all the system's memory (a situation that is particularly hard for most programs to handle), the power might fail or experience a voltage spike, or the user might trip over the computer's power cord.

In all these cases, a program has no chance to update its settings. Some programs even leave their settings in an undefined state so they don't have the same values they did the last time the program started.

Tale from the Trenches

My system has had a *lot* of different software installed and removed over the last couple years. I often review demonstration and beta versions of products, so over time my system has become a little weird. Right now, I'm running the VB.NET Beta version 1 and, like all beta software, it sometimes crashes. When it does, it does not update its MRU list. The next time I start the development environment, I can't just select the project I was working on from the File menu. I need to navigate to the project and load it myself. This is true of previous versions of Visual Basic, as well.

Occasionally when the VB.NET beta crashes, it messes up Internet Explorer, too. Internet Explorer loses its Content Advisor settings, so the next time I try to open NASA's Astronomy Picture of the Day (http://antwrp.gsfc.nasa.gov/apod/), I get an error because that site is not rated.

Hopefully the later releases will be harder to crash, but this will always be an issue. No program can protect itself from power failures.

Although this problem is common in commercial software, it is easy to solve. Just make the program update its settings as soon as they change. As soon as the program loads a new file, update the MRU list. Whenever the user resizes a form, save the new width and height. Unless you need to save hundreds of settings all at once, calling SaveSetting or saving these changes into a database will be too fast for the user to notice.

SETTING EXAMPLES

The Registry example program, shown in Figure 9.2, saves and restores settings in the Registry. Enter a section, key, and value and click the Save Setting button to save the setting. If you enter a section and key and click the Get Setting button, the program retrieves the value and displays it in the Setting text box.

Enter a section and a key and click the Delete Setting button to delete that setting. Omit the key to delete the entire section.

Finally, enter a section and click the Get All Settings button to list all the values stored in that section.

Figure 9.2
The Registry program saves and restores values from the Registry.

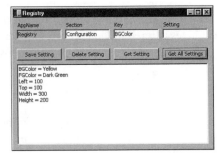

The SavePosition example program, shown in Figure 9.3, loads and saves its size and position in the Registry. Move and resize the program's form and then close it. When you restart the program, the form appears where you left it.

Figure 9.3
SavePosition saves and restores its size and position in the Registry.

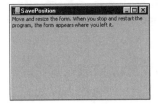

SavePosition is surprisingly simple. The following shows the program's most interesting code:

```
Private Const APP_NAME As String = "SavePosition"
Private Const SECTION_NAME As String = "Position"
    ...
' Restore the form's previous position.
Private Sub LoadSettings()
    Me.SetDesktopBounds( _
        GetSetting(APP_NAME, SECTION_NAME, "Left", "100").ToInt32(), _
        GetSetting(APP_NAME, SECTION_NAME, "Top", "100").ToInt32(), _
        GetSetting(APP_NAME, SECTION_NAME, "Width", "300").ToInt32(), _
        GetSetting(APP_NAME, SECTION_NAME, "Height", "200").ToInt32())
End Sub

' Save the form's new position.
Public Sub Form1_Move(ByVal sender As Object, _
  ByVal e As System.EventArgs) Handles Form1.Move
    SaveSetting(APP_NAME, SECTION_NAME, "Left", Me.Left.ToString)
    SaveSetting(APP_NAME, SECTION_NAME, "Top", Me.Top.ToString)
End Sub
```

```
' Save the form's new dimensions.
Public Sub Form1_Resize(ByVal sender As Object, _
   ByVal e As System.EventArgs) Handles Form1.Resize
     ' Save the width and height.
     SaveSetting(APP_NAME, SECTION_NAME, "Width", Me.Width.ToString)
     SaveSetting(APP_NAME, SECTION_NAME, "Height", Me.Height.ToString)
End Sub
```

You can use similar techniques to save and restore other properties that the user can modify, for example, the text in TextBoxes, values entered in ComboBoxes, dimensions of rows and columns in grid controls, and the state of CheckBoxes and OptionButtons.

RESOURCE FILES

Resource files let you separate your program's code and behavior from the text and other content it displays. The most common use for resource files is *localization*, giving the program different appearances for different languages. For example, an application might have a menu item labeled "New Document" when it is run in a computer set up for English. When run on a computer set up for German, the menu item might say "Neues Dokument."

Tip

Although you should get a native speaker to check your internationalized applications, you can get started using a translation Web site such as Alta Vista's Babelfish site at http://babelfish.altavista.com/translate.dyn.

Building and using resource files is easy in Visual Basic. First, design the form you want to localize. Localizing the form will be easiest if you build the form as completely as possible before you start using resource files.

Next, open the form. In the Properties window, change the Localizable property to True. At that point, Visual Basic creates a resource file to hold important properties of the form and its controls.

To look at the file, click the Show All Files button in the Solution Explorer's toolbar. Beneath the form, you will see the resource file. It will have the same name as the form but with a "resx" extension. Double-click this file to see its XML code as shown in Figure 9.4. The top entry visible in Figure 9.4 represents the mnuFileOpen menu item's Text property and has the value "&Open." The next entry says that menu's Shortcut value is "CtrlO."

With a little patience, you can figure out what the other entries in this file mean. If you click the Data button at the bottom of the file's display, you can view the values in the grid shown in Figure 9.5.

Using this display, you can edit the values stored in the resource file. By clicking the grid's bottom row, you can add new properties that do not correspond to any of the form's controls.

Figure 9.4
Double-click on a resource file to view its XML code.

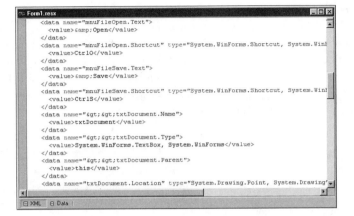

Figure 9.5
Clicking the Data button enables you to view a resource file's values in a grid.

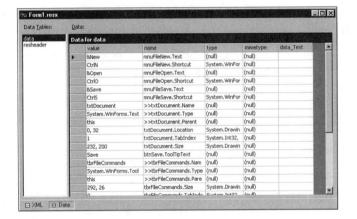

When you have finished looking at the resource file, close it and reopen the form itself and look at its Language property. Initially this is (Default). When the program runs, it uses the values in this resource file whenever a value is not specified in the current language-specific resource file. For example, if you are running the program on a German system and the German resource file does not specify a value for the mnuFileNew menu item's Text property, the program falls back to the default resource file and sets the property to "&New."

Now change the form's Language property to one of the values available in its drop-down list. The development environment says the new Language setting will take effect when you close and reopen the form designer. Close the form and reopen it. The form looks the same but any changes you make to its properties are stored in a new resource file. The new file begins with the form's name, followed by the language abbreviation, followed by the resx extension. For example, the file named Form1.es-MX.resx is a resource file for Form1 using the language Spanish (es = Español) as spoken in Mexico (MX).

When you run the program, Visual Basic automatically selects the right resource file for your system and uses its values to initialize the form and its controls. The code that does this is automatically generated and is normally hidden in the code window. You can view this code by clicking the plus sign to the left of the text "Windows Form Designer generated code" in the code window. The code that reads the resources looks like this:

```
Dim resources As System.Resources.ResourceManager = _
    New System.Resources.ResourceManager(GetType(Form1))
    ...
mnuFileNew.Text = CType(resources.GetObject("mnuFileNew.Text"), String)
mnuFileNew.Shortcut = CType(resources.GetObject("mnuFileNew.Shortcut"), _
    System.WinForms.Shortcut)
    ...
mnuFileOpen.Text = CType(resources.GetObject("mnuFileOpen.Text"), String)
mnuFileOpen.Shortcut = CType(resources.GetObject("mnuFileOpen.Shortcut"), _
    System.WinForms.Shortcut)
    ...
```

First this code creates a `ResourceManager` object. It then uses the `ResourceManager`'s `GetObject` method to read the values it needs from the appropriate resource file.

You can use similar code to load resource values other than control properties. For example, the following code displays a message. The message text is defined by the `ButtonNotImplemented` resource and the message box's title is defined by the `NotReady` resource:

```
' Say this button is not yet implemented.
Private Sub ButtonNotImplemented()
    Dim resource_manager As _
        New System.Resources.ResourceManager(GetType(Form1))

    MsgBox( _
        CType(resource_manager.GetObject("ButtonNotImplemented"), String), _
        Microsoft.VisualBasic.MsgBoxStyle.Exclamation, _
        CType(resource_manager.GetObject("NotReady"), String))
End Sub
```

The ResourceFile example program, shown in Figure 9.6, uses this code to display a message whenever you click one of its buttons. It uses similar code to display a message when you invoke one of its menu items.

Figure 9.6
`ResourceFile` displays a message with text taken from a resource file.

If you are building an international application, you can use resource files to demonstrate internationalization features in your prototype quickly.

Using these techniques, you can also build other kinds of data into a resource file. Resource files are really designed for internationalization, however, and the tools Visual Basic gives you are a bit clumsy for this sort of thing. Putting an array of values into a resource file using Visual Basic's grid display would be time consuming and updating a resource file at runtime is possible but not trivial. For these kinds of operations, you are probably better off using a more dynamic storage method such as a text file, XML file, or database.

TEXT FILES

A prototype can save and restore values in an ordinary text file. This method has several advantages. It is very simple and easy to understand. You can edit text files using any text editor so you don't need to use a special editor such as Visual Basic's XML or resource file editor. Text files are easy to distribute—you just copy them into the directory where you want them. You can also share text files among multiple computers by storing them in a shared directory.

You can make several different versions of the file to handle different prototyping situations. For example, you could have one file containing parameters for the program to use for a typical user, another for users with supervisor privileges, another for system managers, and so forth.

One potential disadvantage to text files is you could spend a lot of effort parsing values out of them. Converting a series of text characters into strings, numbers, and other data values can be time consuming.

Fortunately, Visual Basic provides tools that make this easy. The Write statement saves values into a text file surrounded by delimiters that make the values easy to read later. The Input statement reads values saved by the Write statement. For example, a text file written by the Write statement containing four integers and a string might look like this:

```
840,11,173,72,"Test 'string'",
```

The Input statement knows how to separate the values at the commas and how to read the string enclosed in quotes.

One troublesome detail, however, is that the Write statement doesn't like double quotes. If a string includes a double quote, Write gets confused and hangs. In some cases, you might be able to convert the double quotes into single quotes. If you really need to store a double quote, you will need to find some other way to encode it in the string.

The TextFile example program, shown in Figure 9.7, uses the code in Listing 9.1 to load and save values in a text file. Position the form and enter text in its text box. The next time you run the program, it returns to its last position and redisplays the text you entered.

Figure 9.7
TextFile loads and
saves data in a text
file.

LISTING 9.1   THE TEXTFILE EXAMPLE USES THIS CODE TO LOAD AND SAVE DATA IN A
TEXT FILE.

```
Public Sub New()
    MyBase.New

    Form1 = Me

    'This call is required by the Win Form Designer.
    InitializeComponent

    ' Load the saved data.
    LoadData()
End Sub

' Save the current data.
Public Sub Form1_Closing(ByVal sender As Object, _
  ByVal e As System.ComponentModel.CancelEventArgs) Handles Form1.Closing
    SaveData()
End Sub

' Save the data.
Private Sub SaveData()
    Dim file_name As String
    Dim file_num As Integer

    ' Open the file for writing.
    file_name = DataFileName()
    file_num = FreeFile()
    Open(file_num, file_name, OpenMode.Output, _
        OpenAccess.Write, OpenShare.LockWrite)

    ' Save the form's position and contents.
    Write(file_num, Me.Left)
    Write(file_num, Me.Top)
    Write(file_num, Me.Width)
    Write(file_num, Me.Height)
    Write(file_num, Replace(txtContents.Text, """", "'"))

    ' Close the file.
    Microsoft.VisualBasic.Compatibility.VB6.Close(file_num)
End Sub

' Load data saved during the last run.
Private Sub LoadData()
    ' File access variables.
    Dim file_name As String
    Dim file_num As Integer
```

LISTING 9.1   CONTINUED

```
      ' Data variables. Initialize the data values to defaults
      ' in case the file does not exist.
      Dim saved_left As Integer = 100
      Dim saved_top As Integer = 100
      Dim saved_width As Integer = 300
      Dim saved_height As Integer = 200
      Dim saved_contents As String = ""

      ' Ignore any errors while you read the file.
      On Error Resume Next

      ' Open the file for reading.
      file_name = DataFileName()
      file_num = FreeFile()
      Open(file_num, file_name, OpenMode.Input, _
          OpenAccess.Read, OpenShare.Shared)

      ' Get the form's position.
      Input(file_num, saved_left)
      Input(file_num, saved_top)
      Input(file_num, saved_width)
      Input(file_num, saved_height)
      Input(file_num, saved_contents)

      ' Set the form's position and contents.
      Me.StartPosition = FormStartPosition.Manual
      Me.SetBounds(saved_left, saved_top, saved_width, saved_height)
      txtContents.Text = saved_contents
      txtContents.Select(0, 0)

      ' Close the file.
      Microsoft.VisualBasic.Compatibility.VB6.Close(file_num)
End Sub

' Application.StartupPath gives the bin directory. Go one level
' up and then down into the Data directory.
Private Function DataFileName() As String
    Dim file_name As String

    file_name = Application.StartupPath()
    file_name = Microsoft.VisualBasic.Left$(file_name, len(file_name) - 3)
    file_name = file_name & "Data\Values.dat"

    Return file_name
End Function
```

Text files do have a couple of disadvantages. First, they can only contain text data. Although you could write routines to encode and decode binary information in text strings, you would be better off storing pictures, executable programs, and other binary data in a database or in resource files.

A program also cannot update pieces of a text file in the middle. If you want to update a single value in the middle of the file, you need to rewrite the whole file. That is not a problem if you only save the values once when the program is about to exit as TextFile does. It does prevent you from saving a value as soon as it is modified as described in "The Registry" earlier in this chapter.

INI FILES

An INI file is an old-style initialization file. Microsoft discontinued its use when it introduced the Registry. Ironically, Microsoft still uses INI files in many of its products and you will find several on the VS.NET CD-ROM.

INI files are text files with a special format. The file is broken into sections. Section titles are surrounded by square brackets. Each section contains lines that hold an item name and its value separated with an equal sign. For example, a small INI file might look like this:

```
[Configuration]
Left=100
Top=100
Width=400
Height=300

[Colors]
BGColor=White
FGColor=Black
```

Because Microsoft officially discontinued the use of INI files, Visual Basic tools for manipulating them have been slowly disappearing. At this point, you probably should think of them as text files with a special format rather than as standard format initialization files. They have all the same strengths and weaknesses as text files as described in the previous section.

You can easily write routines to save and load files with this format. You might be better off, however, using XML files instead. An XML file can store the information in a roughly equivalent format:

```
<?xml version="1.0" encoding="utf-8"?>
<AllValues>
  <Configuration>
    <Left>100</Left>
    <Right>100</Right>
    <Width>400</Width>
    <Height>300</Height>
  </Configuration>
  <Colors>
    <BGColor>White</BGColor>
    <FGColor>Black</FGColor>
  </Colors>
</AllValues>
```

The following section has more to say about XML files.

XML FILES

XML files are nothing more than fancy text files. They don't do anything by themselves but recently a lot of applications have been modified to do things with them. For example, Web browsers can display their contents quickly and easily.

VB.NET includes a lot of tools that use XML files either directly or indirectly. In particular, ADO.NET uses XML to send data to and from a database. That means if your program uses ADO.NET, it uses XML implicitly.

VB.NET also provides methods for directly editing and manipulating XML files both at design time and at runtime. That makes XML files a good candidate for storing and retrieving data in a Visual Basic prototype.

The following sections barely scratch the surface of all you can do with XML. They only show how you can use XML files to save and load data quickly in a prototype. For a more complete treatment of XML files, consult a book that discusses XML use in Visual Basic.

XML FILES AT DESIGN TIME

To add an XML file to a Visual Basic project, choose Project, Add New Item. Select the XML File item and click OK. Initially, the new file contains a single line describing the XML version:

```
<?xml version="1.0" encoding="utf-8"?>
```

When you open the file, the Visual Basic development environment's XML editor displays the file as shown in Figure 9.8. Here you can edit the file's raw XML text.

Figure 9.8
The XML file
`Values.xml` is
shown in Visual
Basic's XML editor.

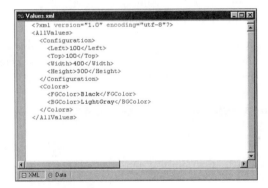

If you compare the file shown in Figure 9.8 to the INI file described in the previous section, you can see how the XML file is arranged. The AllValues element contains all the data values. The values are divided into Configuration and Colors sections. The items in each section have names (Left, Width, FGColor, and so on) and contain text (100, 400, Black, and so on).

If you click the Data button at the bottom of the XML editor, the editor displays the XML file as a sequence of tables as shown in Figure 9.9. The tables correspond to the two top-level XML elements Configuration and Colors.

Figure 9.9
Clicking on the Data button brings up the XML editor's Data view.

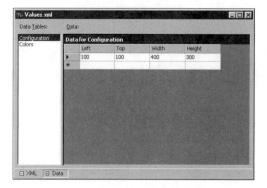

Each table displays the values contained by the corresponding node in the XML file. As Figure 9.9 shows, the Configuration element contains the Left, Right, Width, and Height elements. You can change an item's value by clicking it and then entering a new value. If you click the editor's XML button, you can see that the new value is incorporated into the XML file's textual representation.

XML FILES AT RUNTIME

There are several ways a Visual Basic program can manipulate XML files at runtime. The method described here uses the System.Xml namespace's XML objects. To use those objects, you need to give your program a reference to them.

Choose Project, Add Reference. On the .NET Framework tab, scroll down to the System.XML.dll entry. Double-click the entry to add it to the list of selected components as shown in Figure 9.10. Then click the OK button.

Figure 9.10
Add a reference to System.XML.dll.

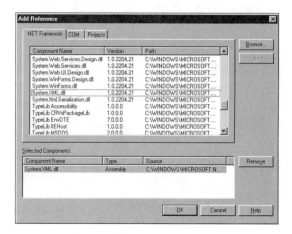

Now the program can use the `System.Xml` objects to manipulate XML files. The XMLFile example program, shown in Figure 9.11, uses an XML file to save and restore its position, and its foreground and background colors.

Figure 9.11
XMLFile saves and restores values from an XML file.

XMLFile loads its data using the following code. The `LoadData` routine begins by declaring an `XmlDocument` variable and three `XmlNode` variables. It sets the form's `StartPosition` property to `FormStartPosition.Manual`, so Windows doesn't automatically reposition the form when it is displayed.

`LoadData` then uses the `XmlDocument`'s `Load` method to open the XML file holding the program's data. The `DataFileName` helper function returns the location of the XML data file.

The routine then uses the Item method to find the document's AllValues node. It uses that node's Item method to find its Configuration and Colors nodes.

Finally, `LoadData` uses the `Item` method provided by the Configuration and Colors nodes to get the data they contain:

```
' Load data saved during the last run.
Private Sub LoadData()
    Dim doc As New Xml.XmlDocument()
    Dim all_values As Xml.XmlNode
    Dim configuration As Xml.XmlNode
    Dim colors As Xml.XmlNode

    ' Don't let Windows position the form.
    Me.StartPosition = FormStartPosition.Manual

    ' Open the XML document.
    doc.Load(DataFileName())

    ' The XML document's structure is
    '    Document
    '        AllValues
    '            Configuration
    '                Left
    '                Top
    '                Width
    '                Height
    '            Colors
    '                BGColor
    '                FGColor
    all_values = doc.Item("AllValues")
    configuration = all_values.Item("Configuration")
    colors = all_values.Item("Colors")
```

```
    ' Read the configuration values.
    Me.Left = configuration.Item("Left").InnerText.ToInt32()
    Me.Top = configuration.Item("Top").InnerText.ToInt32()
    Me.Width = configuration.Item("Width").InnerText.ToInt32()
    Me.Height = configuration.Item("Height").InnerText.ToInt32()

    ' Read the foreground color values.
    Select Case colors.Item("FGColor").InnerText
        Case "Red"
            optFGColorRed.Checked = True
        Case "White"
            optFGColorWhite.Checked = True
        Case "Black"
            optFGColorBlack.Checked = True
        Case "Green"
            optFGColorGreen.Checked = True
    End Select

    ' Read the background color values.
    Select Case colors.Item("BGColor").InnerText
        Case "LightGray"
            optBGColorLightGray.Checked = True
        Case "White"
            optBGColorWhite.Checked = True
        Case "Black"
            optBGColorBlack.Checked = True
        Case "Green"
            optBGColorGreen.Checked = True
    End Select
End Sub

' Application.StartupPath gives the bin directory. Go up one level.
Private Function DataFileName() As String
    Dim file_name As String

    file_name = Application.StartupPath()
    file_name = Microsoft.VisualBasic.Left$(file_name, len(file_name) - 3)
    file_name = file_name & "Values.xml"

    Return file_name
End Function
```

XMLFile uses the following code to save its data into the XML file before the program exits. When the form's Closing event fires, the program calls the SaveData subroutine. SaveData begins by opening the XML file and locating the AllValues, Configuration, and Colors nodes similar to how the LoadData subroutine does. It then updates the values contained in the items within those nodes so they match the values the program is currently using. SaveData finishes by calling the XmlDocument's Save method to write the data back into the XML file:

```
' Save the data.
Public Sub Form1_Closing(ByVal sender As Object, _
  ByVal e As System.ComponentModel.CancelEventArgs) Handles Form1.Closing
    SaveData()
End Sub
```

```
' Save the data.
Private Sub SaveData()
    Dim doc As New Xml.XmlDocument()
    Dim all_values As Xml.XmlNode
    Dim configuration As Xml.XmlNode
    Dim colors As Xml.XmlNode
    Dim node As Xml.XmlNode

    ' Open the XML document.
    doc.Load(DataFileName())

    ' Get the section nodes.
    all_values = doc.Item("AllValues")
    configuration = all_values.Item("Configuration")
    colors = all_values.Item("Colors")

    ' Update the configuration information.
    configuration.Item("Left").InnerXml = Me.Left.ToString
    configuration.Item("Top").InnerXml = Me.Top.ToString
    configuration.Item("Width").InnerXml = Me.Width.ToString
    configuration.Item("Height").InnerXml = Me.Height.ToString

    ' Update the foreground color information.
    If optFGColorRed.Checked Then
        colors.Item("FGColor").InnerXml = "Red"
    ElseIf optFGColorWhite.Checked Then
        colors.Item("FGColor").InnerXml = "White"
    ElseIf optFGColorBlack.Checked Then
        colors.Item("FGColor").InnerXml = "Black"
    ElseIf optFGColorGreen.Checked Then
        colors.Item("FGColor").InnerXml = "Green"
    End If

    ' Update the background color information.
    If optBGColorLightGray.Checked Then
        colors.Item("BGColor").InnerXml = "LightGray"
    ElseIf optBGColorWhite.Checked Then
        colors.Item("BGColor").InnerXml = "White"
    ElseIf optBGColorBlack.Checked Then
        colors.Item("BGColor").InnerXml = "Black"
    ElseIf optBGColorGreen.Checked Then
        colors.Item("BGColor").InnerXml = "Green"
    End If

    ' Save the XML document.
    doc.Save(DataFileName())
End Sub
```

XML files have capabilities far beyond those used here. They can store many different types of data and can represent complex data structures with elements containing other elements to any depth you need.

XML files still suffer from some of the limitations of other text files. Notably, you cannot update an XML file in the middle. Although you can make changes to any part of an XmlDocument that represents an XML file, the entire file must be written at some point if you want to save the values. That makes it difficult to save values as soon as they change.

XML WITH MULTIPLE RECORDS

The XMLFile program described in the previous section uses an XML file to store configuration information. The XML file contains sections with unique names. Each section contains values that have unique names within that section. Because the names are unique at each level, the program can use the Item method to locate the values quickly and easily. This method is convenient but it doesn't take full advantage of an XML file's capabilities.

In addition to holding values with unique names like this, XML files can contain multiple rows of data with the same field names. To create this kind of data, repeat the data fields that define the records in the XML file. Figure 9.12 shows an XML file containing four Person records.

Figure 9.12
This XML file contains multiple Person records.

This XML file's Data view is shown in Figure 9.13. Click a cell and type a new value to modify the data. Click the row marked with an asterisk to add a new record to the file.

Figure 9.13
This is the Data view of an XML file containing multiple Person records.

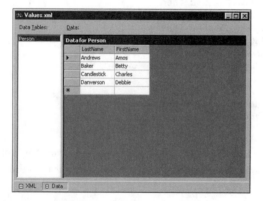

In a multi-record XML file, nodes that represent the same kind of row must have the same name. That means a program that uses this kind of file cannot locate the nodes using their names as the XMLFile program does. However, the program can access these nodes using their indices within their parent nodes.

The XMLFile2 example program, shown in Figure 9.14, saves and restores four records from an XML file. If you change the values and exit, the program saves the new values in the XML file. When you start the program again, it redisplays the new values.

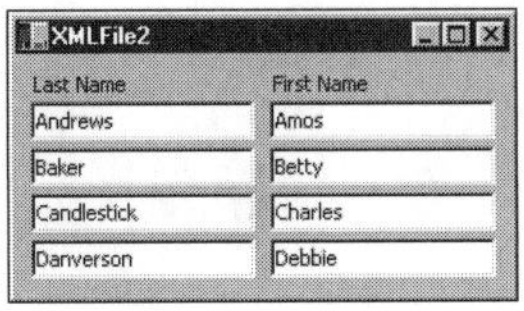

Figure 9.14
XMLFile2 displays
four records from a
multi-record XML file.

XMLFile2 uses the following code to save and load its data. The LoadData subroutine opens the XML file into an XmlDocument object. LoadData uses the XmlDocument's Item method to find the AllValues node.

The routine then uses that node's ChildNodes method to get its first four child nodes. A more general program would loop through all the nodes contained in the ChildNodes collection.

Each of the nodes returned by ChildNodes represents one Person record in the XML file. Because each Person record has only one LastName and FirstName node, the program can use the Person node's Item method to locate its fields.

The SaveData subroutine saves the modified data when the program exits. SaveData begins by loading the XML file and removing all the child nodes from its AllValues node. It then calls the AddPerson helper routine to create the new Person nodes. When the node structure is up to date, the program calls the XmlDocument's Save method to save the new version of the XML file.

The AddPerson subroutine creates a new Person node and adds it to the XmlDocument's AllValues node. It then creates new LastName and FirstName nodes and adds them to the new Person node:

```
Public Sub New()
    MyBase.New

    Form1 = Me

    'This call is required by the Win Form Designer.
    InitializeComponent

    ' Load saved data.
    LoadData()
End Sub

' Save the data.
Public Sub Form1_Closing(ByVal sender As Object, _
  ByVal e As System.ComponentModel.CancelEventArgs) Handles Form1.Closing
```

```
        SaveData()
    End Sub

    ' Load data saved during the last run.
    Private Sub LoadData()
        Dim doc As New Xml.XmlDocument()
        Dim all_values As Xml.XmlNode
        Dim person As Xml.XmlNode

        ' Open the XML document.
        doc.Load(DataFileName())

        ' The XML document's structure is
        '    Document
        '        Person
        '        Person
        '        Person
        '        ...
        all_values = doc.Item("AllValues")

        ' Read the people's names.
        person = all_values.ChildNodes(0)
        txtLastName0.Text = person.Item("LastName").InnerText
        txtFirstName0.Text = person.Item("FirstName").InnerText
        person = all_values.ChildNodes(1)
        txtLastName1.Text = person.Item("LastName").InnerText
        txtFirstName1.Text = person.Item("FirstName").InnerText
        person = all_values.ChildNodes(2)
        txtLastName2.Text = person.Item("LastName").InnerText
        txtFirstName2.Text = person.Item("FirstName").InnerText
        person = all_values.ChildNodes(3)
        txtLastName3.Text = person.Item("LastName").InnerText
        txtFirstName3.Text = person.Item("FirstName").InnerText

        ' Start with no text selected.
        txtLastName0.Select(0, 0)
    End Sub

    ' Save the data.
    Private Sub SaveData()
        Dim doc As New Xml.XmlDocument()
        Dim all_values As Xml.XmlNode

        ' Open the XML document.
        doc.Load(DataFileName())

        ' Get the section nodes.
        all_values = doc.Item("AllValues")

        ' Remove all the Person nodes.
        all_values.RemoveAll()

        ' Add the Person nodes.
        AddPerson(doc, all_values, txtLastName0.Text, txtFirstName0.Text)
        AddPerson(doc, all_values, txtLastName1.Text, txtFirstName1.Text)
        AddPerson(doc, all_values, txtLastName2.Text, txtFirstName2.Text)
        AddPerson(doc, all_values, txtLastName3.Text, txtFirstName3.Text)
```

```
      ' Save the XML document.
      doc.Save(DataFileName())
End Sub

' Add a new Person record to the document.
Private Sub AddPerson(ByVal doc As Xml.XmlDocument, _
  ByVal all_values As Xml.XmlNode, ByVal last_name As String, _
  ByVal first_name As String)
    Dim person_node As Xml.XmlNode
    Dim name_node As Xml.XmlNode

    ' Create the Person node.
    person_node = doc.CreateElement("Person")
    all_values.AppendChild(person_node)

    ' Create the LastName node.
    name_node = doc.CreateElement("LastName")
    name_node.InnerText = last_name
    person_node.AppendChild(name_node)

    ' Create the FirstName node.
    name_node = doc.CreateElement("FirstName")
    name_node.InnerText = first_namees
    person_node.AppendChild(name_node)
End Sub

' Application.StartupPath gives the bin directory. Go up one level.
Private Function DataFileName() As String
    Dim file_name As String

    file_name = Application.StartupPath()
    file_name = Microsoft.VisualBasic.Left$(file_name, len(file_name) - 3)
    file_name = file_name & "Values.xml"

    Return file_name
End Function
```

The XMLFile program uses nodes with unique names to quickly find configuration values. The XMLFile2 program uses multiple records containing the same fields to load several Person records. You can also mix these two techniques. For example, you might create a Settings section that contains one or more subsections, each holding configuration values with unique names. In the same XML file, you could also have a RecordData section that holds a series of data records. By combining both of these methods, a single XML file can store settings like the Registry does and hold large amounts of record-oriented data like a database does.

DATABASES

A full-fledged database is the most powerful method for storing and retrieving data. A database can store practically any kind of data, sort and search the data for specific values, return combinations of data pulled from several related tables, validate data values, and even contain stored procedures that execute database code.

A database can be stored locally on the same system as the prototype, or it can be shared across a network so many users can access the same data. All these features make a database an ideal place to store prototype data.

You can use separate tables for different kinds of data that should be shared among users.

You can also make a separate table to hold user configuration information. That table can include a UserName field used as a key. A program can use this table to load the configuration information quickly for each individual user. If the database is shared across a network, each user can use his or her personal configuration settings from every computer in your network.

Unfortunately this convenience requires a little extra work. At a minimum, you will need to build a logon screen so the prototype knows which user is running it. A more complete system would also include user privilege information that used similar methods to control user access to different parts of the prototype. If you implement user privileges, you also need to provide tools for managing those privileges, adding new users to the system, and so forth. Although providing a logon screen is easy, some of these other features can be complicated enough that you might want to leave them out of the prototype.

The Database example program, shown in Figure 9.15, works similar to XMLFile2 except it uses ActiveX Data Objects (ADO) to load and save its data in an Access database. Chapter 10, "ADO Versus ADO.NET," discusses why you might want to use ADO instead of the newer ADO.NET in prototypes.

Figure 9.15
The Database program loads and saves data in an Access database.

ADO is included in the Microsoft Data Access Controls (MDAC). Currently you can download the latest version of MDAC at www.microsoft.com/data/download.htm.

To use ADO in a Visual Basic project, you need to add a reference to it. Choose Project, Add Reference. Find the ADO library shown in Figure 9.16. Double-click the library to select it and then click the OK button.

At the top of the program's main form, include this Imports statement:

```
Imports ADODB
```

Now you can create ADO objects and use them to manipulate the database.

The Database program uses the following code to load and save its data. The LoadData subroutine sets a Connection object's ConnectString property to specify the database and database engine the Connection should use. The routine then calls the Connection's Open method to open the database.

Figure 9.16
Before you can use
ADO, you need to
add a reference to it.

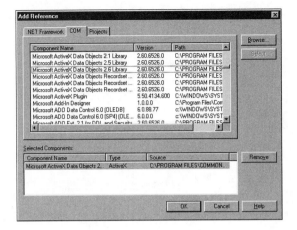

The program uses the `Connection` object's `Execute` method to select records from the database and place the results in a `Recordset` object. `LoadData` moves through the `Recordset`'s records pulling out the values it needs from each. Notice that the `SELECT` statement uses an `ORDER BY` clause to order the records. If you modify the values displayed by the program so they are out of order, the program will reload them in sorted order the next time it runs.

After it has loaded the data, the `LoadData` routine closes its `Recordset` and `Connection`.

The `SaveData` subroutine creates a `Connection` object and opens the database just as `LoadData` does. It executes a `DELETE` statement to remove all the records currently in the People table. `SaveData` then calls the helper routine `AddPerson` to create the new records before it closes its `Connection`.

The `AddPerson` subroutine executes an `INSERT` statement to create a new record in the People table.

```
Public Sub New()
    MyBase.New()

    Form1 = Me

    'This call is required by the Win Form Designer.
    InitializeComponent()

    ' Load saved data.
    LoadData()
End Sub

' Save the data.
Public Sub Form1_Closing(ByVal sender As Object, _
    ByVal e As System.ComponentModel.CancelEventArgs) Handles Form1.Closing
    SaveData()
End Sub

' Load data saved during the last run.
Private Sub LoadData()
```

```
        Dim db_connection As New Connection()
        Dim query As String
        Dim rs As Recordset

        ' Connect to the database.
        db_connection.ConnectionString = _
            "Provider=Microsoft.Jet.OLEDB.4.0;" & _
            "Data Source=" & DataFileName() & ";" & _
            "Persist Security Info=False"
        db_connection.Open()

        ' Open the Recordset.
        query = _
            "SELECT LastName, FirstName " & _
            "FROM People " & _
            "ORDER BY LastName, FirstName"
        rs = CType(db_connection.Execute(query, , CommandTypeEnum.adCmdText), _
            Recordset)

        ' Process the records.
        txtLastName0.Text = rs.Fields("LastName").Value.ToString()
        txtFirstName0.Text = rs.Fields("FirstName").Value.ToString()
        rs.MoveNext()

        txtLastName1.Text = rs.Fields("LastName").Value.ToString()
        txtFirstName1.Text = rs.Fields("FirstName").Value.ToString()
        rs.MoveNext()

        txtLastName2.Text = rs.Fields("LastName").Value.ToString()
        txtFirstName2.Text = rs.Fields("FirstName").Value.ToString()
        rs.MoveNext()

        txtLastName3.Text = rs.Fields("LastName").Value.ToString()
        txtFirstName3.Text = rs.Fields("FirstName").Value.ToString()

        ' Close the Recordset and Connection.
        rs.Close()
        db_connection.Close()

        ' Start with no text selected.
        txtLastName0.Select(0, 0)
    End Sub

    ' Save the data.
    Private Sub SaveData()
        Dim db_connection As New Connection()

        ' Connect to the database.
        db_connection.ConnectionString = _
            "Provider=Microsoft.Jet.OLEDB.4.0;" & _
            "Data Source=" & DataFileName() & ";" & _
            "Persist Security Info=False"
        db_connection.Open()

        ' Delete the existing records.
        db_connection.Execute("DELETE FROM People", , CommandTypeEnum.adCmdText)
```

```
    ' Create the new records.
    AddPerson(db_connection, txtLastName0.Text, txtFirstName0.Text)
    AddPerson(db_connection, txtLastName1.Text, txtFirstName1.Text)
    AddPerson(db_connection, txtLastName2.Text, txtFirstName2.Text)
    AddPerson(db_connection, txtLastName3.Text, txtFirstName3.Text)

    ' Close the database.
    db_connection.Close()
End Sub

' Add a new People record. Note that the INSERT statement will
' get confused if a text field contains an apostrophe so you
' replace any apostrophes with double apostrophes. That tells
' the database to include a single apostrophe.
Private Sub AddPerson(ByVal db As Connection, _
  ByVal last_name As String, ByVal first_name As String)
    db.Execute( _
        "INSERT INTO PEOPLE (LastName, FirstName) VALUES (" & _
        "'" & Replace(last_name, "'", "''") & "', " & _
        "'" & Replace(first_name, "'", "''") & "')")
End Sub

' Application.StartupPath gives the bin directory. Go up one level.
Private Function DataFileName() As String
    Dim file_name As String

    file_name = Application.StartupPath()
    file_name = Microsoft.VisualBasic.Left$(file_name, len(file_name) - 3)
    file_name = file_name & "Values.mdb"

    Return file_name
End Function
```

This example deletes all the People records and then recreates them whenever it must save its data. You could modify the program to use an UPDATE statement to update the field values in the records instead. In this example, the difference would be small. In a more interesting application, however, this would allow the program to update only the values that had changed while leaving the others alone.

Chapter 11, "Database Tips and Tools," describes some tips and tricks to make using databases easier in a prototype. That chapter does not cover everything there is to know about databases, however. Database programming is a huge topic and there are several good books on using databases in Visual Basic. See one of these books for more information.

SUMMARY

Which method you use to save and restore data depends on the amount and type of the data, and how you plan to use it.

If a program needs values that never change, consider compiling them into the source code. This is easy and doesn't require some other file, such as an XML or database file, to be available when the prototype runs. That makes installing the prototype easier. If the values change at all, no matter how infrequently, this solution won't work.

If you have relatively few items, Visual Basic's Registry functions SaveSetting, DeleteSetting, GetSetting, and GetAllSettings are a good choice. They are fast, easy to use, and they let you save a single setting quickly without saving all the others. They are stored in a specific computer's Registry, however, so they don't work very well if you need to share data among computers.

Resource files can contain all kinds of data, including pictures. They are just files, so you can let multiple computers use them by putting them in a shared directory. Resource files are really intended for internationalization and that's what they do best. Although you might be able to figure out how to modify them at runtime, it's probably more trouble than it's worth. They are best for data you will read but not modify.

Text files have most of the advantages of resource files, however, they cannot easily store pictures or other binary data. You can write to them so you can use a text file for data that you must read and modify.

XML files are really just text files with some additional structure. They have the same advantages as text files. For example, you can read and write them and share them by putting them in a shared directory. They are relatively easy to edit at design time using Visual Basic's XML editor and they are easy to manipulate at runtime using Visual Basic's XML tools. Their added structure makes it easy to find specific pieces of data.

Finally, databases provide the most features. They let you read, update, delete, sort, and search the data. They can perform multi-table joins, can hold almost any kind of data, and can even contain stored procedures that perform complex tasks. You can store a database locally or you can allow many computers to share it. The one disadvantage of databases is their complexity. If you use one, you will need to learn at least the fundamentals of database management.

Table 9.1 summarizes the strengths and weaknesses of each of these data storage methods.

TABLE 9.1   DATA STORAGE STRENGTHS AND WEAKNESSES

Method	Strengths	Weaknesses
Compiled-In data	Easy Fast No external files to keep track of	Cannot modify data at runtime Hard to change the data
The Registry	Easy Fast Can change one value without changing others	Hard to share between computers

TABLE 9.1   CONTINUED

Method	Strengths	Weaknesses
Resource Files	Can hold many data types Internationalization Can be shared	Hard to modify at runtime
Text files	Simple Can be shared	Hard to store binary data
XML files	Extra structure makes organizing data easier Can hold many data types Can be shared	Cannot update one value without updating the others
Databases	Can sort, search, and perform joins Can hold stored procedures Can hold many data types Can update one value without modifying the others Can be shared Can provide user-level protection	Complex

PART

III

CH

9

ADO VERSUS ADO.NET

In this Chapter

ActiveX Data Objects (ADO) and ADO.NET are two methods for manipulating databases. Both provide methods for selecting, creating, updating, and deleting records in database tables. How they provide these features, however, differs. Which method is more appropriate for a particular application depends on how the application manipulates its data.

ADO and ADO.NET differ in four main respects: maturity, connection method, data structure, and modification method. The next few sections describe these differences. The chapter finishes with a summary of those differences and a discussion of some tips for picking a database access method when you build a prototype.

MATURITY

ADO is the older technology. It has been around for a while, is relatively stable, and many Visual Basic programmers have a lot of experience using it.

ADO.NET is being introduced with Visual Studio.NET. ADO.NET is largely based on ADO. Therefore, if you know how to use ADO, you already know how to use many of the features of ADO.NET. Few programmers have had a chance to use the new features for very long, however, so some changes may occur in the short term.

Microsoft envisions ADO.NET as the data access method of the future, but it also acknowledges that ADO.NET's connectionless data access methods will not work for all applications. For applications that need an explicit database connection, Microsoft recommends that you continue to use ADO. For that reason, it is likely that ADO will be available for at least several more years. Microsoft will probably not drop support for ADO until it can replace all of its functionality.

If you have a lot of experience with ADO, you are likely to be more productive using it than trying to learn ADO.NET. The short timeframes common for prototypes might be the only reason you need to pick ADO.

On the other hand, one of the main benefits of prototypes is they let you try new technology. If you have the time, and ADO.NET provides the features you need in the final application, you should consider using it in the prototype to gain experience. ADO.NET is similar in many ways to ADO, so learning the basics of ADO.NET should not take much extra time.

CONNECTION METHOD

Many programs that use ADO explicitly manage their database connections. They open a connection to the database, manipulate the data, and then close the database connection. A program can perform many actions while the database connection is open. Some programs open the database connection when they start and close it only when they exit. The connection stays open throughout the program's lifetime, possibly for hours.

ADO also supports a connectionless mode of operation in which database connections are made automatically as needed. Any time the program accesses the database, ADO implicitly connects to the databases, performs its task, and then disconnects from the database. This mode of operation makes less sense for desktop applications where the program pays a small performance penalty for connecting and disconnecting from the database every time it takes action.

ADO.NET takes a more Web-oriented approach. It assumes applications use a large number of Web services running on different computers throughout the network. The application needs to connect to many different data sources, each for only a brief time. In this case, using connectionless database access prevents an application from holding a database connection open for a long period of time, tying up resources on the server. For a large Web application, that can be important. If too many clients hold connections to a server at once, the server might be unable to respond to new connection requests.

DATA STRUCTURE

When a program selects records from a database, ADO returns the results in a Recordset. ADO.NET returns results in a DataSet. Both Recordsets and DataSets provide methods for manipulating data. Which one is better for a particular program depends on how the program needs to manipulate the data. Before you can decide on an approach, you need to know a little about Recordsets and DataSets. The next two sections give a brief overview of the two.

RECORDSETS

A *Recordset* is an object that represents the results of a database select operation. A Recordset's data looks a lot like an array or database table. The Recordset contains a series of records, each holding a series of fields that represent the selected data items.

A Recordset has this two-dimensional structure even if it includes fields taken from more than one database table. When the data is stored in the Recordset, all of the fields are equal.

Because of this flat structure, a Recordset that contains data from more than one table cannot modify that data. The Recordset doesn't keep track of which fields come from which records in which tables, so it doesn't know how to update the values. If a program must update the data, it must access the tables individually.

Figure 10.1 shows a Recordset graphically. This Recordset includes fields taken from a master table and corresponding fields taken from a detail table.

Program DBRecordset, shown in Figure 10.2, loads a simple master/detail Recordset and displays the results. Each line in the text box shows the fields in one of the Recordset's rows, separated by commas. The first two fields are the DepartmentName and DepartmentId fields from the database's Departments table. The rest of the fields list records from the Employees table that have a matching DepartmentId value.

Figure 10.1
A Recordset flattens the returned data's structure.

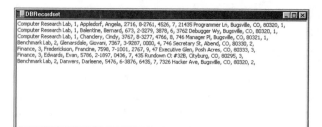

Figure 10.2
Program DBRecordset displays the Recordset fields returned by a master/detail query.

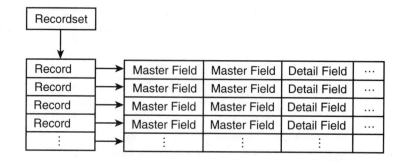

Program DBRecordset includes a reference to Microsoft's Data Access Objects (ADO) library. For information on adding a reference to the ADO library, see the "Databases" section of Chapter 9, "Loading Data."

DBRecordset uses the code shown in Listing 10.1 to load and display its Recordset. The LoadData routine begins by opening a connection to the database. The DataFileName function returns the name of the database used by this program. The database is an Access 7.0 file named People.mdb and stored in the project's Data subdirectory. You could replace the call to DataFileName with a hard-coded file name.

After connecting to the database, the program executes an SQL query to select the records in the Departments table and the corresponding Employees records. The routine loops through each of the Recordset's records, adding its field values to the output string. When it has processed every record, the subroutine displays the output string, and closes the Recordset and database connection.

LISTING 10.1   DBRECORDSET USES THIS CODE TO LOAD AND DISPLAY THE RECORDS IN AN ADO RECORDSET.

```
' Load and display the data.
Private Sub LoadData()
    Dim db_connection As New Connection()
    Dim query As String
    Dim rs As Recordset
    Dim txt As String
    Dim fld As Field
```

LISTING 10.1   CONTINUED

```
' Open the database.
db_connection.ConnectionString = _
    "Provider=Microsoft.Jet.OLEDB.4.0;" & _
    "Data Source=" & DataFileName() & ";" & _
    "Persist Security Info=False"
db_connection.Open()

' Open the Recordset.
query = _
    "SELECT * " & _
    "FROM Departments, Employees " & _
    "WHERE Departments.DepartmentId = Employees.DepartmentId"
rs = CType(db_connection.Execute(query, , CommandTypeEnum.adCmdText), _
    Recordset)

' Process the records.
Do While Not (rs.EOF)
    ' Add this record to the string.
    For Each fld In rs.Fields
        txt = txt & fld.Value.ToString() & ", "
    Next fld
    txt = txt & CrLf

    ' Move to the next record.
    rs.MoveNext()
Loop

' Display the result.
txtResults.Text = txt
txtResults.Select(0, 0)

' Close the Recordset and Connection.
rs.Close()
db_connection.Close()
End Sub
```

The Recordset used by program DBRecordset does not preserve the structure of the query's master and detail records; however, at least it is relatively simple.

DATASETS

Like a Recordset, a *DataSet* represents database records. If the values come from more than one table, however, the DataSet preserves the table structure internally. It keeps a copy of each table.

Each table is represented by a DataTable object. Each DataTable object contains a collection of DataRow objects that represent the rows of data. Each DataRow object contains a collection of objects that represent the values in that database record.

The DataRow object's GetChildRows method provides a link from the DataRow object in a master or parent table to rows in detail or child tables. By using this method to link master and detail rows, the DataSet preserves the tables' separate structures.

PART

III

CH

10

Because it keeps track of the table structures, a DataSet can update data even in multi-table queries. The DataTable object's NewRow method adds a new record to the table. The DataRow object's Delete method deletes the corresponding row of data. The DataRow's BeginEdit method opens the object's fields for editing. The program can then use the EndEdit or CancelEdit methods to accept or cancel any changes that it has made since it called BeginEdit.

Figure 10.3 shows a DataSet graphically. In this picture, the first table is a master table and the second provides detail that goes with the master table's data. The dashed lines represent the relationship between master records and detail records. This picture shows a single link from each master row to one detail row. In general, a master row could have zero, one, or more detail rows.

Figure 10.3
A DataSet preserves the database's table structure.

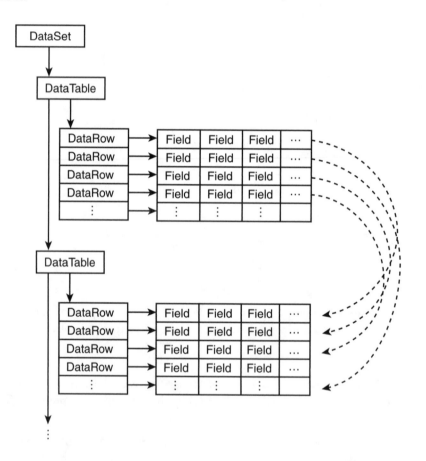

When you compare Figures 10.1 and 10.3, you see that Recordsets and DataSets represent data in very different ways.

Program DataSet, shown in Figure 10.4, loads employee department data from a database into a DataSet object. It defines a relationship matching records in the Employees and Departments tables that have the same value for the DepartmentId field.

The upper text box lists every record in the DataSet. The lower text box lists the records in the Departments table. For each Departments record, the program lists the corresponding Employees records with matching DepartmentIds.

Figure 10.4
Program DataSet displays the Recordset fields returned by a master/detail query.

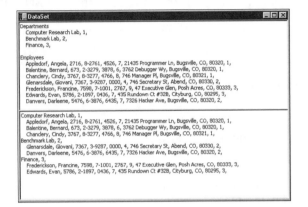

Program DataSet uses the code in Listing 10.2 to load and display its data. When the form loads, its New subroutine calls LoadData to load the DataSet. It uses AllTableRows to display all the rows for each table. It then uses DepartmentsWithEmployees to display the Departments records with their corresponding Employees records.

Subroutine LoadData begins by defining a connection to the database. It then creates an ADOCommand object that selects the records in the Departments table. It creates an ADODataSetCommand object that references this ADOCommand and invokes its FillDataSet method to load the table's data into the program's DataSet variable named data_set. LoadData repeats this process to load the data from the Employees table.

Next, LoadData creates two DataColumn objects to represent the DepartmentId fields in the two tables. Finally, it builds a DataRelation object to link the two DataColumn objects. This DataRelation represents the master/detail relationship between the Departments and Employees tables.

Subroutine AllTableRows returns a string listing all of the records in every table in the DataSet. It iterates through the DataTable objects in the DataSet's Tables collection. For each table, the routine iterates through the DataTable's Rows collection. For each row, AllTableRows loops through the table's columns to retrieve the table's column names. Finally, it uses the column names as indices into the current DataRow object to get the row's value for that column. AllTableRows concatenates the field values and returns the result.

Subroutine DepartmentsWithEmployees shows how to manipulate tables that have a master/detail relationship. The routine begins by setting references to the Departments and Employees tables, and to the DataRelation object that joins them. It then iterates through the rows in the Departments table and adds that row's field values to the output string, much as subroutine AllTableRows does. Then it uses the row's GetChildRows method to get an array of rows in the Employees table related to the current Departments row via the

DataRelation object linking the two tables. DepartmentsWithEmployees examines the child rows and adds their field values to the output.

LISTING 10.2   PROGRAM DATASET USES THIS CODE TO LOAD AND DISPLAY ITS DATA.

```
Public Sub New()
    MyBase.New()

    Form1 = Me

    'This call is required by the Win Form Designer.
    InitializeComponent()

    ' Load the DataSet.
    Dim data_set As New System.Data.DataSet()
    LoadData(data_set)

    ' Display the rows for all tables.
    txtAllTableRows.Text = AllTableRows(data_set)
    txtAllTableRows.Select(0, 0)

    ' Display the rows for Employees with detail.
    txtDepartmentsWithEmployees.Text = DepartmentsWithEmployees(data_set)
    txtDepartmentsWithEmployees.Select(0, 0)

    ' Close the DataSet.
    data_set = Nothing
End Sub

' Load a DataSet and display its data.
Private Sub LoadData(ByVal data_set As System.Data.DataSet)
    Dim connect_string As String
    Dim db_connection As System.Data.ADO.ADOConnection
    Dim employees_cmd As New System.Data.ADO.ADOCommand()
    Dim employees_ds_cmd As New System.Data.ADO.ADODataSetCommand()
    Dim departments_cmd As New System.Data.ADO.ADOCommand()
    Dim departments_ds_cmd As New System.Data.ADO.ADODataSetCommand()
    Dim departments_data_column As System.Data.DataColumn
    Dim employees_data_column As System.Data.DataColumn
    Dim data_relation As System.Data.DataRelation

    ' ***********************
    ' Connect to the database.
    ' ***********************
    connect_string = _
            "Provider=Microsoft.Jet.OLEDB.4.0;" & _
            "Data Source=" & DataFileName() & ";" & _
            "Persist Security Info=False"
    db_connection = New System.Data.ADO.ADOConnection(connect_string)

    ' **********************************
    ' Get data from the Departments table.
    ' **********************************
    ' Define the ADOCommand object.
    departments_cmd.ActiveConnection = db_connection
    departments_cmd.CommandText = "SELECT * FROM Departments"
```

LISTING 10.2   CONTINUED

```
    ' Define the ADODataSetCommand object.
    departments_ds_cmd.SelectCommand = departments_cmd

    ' Add a mapping between the departments and Departments tables.
    departments_ds_cmd.TableMappings.Add("Table", "Departments")

    ' Get the data.
    departments_ds_cmd.FillDataSet(data_set)

    ' **********************************
    ' Get data from the Employees table.
    ' **********************************
    ' Define the ADOCommand object.
    employees_cmd.ActiveConnection = db_connection
    employees_cmd.CommandText = "SELECT * FROM Employees"

    ' Define the ADODataSetCommand object.
    employees_ds_cmd.SelectCommand = employees_cmd

    ' Add a mapping between the Employees and Departments tables.
    employees_ds_cmd.TableMappings.Add("Table", "Employees")

    ' Get the data.
    employees_ds_cmd.FillDataSet(data_set)

    ' ******************************************
    ' Create a relation between the two tables.
    ' ******************************************
    departments_data_column = _
        data_set.Tables("Departments").Columns("DepartmentId")
    employees_data_column = data_set.Tables("Employees").Columns("DepartmentId")
    data_relation = New System.Data.DataRelation( _
        "departments_to_employees", departments_data_column,
employees_data_column)
    data_set.Relations.Add(data_relation)
End Sub

' Return a string listing all rows for all tables.
Private Function AllTableRows(ByVal data_set As System.Data.DataSet) As String
    Dim txt As String
    Dim data_table As DataTable
    Dim data_row As DataRow
    Dim data_column As DataColumn

    ' For each table in the DataSet...
    For Each data_table In data_set.Tables
        txt = txt & data_table.TableName & CrLf

        ' For each row in the table...
        For Each data_row In data_table.Rows
            txt = txt & "        "
            ' For each column in the row...
            For Each data_column In data_table.Columns
                ' Add the column to the output.
```

PART

III

CH

10

LISTING 10.2   CONTINUED

```
                    txt = txt & data_row(data_column.ColumnName).ToString & ", "
            Next data_column
            txt = txt & CrLf
        Next data_row
        txt = txt & CrLf
    Next data_table

    ' Return the results.
    Return txt
End Function

' Return a string listing the Departments table with
' employee detail.
Private Function DepartmentsWithEmployees(ByVal data_set As System.Data.DataSet) _
  As String
    Dim txt As String
    Dim relation As DataRelation
    Dim master_table As DataTable
    Dim master_row As DataRow
    Dim master_column As DataColumn
    Dim detail_table As DataTable
    Dim detail_rows() As DataRow
    Dim detail_column As DataColumn
    Dim i As Integer

    ' Get the relation between the Employees and Departments tables.
    relation = data_set.Relations("departments_to_employees")

    ' Get the master and detail tables.
    master_table = data_set.Tables("Departments")
    detail_table = data_set.Tables("Employees")

    ' Display the Employees rows.
    For Each master_row In master_table.Rows
        ' Display the master information.
        For Each master_column In master_table.Columns
            txt = txt & master_row(master_column.ColumnName).ToString & ", "
        Next master_column
        txt = txt & CrLf

        ' Display the detail information.
        detail_rows = master_row.GetChildRows(relation)
        For i = 0 To UBound(detail_rows)
            txt = txt & "        "
            For Each detail_column In detail_table.Columns
                txt = txt & _
                    detail_rows(i)(detail_column.ColumnName).ToString & ", "
            Next detail_column
            txt = txt & CrLf
        Next i
    Next master_row

    ' Return the results.
    Return txt
End Function
```

LISTING 10.2 CONTINUED

```
' Application.StartupPath gives the bin directory. Go one level
' up and then down into the Data directory.
Private Function DataFileName() As String
    Dim file_name As String

    file_name = Application.StartupPath()
    file_name = Microsoft.VisualBasic.Left$(file_name, len(file_name) - 3)
    file_name = file_name & "Data\People.mdb"

    Return file_name
End Function
```

This method is a lot more work than loading a Recordset in ADO, but it gives the program much greater flexibility. Using the DataSet's objects, a program can examine and modify every bit of the loaded data.

MODIFICATION METHOD

The last major way in which ADO Recordsets and ADO.NET DataSets differ is how they update databases.

Normally, when a program modifies a Recordset's fields and accepts the changes, the changes are immediately transmitted back to the database. This method makes sense for many desktop applications. It makes changes to the database quickly, so other programs that share the same database see changes right away.

Note

Some Recordsets can also hold onto changes and send them to the database all at once in batch mode.

A DataSet always works in batch mode. It holds onto its changes and only updates the database when the program explicitly uses an ADODataSetCommand's Update method on the DataSet. Then the ADODataSetCommand only updates records that have actually been modified. It doesn't bother to tell the database when a record has remained unchanged since it was loaded.

Batch updates reduce the number of trips the program makes to the database over time. Instead of making a trip to the database every time a record is modified, the program only needs to make send data to the database when it is ready to update modified values.

One problem with batch updates is they do not save any changes if the program crashes before it makes the update. If you make a lot of changes to the data before calling the ADODataSetCommand's Update method, you can lose a lot of work.

Another problem with batch mode updates is they can cause a *race condition*. In a race condition, two programs race for the same record. In this case, the program that gets to the record second wins because its changes overwrite any changes made by the first program.

DataSets use batch updates because of ADO.NET's Web orientation. Many large Web projects only allow users to view and add records. Rarely do users modify or delete records. All of these operations are typically localized within the database and they have very short durations.

Example

Suppose you use a Web service to subscribe to a mailing list. You go to a Web site, fill in a username, email address, and password, and click the Submit button. ADO.NET tries to make a new record for you using the username as the record's key. If someone already has that username, the process fails and displays an error message. Then you can try again with a different username.

The only way this operation can create a race condition is if another user is trying to grab the same username at exactly the same time. In that case, one of you gets the name first and the other is out of luck. That is no different from the case where the first person took that username an hour ago. Either way, someone got there first, and it doesn't really matter to the database which user won. You mutter under your breath about someone taking your favorite name, "Code Warrior," and you enter another one. No big deal.

Now let's suppose you want to update or delete your mailing list entry. The Web site makes you log on with the username and password you used to join the list. Because you need to log on, no one else can edit your record at the same time you are, so you cannot get a race condition. If you are silly enough to try to edit the record simultaneously in two different Web browser windows at the same time, you can get a race condition and you deserve whatever confusion you cause yourself.

Contrast the previous scenario with the one that follows.

Example

Suppose you are one of several customer service clerks entering customer payment data. At 8:30 you begin your day and fire up you customer maintenance program. The program grabs the customer account data using an ADO.NET DataSet.

You enter payments for a hundred or so customers, watching the clock all the while. When noon finally rolls around, you shutdown to go to lunch. When the program exits, it performs a batch update of the customer data and the changes you have made are saved.

A few minutes later, one of your co-workers also quits for lunch. Unfortunately a few customers made two payments during this payment period, and you processed one while your colleague processed the other. Because his program stopped second, he wins the race and his update gets saved to the database, replacing yours.

As if that wasn't bad enough, you don't even know there is a problem. Only one of each of these customers' payments was recorded but you don't know which payments, which customers, or even that anything at all is wrong.

The possibility of race conditions make batch updates most useful when you know no one else is working on the same record you are. For example, when you need to enter a password to access the record. Race conditions also pose no problem if the users only view the data and never update it. Race problems can be cause trouble when multiple users might want to modify the same data at the same time.

SUMMARY

Table 10.1 summarizes the major differences between ADO and ADO.NET.

TABLE 10.1   DIFFERENCES BETWEEN ADO AND ADO.NET

	ADO	ADO.NET
Maturity	Mature technology	New technology
Connection	Uses explicit connections	Connectionless
Data structure	Recordset	DataSet
Updates	Immediate or batch	Batch

PART

III

CH

10

For throwaway prototypes, these issues are largely irrelevant. A throwaway prototype isn't around long enough for maturity to be a big problem. The prototype will probably be obsolete before ADO.NET's next release anyway. If you want to gain some experience with ADO.NET, give it a try. If you are pressed for time and know ADO better, use it instead.

Whether the prototype uses connectionless data access methods or not isn't a big issue unless you need to build a huge, scalable prototype. If the prototype only needs to work on one or two computers at the same time, you can use ADO or ADO.NET. ADO can provide either persistent connections or connectionless access. You can use ADO if you want to keep your options open.

Recordsets and DataSets both provide methods for manipulating a database. Which is easier depends on what you need to do and on your previous experience. If you need to modify records in master/detail relationships, a DataSet might make your job easier. If you don't mind working with individual tables and you have more experience with Recordsets, use ADO.

Finally, if only one instance of the prototype is running at a time, it doesn't matter whether you use immediate or batch updates. If there are no other processes running that can cause a race condition, the prototype can update the data whenever it's convenient, without fear of interference. As long as the prototype doesn't crash before it saves the modified data, the customers won't know exactly when the data is saved and they won't care.

For a throwaway prototype, you might as well use the technology that makes you most comfortable. For an evolutionary prototype, the choice between ADO and ADO.NET is more important. You need to weigh the program's architectural needs and decide which technology gives you the best features.

If all else is equal, I use ADO. It is the more mature technology, can provide persistent connections or connectionless data access, and can make either immediate or batch data updates. ADO gives you more flexibility than ADO.NET, which requires connectionless data access and batch updates.

CHAPTER 11

DATABASE TIPS AND TOOLS

In this Chapter

This chapter describes several database tips and tools I have found useful in building prototypes. This chapter doesn't cover everything there is to know about databases. In fact, it doesn't really even cover the basics. It assumes you know a little bit about database programming already. If you already know the fundamentals, you should be able to apply these tips and tools to help your prototype use a database as quickly as possible.

Database programming is a huge topic, and there are several good books about using databases in Visual Basic, including *Beginning Visual Basic 6 Database Programming* by John Connell (Wrox Press, 1998) and *Beginning SQL Server 2000 for Visual Basic Developers* by Thearon Willis (Wrox Press, 2000).

The programs in this chapter use ADO. For a discussion of the reasons why you might pick ADO rather than ADO.NET, see Chapter 10, "ADO Versus ADO.NET."

This chapter also uses data access objects designed for use with OLE DB databases, such as `ADOConnection` and `ADODataSetCommand`. If you use SQL Server version 7.0 or later, you can use versions of these objects designed for use with SQL Server. The `SQLConnection` and `SQLDataSetCommand` classes avoid an extra OLE DB layer of code that the ADO objects use, so the SQL versions should be faster when you use SQL Server.

THE BOUND DATAGRID

The Data Form Wizard is used to quickly build an application that displays data in a DataGrid control. For instructions on using the Data Form Wizard, see Chapter 8, "Wizards."

Unfortunately the program the Data Form Wizard builds is fairly complicated and confusing. Using a DataGrid to display data without the wizard is not very hard.

To use the DataGrid, start a new project. Next, create an `ADODataSetCommand` object to select the records you want to display. To do that, select the Toolbox's Data tab. Drag an `ADODataSetCommand` object onto the form so the DataSetCommand Configuration Wizard appears. Use the wizard to define the `ADODataSetCommand` object and the `ADOConnection` object that attaches it to the database. For more explicit instructions, see the section "Create an `ADODataSetCommand`" in Chapter 8.

Next, select the `ADODataSetCommand` object and invoke the DataClass menu's Generate DataSet command. Enter the name you want to give the DataSet class. For example, you might call the class `dsEmployees`. Check the Add an instance of this class to the designer check box and click OK. This creates a new DataSet class with methods for manipulating the records selected by the `ADODataSetCommmand` object, and it adds an instance of the class to your project.

To see the source code Visual Basic generated, click the Show All Files button at the top of the Solution Explorer. Click the plus sign to the left of the DataSet class entry `dsEmployees.xsd`. The class source code `dsEmployees.vb` is beneath this entry. Double-click this file to see the code generated by Visual Basic.

When you have finished looking at this code, reopen the form and select the Toolbox's Win Forms tab. Add a DataGrid control to the form, select the new control, and click on its Dock property in the Properties window. Click the down arrow to its right and pick the large rectangle in the middle of the popup. That sets the control's Dock property to Fill so the control fills the form.

Select the control's DataSource property and click the down arrow to its right. Select the DataSet class method named after the table from which you are selecting data. For example, if the ADODataSetCommand named dsPeople uses the SQL statement SELECT * FROM Employees, then you should select the DataSource named dsPeople.Employees.

Now you just need to add some code to make the program load and save data in the database. At the end of the form's New subroutine, add a call to the LoadData routine. Then add the Form1_Closing, LoadData, and SaveData routines as shown in Listing 11.1.

LoadData calls the ADODataSetCommand object's FillDataSet method. That method loads the data selected by the ADODataSetCommand object into a DataSet. LoadData then calls the related DataSet class object's Merge method to merge the newly loaded data with the values already loaded by the object, though currently it has no data loaded. The DataGrid control's DataSource is bound to this object's Employees method, so it automatically displays the results.

The Form1_Closing subroutine simply invokes the SaveData subroutine. SaveData calls the DataSet object's GetChanges method to make a new DataSet consisting of changes to the data. If the DataSet of changes is not empty, SaveData calls the ADODataSetCommand object's Update method to make it save the changes to the database.

LISTING 11.1   BOUNDDATAGRID USES THIS CODE TO LOAD AND SAVE CHANGES TO ITS DATA.

```
Public Sub New()
    MyBase.New()

    Form1 = Me

    'This call is required by the Win Form Designer.
    InitializeComponent()

    ' Load the data.
    LoadData()
End Sub

' Save modified data.
Public Sub Form1_Closing(ByVal sender As Object, _
    ByVal e As System.ComponentModel.CancelEventArgs) Handles Form1.Closing
    SaveData()
End Sub

' Load the data into the DataGrid.
Private Sub LoadData()
Dim ds As New DataSet()
```

LISTING 11.1   CONTINUED

```
    Me.ADODataSetCommand1.FillDataSet(ds)
    dsEmployees1.Merge(ds)
End Sub

' Save changes to the data.
Private Sub SaveData()
    Dim changes As DataSet

    ' Get a DataSet holding only the changes.
    changes = dsEmployees1.GetChanges()

    ' Make sure there were some changes.
    If Not (changes Is Nothing) Then
        ' There were changes. Save them.
        ADODataSetCommand1.Update(changes)
    End If
End Sub
```

Program BoundDataGrid, shown in Figure 11.1, demonstrates this method. Click a grid cell to enter a new value. Click any cell in the bottom row marked with an asterisk to create a new record. Click to the left of the leftmost cell to select a record, and then press **Delete** to delete that record. When you close the form, the program saves any changes you made into the database. When you restart the program, you see the modified data.

Figure 11.1
A DataGrid control bound to a DataSet lets a program display and edit data effortlessly.

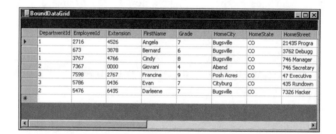

Using this technique, you can let a program manage a database table with just a few lines of code. This method does not help manage any master/detail relationships among tables, but it is sufficient for isolated tables that define system parameters and lists such as user privileges, item costs, states and cities, and so on. This kind of table determines how the program acts and is independent of the data entered by the user. For example, the States table would contain the states the program lists in a customer address dropdown box. No matter what kind of data the user enters, the list of possible states is the same.

If you use a grid to manage these sorts of system parameters like this, you need to restrict access to the form. You probably don't want every user to be able to change the program's list of states.

DATABASE INDEPENDENCE

Visual Basic comes with a bewildering assortment of data access methods. You can use controls bound directly to a database. You can manipulate a database with ADO using the Microsoft Data Access controls (MDAC), or with ADO.NET using the objects in the System.Data.ADO namespace. You can even use an XML file to load an ADO.NET DataSet and treat the data as if it is stored in a true database.

You can use a wide variety of database engines including Access, FoxPro, SQL Server, Oracle, Informix, and other Open Database Connectivity (ODBC) data providers. Some of these database products come with their own tools that you can use to manage the database, build and maintain tables, save and load data in files, execute SQL scripts, and so on.

There are so many combinations that you could easily drive yourself crazy trying to understand them all and figure out which is best. This is particularly true when you are building a prototype. Unless you are building the prototype explicitly to try the different data access methods and become comfortable with them, you don't have a lot of time to waste trying them all.

Tales from The Trenches

Sometimes, no matter how much research you do, you end up selecting the wrong database and access method. Ideally, you begin a project knowing what database engine and data access method you are going to use. You stick with the decisions throughout the project and make as few changes as possible during subsequent releases.

Unfortunately, this doesn't always work. Large database systems, such as SQL Server, Oracle, and Informix, are expensive. On a large project that runs on many computers, there's a huge amount of money at stake. That gives management incentive to switch back and forth between vendors to get the best deal.

In the prototypes I've built, the underlying database was one of the most frequently changed items. In one project, the target database switched back and forth more than half a dozen times. In the end, the database was changed just before the final release, and we had to modify the prototype at the last minute to use the new database. Fortunately, most of these databases are similar enough that you can switch from one to another without too much difficulty, if you plan ahead. If you avoid features specific to a particular database, you can make any last minute changes easier.

Surprisingly, one of the other most frequently changed items in the prototypes I've worked on was the hardware platform. This was for the same reason: Hardware is expensive. When you buy a couple hundred workstations, there's a lot of money at stake. Fortunately, Visual Basic runs very similarly on the different hardware platforms on which it runs, so this isn't a huge issue.

PART

III

CH

11

You can minimize the dangers of selecting the "wrong" database and access method by keeping the database at arm's length. Isolate the data access code in routines in a BAS module or inside data access classes. This way, if you need to change the data access method or database later, you know where all the code is.

The data access routines do not need to do much. They can be thin layers above the actual data access objects provided by Visual Basic. All they really need to do is localize all the code that deals directly with the database in one or two places where you can find it easily.

ADO TOOLS

Program ADOTools, shown in Figure 11.2, uses a DBConnection class to separate itself from the database. Click the List Tables button to see a list of the tables in the database. Click a table name to see a list of the fields in that table. Enter a SQL SELECT statement in the Query box and click the Execute button to make the program execute the query and display the results in two lists using two different methods.

Enter a database action statement or pick one from the Action Statement ComboBox and click **Execute** to make the program execute the statement. This procedure is very flexible and, if you know the right SQL syntax, enables you to make all sorts of changes to the database. These include creating and dropping tables; adding and removing stored procedures; inserting, updating, and deleting records; and more.

Program ADOTools also shows how to build a list of paired values from a database table. Several of the projects I have built used lookup tables to define codes. In this example, the AccountStatuses table contains two fields: AccountStatusName and AccountStatusCode. Each entry defines the code for some status value. For example, the status Suspended has the code S. These programs need to map statuses to codes frequently so the program caches the codes to save time. Select a status from the AccountStatus ComboBox and click the > button to see the corresponding code. Select a status code from the AccountStatusCode list and click the < button to see the matching status value.

Figure 11.2
Program ADOTools demonstrates some of the functions provided by the DBConnection class.

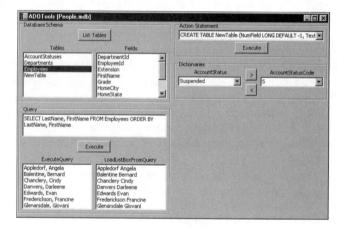

Program ADOTools uses two classes, DBConnection and PairedValues, to make managing data easier.

DBConnection

The DBConnection class shown in Listing 11.2 helps program ADOTools manage its database. This class is designed to work with Access databases using ADO. You could build similar classes to work with other kinds of databases or to use ADO.NET.

The class stores the name of the database it has opened in its `m_DatabaseName` variable. It keeps a reference to the ADO `Connection` object that is connected to the database in its `m_Connection` variable. The `ADOConnection` class provides two public properties—`DatabaseName` and `DatabaseTitle`—that return the database's complete file name and its file title (the name without the directory path).

The `OpenDatabaseAccess` method opens an Access database. It first calls the `CloseDatabase` method which closes the database if one is currently open. The routine then allocates a new `Connection` object and uses it to open the database.

The `CloseDatabase` routine blanks the database name. If the `m_Connection` object is not Nothing, the routine invokes the `m_Connection` object's `Close` method and sets it to Nothing so it doesn't try to do this again later. This is the last of the record keeping routines. The rest of the routines are a bit more interesting.

Function `ExecuteQuery` executes a SQL `SELECT` statement and returns the resulting ADO Recordset. The calling program can then loop through the Recordset, examining the values returned. `ExecuteQuery` is quite simple. It calls the `Connection` object's `Execute` method and passes it to the query to execute. `Execute` returns a Recordset containing the selected records, and the `ExecuteQuery` method simply returns that Recordset.

By returning a Recordset, the `ExecuteQuery` function ties itself to the ADO implementation. For example, suppose your program uses `ExecuteQuery` to select some records. It loops through the returned Recordset and adds each record's value to a ListBox control. If you later change the `DBConnection` class so it accesses data using ADO.NET instead of ADO, `ExecuteQuery` needs to return values using a DataSet instead of a Recordset. Because your program assumes `ExecuteQuery` returns a Recordset, you now need to modify your program, as well.

You can avoid this dependence by moving the routines that rely on the Recordset into the `DBConnection` class. The `LoadListBoxFromQuery` routine does just that. Rather than using `ExecuteQuery` to get a list of values for its ListBox, the program can just call `LoadListBoxFromQuery`. This routine calls `ExecuteQuery` and then uses the returned Recordset to fill the ListBox. Although `LoadListBoxFromQuery` needs to know that `ExecuteQuery` returns a Recordset, your main program does not. If you change the `DBConnection` class so it uses ADO.NET, you need to update `LoadListBoxFromQuery`, but your program should still work without changes.

The `LoadComboBoxFromQuery` routine is exactly the same as `LoadListBoxFromQuery`, except it loads a ComboBox control instead of a ListBox.

Subroutines `GetTableNames` and `GetFieldNames` are a little different from the other routines. Instead of returning information about the data, they return information about the database itself. You are less likely to need this sort of information because you are probably developing the database your prototype uses while you build the prototype. Still, this can sometimes be useful. For example, you might let the user select the fields in a table to be included in a report. In that case, you could use the `GetFieldNames` method to build the list of fields.

The `GetTableNames` method calls the `Connection` object's `OpenSchema` method, and passes it the parameter `adSchemaTables` to make a Recordset that lists the names of the tables in the database. It then returns the Recordset containing the table names. Just as the `LoadListBoxFromQuery` routine hides the use of Recordsets inside the `DBConnection` class, you can make a `LoadListBoxWithTableNames` routine to separate the main program from the need for Recordsets here.

The `GetFieldNames` method calls the `Connection` object's `OpenSchema` method, and passes it the name of the table of interest and the flag `adSchemaColumns` to get a list of the fields in the table.

Note that you can also find the column names with ADO by selecting all of the fields in a `SELECT` statement. For example, if you use `ExecuteQuery` to execute the statement `SELECT * FROM Employees`, the records in the resulting Recordset contain `Field` objects that give the names of the database fields. If you just want the field names but don't want to select any data, use the `GetFieldNames` method. If you want to select data and know the names of the fields you selected, use `ExecuteQuery` and then look at the names of the fields in the Recordset.

The last method in the `DBConnection` class is `ExecuteActionStatement`. This command is similar to `ExecuteQuery` except this routine assumes it is executing an action statement such as `DROP TABLE` or `INSERT`. These statements do not select records, so this routine does not return a Recordset.

LISTING 11.2   THE DBCONNECTION CLASS SEPARATES A PROGRAM FROM DIRECT DATABASE ACCESSES.

```
Imports ADODB
Imports Microsoft.VisualBasic.ControlChars

' Represents and manipulates a database.
Public Class DBConnection
    Private m_DatabaseName As String
    Private m_Connection As Connection

    ' Close the database connection if it is open.
    Public Sub Dispose()
        CloseDatabase()
    End Sub

    ' Return the name of the open database.
    Public ReadOnly Property DatabaseName() As String
        Get
            DatabaseName = m_DatabaseName
        End Get
    End Property

    ' Return the last part of the database name.
    Public ReadOnly Property DatabaseTitle() As String
        Get
            Dim pos As Integer
```

LISTING 11.2   CONTINUED

```vb
            pos = InStrRev(m_DatabaseName, "\")
            If pos = 0 Then
                DatabaseTitle = m_DatabaseName
            Else
                DatabaseTitle = Mid$(m_DatabaseName, pos + 1)
            End If
        End Get
    End Property

    Public Sub OpenDatabaseAccess(ByVal database_name As String)
        ' Close the database if it is open.
        CloseDatabase()

        ' Try to open this database.
        m_Connection = New Connection()
        m_Connection.ConnectionString = _
            "Provider=Microsoft.Jet.OLEDB.4.0;" & _
            "Data Source=" & database_name & ";" & _
            "Persist Security Info=False"
        m_Connection.Open()

        ' Save the new database name.
        m_DatabaseName = database_name
    End Sub

    ' Close the database if it is open.
    Public Sub CloseDatabase()
        ' Blank the database name.
        m_DatabaseName = ""

        ' Close the connection if it is open.
        If Not m_Connection Is Nothing Then
            m_Connection.Close()
            m_Connection = Nothing
        End If
    End Sub

    ' Execute a query and return the resulting forward-only,
    ' read-only Recordset.
    Public Function ExecuteQuery(ByVal query As String) As Recordset
        Dim rs As Recordset

        ' Open the Recordset.
        rs = CType(m_Connection.Execute(query, , CommandTypeEnum.adCmdText), _
            Recordset)

        ' Return the Recordset.
        Return rs
    End Function

    ' Load a ListBox with values returned by a query.
    Public Sub LoadListBoxFromQuery(ByVal lst As System.WinForms.ListBox, _
        ByVal query As String, Optional ByVal separator As String = ", ")
        Dim rs As Recordset
        Dim txt As String
```

LISTING 11.2   CONTINUED

```
        Dim field_num As Integer

        lst.Items.Clear()
        rs = ExecuteQuery(query)
        Do While Not rs.eof
            ' Combine the returned field values into a string.
            txt = New String(rs.Fields(0).Value.ToString())
            For field_num = 1 To rs.Fields.Count - 1
                txt = txt & separator & _
                    rs.Fields(field_num).Value.ToString()
            Next field_num

            ' Add the string to ListBox.
            lst.Items.Add(txt.ToString())

            ' Move to the next record.
            rs.MoveNext()
        Loop

        rs.Close()
        rs = Nothing
    End Sub

    ' Load a ComboBox with values returned by a query.
    Public Sub LoadComboBoxFromQuery(ByVal cbo As System.WinForms.ComboBox, _
      ByVal query As String, Optional ByVal separator As String = ", ")
        Dim rs As Recordset
        Dim txt As String
        Dim field_num As Integer

        cbo.Items.Clear()
        rs = ExecuteQuery(query)
        Do While Not rs.eof
            ' Combine the returned field values into a string.
            txt = New String(rs.Fields(0).Value.ToString())
            For field_num = 1 To rs.Fields.Count - 1
                txt = txt & separator & _
                    rs.Fields(field_num).Value.ToString()
            Next field_num

            ' Add the string to ComboBox.
            cbo.Items.Add(txt.ToString())

            ' Move to the next record.
            rs.MoveNext()
        Loop

        rs.Close()
        rs = Nothing
    End Sub

    ' Return a Recordset containing the database's table names.
    ' The Recordset item of interest is TABLE_NAME.
    Public Function GetTableNames() As Recordset
        Dim rs As Recordset
```

LISTING 11.2 CONTINUED

```
        ' Use OpenSchema and get the table names.
        rs = CType(m_Connection.OpenSchema( _
            SchemaEnum.adSchemaTables, _
            New Object() {Nothing, Nothing, Nothing, "Table"}), _
            Recordset)

        Return rs
    End Function

    ' Return a Recordset containing the table's field names.
    ' The Recordset item of interest is COLUMN_NAME.
    Public Function GetFieldNames(ByVal table_name As String) As Recordset
        Dim rs As Recordset

        ' Use OpenSchema and get the field names.
        rs = CType(m_Connection.OpenSchema( _
            SchemaEnum.adSchemaColumns, _
            New Object() {Nothing, Nothing, table_name}), _
            Recordset)

        Return rs
    End Function

    ' Execute an action statement. Return an error message
    ' if there is a problem. Reutrn Nothing if everything is ok.
    Public Function ExecuteActionStatement(ByVal statement As String) As String
        ' Execute the statement.
        Try
            m_Connection.Execute(statement, , _
                CommandTypeEnum.adCmdText)
            Return Nothing
        Catch e As Exception
            ' Return an error message. The exception's
            ' message is not very pretty and the stack trace
            ' would overwhelm a user, but this information
            ' is ok in a prototype.
            Return e.Message & CrLf & CrLf & "Stack Trace:" & _
                CrLf & e.StackTrace.ToString()
        End Try
    End Function
End Class
```

PairedValues

The PairedValues class shown in Listing 11.3 keeps track of two sets of paired values. In program ADOTools, the values are status names and status codes.

The class stores its values in two Dictionary objects. Each Dictionary object holds one set of values using the other set of values as keys. For example, in program ADOTools, the first Dictionary object holds status names using the corresponding status codes as keys. The second Dictionary object stores status codes with the matching status names as keys.

The LoadFromRecordset method loops through the records in an ADO Recordset and calls AddValuePair to add entries for each of the records in the Recordset. Subroutine AddValuePair first verifies that neither of the paired values already appears in the `Dictionary` objects. It then adds each value to the appropriate `Dictionary` object using the other value as its key.

Finally, the `Value1` and `Value2` functions return an item's associated paired value. For example, if the Suspended status name has the status code S, then `Value1("S")` would return Suspended and `Value2("Suspended")` would return S.

LISTING 11.3   THE PAIREDVALUE CLASS LETS A PROGRAM BUILD LOOKUP TABLES EASILY.

```
Imports ADODB

' Associate sequences of two paired values.
Public Class PairedValues
    Private m_Value1 As New Collections.Dictionary()
    Private m_Value2 As New Collections.Dictionary()

    ' Clear the currently loaded values.
    Public Sub ClearValues()
        m_Value1.Clear()
        m_Value2.Clear()
    End Sub

    ' Load the pairs from a Recordset's first two columns.
    Public Sub LoadFromRecordset(ByVal rs As Recordset)
        ' Clear the value pairs.
        ClearValues()

        ' Load the value pairs.
        Do While Not (rs.EOF)
            AddValuePair(rs.Fields.Item(0).Value.ToString, _
                rs.Fields.Item(1).Value.ToString)
            rs.MoveNext()
        Loop
    End Sub

    ' Add a value pair.
    Public Sub AddValuePair(ByVal value1 As String, ByVal value2 As String)
        ' Make sure these values aren't already present.
        If m_Value1.Contains(value2) Then
            Throw New DuplicateNameException("Value 2 '" & value2.ToString & _
                "' is already present")
        End If
        If m_Value2.Contains(value1) Then
            Throw New DuplicateNameException("Value 1 '" & value1.ToString & _
                "' is already present")
        End If

        ' Save the values.
        m_Value1.Add(value2, value1)
        m_Value2.Add(value1, value2)
    End Sub

    ' Return the value1 for a value2.
    Public Function Value1(ByVal value2 As String) As String
        Return m_Value1.Item(value2).ToString
    End Function
```

LISTING 11.3   CONTINUED

```
' Return the value2 for a value1.
Public Function Value2(ByVal value1 As String) As String
    Return m_Value2.Item(value1).ToString
End Function

End Class
```

ADOTOOLS

Using the DBConnection and PairedValues classes keeps program ADOTools reasonably simple. Listing 11.4 shows the most interesting parts of the ADOTools code.

The program's LoadDatabase routine finds the program's database and connects its DBConnection object to the database using the OpenDatabaseAccess method. It then performs some user interface chores such as displaying the database name and enabling some buttons.

LoadAccountStatuses calls the DBConnection object's LoadComboBoxFromQuery method twice to display account status names and codes from the AccountStatuses table. It then allocates a new PairedValues object and uses its LoadFromRecordset method to initialize it with all of the account status names and codes in the AccountStatuses table.

When the user clicks the > button, the program's btnFindAccountStatusCode_Click event handler calls the PairedValues object's Value2 method to get the account status code that matches the selected account status name. When the user clicks the < button, the program's btnFindAccountStatusName_Click event handler calls the PairedValues object's Value1 method to get the account status name that matches the selected account status code.

When the user clicks the List Tables button, the program calls the subroutine ListTables. This subroutine calls the DBConnection object's GetTableNames method to fetch a Recordset listing the database's tables. It loops through the Recordset adding the tables to a list.

When the user clicks a table in this list, the program calls subroutine ListFields. This subroutine works much as GetTableNames does. It calls the DBConnection object's GetFieldNames routine to get a Recordset listing the selected table's fields. It then loops through the Recordset, adding the names to a list.

When the user clicks the Execute button in the Query area, the program executes the entered query in two ways. First, it calls the DBConnection object's ExecuteQuery method to get a Recordset containing the returned records. For each record in the Recordset, the routine concatenates the record's fields to form a single string. It adds that string to a list.

Next, the program fills another list with the selected records by calling the DBConnection object's LoadListBoxFromQuery method. This is much easier than using ExecuteQuery.

Finally, when the user clicks the Execute button in the Action Statement area, the program calls the DBConnection object's ExecuteAction method to perform the selected action. It then calls ListTables to update the list of tables because the example action statements in this program add and drop a table.

LISTING 11.4 PROGRAM ADOTOOLS USES THE DBCONNECTION AND PAIREDVALUES CLASSES TO MANIPULATE A DATABASE.

```
' Load the database.
Private Sub LoadDatabase()
    Dim database_name As String

    ' StartupPath is in the bin directory. Go up one
    ' level and down to the Data directory.
    database_name = Application.StartupPath()
    database_name = Microsoft.VisualBasic.Left$(database_name, _
        len(database_name) - 3)
    database_name = database_name & "Data\People.mdb"

    ' Open the database.
    m_DBConnection.OpenDatabaseAccess(database_name)

    ' Display the database name in the form's caption.
    Form1.Text = "ADOTools [" & m_DBConnection.DatabaseTitle & "]"
    btnListTables.Enabled = True
    btnExecuteQuery.Enabled = True
    btnExecuteAction.Enabled = True
    txtQuery.Enabled = True
End Sub

' Load the AccountStatusName/AccountStatusCode pairs.
Private Sub LoadAccountStatuses()
    Dim rs As Recordset

    ' Load the ComboBoxes.
    m_DBConnection.LoadComboBoxFromQuery(cboAccountStatusName, _
    "SELECT AccountStatusName FROM AccountStatuses ORDER BY AccountStatusName")
    m_DBConnection.LoadComboBoxFromQuery(cboAccountStatusCode, _
    "SELECT AccountStatusCode FROM AccountStatuses ORDER BY AccountStatusCode")

    ' Load the paired account status names and codes.
    rs = m_DBConnection.ExecuteQuery( _
        "SELECT AccountStatusName, AccountStatusCode FROM AccountStatuses")
    m_AccountStatusPairs = New PairedValues()
    m_AccountStatusPairs.LoadFromRecordset(rs)
    rs.Close()
    rs = Nothing
End Sub

' Display the account status code for the selected
' account status name.
Protected Sub btnFindAccountStatusCode_Click(ByVal sender As Object, _
  ByVal e As System.EventArgs)
    cboAccountStatusCode.Text = _
        m_AccountStatusPairs.Value2(cboAccountStatusName.Text.ToString())
End Sub

' Display the account status name for the selected
' account status code.
Protected Sub btnFindAccountStatusName_Click(ByVal sender As Object, _
  ByVal e As System.EventArgs)
```

LISTING 11.4 CONTINUED

```
        cboAccountStatusName.Text = _
            m_AccountStatusPairs.Value1(cboAccountStatusCode.Text.ToString())
End Sub

' List the database tables.
Protected Sub btnListTables_Click(ByVal sender As Object, _
  ByVal e As System.EventArgs)
    ListTables()
End Sub

' List the database's tables.
Private Sub ListTables()
    Dim rs As Recordset

    ' Clear the field list.
    lstFields.Items.Clear()

    ' Load the list of tables.
    lstTables.Items.Clear()
    rs = m_DBConnection.GetTableNames()
    Do While Not rs.eof
        lstTables.Items.Add( _
            rs.Fields.Item("TABLE_NAME").Value.ToString)
        rs.MoveNext()
    Loop
    rs.Close()
    rs = Nothing

    lstTables.Enabled = True
End Sub

' Display the fields in the selected table.
Protected Sub lstTables_SelectedIndexChanged(ByVal sender As Object, _
  ByVal e As System.EventArgs)
    ListFields()
End Sub

' Display the fields in the selected table.
Private Sub ListFields()
    Dim rs As Recordset

    ' Clear the list.
    lstFields.Items.Clear()

    ' Make sure a table is selected.
    If lstTables.SelectedIndex >= 0 Then
        ' A table is selected. Display its fields.
        ' Load the list of fields in this table.
        rs = m_DBConnection.GetFieldNames(lstTables.SelectedItem.ToString)
        Do While Not rs.eof
            lstFields.Items.Add( _
                rs.Fields.Item("COLUMN_NAME").Value.ToString)
            rs.MoveNext()
        Loop
        rs.Close()
```

PART

III

CH

11

LISTING 11.4 CONTINUED

```
            rs = Nothing
        End If

        lstFields.Enabled = True
    End Sub

    ' Execute the query.
    Protected Sub btnExecuteQuery_Click(ByVal sender As Object, _
      ByVal e As System.EventArgs)
        Dim rs As Recordset
        Dim txt As String
        Dim field_num As Integer

        ' Load lstRecordset using a Recordset.
        lstRecordset.Items.Clear()
        rs = m_DBConnection.ExecuteQuery(txtQuery.Text)
        Do While Not rs.eof
            ' Combine the returned field values into a string.
            txt = New String(rs.Fields(0).Value.ToString())
            For field_num = 1 To rs.Fields.Count - 1
                txt = txt & ", " & _
                    rs.Fields(field_num).Value.ToString()
            Next field_num

            ' Add the string to lstRecordset.
            lstRecordset.Items.Add(txt.ToString())

            ' Move to the next record.
            rs.MoveNext()
        Loop
        rs.Close()
        rs = Nothing

        ' Load lstList using LoadListBoxFromQuery.
        m_DBConnection.LoadListBoxFromQuery(lstList, txtQuery.Text, _
            " ")
    End Sub

    ' Execute an action statement.
    Protected Sub btnExecuteAction_Click(ByVal sender As Object, _
      ByVal e As System.EventArgs)
        ' Execute the statement.
        m_DBConnection.ExecuteActionStatement(cboAction.Text)

        ' Update the list of tables.
        ListTables()
    End Sub
```

DSNs

Windows Data Source Names (DSNs) provide a big help in isolating programs from specific database types. A DSN defines a connection to a database. The program can then connect to the database using the DSN rather than information about the database itself.

If you later need to switch databases, you can change the DSN's definition. The program can still connect to the DSN without knowing that the DSN has changed.

CREATING DSNs

To create a DSN, click the computer's Start menu, open the Settings submenu, and select the Control Panel command. On the Control Panel, double-click the ODBC Data Sources applet to start the ODBC Data Source Administrator.

Click the User DSN tab to create a User DSN. A program can only use a User DSN if the user who is running the program is the user who created the DSN.

Click the System DSN tab to create a DSN that can be shared by all the users on the computer. To create a System DSN, you need administrator privileges on the computer. Figure 11.3 shows the ODBC Data Source Administrator's System DSN tab. This computer already has DSNs named IFTA and MQIS defined.

Figure 11.3
The System DSN tab on the ODBC Data Source Administrator enables you to add a new system DSN.

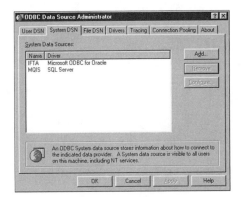

PART

III

CH

11

Click the File DSN tab to create a DSN with connection information stored in a file. A File DSN is an INI file containing values that describe the database connection.

After you have selected the appropriate tab, click the Add button. The ODBC Data Source Administrator displays the dialog shown in Figure 11.4.

Figure 11.4
Before you can create a DSN, you must select the new DSN's database driver.

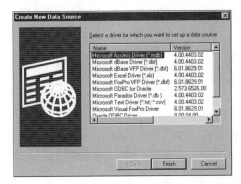

Select the database driver you want to use and click Finish. What comes next depends on the type of database you are using. Figure 11.5 shows the dialog that appears when you use the Microsoft Access driver. Enter the name you want to give the new DSN and a brief description. Click the Select button to select the Access database file. When you are finished, click the OK button.

Figure 11.5
The fields needed to define a DSN depend on the driver. This figure shows how to define a DSN using the Microsoft Access driver.

At this point, the ODBC Data Source Administrator creates the DSN and adds it to its list.

DSNs IN DATA CONNECTIONS

After you have defined a DSN, your programs can use it to connect to a database without knowing all the connection's details. To create a data connection object that connects to the DSN, open the Server Explorer and double-click the Add Connection item. The Data Link properties dialog appears as shown in Figure 11.6.

Figure 11.6
The Data Link Properties dialog lets you create a data connection.

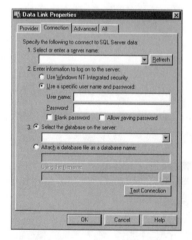

Initially, this dialog assumes you are using a SQL Server database. The whole point of using a DSN is to separate the data connection from the database itself, so you don't want to specify SQL Server here. Click the Provider tab to select a different data provider. Select Microsoft OLE DB Provider for ODBC Drivers because the DSN you created is an ODBC object. Figure 11.7 shows the result.

Figure 11.7
To use a DSN, select Microsoft OLE DB Provider for ODBC Drivers.

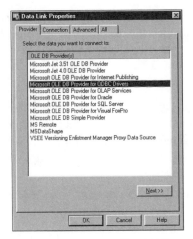

After you have selected the ODBC driver, return to the Connection tab. Make sure the Use data source name option is selected, and select the DSN from the dropdown list. If the database requires a username and password, enter them. Then click the Test Connection button to verify that Visual Basic can connect to the DSN. Figure 11.8 shows the dialog selecting the DSN named DSN_Example.

PART
III

CH
11

Figure 11.8
Select the DSN from the dropdown list and click the Test Connection button.

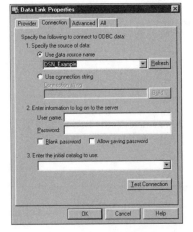

Now you can use the new connection in your program. For example, you could use the Data Form Wizard to quickly build a form that displays the data contained in the database referenced by the DSN. For more information, see the "Data Form Wizard" section in Chapter 8.

DSNs IN CODE

You can also use a DSN to connect to a database in your Visual Basic source code. Listing 11.5 displays data loaded from the DSN named DSN_Example. The LoadData subroutine begins by creating an `ADODB.Connection` object and setting its `ConnectionString` to indicate the DSN. Notice that the program only identifies the DSN by its name. If you later changed the DSN's definition, the program would happily load the new database indicated by the DSN.

After setting the `Connection`'s `ConnectionString`, `LoadData` opens the `Connection` object. It uses that object's `Execute` method to query the database and create a Recordset containing the results. `LoadData` then iterates through the Recordset's records, adding the LastName and FirstName fields to the ListBox named `lstEmployees`. Finally, `LoadData` closes the `Recordset` and `Connection` objects.

LISTING 11.5   PROGRAM DSN USES THIS CODE TO CONNECT TO A DSN PROGRAMMATICALLY.

```
' Load the data.
Private Sub LoadData()
    Dim db_connection As New ADODB.Connection()
    Dim rs As ADODB.Recordset

    ' Open the connection using the DSN.
    db_connection.ConnectionString = "Data Source=DSN_Example"
    db_connection.Open()

    ' Select the employee names.
    rs = CType(db_connection.Execute( _
            "SELECT LastName, FirstName " & _
            "FROM Employees " & _
            "ORDER BY LastName, FirstName", , _
            ADODB.CommandTypeEnum.adCmdText), _
        ADODB.Recordset)

    ' Display the names.
    lstEmployees.Items.Clear()
    Do While Not rs.EOF
        lstEmployees.Items.Add( _
            rs.Fields.Item("LastName").Value.ToString & ", " & _
            rs.Fields.Item("FirstName").Value.ToString)
        rs.MoveNext()
    Loop

    ' Close the Recordset and Connection.
    rs.Close()
    db_connection.Close()
End Sub
```

Program DSN, shown in Figure 11.9, uses this code to display the names of employees in the `DsnTest.mdb` database. Note that the program does not work until you define a DSN named `DSN_Example` connecting to the database.

To use the ADODB `Connection` and `Recordset` objects, program DSN needs a reference to the Microsoft ActiveX Data Objects (ADO) library. The section "ADO Tools" later in this chapter shows you how to set that reference.

Figure 11.9
Program DSN displays records fetched using a DSN.

FINDING DATABASES

If a program uses an ADODataConnection object to bind to a database at design time, the database's location is built into the object so the program does not need to find the database at runtime. It simply uses the ADOConnection object, and that object knows how to find the database.

However, it is often useful to allow a program to open one of several different databases at runtime. This can be particularly helpful for prototypes in which you might want to use different databases to test different scenarios. You might have one database for general level users, one for supervisors, and one for database administrators. Alternatively, different developers might work with their own copies of the database so they can perform tests without interfering with each other.

One way to handle this situation is to give the program several different ADOConnection objects and select the right one at runtime. That method is rather cumbersome, requiring a potentially large number of ADOConnection objects. It also ties the program to particular database locations, so the ADOConnection objects don't work if you need to move the databases later.

A better solution is to connect to the database at run time. The previous section shows how to use DSNs to connect to a database at run time.

Another method is to locate the database file at runtime and open it. The database file can be stored in a location relative to the prototype code. When you make a VB.NET project, Visual Basic creates a new directory to hold its files. Inside that directory, it also creates two subdirectories named bin and obj. When you run the program from the development environment, you execute an exe file inside the bin directory. If the program looks at the Application object's StartupPath method, it sees the path to the executable in the bin directory. Starting from that point, the program can locate a database in a nearby directory.

For example, suppose you create a Data directory inside the project directory, and you place several databases there. The program can use Application.StartupPath to find the bin directory, remove the "bin" from the end of the path, and add "Data" to find the databases' directory.

At runtime, the program can locate this directory and present the user with a list of databases. Example program RelativePath, shown in Figure 11.10, does just that. When you invoke the File menu's Open Database command, the program locates its Data directory. It presents a file selection dialog that lets you select one of the database files in that directory.

When you select a file, the program connects to it and displays a list of records in the database's Employees table.

Figure 11.10
Program RelativePath lets the user select a database at runtime.

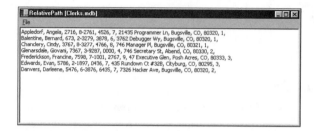

Program RelativePath uses the code shown in Listing 11.6 to find its Data directory, let the user select a database, and read records from that database. When the program starts, it sets some properties for its file selection dialog. It sets the dialog's `Filter` property to select Access database files, and it sets the `CheckFileExists` property to True so the user must select a file that actually exists. It also sets the control's `InitialDirectory` property to the path to the program's Data directory. The `FilePath` function makes this easier. `FilePath` takes a directory path as a parameter and returns the path with the text after the last backslash (\) is removed. For example, `FilePath("C:\VB Prototyping\RelativePath\bin")` returns the string "`C:\VB Prototyping\RelativePath`."

When the user invokes the Open Database command, the `mnuFileOpenDatabase_Click` subroutine displays the file selection dialog. If the user selects a file, the routine then updates the program's title bar caption to include the name of the database selected. The `FileTitle` function makes this a little easier. `FileTitle` takes as a parameter a complete file name and returns the file's name without its directory path. This makes the title bar caption a little less cluttered than it is with the whole file name.

The `mnuFileOpenDatabase_Click` subroutine then updates the file selection dialog's `InitialDirectory` property to the current directory. The next time the user wants to open a database, the dialog starts in this directory.

With the preliminaries out of the way, `mnuFileOpenDatabase_Click` connects to the database and loads some data.

LISTING 11.6   PROGRAM RELATIVEPATH USES THIS CODE TO LET THE USER SELECT A DATABASE AT RUNTIME.

```
Public Sub New()
    MyBase.New()

    Form1 = Me

    'This call is required by the Win Form Designer.
    InitializeComponent()
```

LISTING 11.6   CONTINUED

```
    ' Make the dialog start in the Data directory.
    dlgOpenDatabase.InitialDirectory = _
        FilePath(Application.StartupPath) & "\Data"

    ' Set some other properties.
    dlgOpenDatabase.Filter = _
        "Access Databases (*.mdb)|*.mdb|" & _
        "All Files (*.*)|*.*"
    dlgOpenDatabase.CheckFileExists = True
End Sub

' Let the user select a database to open.
Protected Sub mnuFileOpenDatabase_Click(ByVal sender As Object, _
  ByVal e As System.EventArgs)
    Dim query As String
    Dim db_connection As New ADODB.Connection()
    Dim rs As ADODB.Recordset
    Dim fld As ADODB.Field
    Dim txt As String

    If dlgOpenDatabase.ShowDialog() = DialogResult.OK Then
        ' Display the database name.
        Me.Text = "RelativePath [" & _
            FileTitle(dlgOpenDatabase.FileName) & "]"

        ' Update the dialog's InitialDirectory.
        dlgOpenDatabase.InitialDirectory = FilePath(dlgOpenDatabase.FileName)

        ' Open the database.
        db_connection.ConnectionString = _
            "Provider=Microsoft.Jet.OLEDB.4.0;" & _
            "Data Source=" & dlgOpenDatabase.FileName & ";" & _
            "Persist Security Info=False"
        db_connection.Open()

        ' Open the Recordset.
        query = "SELECT * FROM Employees"
        rs = CType(db_connection.Execute(query, , CommandTypeEnum.adCmdText), _
            Recordset)

        ' Process the records.
        Do While Not (rs.EOF)
            ' Add this record to the string.
            For Each fld In rs.Fields
                txt = txt & fld.Value.ToString() & ", "
            Next fld
            txt = txt & CrLf

            ' Move to the next record.
            rs.MoveNext()
        Loop

        ' Display the result.
        txtResults.Text = txt
        txtResults.Select(0, 0)
```

LISTING 11.6   CONTINUED

```
            ' Close the Recordset and Connection.
            rs.Close()
            db_connection.Close()
        End If
End Sub

' Return the last part of the path.
Private Function FileTitle(ByVal path As String) As String
    Dim pos As Integer

    ' Find the last "\" character.
    pos = InStrRev(path, "\")
    If pos > 0 Then
        ' There is a "\". Take whatever comes after it.
        path = Mid$(path, pos + 1)
    End If

    Return path
End Function

' Return the first part of the path up to but not
' including the final \.
Private Function FilePath(ByVal path As String) As String
    Dim pos As Integer

    ' Find the last "\" character.
    pos = InStrRev(path, "\")
    If pos > 0 Then
        ' There is a "\". Take whatever comes before it.
        path = Microsoft.VisualBasic.Left$(path, pos - 1)
    Else
        ' There is no "\". Return an empty string.
        path = ""
    End If

    Return path
End Function
```

If a program can use different databases selected at run time, the location of the database names is just another piece of data. Program RelativePath looks in its Data directory to see what databases are available. The program could just as easily use GetAllSettings to fetch a list of database locations stored in the system registry. Those databases could be database file names, DSNs, or even URLs specifying the location of a Web service.

LOGONS AND SECURITY

Before a program can use a database, it must connect to the database either explicitly or implicitly. Most of this book's examples use simple Access databases without password protection. Access databases are easy to work with and provide enough functionality for most prototypes.

This level of security is insufficient for most real applications. Anyone can open the database files and make changes using the prototype, Access, or any other database program.

When you build the final application, you are likely to use a more powerful database like Oracle, Informix, or SQL Server. Those databases include good security features, such as separate usernames and passwords for each user. The final application should use those features to provide security.

When the program starts, it should prompt the user for a username and password. This logon screen can double as the program's splash screen and display the program's name and version number. The program should then use the values entered by the user to connect to the database. If the database connection fails, the program should exit. Now the burden of verifying the user's identity is on the database—not on your program—so you don't have to do any work to take advantage of the database's security.

If the prototype uses a database that provides user-level password protection, by all means, use it. Otherwise, it's usually not worth the trouble of building really safe logon security into the prototype. If the prototype uses an Access database without a password, an attacker can simply open the database with Access or an ADO program to modify the data. If you place a single password on the database, you either need to give the password to every user, or you need to code the password into the program. In the first case, the password is not very secure because a lot of people know what it is. In the second case, an attacker can pick apart your code and find the password.

PART

III

CH

11

Rather than spending a lot of time trying to make the prototype secure, create a UserPasswords table with two fields: UserName and Password. When the prototype starts, it can prompt the user for a username and password just as the final application will. Instead of using this information to connect to the database, however, the prototype simply looks the user up in the UserPasswords table and verifies that the password the user entered matches the one that's stored in the table.

This is really not a secure method for password protection. An attacker can easily open the unprotected database and read everyone's passwords. However, this method shows the behavior the final application will use, so it is fine for a throwaway user interface prototype.

Tip

In fact, because the database is unsecured, you should probably tell users not to use any real passwords in the prototype. If someone uses the same password they use on another system, someone reading the UserPasswords table could learn passwords that could do some real damage. Of course, users *should* use different passwords for every system they use, but many do not.

Both the prototype and the final application probably need to include screens that allow the system administrator to add and delete users and change their passwords. The prototype can do this by adding, deleting, and modifying records in the UserPrivileges table. The final application needs to modify the database itself. For example, it could set a user's password using the SQL statement:

```
ALTER USER 'Rod' IDENTIFIED BY 'VB Prototyping'
```

Although the prototype and final application use different methods for managing user passwords, they can both use the same logon and password maintenance screens.

Example program Passwords, shown in Figure 11.11, uses the code shown in Listing 11.11 to validate the user's name and password. If the user enters an invalid username or password, the program displays an error message and quits. If the username and password are correct, the program displays its main form and unloads the logon form.

Figure 11.11
The Passwords logon form requires a username and password before it displays the program's main form.

LISTING 11.7   PROGRAM PASSWORDS USES THIS CODE TO VERIFY USERNAMES AND PASSWORDS.

```
' If the username/password is valid, display the program's
' main form. Otherwise warn the user and exit.
Protected Sub btnOk_Click(ByVal sender As Object, ByVal e As System.EventArgs)
    Dim frmMain As MainForm

    ' Verify the username/password.
    If LogonOk(txtUserName.Text, txtPassword.Text) Then
        ' Display the program's main form.
        frmMain = New MainForm()
        frmMain.Show()

        ' Close this form.
        Me.Close()
    Else
        ' The logon failed. Tell the user.
        MsgBox("Invalid username/password", _
            Microsoft.VisualBasic.MsgBoxStyle.Critical, _
            "Logon Error")

        ' Close this form.
        Me.Close()
    End If
End Sub

' Return True if the username/password is valid.
' This program uses a connectionless Recordset because
' it won't do anything else with the database.
Private Function LogonOk(ByVal username As String, ByVal password As String) _
    As Boolean
    Dim db_name As String
```

LISTING 11.7   CONTINUED

```
    Dim connect_string As String
    Dim query As String
    Dim rs As ADODB.Recordset

    ' Select the record (if any) that holds this username
    ' and password.
    db_name = FilePath(Application.StartupPath) & "\People.mdb"
    connect_string = _
        "Provider=Microsoft.Jet.OLEDB.4.0;" & _
        "Data Source='" & db_name & "';" & _
        "Persist Security Info=False"
    query = _
        "SELECT * " & _
        "FROM UserPasswords " & _
        "WHERE UserName='" & username & "'" & _
        "  AND Password='" & password & "'"
    rs = New ADODB.Recordset()
    rs.Open(query, connect_string)

    ' Return True if we found a record.
    LogonOk = Not (rs.EOF And rs.BOF)

    ' Close the recordset.
    rs.Close()
    rs = Nothing
End Function
```

The UserPasswords table in the example database defines three users: Clerk, Supervisor, and Administrator. Each of these users has its username as its password. For example, the Clerk password is Clerk.

Tip

Be sure you change the passwords for Clerk, Supervisor, and Administrator before you ship the final application. These passwords are fine for demonstrating a prototype but they are much too easy to guess for a finished application. Hackers often break into computers by trying to use default passwords that are installed when the computer is set up.

Tip

To save time during prototype development, you might want to bypass the logon form. When the form loads, it can automatically log on with a particular username and password and then unload itself.

Be sure to remove this code before you run demonstrations for customers. This way, they can see the normal logon process.

PART

III

CH

11

USER PRIVILEGES

Many large-scale business applications have more than one class of user. The names of these classes varies by industry, but usually there are at least three kinds of users. I call these users types clerks, supervisors, and administrators.

Clerks are the typical users who work with the application every day. Usually there are a lot more clerks than supervisors or administrators. For example, think of customer service representatives.

As the name implies, supervisors supervise clerks. They tend to know more about the application domain than clerks. This enables them to fix problems the clerks have. They sometimes also have extra privileges. For example, a supervisor might be able to view a clerk productivity report to which clerks do not have access. They might also be able to enter certain values and perform certain functions that a clerk cannot. For example, a supervisor might be able to waive a customer's late fee.

Administrators are those who manage the application itself. They create users, change passwords, and set program configuration parameters. Administrators usually know the most about the program though they do not always know the most about the application domain.

Tale from the Trenches

Several of the projects I have worked on were designed to replace or enhance existing systems that had grown up over time. In several cases, one or two customers had put together remarkably powerful systems with little or no formal programming education.

It is important that you win these people over at the start. Often they can make or break your project. Fortunately, they usually enjoy experimenting with software and you can get them excited about the new, more powerful application you are building. These people also usually become the administrators for your new application so they don't lose their current prestigious positions as application gurus.

Some applications have additional classes of users. For instance, a sales and inventory system might have sales representatives who generate orders, inventory clerks who manage inventory and order new products when necessary, order fulfillment clerks who process orders and ship them, and corporate managers who can generate reports but who do not modify any data.

You should try to get your customers to make a list of the classes of users and define their capabilities as early in the project as possible. Lots of design decisions are based on what different kinds of users can do, so it's important to know this as soon as possible.

If there are lots of classes, the customer can more easily control who gets access to what. Unfortunately, that can make your job harder and it can cause some confusion among the users if they have trouble telling the classes apart. If there are only a few classes, your job is easier because you don't need to consider as many different situations. In most of the systems I have built, three classes were enough.

DEFINING PRIVILEGES

After you have defined the user classes, you can build a prototype that accounts for them. Start by creating a UserPrivileges table. Give it two fields: UserName and Privilege. Enter records to define the types of privileges each user has. For example, if clerks should be allowed to view the Employees table, you might create an entry where UserName is Clerk, and Privilege is VIEW_EMPLOYEES.

If every user in a particular class has exactly the same privileges, you only need to create one record per class for each privilege you need to define. For each user, create a record that tells that user's class. For example, if Sally is a clerk, you might create a record where UserName is Sally and Privilege is CLERK.

Customers often want the ability to customize each user's privileges individually. They can imagine a user who—for some mysterious reason—should not be allowed to do one certain thing. Or perhaps this user is extra experienced and should be allowed to do something other users cannot.

To handle this case, create separate records in the UserPrivileges table for every user. Then you can set each user's access on an individual basis.

You can still create records for users named Clerk, Supervisor, and Administrator. Give these users the default properties for their class of user. Then, when you create a new user, copy the appropriate records to start the new user with default privileges.

Note that the administrators need to have privileges to modify the privileges table. After all, someone has to do this.

If the program can perform some extremely dangerous operations (such as reformatting a hard disk), you might decide to give the privilege to execute the operation to no one. If an administrator *really* needs to do this, he can grant himself the privilege, perform the operation, and then revoke the privilege again. This prevents people from executing the operation accidentally.

You can use a bound DataGrid control to manage the privileges, at least in the prototype. Users should not modify privileges often, and only one or two administrators should have permission to do this. This means that more than one person should rarely, if ever, need to modify the records at the same time. If that does happen, the program does not need to worry about multiple users interfering with each other and causing race conditions like those described in the "Modification Method" section of Chapter 10, "ADO Versus ADO.NET." Because race conditions are not a big problem, you can use a bound DataGrid control safely.

PART
III

CH
11

USING PRIVILEGES

Now that you've built the UserPrivileges table, the prototype and final application can use it to tailor the program to each user's needs. The easiest way to do this is to make one version of the program that provides all of the features any user could possibly need. It includes all the forms, buttons, and menu items that anyone might need.

When a form loads, it checks the privileges of the user who is currently running the program. It then hides any features that the user should not have by setting the appropriate controls' Visible property to False.

Don't disable these features instead of hiding them. A user who sees a menu item or command button that is disabled might try to figure out how to enable it. If the command is just not allowed, trying to enable the command is likely to frustrate the user and might end with a phone call asking you for help.

Example program Privileges, shown in Figure 11.12, presents different menu items and commands buttons to different users. The example database defines three users: Clerk, Supervisor, and Administrator. Each has its username as its password. For example, the Clerk password is Clerk. When you log in as different users, the program displays the appropriate menus and command buttons.

Figure 11.12
Program Privileges displays different menu items and command buttons for different users.

The Privileges program uses the code shown in Listing 11.8 to configure its main form. The form's constructor uses the user's logon name as a parameter. It stores the name in the m_UserName variable and calls subroutine ConfigureForm.

The ConfigureForm routine creates a new PrivilegeInfo object to help manage the user's privileges. The PrivilegeInfo class is described shortly. ConfigureForm uses the object's LoadPrivileges method to load the user's privileges from the database. It then uses the object's HasPrivilege method to decide which controls to hide for this user.

LISTING 11.8   PROGRAM PRIVILEGES USES A PRIVILEGEINFO OBJECT TO HELP MANAGE USER PRIVILEGES.

```
Private m_UserName As String

Private m_PrivilegeInfo As PrivilegeInfo

Public Sub New(ByVal user_name As String)
    MyBase.New()

    MainForm = Me

    'This call is required by the Win Form Designer.
    InitializeComponent()

    ' Display appropriate controls for this user.
    m_UserName = user_name
    ConfigureForm()
End Sub
```

Listing 11.8 Continued

```
' Configure the form for this user.
Private Sub ConfigureForm()
    Dim db_name As String

    ' Display the user's name in the form's caption.
    Me.Text = "Privileges [" & m_UserName & "]"

    ' Load the user's privilege information.
    db_name = FilePath(Application.StartupPath) & "\People.mdb"
    m_PrivilegeInfo = New PrivilegeInfo()
    m_PrivilegeInfo.LoadPrivileges(m_UserName, db_name)

    ' Hide controls the user shouldn't see.
    ' **********
    ' File menu.
    ' **********
    mnuFilePrint.Visible = m_PrivilegeInfo.HasPrivilege("Print")
    ' Display the separator only if mnuFilePrint is visible.
    mnuFileExitSep.Visible = m_PrivilegeInfo.HasPrivilege("Print")
    ' Everyone gets the exit command so we don't check that.

    ' ************
    ' Orders menu.
    ' ************
    mnuOrdersNew.Visible = m_PrivilegeInfo.HasPrivilege("Orders New")
    btnOrdersNew.Visible = m_PrivilegeInfo.HasPrivilege("Orders New")
    mnuOrdersList.Visible = m_PrivilegeInfo.HasPrivilege("Orders List")
    btnOrdersList.Visible = m_PrivilegeInfo.HasPrivilege("Orders List")
    mnuOrdersApproveLarge.Visible = _
        m_PrivilegeInfo.HasPrivilege("Orders Approve Large")
    ' Hide the whole menu if it doesn't have any visible children.
    CheckMenuForChildren(mnuOrders)

    ' *************
    ' Reports menu.
    ' *************
    ' Either all reports are visible or none are.
    mnuReports.Visible = m_PrivilegeInfo.HasPrivilege("Reports")

    ' ***********
    ' Users menu.
    ' ***********
    mnuUsersNew.Visible = m_PrivilegeInfo.HasPrivilege("Users New")
    mnuUsersPrivileges.Visible = _
        m_PrivilegeInfo.HasPrivilege("Users Privileges")
    ' Hide the whole menu if it doesn't have any visible children.
    CheckMenuForChildren(mnuUsers)
End Sub

' Hide this menu if it doesn't have any visible items.
Private Sub CheckMenuForChildren(ByVal menu_item As MenuItem)
    Dim subitem As MenuItem

    ' Assume the menu has no visible subitems.
    menu_item.Visible = False
```

LISTING 11.8   CONTINUED

```
        ' See if the menu has any visible subitems.
        For Each subitem In menu_item.MenuItems
            If subitem.Visible Then
                ' This subitem is visible. Make the menu visible.
                menu_item.Visible = True
                Exit For
            End If
        Next
End Sub
```

The `PrivilegeInfo` class shown in Listing 11.9 manages a user's privileges. Its `LoadPrivileges` method fetches all of the UserPrivilege table's records for the indicated user. It loops through the records, saving the privilege values into the `m_Privileges SortedList` object. Each privilege is used as its own key in the list. For instance, the "Reports" privilege is stored in the list with key "Reports."

Later the `HasPrivilege` method can tell if the user has a particular privilege by simply asking the `m_Privileges SortedList` object if it contains the corresponding key.

LISTING 11.9   THE PRIVILEGEINFO CLASS MAKES MANAGING USER PRIVILEGES EASY.

```
Public Class PrivilegeInfo

    ' This user's privileges.
    Private m_Privileges As Collections.SortedList

    ' Load this user's privileges. This version uses a
    ' connectionless Recordset because the example doesn't
    ' really need a connection.
    Public Sub LoadPrivileges( _
      ByVal user_name As String, ByVal db_name As String)
        Dim connect_string As String
        Dim query As String
        Dim rs As ADODB.Recordset

        ' Get the user's privileges.
        connect_string = _
            "Provider=Microsoft.Jet.OLEDB.4.0;" & _
            "Data Source='" & db_name & "';" & _
            "Persist Security Info=False"
        query = _
            "SELECT Privilege " & _
            "FROM UserPrivileges " & _
            "WHERE UserName='" & user_name & "'"
        rs = New ADODB.Recordset()
        rs.Open(query, connect_string)

        ' Save the privilege values.
        m_Privileges = New Collections.SortedList()
        Do While Not rs.EOF
            m_Privileges.Add(rs.Fields(0).Value, rs.Fields(0).Value)
            rs.MoveNext()
```

LISTING 11.9   CONTINUED

```
        Loop

        ' Close the recordset.
        rs.Close()
        rs = Nothing
    End Sub

    ' Return True if the user has this privilege.
    Public Function HasPrivilege(ByVal privilege_name As String) As Boolean
        HasPrivilege = m_Privileges.Contains(privilege_name)
    End Function

End Class
```

After you have defined the user classes, using privileges is straightforward. With only a little effort, you can make your prototype look very different for the different user classes.

APPLICATION PARAMETERS

The previous section shows how to use a database to load privileges for the user running the prototype. Using a similar technique, you can load application parameters that are the same for all users. Some examples of parameters that you might want to put in a database table include

- The number of days a customer payment can be late before you print a warning letter
- Your return address and phone number to include on correspondence
- The URL where customers can get extra information
- Colors the program uses to display different types of orders
- URLs for Web services that the program can query for product data
- An important message to display when the user logs on
- The tip-of-the-day

You could put all of these values inside the code either as hard-coded values or, more appropriately, as constants. Using Hard-coded values makes them hard to modify. To change a value, you need to recompile the program and then reinstall it on all of the users' computers. For values that change frequently, like messages to display to the user or a tip-of-the-day, that would be extremely inconvenient.

To handle this situation more easily, add an ApplicationParameter table to the database. Give it two fields: ParameterName and ParameterValue. Now create an ApplicationParameterInfo class that's very similar to the PrivilegeInfo class described in the previous section.

Listing 11.10 shows how the ApplicationParameterInfo class works. The LoadParameters method fetches the parameter values from the database and stores their values in SortedList object using the parameter names as keys. The `ParameterValue` method takes a parameter name as input and returns the parameter's value. If the parameter is missing from the parameter list, `ParameterValue` returns a default value.

LISTING 11.10 THE `ApplicationParameterInfo` CLASS ALLOWS A PROGRAM TO EASILY USE VALUES THAT CHANGE RELATIVELY FREQUENTLY.

```
Public Class ApplicationParameterInfo

    ' The parameter values.
    Private m_Parameters As Collections.SortedList

    ' Load the application parameters. This version uses a
    ' connectionless Recordset because the example doesn't
    ' really need a connection.
    Public Sub LoadParameters(ByVal db_name As String)
        Dim connect_string As String
        Dim query As String
        Dim rs As ADODB.Recordset

        ' Get the parameters.
        connect_string = _
            "Provider=Microsoft.Jet.OLEDB.4.0;" & _
            "Data Source='" & db_name & "';" & _
            "Persist Security Info=False"
        query = _
            "SELECT ParameterName, ParameterValue " & _
            "FROM ApplicationParameters"
        rs = New ADODB.Recordset()
        rs.Open(query, connect_string)

        ' Save the privilege values.
        m_Parameters = New Collections.SortedList()
        Do While Not rs.EOF
            m_Parameters.Add(rs.Fields(0).Value, rs.Fields(1).Value)
            rs.MoveNext()
        Loop

        ' Close the recordset.
        rs.Close()
        rs = Nothing
    End Sub

    ' Return the indicated parameter's value. Return the
    ' default value if the parameter is not in the list.
    Public Function ParameterValue(ByVal parameter_name As String, _
        Optional ByVal default_value As String = "") As String
        Try
            Return m_Parameters.Item(parameter_name).ToString()
        Catch e As Exception
            Return default_value
        End Try
    End Function

End Class
```

Example program ApplicationParameters, shown in Figure 11.13, uses the ApplicationParameterInfo class to load application parameters at runtime.

Figure 11.13
Program
ApplicationParameters
loads values from a
database at runtime.

Program ApplicationParameters uses the code shown in Listing 11.13 to load its parameters. Its LoadApplicationParameters subroutine creates an ApplicationParameterInfo object. It calls the object's LoadParameters method to fetch the parameter values stored in the database. Then the program calls the object's ParameterValue method to retrieve and display several application parameters.

LISTING 11.11   PROGRAM ApplicationParameters USES THIS CODE TO LOAD
PARAMETERS AT RUNTIME.

PART

III

CH

11

```
Public Sub New()
    MyBase.New()

    Form1 = Me

    'This call is required by the Win Form Designer.
    InitializeComponent()

    ' Load the application parameters.
    LoadApplicationParameters()
End Sub

' Load the application parameters and use them to format
' the form.
Private Sub LoadApplicationParameters()
    Dim db_name As String
    Dim clr As Drawing.Color

    ' Load the parameter information.
    m_AppParams = New ApplicationParameterInfo()
    db_name = FilePath(Application.StartupPath) & "\People.mdb"
    m_AppParams.LoadParameters(db_name)

    ' Get the parameters are want.
    Me.BackColor = System.Drawing.Color.FromString( _
        m_AppParams.ParameterValue("BackColor", "&HC0C0C0"))
    Me.ForeColor = System.Drawing.Color.FromString( _
        m_AppParams.ParameterValue("ForeColor", "&H000000"))
    lblTipOfTheDay.Text = "Tip: " & _
        m_AppParams.ParameterValue("TipOfTheDay", "")
    lblBooksURL.Text = _
        m_AppParams.ParameterValue("BooksURL", "")
    lblAllowedDaysLate.Text = _
```

LISTING 11.11   CONTINUED

```
        m_AppParams.ParameterValue("AllowedDaysLate", "")
    lblReturnAddress.Text = _
        m_AppParams.ParameterValue("ReturnAddressStreet", "") & CrLf & _
        m_AppParams.ParameterValue("ReturnAddressCity", "") & CrLf & _
        m_AppParams.ParameterValue("ReturnAddressState", "") & " " & _
        m_AppParams.ParameterValue("ReturnAddressZip", "") & CrLf & _
        m_AppParams.ParameterValue("ReturnAddressPhone", "")

    ' This one isn't in the database. It's here to show
    ' a default value.
    lblTipOfTheDay.BackColor = System.Drawing.Color.FromString( _
        m_AppParams.ParameterValue("TipBackColor", "&HC0C0C0"))
End Sub
```

As is the case with user privileges, two users should rarely need to modify application parameters at the same time. Only one or two system administrators should even have the privilege to do this. If two users don't need to modify the records at the same time, the program doesn't have problems with race conditions like those described in the "Modification Method" section of Chapter 10. In that case, you can safely use a bound DataGrid control to let the program maintain the application parameters with almost no work on your part.

RESERVING DATA

When more than one user tries to update a piece of data at the same time, a race condition can occur as described in the "Modification Method" section in Chapter 10. For example, suppose a customer service representative opens a customer's record and makes some changes. Meanwhile, an accounts receivable clerk opens the same account record to record a payment. Whichever user saves his changes second overwrites the other user's changes.

To prevent race conditions, the program should lock any record it is going to modify. In this example, the service representative would lock the customer record and begin editing. When the accounts receivable clerk tries to open the record, it is locked. The service representative can make any necessary changes without fear of interference. When the service representative is finished, the program updates the records and unlocks it. Now the accounts receivable clerk can edit the record.

Unfortunately, different databases provide different methods for locking records and determining who has a record locked. If you use the database's particular methods, you tie yourself to that database. If you need to switch databases later, you might be in for a lot of work.

A homegrown alternative is to place a ReservedBy field in a table in which you might need to lock records. Before editing a record, the program verifies that this field is blank. It then drops the current username into this field to reserve it. I call this "reserving" the record because the record isn't really locked.

Suppose another instance of the program needs to edit this record. It checks the ReservedBy field and sees the username of the person who has the record reserved. It might display a message like "This record is reserved by Bob." When you see this message, you know right away that you cannot edit the record, and you even know to go pester Bob if you need the record right away.

When the program has finished editing the record, it clears the ReservedBy field to free it.

The fact that the database itself doesn't handle the reservation has a couple of drawbacks. First, the record is not really locked, so another program that doesn't follow the rule of checking the ReservedBy field before updating a record could cause race conditions.

Second, reservations are not automatically removed when a program ends or when the database shuts down. If you have a record reserved and your computer crashes, the reservation remains in the database forever. To solve this problem, your program should have some way to clear these zombie reservations. You should not remove a reservation this way unless you are absolutely certain that the program that placed the reservation is really gone or you could mess up the system. Because this is a potentially dangerous operation, only system administrators and supervisors should be able to do it.

You might also want to write a stored procedure or small program to clear out any zombie reservations when you restart the database. For instance, you can use this SQL statement to clear the reservations for the Orders table:

```
UPDATE Orders SET ReservedBy = NULL
```

Repeat this statement for each table in the database to remove every reservation.

GATEWAY TABLES

You can minimize the number of ReservedBy fields you have to place in the database by using *gateway tables*. A gateway table is one that has a ReservedBy field that represents a reservation for several related tables. If this record is reserved, it is understood that all of the related records are also reserved.

Example
Consider a typical customer database. Each customer has a single record in the Accounts table that has a CustomerId field. This field links the master Accounts table to detail tables that hold Addresses, Orders, Invoices, Payments, and so on.

In this case, you can put a ReservedBy field in the Accounts table and use it as a gateway. If you need to modify any of the records related to a particular account, you reserve the Accounts record. As long as all the programs using the database know that this ReservedBy field controls access to the Accounts, Addresses, Orders, Invoices, and Payments tables, you only need a single gateway field.

This method has the same drawbacks as reservations in general. Reservations are not removed if a program crashes or if the database shuts down. A program that doesn't follow the rules can also cause race conditions. This problem might be even worse with gateway tables because it's more confusing than putting ReservedBy fields in all the tables that need coordination. However, it's a technique I've used successfully in several projects.

UPDATING SAFELY

Whenever you update a record, there is a tiny chance that another program might try to update the same record at the same time. This can occur even if you use the reservation scheme described in the previous section.

Example

Suppose when Program 1 and Program 2 both try to reserve the same record, the reservation steps take place in this order:

1. Program 1 looks at a record's ReservedBy field and sees that it is blank.
2. Program 2 looks at the same record's ReservedBy field and sees that it is blank.
3. Program 1 places its user's username in the field to reserve the record.
4. Program 2 places its user's username in the field to reserve the record.

Now both programs think they have the record reserved and you have a race condition.

The trick to making this reservation safely is to verify that the ReservedBy field is empty and assign it a new value at the same time. For example, the following SQL statement sets the ReservedBy field to Rod, but it does this only if the field is empty when the statement executes.

```
UPDATE Customers SET ReservedBy = 'Rod' WHERE ReservedBy IS NULL
```

If two programs try to grab the field at the same time, one succeeds and puts its user's username in the ReservedBy field. The other fails because ReservedBy is not NULL when it executes the UPDATE statement. After executing this statement, a program should check to see whether its UPDATE statement succeeded and it made the reservation.

SUMMARY

The most important concept in this chapter is the idea of database independence. If you isolate your code from the database, switching databases and installing new versions of your original database later will be much easier. This is particularly important when you are building a prototype and it's not completely clear which type of database is going to be used in the final application. If you are building an evolutionary prototype, you need to keep the code as independent as possible from the particular database you are using. Even if the choice of database has been firmly carved in stone, who knows what next year will bring?

It is often fastest to pick one data access method and assume you will use it during prototype development. You should still try to separate the database code from the program's other code, but you may make certain assumptions. For instance, most of the examples in this chapter assume you want to use ADO rather than ADO.NET. For a throwaway prototype, the choice usually doesn't matter much anyway.

CHAPTER **12**

GENERATING REPORTS

In this Chapter

Most business applications include reports and sometimes they include a *lot* of reports. Some programs I have worked on contained only eight or ten major forms but several dozen reports. Customers can think of countless ways to organize and rearrange data. After they use your prototype for a while, they will think of even more reports that take advantage of your program's capabilities.

Two main approaches to providing reports are prebuilt reports and reports generated at runtime. The next two sections describe these general approaches and give some tips for building reports in your prototypes. The section after those explains how you can extend the methods for build ad hoc reports to executing more general SQL statements.

PREBUILT REPORTS

Given enough time, you can eventually make the ultimate customized report. You can put text and graphics directly on a form to provide a preview. You can give the report options, such as display at different scales, print, save text into a text file, export into Word format, and so forth. Unfortunately, all of this takes a huge amount of time and effort. Even if you took the time to build this report, it wouldn't help you much with other reports. Unless you build a full-featured general reporting tool, you'll need to do a lot of customized programming to make each report look perfect.

Fortunately, VB.NET comes with Crystal Reports, a general tool for generating reports. Crystal Reports is very flexible and complex, so this book doesn't say too much about it. Entire books have been written about using Crystal Reports, and you can look for details in one of them—for example, *Seagate Crystal Reports 8: The Complete Reference* by George Peck (McGraw-Hill, 2000).

Getting started isn't too hard, however. The rest of this section walks you through an example that displays a list of Employee records using Crystal Reports.

Start a new Windows Application project. Open the Project menu and select Add Component. Select the Crystal Reports template. Name the new report Employees.rpt and click Open.

This launches a series of wizards to help you define the report. The wizards' purposes are relatively straightforward, so they are not described in detail here. You should be able to figure them out with trial and error. The next paragraphs describe the steps for creating one kind of report.

When the Seagate Crystal Reports Gallery shown in Figure 12.1 opens, select the Using the Report Expert option. Then select the Form expert and click OK.

Next, the Data Explorer shown in Figure 12.2 appears. Select the data source you want to use to generate the report. In Figure 12.2, an Access database is selected. It is listed in the Data Explorer's ADO folder because Crystal Reports accesses the data using ADO. If you do not see the data source you want here, click the Make New Recordset item in the ADO folder to connect to a new database.

Figure 12.1
Select a report type from the Crystal Reports gallery.

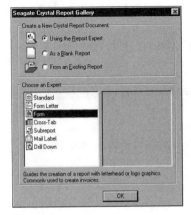

Figure 12.2
Select the report's data source.

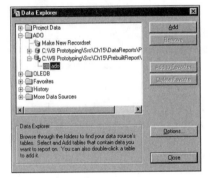

After you select a data source, click the Add button. That brings up the dialog shown in Figure 12.3. Here you can describe the Recordset that generates the report's data. For this example, select the SQL option and enter a SQL query that selects the records you want listed in the report. The query shown in Figure 12.3 performs a join of the Departments and Employees tables. After you enter the query, click the OK button.

Figure 12.3
Define the data in the report's Recordset.

When the Select Recordset dialog closes, the Data Explorer reappears. You don't need the Data Explorer right now, so click the Close button. Now the Form Report Expert shown in Figure 12.4 takes center stage. You have already selected a data source, so click Next to go to the Fields tab.

Figure 12.4
The Form Report Expert lists the ADO Recordset that Crystal Reports will use to build the report.

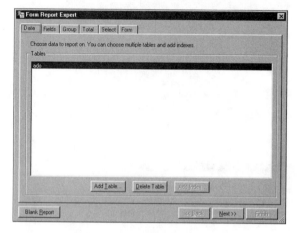

The Fields tab shown in Figure 12.5 lists the fields available in the Recordset. Select the fields you want to include in the report from the list on the left. Click the Add button to move them into the list of included fields. There is a lot more you can do to format the report, but for now just click the Finish button.

Figure 12.5
Use the Form Report Expert's Fields tab to select the report's fields.

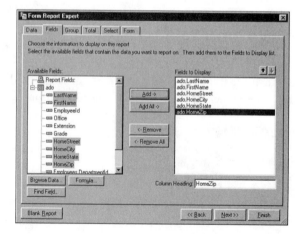

At this point, the Form Report Expert creates a new Crystal Reports object and adds it to your project. Initially, the report is not very well formatted. The fields you selected are probably wider than they need to be, and they don't all fit on one line.

Spend some time editing the report. Resize and arrange the fields, add headers and footers, and resize the report's sections so they make sense. This is another situation where Crystal Reports can do a lot more than there's room to describe here.

When you have finished arranging the report, only one task remains: displaying the report. Add a new form named EmployeesReportForm.vb to the project. From the Win Forms tab of the toolbox, place a CrystalReportViewer control on the form. Set the control's Dock property to Fill so it fills the whole form. Then click its ReportName property. Click the drop-down arrow to the right of the property value. The drop-down list should include the report you just built. Select it. That binds the CrystalReportViewer control to the report so it knows where to get the report it should display.

Go back to the program's main form. Add a button with text Employees Report to the form and give it code to display the report form you created similar to this:

```
' Display the Employees report.
Protected Sub btnEmployeesReport_Click(ByVal sender As Object, _
  ByVal e As System.EventArgs)
    Dim report_form As New EmployeesReport()

    report_form.ShowDialog()
End Sub
```

That's all you need to do. Notice that the only code you had to write is the code that displays the report form. Generating the report and displaying it in the CrystalReportViewer control is automatic.

Run the program. When you click the Employees Report button, the program displays the report form. Program PrebuiltReport, shown in Figure 12.6, demonstrates this technique for displaying reports.

PART

III

CH

12

Figure 12.6
Example program
PrebuiltReport dis-
plays a report gener-
ated by Crystal
Reports.

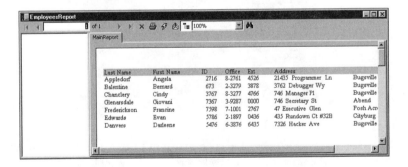

Although building reports using Crystal Reports takes a lot of steps, each individual step is simple. That makes report building a good task to assign to less experienced developers. In fact, building these reports is straightforward enough that you might be able to let your customers build some. If your customer provides experts to help you with the project domain, they probably know what kinds of reports they need better than you do. Letting customers build reports enables them to determine exactly what they get, saves you time, and helps increase customer buy-in.

REPORTS GENERATED AT RUNTIME

It is possible to build reports using Crystal Reports objects at runtime, but it is difficult. Without knowing ahead of time where the data will come from and which fields will be displayed, it's hard to format the report nicely. Fetching the data is relatively easy, but displaying it with nice column names and properly aligned columns is difficult.

If a program's code selects the data using ADO or ADO.NET, it can use the returned Recordset or DataSet to display the data. The DataSets provided by ADO.NET are particularly helpful because they provide methods for representing the returned data in extensible markup language (XML). Other programs can import XML data and display it. For example, after loading a DataSet, a program can use the DataSet's WriteXml method to save the XML into a file. Other Visual Basic programs can load the XML file and manipulate the data, and a Web browser can display the XML file using an appropriate style sheet.

Example program AdHocQuery, shown in Figure 16.7, enables you to create and execute queries at runtime. Enter one or more SELECT statements separated by semi-colons in the Queries box and click the Execute button. The program executes each query and adds the results to a DataSet. It then attaches the DataSet to a DataGrid control to display the results. The grid in Figure 12.7 shows the results of the first query, SELECT * FROM Employees.

Figure 12.7
Example program AdHocQuery enables the user to execute queries at runtime.

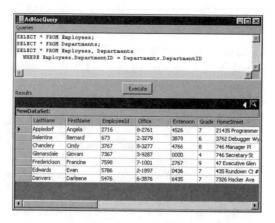

Program AdHocQuery uses the code shown in Listing 12.1 to execute queries. Considering how flexible the program is, the code is remarkably simple.

When you click the Execute button, the program opens a connection to the database. You can make the query connectionless by making the code use a connection string instead of an ADOConnection object when it creates the ADODataSetCommand object. Because this version executes several commands on the same connection, it saves time by using a single connection object instead of opening and closing a new connection for each command.

The program then uses Visual Basic's Split function to break the string holding all the queries into an array of strings where each array entry holds one query. Next, it loops through this array creating an `ADODataSetCommand` object for each query. It uses that object's `FillDataSet` method to add the query results to the DataSet. After it has repeated this step for each query, the DataSet contains separate `DataTable` objects representing the output from each query.

Next, the program attaches the DataSet to its DataGrid control to display the data. The DataGrid automatically lets you select the query result you want to view, sort the results, resize columns, and so on.

LISTING 12.1   PROGRAM ADHOCQUERY USES THIS CODE TO EXECUTE A SERIES OF DATABASE COMMANDS.

```
' Execute the query and display the results.
Protected Sub btnExecute_Click(ByVal sender As Object, ByVal e As
System.EventArgs)
    Dim db_name As String
    Dim connect_string As String
    Dim db_connection As ADOConnection
    Dim queries() As String
    Dim i As Integer
    Dim data_set_command As ADODataSetCommand
    Dim ds As New DataSet()

    ' Create the ADODataSetCommand.
    db_name = FilePath(Application.StartupPath) & "\People.mdb"
    connect_string = _
        "Provider=Microsoft.Jet.OLEDB.4.0;" & _
        "Data Source=" & db_name & ";" & _
        "Persist Security Info=False"

    ' Connect to the database.
    db_connection = New ADOConnection(connect_string)

    ' Separate the queries at semi-colons.
    queries = Split(txtQueries.text, ";")

    ' Execute each query.
    For i = 0 To UBound(queries)
        ' Execute the query.
        data_set_command = New ADODataSetCommand(queries(i), db_connection)

        ' Fill the DataSet with the ADODataSetCommand's results.
        data_set_command.FillDataSet(ds, "Results" & i.ToString)
    Next i

    ' Connect the DataGrid to the DataSet.
    grdResults.DataSource = ds
End Sub
```

PART

III

CH

12

You can easily modify program AdHocQuery to let the user select the database to use, save the queries' results into an XML file for further processing, load or save the queries from a text file, and so forth.

When you build the prototype—and later the final application—you need to decide whether you want to include a feature to execute ad hoc queries.

Most of my customers have wanted this sort of feature either embedded in the application or as a separate program. They also wanted it to be available only to supervisors and system administrators. This tool lets these more experienced users generate new reports quickly and easily, but it might confuse less experienced users.

Database products like Informix and Oracle provide similar tools for executing ad hoc queries, but they can be hard to use. They are also usually much more powerful than this program is. Some of these tools let the user delete records, drop tables, and make other potentially disastrous changes to the database itself. Building a tool of your own lets you control how much power the user has. For example, your program can examine the commands before it executes them. If it sees a command that uses a table that should be hidden from the user, it can refuse to execute that command.

EXECUTING SCRIPTS

Program AdHocQuery, described in the previous section, enables the user to execute queries at runtime. It's only a little more complicated to let the user execute statements that modify the database. For example, the user could use INSERT, UPDATE, and DELETE statements to add, modify, and delete records.

Program AdHocQuery uses an ADO Connection object's Execute method to perform a query and get a Recordset containing the query's results. A program can also use Execute to perform an action statement that does not return any records. The DBConnection class described earlier in this chapter shows how to execute both kinds of statements.

Program SQLScript, shown in Figure 12.8, enables you to execute queries and execute action statements at runtime. Enter a series of SQL statements separated by semi-colons and then click the **Execute** button. The program executes each statement separately and displays the results.

Program SQLScript uses the code shown in Listing 12.2 to execute queries and action statements. First it uses Visual Basic's Split statement to split the single string containing all the SQL commands into an array of strings each containing one command. It then loops through the commands, executing each.

For each command, the program calls subroutine RemoveComments. This routine removes text following two dashes (—) up to the end of the line. It then removes any text that lies between a /* and */ pair. This lets you embed two different kinds of comments in long script files.

After the comments have been removed from the command, the program looks at the command's first six letters. If the command begins with the word SELECT, the program calls its ExecuteQuery function to get the formatted results of the query.

Figure 12.8
Example program
SQLScript enables the
user to execute
queries and action
statements at run-
time.

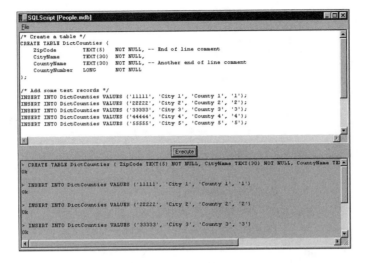

If the SQL statement does not start with SELECT, the program assumes it is an action statement. It calls the DBConnection object's ExecuteActionStatement method to perform the
action, and it then displays either a success message or the error message returned by
ExecuteActionStatement.

The ExecuteQuery routine calls the program's DBConnection object's ExecuteQuery method to
get a Recordset containing the query's results. It then loops through the first record's fields,
storing the width of each field's column name in the col_wid array. Next the program loops
through each record making sure each column width is big enough to hold the column's
value. The program adds a three-character margin to each column and then loops through
the column names again, adding them to the return result. It finishes by looping through
the records one more time, adding their values to the result.

PART

III

CH

12

LISTING 12.2   PROGRAM SQLSCRIPT USES THIS CODE TO EXECUTE SELECT STATEMENTS AND
STATEMENTS THAT MODIFY THE DATABASE.

```
' Execute the script.
Protected Sub btnExecute_Click(ByVal sender As Object, ByVal e As
System.EventArgs)
    Dim all_cmds As String
    Dim cmds() As String
    Dim cmd_num As Integer
    Dim cmd As String
    Dim result As String

    ' Break the command lines apart.
    cmds = Split(txtScript.Text, ";")

    ' Execute the commands.
    txtResults.Text = ""
    For cmd_num = 0 To UBound(cmds)
        ' Remove comments from the command.
        cmd = RemoveComments(cmds(cmd_num))
```

LISTING 12.2   CONTINUED

```
            If Len(cmd) > 0 Then
                ' Format the command for output.
                txtResults.AppendText("> " & cmd & CrLf)
                Application.DoEvents()

                ' Get the first word from the command.
                If UCase$(Microsoft.VisualBasic.Left$(cmd, 6)) = "SELECT" Then
                    ' Execute this SELECT statement.
                    txtResults.AppendText(ExecuteQuery(cmd) & CrLf)
                Else
                    ' Execute this action statement.
                    result = m_DBConnection.ExecuteActionStatement(cmd)
                    If result Is Nothing Then
                        txtResults.AppendText("Ok" & CrLf & CrLf)
                    Else
                        txtResults.AppendText(result & CrLf & CrLf)
                    End If
                End If

                Application.DoEvents()
            End If ' End if Len(cmd) > 0 ...
        Next cmd_num
End Sub

' Remove comments from the text. Then replace Cr and Lf
' characters with spaces.
Private Function RemoveComments(ByVal one_cmd As String) As String
    Dim pos1 As Integer
    Dim pos2 As Integer

    ' ****************************
    ' Remove end of line comments.
    ' ****************************
    ' Find the first " — ".
    pos1 = InStr(one_cmd, " — ")
    Do While pos1 > 0
        ' Find the ending CrLf.
        pos2 = InStr(pos1 + 2, one_cmd, CrLf)
        If pos2 = 0 Then pos2 = Len(one_cmd)

        ' Remove the text between.
        one_cmd = one_cmd.Remove(pos1 - 1, pos2 - pos1)

        ' Find the next " — ".
        pos1 = InStr(pos1, one_cmd, " — ")
    Loop

    ' *************************
    ' Remove /* .. */ comments.
    ' *************************
    ' Find the first "/*".
    pos1 = InStr(one_cmd, "/*")
    Do While pos1 > 0
        ' Find the ending */.
        pos2 = InStr(pos1 + 2, one_cmd, "*/")
        If pos2 = 0 Then pos2 = Len(one_cmd)
```

LISTING 12.2   CONTINUED

```
        ' Remove the text between.
        one_cmd = one_cmd.Remove(pos1 - 1, pos2 - pos1 + 2)

        ' Find the next "/*".
        pos1 = InStr(pos1, one_cmd, "/*")
    Loop

    ' Replace Cr and Lf with space.
    one_cmd = Replace(one_cmd, Cr, " ")
    one_cmd = Replace(one_cmd, Lf, " ")
    Do While InStr(one_cmd, "  ") > 0
        one_cmd = Replace(one_cmd, "  ", " ")
    Loop

    ' Return whatever is left.
    Return one_cmd.Trim()
End Function

' Execute a query and return the results in a multi-row string.
Private Function ExecuteQuery(ByVal query As String) As String
    Dim rs As ADODB.Recordset
    Dim col_wid() As Integer
    Dim c As Integer
    Dim value As String
    Dim txt As String

    ' Execute the query.
    rs = m_DBConnection.ExecuteQuery(query)

    ' If we got no data, say so.
    If rs.EOF And rs.BOF Then
        rs.Close()
        Return "<No records selected>"
    End If

    ' See how wide the column names are.
    ReDim col_wid(rs.Fields.Count)
    For c = 0 To rs.Fields.Count - 1
        value = rs.Fields.Item.Name
        If col_wid < Len(value) Then
            col_wid = Len(value)
        End If
    Next c

    ' See how wide the values are.
    Do While Not rs.EOF
        For c = 0 To rs.Fields.Count - 1
            value = rs.Fields.Item.Value.ToString
            If col_wid < Len(value) Then
                col_wid = Len(value)
            End If
        Next c
        rs.MoveNext()
    Loop
```

PART
III

CH
12

LISTING 12.2   CONTINUED

```
    ' Add a margin to each column.
    For c = 0 To rs.Fields.Count - 1
        col_wid = col_wid + 3
    Next c

    ' Add the field names to the return string.
    For c = 0 To rs.Fields.Count - 1
        txt = txt & rs.Fields.Item.Name.PadRight(col_wid)
    Next c
    txt = txt & CrLf
    For c = 0 To rs.Fields.Count - 1
        txt = txt & New String(CType("-", Char), col_wid - 3) & "   "
    Next c
    txt = txt & CrLf

    ' Build the return string.
    rs.MoveFirst()
    Do While Not rs.EOF
        For c = 0 To rs.Fields.Count - 1
            value = rs.Fields.Item.Value.ToString
            txt = txt & value.PadRight(col_wid)
        Next c
        txt = txt & CrLf
        rs.MoveNext()
    Loop

    rs.Close()
    Return txt
End Function
```

This kind of script execution code can be handy, particularly during prototype development. It lets you make quick changes to the database or create new data without working through your program's user interface or the database's own tools.

Tale from the Trenches

In several of the applications I have worked on, I used scripts to manage the database. The first script contained a series of DROP TABLE statements to drop all of the application's tables.

The order of the DROP statements in this script was important because some of the tables contained integrity constraints. For example, the Accounts table might contain an AccountRepresentative field that refers to a record in the Employees table. If you tried to drop the Employees table first, records in the Accounts table would refer to non-existent Employees records. That would cause an error so the program would fail to drop the Employees table. In this case, the script must drop the Accounts table first. The easiest way to keep the scripts synchronized was to drop tables in the reverse order in which they were created.

One or more scripts contained CREATE TABLE statements to build the tables needed by the application. A final series of scripts contained INSERT statements to populate the database with test data for the prototype.

Managing the database using scripts in this way has the advantage that you can store the scripts in your source code control system. If you keep the scripts synchronized with the prototype, you can always find a version of the scripts that will work with a particular version of the prototype.

Using scripts also makes it easy to work with more than one set of data. For each different prototype scenario, you can have a different series of scripts that use INSERT statements to populate the database.

Your program can use similar techniques to execute action statements in code. You can use the ActiveX Data Objects extensions library (ADOX) objects to manipulate the database in an object-oriented way, but nothing beats the simplicity of a good old CREATE TABLE statement.

This is a much more powerful tool than the program AdHocQuery. In the wrong hands, program SQLScript could delete tables, corrupt records, and wreak all sorts of other mischief. For those reasons, you might think this tool should not be included in an application or even a prototype. Depending on your users, you might be right.

However, many of the customers I have worked with needed these more powerful functions. They often had to perform complex database management tasks and they either needed a script execution tool like this one or they had to use the tools that came with the database engine.

If you do include this kind of tool in your program, there are a few things you can do to make it a little safer. First, make the tool available only to the most experienced system administrators. A typical user has no business messing around with the database's internal structure.

Build and test some useful scripts and keep them where the system administrators can find them. They can load these scripts and modify them rather than trying to create new scripts from scratch.

Make sure the users understand the dangers that come with this sort of tool. Present a message box before you execute a script reminding the user that they could do irreparable damage to the database and make them confirm that they want to continue. Encourage them to contact you or the database administrator before executing any script that they are not sure is safe. Telling the users how serious the consequences of these scripts can be is usually enough to keep the database safe. In the projects where I have included this sort of tool, there have never been any problems with users accidentally destroying the database.

Program SQLScript examines the beginning of each command to see if it is a SELECT statement. You can similarly check for other commands. For example, you could prevent the program from executing DROP TABLE and CREATE TABLE commands, or you might allow only INSERT commands. That way, you can control the types of operations the users perform and the amount of damage they can do.

Finally, make sure a good backup system is in place before you let users make drastic changes to the database. If all else fails, you can always restore the most recently saved backup.

SUMMARY

If you know what reports the customer needs, and you have the time, you can build them using Crystal Reports. If you are pressed for time during prototyping, you can build a representative sample of the reports and tell the customers that the others will be similar. If the customers can afford to provide you with domain experts who know a bit about computers, these individuals can build their own reports. Then you just need to provide menus and buttons to display them.

No matter how many reports you include in your system, the customers will eventually think of something else they want. In the long term, you might want to add the new reports to a future release of the program. In the short term, you can provide an ad hoc query tool to enable users to invent their own reports as needed. That might not produce the prettiest result, but it gives you the flexibility to provide new reports quickly in the prototype and later releases.

CHAPTER **13**

ERROR HANDLING

In this Chapter

Ideally, a program never generates any errors, so it never bothers the user with them. Unfortunately, catching and handling every conceivable error can be extremely difficult. Even if the program contains no bugs in its own code, it might run into errors that lie outside of its control. For example, the user might accidentally delete a file the program needs or the program might need to access a Web site that is down.

Fortunately, a prototype's error handling needs are a little simpler than those of a finished application. The prototype does not necessarily need to handle every possible error in the most graceful way. For example, a prototype might simply present an error message to the user instead of trying to solve a problem itself.

This chapter begins with a quick overview of Visual Basic's error handling statements. It then describes some guidelines you can use to make error handling easier in a prototype.

ERROR HANDLING OVERVIEW

Visual Basic provides two distinct styles of error handling. Visual Basic 6 and earlier versions use an "unstructured" GoTo approach. When the program encounters an error, control goes to a section of error handling code. VB.NET introduced a more structured form of error handling that ties error handling code more closely to the code that might generate the error.

The following sections describe these two styles. You can use either style or a combination of both in your VB.NET prototypes. The "Unstructured Versus Structured Error Handling" section later in this chapter discusses the advantages and disadvantages of each and gives some guidelines you can use to make error handling easier in Visual Basic prototypes.

The Errors example program, shown in Figure 13.1, demonstrates many of the error handling techniques described in this chapter. Because it doesn't do much visibly, you should step through its code in the debugger to see how it demonstrates Visual Basic's error handling capabilities.

Figure 13.1
Program Errors demonstrates many of the error handling concepts described in this chapter.

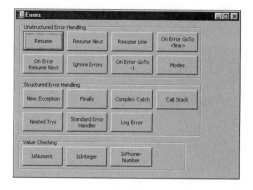

THE Err OBJECT

The Err object represents the last error that occurred. Its properties give a program access to information about the error. The Err object's most important properties and methods are:

- Number—The error number that defines this error. If this is zero, no error has occurred since the Err object was reset.

- Description—A description of the error.

- Source—A string naming the object that generated the error. This is usually an object's class name or a subroutine name.

- Clear—Clears the current error.

- GetException—Returns an Exception object representing the Err object's values. See the next section for information about Exception objects.

- Raise—Raises an error. Parameters specify the error's number, description, and so on.

When you define your own errors, add the constant vbObjectError to offset values to define your own error number. For example:

```
Public Enum MyErrorEnum
    err_InvalidMode = vbObjectError + 10001
    err_UnknownMode = vbObjectError + 10002
    err_ColorMismatch = vbObjectError + 10003
        :
End Enum
```

Using this constant ensures that your error codes do not conflict with those defined by Microsoft.

Exception OBJECTS

Like the Err object, an Exception object represents the last error that occurred. Its properties give a program access to information about the error. An Exception object's most important properties and methods are:

- Message—A message describing the error.

- Source—The name of the object or application that raised the exception.

- TargetSite—The method that generated the exception.

- StackTrace—A string listing the routines in the call stack. This shows the series of subroutine calls that lead to the exception. It is generally useful to developers but meaningless to users.

- InnerException—Returns a nested Exception object. If the program catches an exception and then raises a new exception, it can save the original Exception object here.

To define a new exception class, a program creates a class that is derived from another exception class. Usually the parent class is the Exception class itself, though it could be any class that inherits from the Exception class. The following code shows how you could define a new BadColorsException class.

PART

III

CH

13

```
Imports System.Runtime.Serialization

Public Class BadColorsException
    Inherits Exception

    ' Normally exception classes should provide these
    ' four constructors.
    Public Overloads Sub New()
        MyBase.New("These are bad colors")
    End Sub

    Public Overloads Sub New(ByVal message As String)
        MyBase.New(message)
    End Sub

    Public Overloads Sub New(ByVal info As SerializationInfo, _
      ByVal context As StreamingContext)
        MyBase.New(info, context)
    End Sub

    Public Overloads Sub New(ByVal message As String, _
      ByVal innerException As Exception)
        MyBase.New(message, innerException)
    End Sub

End Class
```

After it has defined a new Exception class, the program can throw the exception as in these two examples:

```
' Throw an exception with the default message.
Throw New BadColorsException()

' Throw an exception with its own message.
Throw New BadColorsException("Invalid background color")
```

Example program Errors demonstrates this class. When you click the New Exception button, the program throws a BadColorsException, catches the exception, and displays an error message.

UNSTRUCTURED ERROR HANDLING

Visual Basic 6 and earlier versions use the On Error GoTo statement to enable an error handler. If an error occurs while an error handler is enabled, the error handler becomes active and control passes to it. Visual Basic provides a couple different methods for returning control to the main code sequence when the error handler has finished its job. The next few sections explain Visual Basic's statements for using this kind of error handling.

ERROR-HANDLING MODE

When an error handler runs, Visual Basic enters a special error-handling mode. In this mode, error handling does not work normally and the error handler cannot catch another error. If another error occurs, control leaves the routine that contains the error handler and passes back up the call stack. If the calling routine has its own error handler, it might catch the error but control has left the routine that originally caught the error.

To ensure that control doesn't get lost this way, don't put any statements in an error handler that might cause another error.

If an error handler must take some action that might fail, put that action in a separate subroutine with its own error handling code. That routine can trap any errors and prevent them from returning to the error previous handler. The error handler calls this subroutine and is protected by the subroutine's error handling.

Other error handling statements also do not work normally in error-handling mode. For example, if an error handler uses an On Error GoTo statement to enable a new error handler, the change does not actually take place until after the current error handler finishes running.

To avoid confusion, keep error handlers as simple as possible. If an error handler must do something complicated, put it in a new subroutine.

LEAVING ERROR-HANDLING MODE

A program can leave error-handling mode in several ways. Some of these methods return control to the routine that contains the error handler. Others return control to the routine that called that one.

Exit Sub

The `Exit Sub`, `Exit Function`, and `Exit Property` statements make control immediately return from the subroutine, function, or property procedure where the error handler is executing. The program continues executing with the statement after the one that called this subroutine.

This method is appropriate when the error handler cannot fix the error and the subroutine cannot continue. It is probably the most common method for exiting error-handling mode. The routine catches an error, displays an error message, and then exits.

```
Private Sub DoSomething()
    On Error GoTo Oops
    ' Do some stuff.
        :
    Exit Sub

Oops:
    MsgBox("Error in DoSomething", _
        MsgBoxStyle.Exclamation, _
        "Error")
    Exit Sub
End Sub
```

```
End Sub
```

If the error handler is the last thing in the subroutine, function, or procedure, then the next statement after the error handler code is End Sub, End Function, End Get, or End Set. In these cases, the subroutine ends after the error handler just as if it had executed Exit Sub, Exit Function, or Exit Property.

Resume

The Resume statement makes execution return to the statement that generated the error. If the error handler did nothing to solve the problem, this immediately raises the error again. The most common use for this statement is when the user might be able to fix the problem.

For example, the following code tries to read the file A:\Readme.txt. If it cannot open the file, the routine presents a message box warning the user and displaying two buttons: Retry and Cancel. If the user clicks the Cancel button, the subroutine exits without doing anything else. However, depending on what the problem is, the user might be able to fix the problem that prevented the routine from reading the file. The user might be able to close another application that has the file locked, insert the correct floppy disk, close the floppy drive door, and so on. If the user fixes the problem and clicks Retry, the subroutine tries to open the file again.

```
' Demonstrate the Resume statement.
Protected Sub DemonstrateResume()
    Dim file_num As Integer
    Dim txt As String
    Dim file_stream As FileStream
    Dim stream_reader As StreamReader

    ' Open the file A:\Readme.txt.
    On Error Goto OpenError
    file_stream = New FileStream("A:\Readme.txt", _
        IO.FileMode.Open, _
        IO.FileAccess.Read, _
        IO.FileShare.Read)
    On Error Goto 0

    ' Read and display the file.
    stream_reader = New StreamReader(file_stream)
    txt = stream_reader.ReadToEnd()
    stream_reader.Close()
    file_stream.Close()
    MsgBox(txt, MsgBoxStyle.OKOnly, "A:\Readme.txt")
    Exit Sub

OpenError:
    Dim msg As String

    msg = "Error " & Err.Number & _
        " opening file A:\Readme.txt." & CrLf & _
        Err.Description
```

```
        Select Case MsgBox(msg, MsgBoxStyle.RetryCancel, _
          "Open Error")
            Case MsgBoxResult.Retry
                ' Try again.
                Resume
            Case MsgBoxResult.Cancel
                ' The user wants to cancel.
                Exit Sub
        End Select
End Sub
```

Example program Errors uses this code to demonstrate the Resume statement. When you click the Resume button, the program tries to read the file A:\Readme.txt. It uses Resume to keep trying until it succeeds or you tell it to stop. You might want to step through the code in the debugger to see how it works.

Resume Next

The Resume Next statement makes control return to the statement after the one that generated the error. This is most useful when the error handler can correct the error. The following code shows how a program could use Resume Next to assign a default value to a variable when the user enters an invalid value.

```
' Demonstrate the Resume Next statement.
Protected Sub DemonstrateResumeNext()
    Dim X As Single

    On Error Goto XError
    X = CSng(InputBox("X"))
    MsgBox("X = " & X, MsgBoxStyle.OKOnly, "X")
    Exit Sub

XError:
    ' Use a default value.
    X = 1.23
    Resume Next
End Sub
```

Example program Errors uses this code to demonstrate the Resume Next statement. Click the Resume Next button. Enter a non-numeric value to trigger the error handler. You might want to step through the code in the debugger to see how it works.

PART
III
CH
13

Resume <line>

The Resume <line> statement makes the program resume execution at the specified line number or label. The following example opens a file and tries to read three numbers from it. If it cannot read a number, the rest of the file probably does not have the right format. The ReadError error handler displays an error message and skips the rest of the code that reads values from the file. The next statement the routine executes is the one that closes the file. Using this code, the routine is certain that the file is closed whether it reads all of the values successfully or not.

```
' Demonstrate the Resume <line> statement.
Protected Sub DemonstrateResumeLine()
```

```
        Dim file_name As String
        Dim file_num As Integer
        Dim X As Single
        Dim Y As Single
        Dim Z As Single

        ' Open the file Values.dat.
        On Error Goto OpenError
        file_name = FilePath(Application.StartupPath) & "\Values.dat"
        file_num = FreeFile()
        Open(file_num, file_name, OpenMode.Input, _
            OpenAccess.Read, OpenShare.Shared)

        ' Read the values from the file.
        On Error Goto ReadError
        Input(file_num, X)
        Input(file_num, Y)
        Input(file_num, Z)
CloseFile:
        ' Close the file.
        Compatibility.VB6.Close(file_num)

        ' Display the values.
        MsgBox( _
            "X = " & X & CrLf & _
            "Y = " & Y & CrLf & _
            "Z = " & Z, _
            MsgBoxStyle.Information, _
            "Values")
        Exit Sub

OpenError:
        Dim msg As String

        msg = "Error " & Err.Number & _
            " opening file " & file_name & "." & CrLf & _
            Err.Description
        Exit Sub
ReadError:
        MsgBox("Error reading values", MsgBoxStyle.Exclamation, "Read Error")
        Resume CloseFile
End Sub
```

Click the Resume Line button to make program Errors demonstrate the Resume <line> statement.

Note that Resume Line can make the program jump to new lines in a very unstructured way. This can make debugging and modifying the code difficult. To avoid problems later on, use Resume <line> sparingly or not at all. A better solution for this example is to open the file in this subroutine, call another routine to read the file's values, and then close the file in this routine. That way, if an error occurs while reading the values, this routine can continue execution after that subroutine finishes with a Resume Next statement.

ENABLING ERROR-HANDLING MODE

Visual Basic includes several statements for enabling and disabling error-handling mode. The two basic forms of unstructured error handling begin with the `On Error GoTo <line>` and `On Error Resume Next` statements.

On Error GoTo <line>

The `On Error GoTo <line>` statement enables an error handler. When an error occurs, control passes to the code at the line number or label specified by `<line>`. For example, the following code enables the `GoToDanger1` error handling code and then executes some code. If the code causes an error, the program enters error-handling mode and control jumps to the line labeled `GoToDanger1`. The error handler calls the `PresentError` subroutine and then exits subroutine `DoSomething`.

```
Protected Sub DoSomething()
    On Error Goto GoToDanger1

    ' Execute some code.
        :

    Exit Sub    ' Do not fall into the error handler code.

GoToDanger1:
    MsgBox("Error in DoSomething")
End Sub
```

Note that this code includes an `Exit Sub` statement before the error handler code. If this line was missing and subroutine `DoSomething` did not encounter any errors, it would finish executing all of its normal code and then move past the line labeled `GoToDanger1` into the error handling code.

To make program Errors demonstrate the `On Error GoTo <line>` statement, click its `On Error GoTo <line>` button. You might want to step through the code in the debugger to see how it works.

On Error Resume Next

The `On Error Resume Next` statement makes a program continue running even if it encounters an error. It can use the `Err` object to see if an error occurred after each statement that might raise an error. The following begins with the `On Error Resume Next` statement. It calls subroutine `DoSomethingDangerous` and then sees whether `Err.Number` is zero. If `Err.Number` is not zero, an error occurred in `DoSomethingDangerous`. The subroutine displays an error message and exits.

If there is no error so far, the code continues and calls subroutine `DoSomethingElseDangerous`. Again it checks `Err.Number` to see if an error occurred.

```
' Demonstrate On Error Resume Next.
Protected Sub OnErrorResumeNext()
    On Error Resume Next
    DoSomethingDangerous()
```

```
    ' See if there was an error.
    If Err.Number <> 0 Then
        MsgBox("Error doing something dangerous")
        Exit Sub
    End If

    DoSomethingElseDangerous()

    ' See if there was an error.
    If Err.Number <> 0 Then
        MsgBox("Error doing something else dangerous")
        Exit Sub
    End If
End Sub
```

Example program Errors demonstrates this code when you click the On Error Resume Next button. You might want to step through the code in the debugger to see how it works.

On Error Resume Next can be useful when you don't really care whether a command raises an error. This is particularly helpful when you are building a prototype and you don't want to try to fix any errors that occur.

For example, suppose the user enters a text string that should be a numeric value. If the user enters a non-numeric value, you don't really care what happens to the value, but you don't want the program to crash. The following code shows how you could use On Error Resume Next to ignore the user's invalid input.

```
Dim interest_rate As Single

On Error Resume Next
interest_rate = CSng(InputBox("Interest Rate"))
```

The following version of this code first initializes the interest_rate variable to 0.1. If the user enters a non-numeric value in the input box, interest_rate keeps this default value.

```
Dim interest_rate As Single = 0.1

On Error Resume Next
interest_rate = CSng(InputBox("Interest Rate"))
```

Program Errors uses similar code to ignore errors when you enter a numeric value. When you click the Ignore Errors button, the program displays an input box. The program tries to store the value you enter in a Single variable. If you enter a non-numeric value, the program ignores the error and the variable keeps its default value of 0.1.

Note that Err.Number is not automatically cleared when the next statement executes. If a statement causes an error and you ignore it, Err.Number might still hold the error value until after the next statement. If you then check Err.Number to see if the second statement failed, you might see the first statement's error information and incorrectly conclude that the second statement raised the error.

If you are going to ignore an error completely, use Err.Clear to clear out any error information before you start checking for new errors.

```
On Error Resume Next

' Ignore these errors.
x = CSng(InputBox("X"))
y = CSng(InputBox("Y"))
z = CSng(InputBox("Y"))

' Do not ignore errors in the call to DoSomething.
Err.Clear()
DoSomething()
If Err.Number Then ...
```

On Error GoTo 0

The On Error GoTo 0 statement disables the subroutine's currently enabled error handler. It is generally a good idea to either disable an error handler or replace it with another one after it has served its purpose. Then if an error occurs later, the program either catches it with a more appropriate error handler or halts so you can see where the unexpected error occurred.

```
On Error Resume Next

' Ignore these errors.
x = CSng(InputBox("X"))
y = CSng(InputBox("Y"))
z = CSng(InputBox("Y"))

' Do not ignore further errors.
On Error GoTo 0
    :
```

On Error GoTo -1

The On Error GoTo -1 statement clears the current exception object if there is one. It resets the Err object so it does not represent any error.

In the following code, the On Error GoTo -1 statement clears the divide by zero exception. When the program then calls the Err object's GetException method, that method returns Nothing.

```
' Demonstrate On Error GoTo -1.
Protected Sub OnErrorGoToMinusOne()
    Dim exc As Exception
    Dim i As Integer
    Dim j As Integer

    ' Continue if there is an error.
    On Error Resume Next

    i = 0
    j = 1 \ i

    ' Display the error message.
    exc = Err.GetException()
    MsgBox(exc.Message)
```

```
    ' Clear the exception.
    On Error Goto -1

    ' See if the exception still exists.
    exc = Err.GetException()
    If exc Is Nothing Then
        MsgBox("The exception is Nothing")
    Else
        ' This should never happen.
        MsgBox(exc.Message)
    End If
End Sub
```

To make program Errors demonstrate this statement, click its On Error GoTo -1 button.

STYLE CONVENTIONS

Visual Basic's unstructured error handling statements are quite flexible. In fact, they are flexible enough to cause some confusion. When an error handler finishes, it can pass control back to the line that caused the error, to the following line, to some other line, or even out of the routine that contains the error handler.

Unstructured error handling does not tell the program whether it is running in normal or error-handling mode. It gives no indication whether a piece of code is intended to be normal code or an error handler. In fact, the same piece of code might execute in normal mode in some cases and as an error handler in others.

Example program Errors uses the following code to show how code can execute in either normal or error handling mode. Click the Modes button to make the program run this routine.

This subroutine prompts you for the number of values it should read from a file. It opens the file and tries to read the values. The file included with the example contains two numbers and a string. If you tell the program to read zero, one, or two values, the routine succeeds and the final statements execute in normal mode. If you tell the program to read more than two values, the program fails and the last statements execute in error-handling mode.

```
' Demonstrate code that can run either in normal or
' error-handling mode.
Protected Sub DemonstrateModes()
    Dim file_name As String
    Dim file_num As Integer
    Dim num_values As Integer
    Dim values() As Single
    Dim i As Integer
    Dim txt As String
    Dim mode As String

    ' See how many values the user wants us to read.
    num_values = CInt(InputBox("# Values"))
    ReDim values(num_values)

    ' Open the file Values.dat.
    file_name = FilePath(Application.StartupPath) & "\Values.dat"
```

```
    file_num = FreeFile()
    Open(file_num, file_name, OpenMode.Input, _
        OpenAccess.Read, OpenShare.Shared)

    ' Read the values from the file.
    mode = "Error-handling mode"
    On Error Goto CloseFile
    For i = 0 To num_values - 1
        Input(file_num, values(i))
    Next i
    mode = "Normal mode"

CloseFile:
    ' Close the file.
    Microsoft.VisualBasic.Compatibility.VB6.Close(file_num)

    ' Display the values.
    txt = mode & CrLf
    For i = 0 To num_values - 1
        txt = txt & values(i) & CrLf
    Next i
    MsgBox(txt, MsgBoxStyle.Information, "Values")
End Sub
```

All of these potentially confusing issues have led to several stylistic conventions for using unstructured error handling. You should follow them whether you are building a prototype or a finished application.

- Error handling code always goes at the end of a subroutine, never in the middle.

- Always put an Exit Sub statement before the first error handler. Do not let execution drop into the first error handler. Do not use the same code in both normal and error handling modes.

- Always end an error handler with some sort of Resume or Exit statement. Don't let execution drop into the next error handler or onto the End Sub statement.

- Do not change the error handling within an error handler. For example, do not execute On Error GoTo to change the enabled error handler inside another error handler.

- Keep error handlers relatively simple. Move complex functions into separate routines.

- Use Resume <line> sparingly; it's confusing.

STRUCTURED ERROR HANDLING

The structured error handling introduced by VB.NET tries to remove much of the confusion allowed by the flexibility of unstructured error handling. The basic format of a structured error handler is:

```
Try
    try_statements...
Catch
    catch_statements...
Finally
    finally_statements...
End Try
```

PART

III

CH

13

The values in this construction are

- *try_statements*—The statements that might generate an error.
- *catch_statements*—The statements that should execute if an error occurs.
- *finally_statements*—The statements that should be executed after all error handling statements are finished.

The following code demonstrates a basic error handler with Finally statements. When the program prompts you, enter a number to let the program proceed without an error. Enter a letter to generate a FormatException error. In either case, the Finally statement runs after all the other statements are finished.

```
' Demonstrate an unhandled exception.
Protected Sub DemonstrateFinally()
    Dim X As Integer

    Try
        X = CInt(InputBox("X"))
    Catch exc As FormatException
        MsgBox(exc.Message, MsgBoxStyle.Exclamation, "Error")
    Finally
        MsgBox("Finally", MsgBoxStyle.Information, "Finally")
    End Try
End Sub
```

Example program Errors demonstrates Try...Catch...Finally. When you click its Finally button, the program displays an input box. It tries to convert the value you enter into an integer. If the value you enter is non-numeric, a Catch statement catches the error and displays a message. Whether you enter a valid integer or not, the Finally statement displays another message.

More complex variations on the Try...Catch...Finally statements enable you to catch more than one type of exception, catch generic exceptions, and catch exceptions when a certain condition occurs. For instance, the following code uses separate Catch statements to capture overflow and divide-by-zero exceptions. A third Catch statement handles all other errors. The RaiseException subroutine prompts the user for an error code and raises the corresponding exception so you can test this code.

```
' Demonstrate a complex Try ... Catch ... Finally statement.
Protected Sub DemonstrateComplexCatch()
    Try
        RaiseException()
    Catch overflow_exception As OverflowException
        ' Catch overflow exceptions (6).
        MsgBox(overflow_exception.Message, MsgBoxStyle.Exclamation, "Overflow")
    Catch divide_by_zero_exception As DivideByZeroException
        ' Catch divide-by-zero exceptions (11).
        MsgBox(divide_by_zero_exception.Message, MsgBoxStyle.Exclamation, _
            "Divide By Zero")
    Catch generic_exception As Exception
        ' Catch other exceptions.
        MsgBox(generic_exception.Message, MsgBoxStyle.Exclamation, "Other Error")
```

```
      End Try
End Sub

' Raise an exception.
Private Sub RaiseException()
    Err.Clear()
    Err.Raise(CInt(InputBox( _
        "Exception # (6 = Overflow, 11 = DivideByZero, '' for other)")))
End Sub
```

Program Errors demonstrates this code if you click the Complex Catch button. You might want to step through the code in the debugger to see how it works.

ERRORS AND THE CALL STACK

Suppose a program enables an error handler using either structured or unstructured methods. When an error occurs, the error handler activates and control passes to it.

If the routine that caused the error does not have an error handler enabled, control passes up the call stack to the subroutine that called this one. If that routine has an error handler enabled, the error handler takes over. Otherwise, control passes up the call stack again.

Control continues passing up the call stack until an error handler catches the error. If no routine in the call stack has an enabled error handler, the error remains uncaught and the program crashes.

In the following code, subroutine CallStack1 enables the error handler at line CallStack1Error and then calls subroutine CallStack2. Subroutine CallStack2 performs a command that raises a divide by zero error.

Subroutine CallStack2 does not have an error handler enabled, so control passes up the call stack to subroutine CallStack1. This routine has an error handler enabled so the program enters error-handling mode and control jumps to the line labeled CallStack1Error.

```
Protected Sub CallStack1()
    On Error Goto CallStack1Error
    CallStack2()
    Exit Sub

CallStack1Error:
    Dim exc As Exception

    exc = Err.GetException()
    MsgBox("Error caught in CallStack1." & CrLf & _
        Err.Description & CrLf & _
        exc.StackTrace(), _
        MsgBoxStyle.Exclamation, _
        "Error")
    Exit Sub
End Sub

' Do something that raises an error. This routine does not
' have an error handler so control passes up the call stack.
Private Sub CallStack2()
```

```
        Dim i As Integer
        Dim j As Integer

        j = 0
        i = 1 \ j
End Sub
```

Note that the `Err` object is initialized when the error occurs—not when it is caught. In this example, the exception's stack trace starts where the error occurred in subroutine `CallStack2`, not where it is caught in `CallStack1`. That is very important to you as a developer. Even if an error handler catches the error at the very top of the call stack, the stack trace shows you exactly where the error occurred. That means you can protect a very deep series of subroutine calls with a single error handler at the top of the stack.

The `StackTrace` method lists the routines in the stack in the reverse order in which people normally think of a stack. The subroutine that caused the error is at the top. The routine that called that one is listed next. As the trace moves up the call stack, it continues listing the routines downward in its output.

Example program Errors displays the stack trace shown in Figure 13.2 when you click its CallStack button. Subroutine `CallStack1` calls subroutine `CallStack2`, which tries to divide by zero. `CallStack2` generates the error, so it is listed at the top. Subroutine `CallStack1` is next in the call stack, so it is listed next.

Figure 13.2
A stack trace lists the routine that caused the error on the top.

UNSTRUCTURED VERSUS STRUCTURED ERROR HANDLING

Structured error handling avoids some confusion by clearly showing what code is protected by what error-handling code. Code in the `Try` section is being protected. Code in the `Catch` sections is error-handling code. Code in the `Finally` section is code executed after the error handling code finishes.

Structured error handling also makes it completely clear when error handling is enabled. For example, suppose an `If` statement executes an `On Error` statement to enable or disable error handling only if some expression is true. When the `If` statement ends, it's unclear whether error handling is enabled.

```
If Len(txt) > 0 Then
    On Error GoTo BadXValue
    X = CSng(txt)
End If

' Is error handling enabled here or not?
```

With structured error handling, it's always obvious whether an error handler is enabled. If the code is inside a `Try` section, error handling is enabled. If the code is not in a `Try` section, it is not protected, at least not locally.

Structured error handling can also be nested. One `Catch` section can contain another `Try...Catch...Finally` structure, as shown in the following code.

```
' Demonstrate nested Try statements.
Protected Sub DemonstrateNestedTrys()
    Dim X As Integer

    Try
        X = CInt(InputBox("First value"))
    Catch exc1 As Exception
        Try
            X = CInt(InputBox("Invalid format. Try again."))
        Catch exc2 As Exception
            MsgBox(exc2.Message, MsgBoxStyle.Exclamation, "Error")
        End Try
    End Try
End Sub
```

Example program Errors demonstrates this code when you click its Nested `Trys` button.

Unstructured error handling cannot use nested error handlers because its error handlers run in a special error-handling mode. While it is in error-handling mode, the routine cannot catch other errors. To do something like this using `On Error` statements, you would have to put the second chunk of code in a separate subroutine and call it from the first error handler.

Of course, nested `Try...Catch...Finally` statements can be rather confusing, so it might be better to put the second chunk of code in a separate subroutine in either case.

Unstructured error handling has its own advantages. The `On Error Resume Next` statement lets a routine ignore errors quickly and easily. Whenever a `Try` section encounters an error, it jumps to a `Catch` section. After it's there, it cannot return to the `Try` section because structured error handling does not allow the `Resume` statement. That means you cannot ignore more than one error in a single `Try...Catch...Finally` structure. If you want to ignore every error in a subroutine, you need to protect every statement with its own `Try...Catch...Finally` statements. Compare the structured and unstructured error handling in the following code.

PART
III

CH
13

```
' Ignore all errors using unstructured error handling.
Private Sub IgnoreErrorsUnstructured()
    On Error Resume Next
    X = CInt(InputBox("X"))
    Y = CInt(InputBox("Y"))
    Z = CInt(InputBox("Z"))
    etc.
End Sub


' Ignore all errors using structured error handling.
Private Sub IgnoreErrorsStructured()
    Try
```

```
            X = CInt(InputBox("X"))
        Catch
        End Try

        Try
            Y = CInt(InputBox("Y"))
        Catch
        End Try

        Try
            Z = CInt(InputBox("Z"))
        Catch
        End Try

        etc.
End Sub
```

This issue is particularly relevant for throwaway prototypes. Many prototype routines don't try very hard to correct errors. You don't really want to spend a lot of effort protecting the program from odd cases in which test data files are missing or have the wrong format, because those files won't be part of the final application. If something goes wrong, you don't want the program to crash, but you don't need it to go to heroic lengths to produce the right result.

In that case, a simple `On Error Resume Next` statement is much simpler than a long series of `Try...Catch...Finally` statements.

Unstructured error handling also gives you more options for returning after an error handler executes. You can exit the subroutine, repeat the command that caused the error, resume at the statement that follows that one, or even jump to some other statement. Some of these—like jumping to another line of code—can be very confusing, so you probably shouldn't use them. Repeating the command that caused the error, however, can be extremely useful.

The section called "Resume," earlier in this chapter, shows an example that tries to open a file. If the file is missing, the program lets the user try to fix the problem and then it tries to open the file again. To make this same test using a structured error handling, the program needs to repeat the `Try...Catch...Finally` sequence inside a loop as shown in the following code. Whether you find this more or less natural than the previous version is a matter of preference.

```
' Demonstrate the Resume statement.
Protected Sub DemonstrateResumeStructured()
    Dim file_stream As FileStream
    Dim stream_reader As StreamReader
    Dim txt As String

    ' Repeat until we succeed.
    Do While file_stream Is Nothing
        Try
            ' Open the file A:\Readme.txt.
            file_stream = New FileStream( _
                "A:\Readme.txt", _
```

```
                    IO.FileMode.Open, _
                    IO.FileAccess.Read, _
                    IO.FileShare.Read)
            Catch exc As Exception
                ' Give the user a chance to fix the problem.
                Dim msg As String

                msg = "Error " & Err.Number & _
                    " opening file A:\Readme.txt." & CrLf & _
                    Err.Description
                If MsgBox(msg, MsgBoxStyle.RetryCancel, "Open Error") = _
                  MsgBoxResult.Cancel Then
                    ' The user wants to cancel.
                    Exit Sub
                End If
            End Try
        Loop

        ' Read and display the file.
        stream_reader = New StreamReader(file_stream)
        txt = stream_reader.ReadToEnd()
        stream_reader.Close()
        file_stream.Close()
        MsgBox(txt, MsgBoxStyle.OKOnly, "A:\Readme.txt")
    End Sub
```

One of the most important features provided by structured error handling is the stack trace. An `Exception` object's `StackTrace` method returns a string that lists the routines on the stack when the error occurred. Knowing the sequence of subroutine calls that produced an error can be invaluable in tracking down the error. The `Catch` statement includes an `Exception` object that can produce the stack trace directly.

Even if you use unstructured error handling, however, you can still get a stack trace. Use the `Err` object's `GetException` method to get a reference to an `Exception` object that describes the problem. Then you can use that object's `StackTrace` method.

```
    On Error GoTo ReadError
    DoSomething()
    etc.
    Exit Sub

ReadError:
    Dim exc As Exception
    exc = Err.GetException()
    MsgBox(exc.StackTrace())
    Exit Sub
End Sub
```

PART

III

CH

13

Whether you use structured or unstructured error handling is largely a matter of style. Both can do roughly the same things, though they do them in slightly different ways. Unstructured error handling offers greater flexibility, but unless you are careful you can use that flexibility to make things more confusing.

To get the most benefit from both systems, try using unstructured error handling with the On Error Resume Next statement when you want to quickly ignore errors in several lines of code. Use Try...Catch...Finally to catch all other errors.

KINDS OF ERRORS

The three basic kinds of errors are expected errors, abnormal errors, and unforeseen errors. The following sections explain what these errors are and how a program should handle them.

EXPECTED ERRORS

Expected errors are situations that you can predict in advance. For instance, if a program asks the user to enter a number, the user might enter a letter or nothing at all. If the program blindly tries to convert the user's input into a number, it might crash.

Expected errors are special conditions that you can anticipate. Because you can guess that these situations might occur, the program does not need to treat these as errors. When the program asks the user to enter a number, it can verify that the value really is a number before it tries to convert the value into a number.

Generally, this technique is better than using error traps to test the value. Unfortunately, Visual Basic does not come with a complete set of routines for determining whether a value has a particular format, so proactive testing isn't always easy. For example, Visual Basic's IsNumeric function returns true for the string 7e300, which represents a number too large to fit in an integer. If you want to assign the string 7e300 to an integer, you cannot use IsNumeric to see if the string is valid.

In cases like this, you can use an error handler to validate the string before you use it. The following code shows a routine that checks whether a string is a valid integer.

```
' Return True if the value is a valid integer.
Private Function IsInteger(ByVal value As String) As Boolean
    Dim test_value As Integer

    On Error Resume Next
    test_value = CInt(value)
    IsInteger = (Err.Number = 0)
End Function
```

You can enhance this routine so it determines whether the value is within specified bounds.

```
' Return True if the value is a valid integer between the given bounds.
Private Function IsInteger(ByVal value As String, _
  Optional ByVal min_value As Integer = -2147483648, _
  Optional ByVal max_value As Integer = 2147483647) As Boolean
    Dim test_value As Integer

    On Error Resume Next
    test_value = CInt(value)
    If err.Number <> 0 Then
        IsInteger = False
```

```
        Else
            IsInteger = (test_value >= min_value) And (test_value <= max_value)
        End If
End Function
```

The following code shows a more elaborate validation routine. It returns True if the input value looks like a United States phone number. It should have either the form ###-#### or ###-###-####, and the first digit in each three-digit group should not be a zero or a one.

```
' Return True if the value is a valid integer between the given bounds.
Private Function IsPhoneNumber(ByVal value As String, _
    Optional ByVal allow_7_digit_number As Boolean = True, _
    Optional ByVal allow_10_digit_number As Boolean = True) As Boolean

    Dim digit As String

    ' See if the number matches a seven digit format.
    If allow_7_digit_number Then
        If value Like "###-####" Then
            ' Don't let the first digit be 0 or 1.
            digit = Microsoft.VisualBasic.Left$(value, 1)
            If (digit = "0") Or (digit = "1") Then Return False
            Return True
        End If
    End If

    ' See if the number matches a ten digit format.
    If allow_10_digit_number Then
        If value Like "###-###-####" Then
            ' Don't let the first digit be 0 or 1.
            digit = Microsoft.VisualBasic.Left$(value, 1)
            If (digit = "0") Or (digit = "1") Then Return False

            ' Don't let the fourth digit (fifth character) be 0 or 1.
            digit = Microsoft.VisualBasic.Mid$(value, 5, 1)
            If (digit = "0") Or (digit = "1") Then Return False
            Return True
        End If
    End If

    Return False
End Function
```

Program Errors demonstrates these routines. When you click the IsNumeric button, the program displays an input box. When you enter a value and click OK, the program uses Visual Basic's IsNumeric function to decide whether the value is numeric. Note that you can enter values like 1e99-, which are technically numeric but might not make sense in your program. You might want to restrict the input to integers, positive integers, or floating point values written with a certain number of digits after decimal point.

If you click the IsInteger button, the program uses the IsInteger function to validate your input. It rejects strings like 1e99- that are numeric but not integers. This version of the routine does accept 1e3+ because that converts into the value 1000, which is a valid integer.

When you click the IsPhoneNumber button, the program uses the `IsPhoneNumber` routine to validate your entry.

Write simple routines like these to see if string values have certain formats. Then use these routines to validate data items proactively before they cause errors. By removing error-handling code from the program's more complex routines, you make these routines easier to understand. You might need to build error-handling code into helper routines like the `IsInteger` function, but those routines are relatively simple.

In a perfect application, no data would enter the system without this kind of validation, so the program would never find an expected error. In a prototype, however, it is tempting to just assign the string value to a variable and then catch or ignore the error. If you can really afford to ignore the error, use `On Error Resume Next`. If you need an error handler to recover from bad values, validate the string before assigning it instead. After you've written your validation routines, this really doesn't take any extra time and makes your prototype easier to understand.

ABNORMAL ERRORS

An abnormal error is a situation that normally should not occur but that you need to handle. The program might try to open a file that is missing or locked by another program, read a registry setting that doesn't exist, or access a Web site when the network is down.

A program can handle some of these conditions as expected errors. For example, it could use the `Dir` statement to verify that a file exists before opening it. But that still doesn't tell the program whether the file is locked.

The only real difference between these conditions and expected errors is the level of difficulty in testing for the condition. You could verify a file's existence before trying to open it, but it's easier to just try to open the file and see if that works.

A finished application might take different actions depending on the kind of error it encountered. If the file was missing, it might use default values. If the file was locked, it might warn the user.

A prototype would probably just give up at this point. It would give the user whatever information it had about the error and then stop trying to open the file.

UNFORESEEN ERRORS

Unforeseen errors are those you didn't imagine in your wildest dreams. You cannot predict them in advance because they are unforeseen by definition. You also cannot tell where they might appear. Even the simplest subroutine might generate one of these little surprises.

Most of these errors are just mistakes and omissions on your part. Use error trapping to catch any of these things you might have missed.

Others of these errors are truly unpredictable. For example, other programs might use up all of your computer's memory and swap space, so your program might be unable to allocate more memory when it calls a subroutine. Another program might use up all of your system's graphics resources so your program would fail when trying to open a new form. There's not much you can do about these exotic errors except catch them and hope for the best.

WHERE TO PROVIDE ERROR HANDLING

Errors can occur anywhere. They usually happen where you least expect them. If you expected them, you would handle them proactively as expected errors and they would cause little trouble.

A program can catch an error in the routine that generates it or in any routine above that one in the call stack. If no routine in the call stack catches the error, the program crashes.

Example
Suppose SubroutineA calls SubroutineB, which calls SubroutineC. If SubroutineC generates an error, it gets the first crack at it. If SubroutineC contains an enabled error handler, that error handler catches the error. If SubroutineC has no error handler enabled, control passes up to SubroutineB.

If SubroutineB has an enabled error handler, it catches the error. If no error handler is enabled in SubroutineB, control passes up to SubroutineA.

If an error handler is enabled in SubroutineA, that error handler catches the error. If SubroutineA contains no enabled error handler, the program crashes.

To completely protect a program from every possible error, you must put error-handling code in every possible call sequence. That does not mean you need to put an error handler in every subroutine. That would work, but you only need to have error handlers in the routines that could lie at the top of the call stack.

In the previous example, that means you must at least put error-handling code in SubroutineA. Otherwise, if SubroutineA generates an error, the program crashes. If the error handler in SubroutineA protects the call to SubroutineB, the error handler protects the entire call stack so SubroutineB and SubroutineC cannot crash the program either.

So where are the routines that could lie at the top of the call stack? If your program starts by executing a Sub Main subroutine, that routine needs an error handler. If your program uses any controls, forms, or other objects that generate events, all of the event handlers must contain error-handling code. This catches any errors generated by code started from Sub Main or an event.

In the early stages of prototype development, it is common to skimp on error handling. The program includes error handlers only where it is obvious that they are needed. As the project continues, the developers find new places where errors occur and they either handle these situations proactively to avoid the errors or they add more error handlers. Over time, the program becomes more robust. Then, right before they deliver the program to customers, the developers add error handling to event handlers and to Sub Main.

PART

III

CH

13

Now the customers should not be able to crash the program. If a customer raises an error that the developers have not seen yet, the program catches the error, displays an error message, and continues. How well the program can continue depends on the program. What's important is that the program displays an error message that pinpoints the error.

Remember that an error's Exception object contains information about the routine where the error occurred, not about the routine where it was caught. That means an error handler, even at the top of the call stack, is able to tell exactly where the error occurred.

There is one other situation where all this error handling is not enough: when an object raises an error asynchronously.

Example
Suppose you build a control that contains a Timer. When the Timer fires, the control checks the system's resources and raises an event if the system memory is more than 90 percent used.

Now suppose the Timer's event handler contains a bug that raises an error. The main program does not call the Timer's event handler, so the main program has no subroutines on the call stack when this event handler runs. That means the main program cannot protect itself from an error generated in the control's Timer event handler. When this error occurs, the program crashes.

The right solution is for the control to catch its own error and handle it. If it needs to tell the main program about the error, it should raise an event for main program to catch.

STANDARD ERROR HANDLING

You should write customized error handlers for expected and abnormal errors. These are places where you know exceptions are likely to occur and you can figure out what to do when something goes wrong. For example, if the program needs to read data from a floppy disk, it should expect the floppy disk to be missing some of the time.

Writing customized error handlers for Sub Main and every event handler in a project can be a big chore. Most of those error handlers don't take special action anyway, so it's not worth building customized error handlers for every routine. Instead, you can build a generic error handling procedure and call it when it is needed.

The following code shows a simple generic error handler. It builds a string containing the error number, an optional context string, the error description, and the stack trace when the error occurred. It then displays the message to the user.

```
' Display the current error.
Private Sub DisplayError(Optional ByVal context As String = "")
    Dim exc As Exception
    Dim txt As String

    exc = Err.GetException()
    txt = "Error " & Err.Number & " " & _
        context & CrLf & exc.Message & CrLf & _
        "Stack Trace:" & CrLf & exc.StackTrace()
```

```
    MsgBox(txt, MsgBoxStyle.Exclamation, "Error")
End Sub
```

The following code shows how a program might use this generic error handler. In a `Try...Catch...Finally` block, this routine calls subroutine `StandardErrorHandler1`. That routine may perform calculations or call other subroutines. If an error occurs anywhere within the call to `StandardErrorHandler1`, the `Catch` block calls subroutine `DisplayError`.

```
Protected Sub UseStandardErrorHandler()
    Try
        StandardErrorHandler1()
    Catch
        DisplayError(" in UseStandardErrorHandler")
    End Try
End Sub
```

Example program Errors demonstrates a standard error handler when you click its Standard Error Handler button. Figure 13.3 shows the result. In this case, subroutine `StandardErrorHandler1` called subroutine `StandardErrorHandler2`, which tried to divide by zero. Subroutine `UseStandardErrorHandler` caught the error and called `DisplayError` to display the error message.

Figure 13.3
A generic error message.

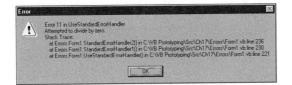

This message can be invaluable to developers, but it is meaningless to users. They don't know what subroutines `UseStandardErrorHandler`, `StandardErrorHandler1`, and `StandardErrorHandler2` do, and they don't have access to the source files so they cannot look at the lines of code that caused the error—not that the code would make sense to them anyway. To the user, this error message just says, "the program bombed." The rest is gibberish.

For a prototype, this might be barely acceptable. If a developer is nearby to take a look at the program whenever an error occurs, you might gain some useful information. Asking the user to write down all this information is pointless. It will annoy your customers and they probably won't copy all the information you need correctly in any case. A much better strategy is to have the standard error handler log the error information so you can look at it later.

PART

III

CH

13

ERROR LOGGING

Instead of displaying an obscure error message to the user, you can build a standard error handler that writes the error into a log file. Because the user never sees this message, you can fill the log with all the information you want. You can include the date and time, user name, stack trace, and anything else you can think of that might help identify the problem.

Depending on the situation, the error routine can also display a message telling the user that something is wrong. If the program can recover from the error, you might decide to hide the problem from the user. It rarely hurts to let the user know something is amiss, particularly in a prototype when a few errors are excusable.

The following subroutine checks its user_message parameter. If user_message is non-blank, the routine displays the message to the user. It also includes a warning that tells the user that the program might have problems now that an error has occurred. You should modify these messages to fit your program.

Next, the routine writes error information into a log file. This is one of the worst possible places the program might encounter an error. The program is already a little suspect because it has generated an exception. If the error logging routine cannot open the log file, the program is really in trouble. In this case, the routine displays a more detailed error message asking the user to call the development team immediately.

You can make program Errors demonstrate this problem. Use the program's Log Error button to make a log file. Then open the file using Word. That locks the file so the program can no longer open it with Append access. Now click the Log Error button again. The program cannot open the file so it presents its panic message.

```
' Display and log the current error.
Private Sub LogError(Optional ByVal context As String = "", _
    Optional ByVal user_message As String = "")
    Dim exc As Exception
    Dim user_txt As String
    Dim log_txt As String
    Dim file_num As Integer

    ' Tell the user what's happening.
    If Len(user_message) > 0 Then
        user_txt = user_message & CrLf & CrLf & _
            "This message has been logged for the developers." & CrLf & _
            "Warning: The program may no longer be stable. " & _
            "Save your work just in case."
        MsgBox(user_txt, MsgBoxStyle.Exclamation, "Error")
    End If

    ' Write a meaningful message to the error log.
    exc = Err.GetException()
    log_txt = Now & CrLf & _
        "Error " & Err.Number & " " & _
        context & CrLf & Err.Description & CrLf & _
        "Stack Trace:" & CrLf & exc.StackTrace() & CrLf & _
        "----------" & CrLf
    Try
        file_num = FreeFile()
        Open(file_num, "C:\Temp\PrototypeErrors.txt", OpenMode.Append)
        Print(file_num, log_txt)
        Microsoft.VisualBasic.Compatibility.VB6.Close(file_num)
    Catch e As Exception
        user_txt = "Error writing to error log (e.Message)." & CrLf & _
            "Please notify the development team immediately." & CrLf & _
            "----------" & CrLf & _
```

```
        log_txt
    MsgBox(user_txt, MsgBoxStyle.Critical, "Severe Error")
  End Try
End Sub
```

This subroutine writes error messages into a log file. There are several other things you could do with the error information. You could write it into a database, email it to the development team, send it to a Web service, or automatically enter it into a bug tracking system. You could even call a pager and display a short error message or numeric code to let a developer know something is wrong.

No matter what you do, be sure to allow for other errors that might occur when you try to handle the first error. If you send an error message to a Web service, be prepared for the service or your network connection to be down. If you save the error information in a networked database, the database or the network might be down. In the worst case, you might need to fall back to displaying a detailed error message and hoping the user can correctly write down the information you need.

SUMMARY

Error handling is important in any application, but it is particularly important in a prototype where errors tend to be more common. During development, provide error handlers only where you expect problems. Before you let your customer experiment with the prototype, add error handling to catch all other possible errors. Use standard error handlers and loggers to simplify error handling for the cases where you don't need customized error handling. With a good error logger, you can capture all the information you need to find a problem without frightening the user with intimidating messages and stack traces.

PART

III

CH

13

WRAPPING UP

In this chapter

When you finish a prototype, it might seem as if your work is over. Depending on the type of prototype you are building, it might have just begun. If you're building a throwaway prototype, you now need to begin final application development. If you are building an evolutionary prototype, finishing one version just means you get to start on the next.

No matter where you go from here, there are several actions you should take before you move on. You should do these things right away while the prototype is still fresh in your mind.

CONDUCT A POSTMORTEM ANALYSIS

Start by analyzing the prototype to see what you can learn from it. Get the prototyping team together and talk about each person's experiences. Include the customers, user advocates, managers, and anyone else who might have something useful to contribute in this meeting.

Find out where people had problems and try to figure out strategies to avoid those problems in the future. Determine which parts of prototype development went smoothly and find out why. See how you can use similar procedures in the future to make other prototyping efforts easier. Think about the code and tools you wrote for this prototype and identify any that may be reusable in future projects. If you wrote a generic wizard, set of dialogs, logon screen, or user privilege database, archive them so you can reuse them later.

Also examine the project proposal and design documents for possible reuse. Very different projects often have common documentation and design elements. Even if a point of sales system and a network flow analysis program have very little in common, the high-level design of their user privileges systems might be very similar. The sections of the proposal that explain why the projects will use Visual Basic on a particular hardware platform might be nearly identical. Examine these documents to see what you can copy and paste into future projects.

If you followed the advice in Chapter 1, "Reasons to Prototype," you began the prototype with a list of things you wanted to learn from the prototype. Review that list and see what you learned. If you were unable to learn something, find out why. Then figure out how you can be certain to learn what you want in the next project.

EXAMPLE

Suppose you want a throwaway prototype to help you predict the time needed to build the final application. As you build the prototype, the customers frequently change their minds about what the application should do. You try to follow the shifting requirements list, but halfway through the prototyping effort management announces that the prototyping period will be cut short. You quickly build all the features you can and then called a halt to development.

In this case, it's very hard to build a reliable estimate of how long it will take to build the final application. Developers initially spent a lot of time working on code that was scrapped by the changing requirements. Near the end of the prototyping period, developers probably concentrated on the easiest features to implement so they could get as much done as possible before the new deadline.

You can probably reduce the dodging specification problem in the future by spending more time on the initial design phase. Make sure the customers thoroughly understand what the application will do and how it will do it before you start building the prototype. Make sure the customers are committed and that they understand how changing the specification will impact the schedule.

You can also solidify the requirements with use cases. A *use case* is a scenario that the users need to perform using the finished application. Make the customers walk through the use cases, listing the steps they would perform to do their jobs using the new application. If you can show how the application helps the users do their jobs, you can reasonably believe that the application requirements are correct. At that point, ask the customers to commit to leaving the requirements alone.

There is less you can do about changing deadlines. You can try to ensure that you have adequate time to finish the prototype when you start, but it's often impossible to predict changes in management or the business environment that might cut a prototyping effort short.

If the deadline is shortened, you can try to stick to your original schedule as much as possible and then stop when time runs out. Instead of working on the easiest tasks first, work on the tasks in the order you had originally planned. This way, you're likely to get a less functional prototype, but you might implement a more representative set of code and have a better understanding of the time you need to finish the application.

Some specific questions to ask the team are

- Did everyone understand what kind of prototype (evolutionary, throwaway, user interface, and so on) you were building from the start? Did you stick to that kind of prototype or did you need to switch, for example, from evolutionary to throwaway?

- What were the prototype's goals (test untried technology, test application architecture, predict schedule, determine feasibility, and so forth)? Did you achieve those goals? Why or why not? How you can ensure that you meet those goals in the future?

- Did the developers carefully evaluate the requirements and determine which release should hold each requested feature? If every feature was included in the first release, your initial feature list might have been too restricted. Try starting with more ideas so you can pick out the most important features for the first release.

- Were the requirements prioritized? Were items identified that could be moved from release 1 to release 2 and vice versa? Giving every item top priority so they all have to be in release 1 makes development much harder. It removes the ability to adjust the feature set to handle unexpected problems. Project completion might be significantly delayed if there are problems.

- Did you stick with the priorities, implementing the most important features first?

- Did the requirements change after development began? Were the changes necessary? Was there some way developers could have discovered the new requirements earlier, perhaps by studying the customers' work environment more carefully?

- Were changes to the requirements documented so anyone could tell what the original and modified requirements were, who requested the changes, and why? Was there some kind of approval process to monitor changes and ensure that only those that were really necessary made it into release 1? Was that process followed? Was the process too tight or too relaxed?

- Did the customers feel the developers understood their application domain?

- Were changes gold-plating, added by developers because they were easy rather than essential?

- Did you make user interface, database, object-oriented, and procedural designs? Did you learn something new from each design? For example, if the object-oriented design was just a reformulation of the database design, you didn't learn anything new.

- Did the developers get customer feedback regularly? One of the most important purposes of a prototype is to get feedback quickly so developers don't waste time building unwanted features.

- Did the customers feel the developers took their suggestions and concerns seriously?

- Was the level of interaction between customers and developers appropriate? Could the developers get feedback from customers when they needed it? Could the customers make suggestions when they had them? Did the customers bury the developers in constant requests for changes and status reports?

- Did the developers consult user-interface experts? Did they build a user interface design and get customer feedback? Then did they build a user interface prototype and get more customer feedback?

- What problems with the initial design did the developers encounter later during development? How could the developers have predicted and avoided those problems during design?

- Were the pieces of the project compartmentalized so different teams could work independently? How could you make the separation between tasks cleaner?

- Were the pieces of the application small enough so each development team could finish its piece on time? How could the application have been broken into smaller pieces?

- Did the developers need to add more people to the project? Was the system broken into enough pieces so you could add more developers without disrupting the original developers? Could more developers have been added if needed?

- Did the bug tracking system work satisfactorily? Were customers able to enter bug reports and change requests into the system? Was someone responsible for reviewing those reports so items were not ignored? Were any items missed?

- Did the version the control system work satisfactorily? Did everyone understand the version numbering scheme?

- Did your progress tracking system work satisfactorily? Did you know how much work was done at all times? Did you know which pieces of the system were the riskiest at all times? How can you improve progress tracking?

- Did the actual schedule match the projected schedule? What things put development off schedule? How can you prevent those in the future?

- Were your schedule calculations correct? For example, did you expect the developers to write 1,000 lines of code per week when they actually only wrote 500? Compile metrics showing how quickly developers produced lines of code, subroutines, and modules so you can predict these times more accurately in the future. Don't forget to include time for testing, integrating different parts of the system, documentation, and other non-programming tasks.

- Is the code self-documenting? Does it contain a good set of comments, even if it is part of a throwaway prototype?
- Did you save time for adequate testing and documentation? If not, how much more time should you have allocated?
- What unexpected problems did you encounter? How can you avoid those problems in the future?

You may need to keep a tight rein on the post-mortem meeting. If the prototype has been particularly frustrating, the meeting might degenerate into a finger-pointing session where everyone piles blame on everyone else. Stay focused on the goal of identifying problems and making sure they won't happen again. While some catharsis is natural and helpful for maintaining a good customer relationship, you don't want the meeting to turn into a name-calling competition.

After you have finished the post-mortem meeting, write up the results and distribute them to everyone involved. Make a special section listing actions you need to take during the next prototype. Then before you start the next prototype, review this list. It does you no good if you don't use it. In the words of philosopher and novelist George Santayana, "Those who cannot remember the past are condemned to repeat it."

EVALUATE INDIVIDUAL PERFORMANCES

Most companies review employee performance on a fixed timetable. Annual or semi-annual reviews determine the employees' job classification and pay scale. A much better time to do this sort of evaluation is right after the employee finishes a prototype, application, or some other large project. Then the employee's performance is fresh in your mind.

Jot down some notes to use in your employees' next performance reviews. If you can, have a mini-review right away so you can discuss the employee's future in the company and things you both can do to best serve the company and the employee.

Determine who exceeded your expectations and give these people extra recognition. Give them bonuses, awards, a special lunch, or just thank them publicly so they know you appreciate their efforts.

Developers who can work independently are particularly valuable in any development effort. Every development team should have a few self-motivated, resourceful members so the lead developers don't have to worry about every part of the project. These developers might also make good team or project leaders in future projects.

Find out who did a good job designing their piece of the application. See who needed to change their design the least. Look for code that did not contain a lot of bugs and did not need to be rewritten repeatedly. Those pieces of code probably had the best design.

PART

III

CH

14

After you have identified the developers who are good at design, see if you can give them more responsibility. You might be able to use these people in higher-level application design tasks. The application-level design sets the stage for the work produced by all of the other developers. You need the best people possible building the overall design.

Look also for team members who did not live up to your expectations and find out why. Was this person assigned to a particularly difficult task or to a task that was new to this developer? Was this developer unable to get help from more experienced developers who were busy doing something else? Does this person need additional training?

Sometimes an employee fails at a task simply because he was assigned to something particularly hard, and anyone who had been assigned to the task would have also failed. In that case, you might want to schedule training for everyone. That makes all of the developers more useful and doesn't single out the one who got stuck with the task that no one in the team could have finished.

Tale from the Trenches

After one project, I did some digging through the bookstores and found a couple of good books on software engineering and user interface design. We bought copies for everyone in the department and let the developers keep them.

No one had to be told what to read. The senior developers skimmed though the books picking up the more advanced techniques they had not seen before. Less experienced developers read the books more thoroughly. People read the books mostly at night and on weekends, so they didn't even take up work time.

Developers like books so this not only helped smooth out some rough spots in the team members' skills, but it also provided a small reward. We all became better programmers for the cost of a few books.

EVALUATE GROUP PERFORMANCES

This is also a good time to think about how different developers work together. Some people who do well in one situation might do poorly in another. It's up to the team leaders and project managers to know how different people work together and to take advantage of the best combinations. You need to figure out how each person works in a team and find the position that takes best advantage of their strengths.

Tale from the Trenches

One developer I knew was just about the perfect database designer. She had the patience and attention to detail needed to design a system with hundreds of database tables. She had the persistence to stick with the design until every piece fit together perfectly. She was also very distracting to the other developers. She would wander into someone's office for a quick question and then chat for an hour or two. Design meetings with her meandered into a maze of digressions that, left unchecked, could go on forever.

The best position for her in a development project was lead database designer, preferably working alone so she didn't have anyone close by to distract her. It still took some effort to keep design meetings on track, but at least she didn't need to have long conversations with other developers on a daily basis. And we still had plenty of time for digressions at lunch.

I worked with another developer who probably knew more about programming for the Unix operating system than anyone else I have ever met. If you had a problem, he could whip out a program to solve it in a matter of minutes. Unfortunately, he would. He was event-driven. Whatever he was working on, no matter how important, he would immediately drop what he was doing to work on your project. Sometimes he would get interrupted in the middle of your task and start on a third.

The best position for this developer was system manager and toolsmith. Then it was officially his job to solve problems for other developers. He still needed some help breaking his event-driven habits. When he was working on a particularly important task, the team leader needed to check with him every now and then to make sure he hadn't gotten distracted. Overall, though, he was much more productive when helping other developers than when he was trying to implement his own piece of the system.

Finally, I knew two developers who worked together on a series of small projects. One wasn't very good at development but had a good grasp of higher-level design issues and project management. The other was a productive developer but had trouble laying out the tasks needed to finish a project. The strengths of one complemented those of the other. Separately they were reasonably productive, but they were much more valuable as a team.

LEARN FROM THE PROTOTYPE

One of the worst mistakes you can make when prototyping is to ignore its results. Stated more bluntly, it's hard to imagine yourself ignoring the results of the prototype you spent so much time building. But it's easier and more common than you think. It's easy to identify schedule problems but then convince yourself that you can solve those problems during the final application development. You convince yourself that you can work a little harder and that you can avoid the problems you identified in the prototype. Unless you make changes to the way you work, however, the problems will not go away.

It's also possible for developers to ignore the user interface and features provided by the prototype when building the final application. This can be a particular problem when the team that builds the final application is different from the prototyping team. Unless you take special care in transferring the knowledge gained from the prototype to the new development team, they might not see the importance of all the prototype's features. Some small detail that you know the customers desperately want in the prototype might be ignored and considered unimportant by the implementation team.

Tale from the Trenches
The "Detailed Specification" section in Chapter 1 contains a Tale From The Trenches describing one such project. We built a prototype and transferred it to a development organization for final implementation. They spent several months working without feedback from the customer or us and built what they thought was the final system. They then spent another few months putting back features they had removed, thinking they were unnecessary.

PART

III

CH

14

Study the prototype and learn what it has to tell you. Then take action. If you are going to ignore the prototype's results, you might as well not build it in the first place.

MAKE GO/NO GO DECISIONS

One of the biggest decisions a prototype can help you make is whether to continue development. If the prototype shows that the project is not feasible, you should stop development immediately to save as much time and money as possible.

Remember that the goal is not to build any old project. The goal is to build a stable, working project that solves the customers' problems. There is no point in stubbornly sticking to a development schedule after you know the project will fail. The instant you are sure the project will fail, you should cancel it. Don't throw good money after bad. You might have "wasted" a few thousand dollars building the prototype, but you can save millions by not finishing development of an application that will fail anyway.

Some reasons you might decide to cancel a project include

- **Development infeasible**—If the project is too complicated for the developers to build with the allowed time and resources, you should either cancel the project, reduce the project's scope, or allocate more resources. It is very common for management to ignore this advice and continue the project anyway, assuming the developers will somehow manage to work faster than they did when prototyping. That never happens.

- **No longer needed**—By the time you finish building the prototype, the application might no longer be needed. Don't build the application just because you said you would. A huge number of applications are built and then never used because they don't solve the customers' problems. Cancel the project and move on to something useful.

- **Quickly changing requirements**—If the requirements changed very quickly during prototype development, you need to determine whether the customers' needs changed or whether the description of the requirements changed. If the developers did not understand the true requirements at the start, it is possible that the customers' needs did not change. In that case, you can continue building the application after you correctly understand the requirements. You might want to build a new prototype first. On the other hand, if the customers' needs changed rapidly due to a quickly changing business environment, any application you build might be obsolete before you finish building it. In that case, cancel the project and cut your losses. If you examine the problem from a new direction, you might find other applications you can build that will help.

- **Unstable code**—Sometimes the prototype's code becomes such a patchwork of changes and bug fixes that the developers cannot produce a correctly working program. Sometimes this is caused by quickly changing requirements. As the requirements change and change again, the developers write and rewrite the code until it doesn't follow the original application architecture closely enough to be stable. You can usually save this kind of project by starting over. Rewrite the requirements and build a new design. Treat the first version of the prototype as a throwaway. Be careful not to reuse any of its code or you will inherit its problems.

- **Immature technology**—You might decide the technology you used to build the prototype is not ready. In that case, you might be able to find alternative tools that will work.

If you cannot find alternatives, cancel the project or defer it until the technology matures. If you work with an immature first version of a product, you might spend more time debugging its code than you spend debugging your own. Let someone else debug the product and then try again when version 2 is available.

Tale from the Trenches

A tax application we built for the State of Minnesota was supposed to allow clients to pay their taxes using several methods including electronic funds transfer (EFT). During development, the EFT software never stabilized. We deferred the EFT part of the application until release 2.0, and clients could still pay by check.

Note that the project would have suffered a serious setback if we had not planned to also allow payment by check. If we had relied completely on EFT, we would have been forced to delay the application's release.

Tip

Some vendors know that customers don't like working with version 1.0 of a product so they give their first version some other number such as 2.0 or 3.2. Before you assume a product has been around for a while, be sure there really was a previous version.

- **Immature environment**—If your application needs to interface with other systems in your customers' environment and those systems are not mature and stable, you could be in trouble. At best, you need to make changes to your code to match changes in the other application. At worst, the changes to the other application could be so large that your program is unable to compensate without a major redesign.

Tale from the Trenches

This doesn't demonstrate an immature environment exactly, but it's interesting and it shows how changes to a related system can cause problems in your application.

A billing software package called ACE (Automated Collections Enhancements) grabbed data from several mainframe systems using terminal emulation. With terminal emulation, the ACE system pretended to be a normal data terminal. To the mainframe systems, it looked just like any human user (one that typed extremely quickly, anyway). It looked at certain codes in the customer records on the mainframe systems to determine whether a customer's phone service should be suspended.

One night, a field on a mainframe system moved to another part of the screen. A human user would have little trouble finding the field in its new position, but ACE couldn't find it. First thing in the morning, ACE started suspending customers who should not have been suspended.

Fortunately, ACE provided lots of status information. The users quickly realized something was wrong and stopped the program but not before it had suspended 750 customers.

While the users started restoring customer service manually, we wrote a quick program to restore service programmatically. A few hours later, everyone was back up and running, though four customers did notice their service had been interrupted before we could fix things.

This problem would have been avoided if the engineers maintaining the mainframe system had warned our users about the change. They just didn't think it was important enough to tell anyone.

PART

III

CH

14

ADJUST PROJECT SCOPE

Sometimes a prototype can lead you to decide that you should cancel a project. A less dramatic conclusion to a prototyping effort is readjusting the project's scope. Often the prototype indicates that the project requirements are too broad to satisfy with the time and resources you have available. In that case, you can reduce the scope of the application by moving some of the lower priority items from release 1.0 to release 2.0.

If you cannot defer enough items until release 2.0 to bring the size of the project under control, you need to take other actions. You might need to redesign the project, breaking it into smaller pieces so more developers can work on it at the same time. Whatever you do, do something. Don't ignore the prototype's results. I know this book has said that before, but it bears repeating.

Tale from the Trenches

The one project I worked on that I truly consider a failure ignored the lessons of the prototype. Three different parts of the application were falling further and further behind schedule. Two parts looked like they would eventually pull through, but the third part looked terminal.

The natural reaction for managers at that point is to pile more people on the project. Unfortunately, we had already used up all of the compartmentalized pieces built into the project architecture. Adding more people only slowed down the current developers while they brought the newcomers up to speed. We just ended up looking over one another's shoulders while one person did all the typing.

What we should have done was step back and reconsider the parts of the application that were in trouble. We should have redesigned them to make them simpler and more compartmentalized. The dying subsystem should have been gutted and reworked from the ground up. It probably would have taken an extra month or two, but it would have given us a chance of success.

Instead, the project manager and I (the lead developer) were called down to corporate headquarters to meet with the program manager and the principle customer representatives. She asked for a status report, and I started to explain what we needed to do to get back on track.

She firmly interrupted, "No. That's not the way it's going to be. We are going to drive a stake in the sand and put in the extra hours to meet our deadlines. I haven't had a project fail on me yet, and I don't intend to now." She went on like that for a couple minutes.

I started to explain that setting a firm deadline and declaring that we *would* meet it would only demoralize the developers who had already been putting in some very long weeks. She interrupted again with an instant replay using different management clichés.

That's when I knew for certain we were doomed. Just as I expected, the developers were demoralized and continued to listlessly plug away at the code, fully expecting to fail. The deadline came and went with us only a little closer to a solution. The program manager was transferred to another part of the company. Eventually the program wandered out of our control into yet another part of the company where it languished.

The project manager and I knew that we could save the project if we were willing to acknowledge the direction the schedule was heading and take action. It would have been painful in the short term, but would probably have worked out in the end.

Later the project manager said he was watching me during the program manager's speech. He said if I had twitched towards the door, he would have raced me to the parking lot.

BUILD A NEW VERSION

If the prototype does not correctly represent the features described in the requirements, you might need to build a new prototype. If you are getting frequent feedback from the customers while building the prototype, the prototype should be more or less on track. In that case, you can modify and extend the current prototype to create a new version.

If you have somehow managed to stray far from what the customers need, you might have to start over and build a new prototype from scratch.

Usually neither of these options is popular because you don't decide to build a new prototype until your allowed prototyping period is over. The customers expect you to move into final application development and might be unwilling to give you more time for prototyping.

Although it might not be popular, you're more likely to get a better result if you allow time to build a new prototype. A new prototype helps you ensure that the customers and developers have the same vision of what the final application will look like. That greatly increases the chances of your building a system that the customers can actually use.

If you are pushed into development without a new prototype, you should first make a complete and detailed list of the ways in which the final application will differ from the current prototype. Make sure the customers and developers agree on what the finished application will look like, even though you cannot demonstrate its features in a prototype.

BEGIN FINAL APPLICATION DEVELOPMENT

Ideally, the prototype development proceeded smoothly. The developers worked closely with the customers to get feedback and adjust the prototype until the final version looks just like the system the customers want. The developers have demonstrated untested technology and understand how all of the parts of the system will fit together. The latest schedule reflects anything you learned from the prototyping effort.

Now you are ready to begin final application development. Declare the prototype finished and make it available to the customers and developers for later reference. Begin the final development effort as if it were a separate project. Start with a fresh bug tracking database, new milestones, and a new development schedule.

Then get to work. If you have built a throwaway prototype, start re-implementing features using careful, high-quality code instead of the quick-and-dirty techniques used in the prototype. Rebuild the user interface and then start adding the features behind the scenes.

At this stage of development, customers often get the feeling that nothing is happening. They don't understand why it takes you months to build a prototype and then more months to rebuild exactly the same thing. Remind them that the prototype code is not high quality and that you need to upgrade the program to production standards. Give the customers regular status reports so they know something is happening, even though it's nothing they can see.

PART

III

CH

14

After you start adding features beyond those demonstrated by the prototype, get feedback from the customers again. Sometimes you can still make minor changes to the application at this point. Be sure the customers understand, however, that the main application architecture was defined and tested by the prototype. After final development starts, large changes can have big consequences in other parts of the application.

TRANSFER PROTOTYPE KNOWLEDGE

If another group of developers is going to build the final application, you need to transfer what you learned by building the prototype to the new group. Give them any documentation you have produced and the prototype itself, so they can see what the customers have in mind.

Transferring information is easiest if one or two of the developers who helped build the prototype move into the new development group. Because they have followed the project from its start, they know all of the countless decisions that were made while building the prototype. They know which features are most important to the customer in a way that the requirements documents cannot easily convey.

These people should have a higher-level view of the application. They might include the project manager, application architects, or team leaders. Moving a low-level programmer into the new group helps with the parts of the application that the programmer worked on in the prototype, but is not much help with the rest of the application.

A good way to make this sort of transfer easier is to include developers who will be in the final application development team in the prototyping effort. Give them offices near the prototype developers for the duration of the prototype development. When the prototype is finished, they move home to join the final application development group.

Tale from the Trenches

I worked at GTE Laboratories in Waltham, Massachusetts on several prototypes. The final development and maintenance organization was GTE Data Services in Tampa, Florida. Our customers usually worked for GTE Telephone Operations and lived in various locations including Dallas, Texas; Fort Wayne, Indiana; and Thousand Oaks, California.

During application development, we often gave our customers offices at GTE Laboratories. On larger projects, one or two customers would move and live in Waltham for months at a time so we could get instant feedback.

Meanwhile, we included developers from GTE Data Services in the prototyping effort. In one project, two of their developers worked with us to develop two of the prototype's subsystems. They later became team leaders in the final development and maintenance team.

That particular project involved some heavy-duty optimization algorithms, a subject that we knew more about than GTE Data Services. We screened résumés and interviewed candidates for GTE Data Services and helped them hire the best person for the job. That person worked closely with our prototype algorithm team and became the final application's algorithm team leader.

Including final application developers in the prototyping team helps them buy into the project. If the transfer is anonymous, the final developers might have the attitude that they need to redesign the system to prove that they are doing their jobs. They might rewrite perfectly good code and change parts of the design that the customers have already approved. If some of the prototype developers transfer over to the final development effort, they have some feeling of ownership for the prototype and are less likely to discard its lessons.

On the other hand, those developers must not become too protective of the prototype. Some decisions will undoubtedly change during the final development effort and these transferred developers must not cling irrationally to their previous work.

CELEBRATE

After you declare the prototype finished, have a wrap party. Finishing a prototype is no small feat, and it deserves some celebration. This gives the developers a chance to blow off steam and realize that this chapter in the application's development is over.

Have a party offsite at an amusement park, lake, dude ranch, bowling alley, or even at the project manager's house. If you have the authority to give everyone a day off, throw the party during normal working hours. Be sure to invite customers, managers, users who provided feedback, and anyone else who helped. The idea is to make everyone feel like they worked together to achieve something significant, not to make someone feel left out.

Hand out shirts, coffee mugs, and toys with phrases such as, "I survived ABS prototype 1.0." It's amazing how much an eight-dollar tee shirt can motivate a developer. Counting overhead and expenses, a typical programmer can easily cost $100,000 or more per year. Adding $50 worth of catering and toys does not significantly change your budget but shows that the team's efforts are appreciated. If you think this is a bit silly, you should know that Microsoft, a company known for keeping developers happy, uses any excuse to shower its programmers with shirts, mugs, mouse pads, and all kinds of toys.

DO OTHER THINGS

Few developers can work at full speed day after day without the quality of their work suffering. Some developers thrive in a high-pressure environment, but most people who work on one high profile prototype after another burn out sooner or later. You can try the usual motivational management techniques of extra responsibility, promotions, and money, but those don't save team members from exhaustion in the long term.

There are several things you can do to keep developers productive. Letting them follow a project from start to completion can give them a break from the frenetic pace demanded by rapid prototyping. The slower speed that usually comes during final development, testing, and implementation can give worn out developers a much needed rest. This also broadens the developers' perspective, letting them see all of the phases of development. Working closely with the application's users at the end of the project helps them appreciate that their application is really doing something useful and can renew their sense of purpose.

On the other hand, many high profile projects face tight deadlines throughout their life-cycles, and following a project through its completion might just keep developers in the pressure cooker longer.

In addition, some developers who are good at one phase of development might be terrible at others. A developer who is great at writing project specifications and designing an application might be worthless when it comes to actual programming. Others who are fantastic programmers cannot stand testing, documentation, or training. Asking these people to follow along on a project so they can gain some perspective might be worthwhile. Routinely forcing them to slog through the phases where they have no talent or interest on every project does not help anyone.

Tale from the Trenches

Almost every experienced developer knows one or two programmers who aren't allowed out in public. They might be so socially inept that they annoy or even anger the customers.

One malady common among developers is excess candor. I've known several developers who didn't know how to filter information before presenting it to managers and customers. When asked why development followed a certain approach, you might hear, "It's really a stupid strategy, but because you idiots told us we had to work with the current operations systems (which, by the way, are absolute garbage and should be completely scrapped), we have to use this ridiculous kludge to do something that should be simple."

It's okay if this developer doesn't experience every stage of application development first hand. These people should be kept away from customers and high-level management at all costs.

Another way to keep developers fresh is to let them do less demanding things between high-pressure projects. One technique is to alternate between high- and low-visibility projects. That lets developers keep doing useful work while giving them a break from more stressful customer interactions.

Tale from the Trenches

At GTE Laboratories, I worked on a mix of high- and low-visibility projects. I might spend a year or two working on an application for GTE Telephone Operations, the huge part of the company that provided telephone service to customers. That application might involve several hundred users and directly affect the service of millions of customers.

After that, I might work defining programming methods for internal use within GTE Laboratories. Not having a multi-billion dollar per year customer made that kind of project much less stressful.

Another way to help developers stay fresh is to let them occasionally work on things that are not directly related to any current project. Let them take some time to learn about a new language, Web programming technique, or database tool. Let them work on something theoretical. Although theoretical work might not have an obvious immediate use, it helps the developers hone their programming skills.

Tale from the Trenches

My manager for most of my stay at GTE Laboratories had an explicit policy that everyone was allowed to attend one major conference, seminar, or training event that was not directly related to current work every other year. In addition to providing a useful break from the current work, this let us explore new technology that might later prove useful.

GTE Laboratories also had a policy of encouraging publication. It produced its own internal technical documents to share information among different parts of the company. It also gave employees a small bonus if they published an article in an external magazine (unless the magazine paid you itself). This not only gave developers a small break from their day-to-day development chores, it got GTE some recognition in the developer community.

One drawback to these approaches is that the most skilled developers are always in the highest demand. Although you might be willing to let a junior programmer spend three months studying Java or software platforms for possible use in future projects, you might have trouble pulling senior developers and project managers out of the work flow long enough to let them recharge.

You might need to fight to give senior developers a chance to relax, but it's important that you do so. Try not to schedule projects so closely together that there is no time in between for the developers to do other things. You need these senior developers the most because they are the most productive. For that same reason, you must ensure that they don't get burned out and leave your company for another company.

Even if you cannot pull developers completely out of the prototyping pipeline, you can help keep them fresh by giving them smaller breaks. A common technique is to hold lunchtime seminars. You can bring in outside speakers to talk about their research.

At GTE Laboratories we often had job candidates give talks about their thesis work. In addition to job candidates, you can ask students from your local university to speak. This helps build a useful relationship between your business and the university that can build on work-study and internship programs.

Finally, your developers can take turns researching a new technology and giving a brief lunchtime summary. Preparing for this week's lunch might reduce a developer's productivity for a day or two, but it gives that person a break, gives the other developers some useful information, and encourages all the developers to explore new ideas together as a team.

SUMMARY

When you finish a prototype, it is natural to want to move on to something else. Often the developers have put in so many long nights that they just want to forget the whole thing for a while.

There are still a few things you need to do, however, to get the most out of the prototyping effort. Analyze the prototype to see what you have learned about the larger application. Reflect on the prototyping experience itself and see what you can learn. Find out what went

PART

III

CH

14

badly and figure out how you can avoid those experiences in the future. Determine how you can repeat the things that went smoothly in the next project.

Be sure to take some time to think about the prototyping team. Let them know their work is appreciated. Give them some time out of the prototyping pipeline to recharge and start the next project fresh.

INDEX